Hotel and Restaurant Guide 2005

Les Routiers is an association of mainly owner-managed establishements. However, membership is not automatic. Many applications are refused because every establishment displaying Les Routiers' symbol must satisfy our rigourous quality criteria.
All opinions included in the Guide entries are based upon the findings of external assessors.

Published 2004 by:
Routiers Limited
190 Earl's Court Road
London SW5 9QG
Tel: 020 7370 5113
Fax: 020 7370 4528
E-mail: info@routiers.co.uk

Book trade distribution:
Portfolio Books Ltd
Unit 5, Perivale Industrial Park
Horsenden Lane South
Greenford, Middlesex
UB6 7RL

ISBN 0-900057-21-1
Copyright © 2004 Routiers Limited

Maps © Routiers Limited 2004
Great Britain Digital Database and
Greater London Digital Data
© Cosmographics Limited.
Maps designed and produced by Cosmographics.
Reproduced by kind permission of Ordnance Survey.
Crown Copyright NC/01/365".
Including mapping content © Automobile Association
Developments Limited 2001 and
© Bartholomew Digital Database.
Greater London Map based on information derived
from satellite imagery and an original ground survey by
Cosmographics. Satellite data provided by USGS and
Infoterra Ltd.

British Library Cataloguing in Publication Data.
A catalogue record for this book is available from the British Library.

Editor:
Melanie Leyshon

Production and Design Editor:
Holly Hall

Design:
Oliver Carter

Editorial Contributors:
Julie Arkell
Alex Chambers
Anita Chaudhuri
Coralie Dorman
Dudley Newbery
Lorna Wing

Location Photographers:
britainonview.com
Annie Hanson
Rebecca Harris
Nicholas Stanley

Cover Photography:
Front: The Crown Hotel
Wells-next-to-Sea, Norfolk
Back: (right) Stone Court Hotel and
Chambers, Maidstone, Kent
(left) Strattons, Swaffham, Norfolk

Maps:
Cosmographics Limited, Watford

Printed in Great Britain by:
London Print and Design plc, Warwick

For Les Routiers:
Director:
Nicholas Stanley
Operations Director:
Imogen Clist
Marketing Manager:
Victoria Borrows

www.routiers.co.uk

Les Routiers Guide - De bons restaurants pas chers et pour tous was originally written for truck drivers who were looking for fairly priced hotels and restaurants. It soon became popular with travelling salesmen, French and foreign tourists.

Today, the red and blue Les Routiers sign has become a cult symbol, standing alongside the Gitannes pack and the Ricard logo as the essence of French style, and the Routiers' original concept of a warm homely welcome and affordable good value is as strong today as when it was first conceived in the 1930s.

Les Routiers Guide - De bons restaurants pas chers et pour tous is a boon for travellers in France, listing simple, inexpensive roadside restaurants and hotels for both truck drivers and motorists.

To obtain a copy visit:

www.routiers.com

Contents

Features

Food Maps
Ever wondered where our members source their quality produce? Our food maps pinpoint their top producers and suppliers of quality foods in 18 culinary hotspots

Drive and Dine
Planned routes that take in spectacular sights and fabulous food and wine

Just off the Motorway
Give the services the cold shoulder and take a quick detour to one of our members

How to use this Guide

Finding an establishment

Les Routiers Hotel and Restaurant Guide 2005 is sectioned into London, England, Scotland, Wales and the Channel Islands. London is ordered alphabetically into Central, East, North, South and West. The countries are listed alphabetically by county, listing town and then establishment name. There are four ways to track down an establishment or establishments.

1. If you are seeking a place in a particular area, first go to the maps at the back of the book. County boundaries are marked in lilac and each establishment has a relevant marker alongside their listing town shown in bold. Once you know the locality, go to the relevant section in the book to find the entry for the hotel, restaurant or other establishment.

2. Page borders are colour coded for each country and also have the appropriate county at the top of each page so you can flick through the book and find the correct area with ease.

3. Turn to the index on page 294 where both establishment names and listing towns appear in alphabetical order.

4. To find a country turn to contents on page 4.

How to read a guide entry

A sample entry is set out on the facing page. At the top of the entry you will find the establishment's name, address, and telephone number and, if it has them, an email and website address. Also, any symbols that may apply to the establishment; an explanation of what these symbols stand for appears beside the sample entry. The middle part of the entry describes accommodation, atmosphere, food, wines and so on, while the final section gives additional statistical information and the map reference number.

Miscellaneous information

Disabled: As disabilities (and needs) vary considerably, Les Routiers has taken the decision not to note whether a place is suitable for the disabled. A more satisfactory course for all concerned is to telephone the hotel or restaurant of your choice and discuss your needs with the manager or proprietor.

Vegetarians: Most restaurants now offer some vegetarian choice. Where there is a wide and imaginative choice, or none at all, it is mentioned in the main body of the entry.

Listing Town and County: Many of our establishments are in the countryside, so their Listing Towns may be a town several miles away. If you are unsure of the county look the town up in the index and it will refer you to the correct page.

Telephone: Two numbers are included here, an 0870 number and normal telephone number, both reach the same destination. We encourage you to use the first 0870 number charged at national rate.

Numbers include the international code for dialling the UK from abroad. To dial from within the UK start the number with the 0 in brackets (0); from outside the UK dial all numbers except the 0 in brackets (0).

Last orders: Times to order by are given for the bar and food where applicable. For each a lunch and dinner last order is given. Where there is only an evening time given, the establishment serves throughout the day.

Closed: Where 'Never' is stated the establishment is open throughout the year. Where 'Rarely' is stated the establishment is open throughout the year bar important holidays (Christmas, New Year). Otherwise dates and days closed are stated.

Listing Town

Name

Address
Telephone: +44(0)870 000000
+44(0)1888 000000
excellentpub@hotmail.com

This quintessentially English hotel dates back to the 18th century and has been revamped by its new owners...

Rooms: 15. Double room from £72, single from £57.. Honeymoon suite available.
Prices: Set menu £18. House wine from £9.95.
Last orders: Bar: 23.30. Food: 21.00.
Closed: 25th December evening - 2nd January.
Food: Modern British.
Other points: No-smoking area. Children welcome. Garden.
Car park. Licence for Civil Weddings.
Directions: Exit 22/M5, turn right at the roundabout towards Weston-super-Mare, A38. Hotel is one mile on the left of the A38 just past Sanders Garden World (on the right). (Map 4, C6)

Directions: These have been supplied by the proprietor of the establishment. The map reference at the end refers to the map section at the back of the Guide.

Symbols:

 Accommodation
 Residents Only
 Pub or Bar
 Teashop or Café
 Food Shop
 Set Menu
★ Award Winner 2003
☆ Award Winner 2004
♥ Free glass of wine
(turn to page 303)

We do not have a food or good wine symbol as it is part of our requirements for membership that all Les Routiers establishments serve good food and wine at reasonable prices.

Rooms: For establishments offering overnight accommodation the number of rooms is given, along with the lowest price for a double and single room. Where this price is per person it is indicated. Prices usually include breakfast. Where the price includes bed, breakfast and dinner it is indicated.

Prices: Set meals usually consist of three courses but can include more. If a set meal has fewer or more than three courses, this is stated. Where no set lunch or dinner is offered, we give the price of the cheapest main course on the menu. House wine prices are by the bottle. Prices are meant as a guideline to the cost of a meal only. All prices include Value Added Tax (VAT).

Other Points:

Credit cards - Very few places don't take credit cards; those that don't are stated here.

Children - Although we indicate whether children are welcome in the establishment, we do not list facilities for guests with babies; we advise telephoning beforehand to sort out any particular requirements.

Dogs - It is specified whether dogs are allowed in the public bar and/or overnight accommodation of the establishment. However, please mention this when booking.

About this Guide

In France the distinctive and coveted red, blue and white Les Routiers plaque identifies independent hotels and restaurants offering good food at good value prices. They are also places where you are guaranteed a warm, friendly welcome. The scheme started in Paris in 1936, but it wasn't until the early 1970s that Les Routiers brand crossed the channel and become a quality mark in Great Britain. The core values are every bit as relevant to visitors here as they are in France. We are careful to pinpoint only those places offering quality and something that little bit different and special. Before they become members, our team of assessors visit the establishments anonymously to ensure they meet our criteria. Around the country, our members now include a wide spectrum of establishments, from small village cafés to rambling country manors.

In the last five years, under the new ownership of Nicholas Stanley, Les Routiers in the UK has evolved and our members have earned an excellent reputation for their high standards, from the food to the furnishings. Les Routiers members make a point of sourcing quality ingredients, local foods wherever possible, and serving home-cooked food and good wine. Accommodation is comfortable and rooms are designed with style. Dine or stay with one of our members and we guarantee that you will experience a level of service that is not always evident in many of the international hotel groups and chain restaurants.

Local Foods

Increasingly, our members are sourcing local and regional produce. Whether that's growing their own vegetables and herbs, buying rare-breed meats, fish from our shores or locally smoked produce, you will be in for a culinary treat. Stay or dine with our members and you will get a real flavour of the specialities of their particular area. To give you an idea of the sort of produce sourced, we are featuring 18 food maps in this guide, highlighting some of the key suppliers and producers. These include farm shops, cheese makers and a flour mill, many of whom you can visit to buy ingredients or to see how they are made.

Master the Menu

Around the country, you will come across many curiously named British dishes. To dispel any fears you may have about sampling Scottish clapshot or Welsh laverbread, we've compiled a glossary of some of the most popular regional dishes so that you can order with confidence.

Which Wine?

Our members have well-annotated wine lists, but choosing can still be a minefield. That's why we asked author of several books on wine and national newspaper writer Julie Arkell to steer us through ordering wines, whether that's top of the range or the house wine. She also reveals how to calculate how much you can drink in terms of alcohol units to safely stay within the drink-drive limits.

Drive and Dine

It's hard to beat a day driving around beautiful countryside, especially when you know there are fabulous places to eat along the way and somewhere to stay at the end of it. We've compiled 10 routes that offer plenty of picturesque sights, landmarks and activities, with Les Routiers members listed where appropriate. Our drives are fully planned, so you can enjoy a relaxing day out.

Just off the Motorway

We've all been there: the motorway service station that short changes you on food, but charges the earth. Check out the 10 maps to find your detour off the motorway to a Les Routiers member, who can offer you something much more appetising. The members suggested are just a short drive from a main motorway junction, but miles ahead on food and accommodation.

Awards

Les Routiers Hotel and Restaurant Awards 2004

All our members pride themselves on offering a warm welcome, quality accommodation and food as well as good value for money. But as in all walks of life, there are always those who excel and stand out, and this year we have chosen those Les Routiers' members who have surpassed the high entry standards in one of the five following categories.

Hotel of the Year

All our hotels are independently run and this is evident in their friendly, personal service, individually designed interiors and comfortable accommodation. Our winners successfully combine warm hospitality with a high standard of décor, and often provide extras and a level of service that you'd expect of a four-star hotel.

Strattons, Swaffham, Norfolk

"It sets itself apart with a distinctive style, from its extraordinarily attractive rooms to exquisite cuisine"

Regional winners

London and the South East - Harlingford, London WC1
South West - Orestone Manor, Torquay, Devon
Central and East Anglia - Strattons, Swaffham, Norfolk
The North - Winder Hall Country House, Cockermouth, Cumbria
Scotland - Balcary Bay Hotel, Castle Douglas, Dumfries and Galloway
Wales and the Welsh Borders - Dunoon Hotel, Llandudno, Conwy

Restaurant of the Year
sponsored by Champagne Mercier

Our restaurants are keen supporters of fresh, local produce in season. This gives us a network of restaurants around the country serving good food at its flavoursome best. Our winners draw on specialist local suppliers to serve imaginative and unpretentious dishes, and we have picked out the following as excellent examples of this philosophy.

Port Na Craig Restaurant, Pitlochry, Perth and Kinross

"Here you can sample the best of Scottish ingredients used imaginatively in contemporary dishes, which are often a twist on classics"

Regional winners

London and the South East - Wheelers, Whitstable, Kent
South West - Allium, Fairford, Gloucestershire
Central and East Anglia - Mussel and Crab, Tuxford, Nottinghamshire
The North - Hazlewood Castle, Tadcaster, West Yorkshire
Scotland - Port Na Craig Restaurant, Pitlochry, Perth and Kinross
Wales and the Welsh Borders - The Bell at Skenfrith, Skenfrith, Monmouthshire

Bed and Breakfast of the Year

Gone are the days when bed and breakfast was considered second best. Our members offer first-class accommodation with a friendly, but not obtrusive, service. The bedrooms and public areas combine a comfortable home-from-home feel with stylish interiors. Our winners surpass in all these elements, and they also offer good food options.

Tor Cottage, Tavistock, Devon

"This is not the normal bed and breakfast experience, but a wonderful retreat in an incredibly unique country cottage environment. Truly unforgettable with wonderful extras"

Regional winners

London and the South East - Jeake's House Hotel, Rye, East Sussex
South West - Tor Cottage, Tavistock, Devon
Central and East Anglia - Thornham Hall & Restaurant,
 Thornham Magna, Suffolk
The North - Lovesome Hill Farm, Northallerton, North Yorkshire
Scotland - The Pend, Dunkeld, Perth and Kinross
Wales and the Welsh Borders - Glangrwyney Court, Crickhowell, Powys

Wine List of the Year

This award recognises a passion for choosing quality wines at value for money prices. We've picked out those members who offer good house options as well as a range of wonderful wines by the glass or bin. It is good to see a restaurant championing and offering such a good variety of organic wines, and that is why among so many other well put together lists Mill Race Organic Restaurant is this year's winner.

Mill Race Organic Restaurant, Leeds, West Yorkshire

"You'll be spoilt for choice when choosing from this line-up of quality all-organic wines that come from around the world"

Regional winners

London and the South East - Swag and Tails, London SW7
South West - Howards House Hotel, Teffont Evias, Wiltshire
Central and East Anglia - World Service, Nottingham, Nottinghamshire
The North - Mill Race Organic Restaurant, Leeds, West Yorkshire
Scotland - Allt-nan-Ros, Onich, Highlands
Wales and the Welsh Borders - The Bear Hotel, Crickhowell, Powys

Café of the Year

Les Routiers' cafés are a varied bunch, ranging from traditional tea rooms and cafés to contemporary conservatories serving all-day homemade snacks. The emphasis is on quality food and friendly service, and all our winners are shining examples of this combination.

Hive on the Quay, Aberaeron, Ceredigion

"Fresh lobster or crab snacks, fabulous honey ice cream and homemade cakes put this harbourside café in the premier league"

Regional winners

London and the South East - Claris's Tea Room, Biddenham, Kent
South West - Organic Farm Shop Café, Cirencester, Gloucestershire
Central and East Anglia - Earsham Street Café, Bungay, Suffolk
The North - The Hazelmere Café and Bakery, Grange-over-Sands, Cumbria
Scotland - Green Welly Stop, Tyndrum, Perth and Kinross
Wales and the Welsh Borders - Hive on the Quay, Aberaeron, Ceredigion

Awards for Supporters of locally produced foods

Hotels and Restaurants winning these awards champion the best of local produce. They are run by food-loving chefs or proprietors who go out of their way to source locally grown fresh vegetables and fruits, buy rare-breed or local meats, often organic, line-caught fresh fish, dairy and other speciality produce from local farm shops.

By doing this they are not only supporting local communities and farmers, but are cutting down on food miles and giving visitors a true taste of the best of British regional food. So whether it's creamy homemade Devon ice cream, fabulous Scottish cheese and oatcakes or English Longhorn beef, you will be in for a feast of fabulous flavours.

Regional winners

London and the South East - Pilgrim's Restaurant, Battle, East Sussex
South West - Roundhouse, Weymouth, Dorset
Central and East Anglia - terroir, Cley next the Sea, Norfolk
The North - Otterburn Tower, Otterburn, Northumberland
Scotland - Mansfield House Hotel, Hawick, Scottish Borders
Wales and the Welsh Borders - The Bistro, Barmouth, Gwynedd

Master the Menu

A guide to classic and curiously named dishes around the country, plus foodies name their favourite British ingredient or dish.

Bara brith: this Welsh 'speckled bread' falls into the high tea category. The speckles are currants and the bread is flavoured with cinnamon and mixed spice.

Bakewell tart: pastry and jam with an almondy cake topping from Derbyshire, where it's still known as Bakewell pudding.

Bashed neeps: mashed swede that's traditionally served with haggis for Scottish Hogmanay and on Burns Night.

Beef wellington: pastry-wrapped beef cooked in the oven and thought to be named for the Duke of Wellington after he defeated Napoleon at Waterloo.

Bubble and squeak: a cholesterol-raising recipe of leftover potatoes and vegetables refried in bacon or duck fat or butter. The squeak comes from the noise the mixture makes when it's reheating in the pan. Great served with boiled hams.

Fish and chips
Antony Worrall Thompson
TV chef and restaurateur

"It's a food that has no boundaries; enjoyed by all! It's the most honest form of fast food eating there is. Ideal for any occasion – eating by the riverside watching the boats go by or as a quick fish supper with friends. It was also the dish I missed the most when I was in the jungle."

Fresh asparagus
Sudi Pigott
Restaurant critic

"I look forward to the beginning of the British asparagus season with anticipation. The fact it's at its peak so fleetingly adds to its appeal. I also love foods you eat with your hands in polite company. I especially enjoy asparagus served simply with melted Somerset butter or dipped into a soft-boiled egg."

Clapshot: this mixture of potato and turnip is popular in Scotland and served instead of ordinary mash, and is much more appetising than its name suggests.

Cock-a-leekie: a hearty chicken, leek and prune stew that's thought to have been introduced to the UK by Belgium weavers in the 14th century.

Cornish pasties: often called Tiddy Oggy in Cornwall, the Cornish pastry comes in many guises, but the classic filling contains beef, onion, potato, carrot and turnip.

Cullen skink: this tasty soup-stew is named after the town of Cullen on the coast of the Moray Firth, Scotland, from where it originates. It's thickened with potato and hard-boiled eggs.

Devils on horseback: prunes wrapped in salty bacon, which make excellent canapés or little starters.

Dressed crab: cooked crabmeat mixed with breadcrumbs and hard-boiled eggs and flavoured with Tabasco and Worcestershire sauce; served in or out of the shell.

Dundee cake: a rich fruit cake characterised by the inclusion of almonds and sherry.

Lancashire hotpot: a hearty slow-roasted lamb, onion and potato hotpot, which would have originally have been cooked at the local bakers before the domestic oven came on the scene.
Laverbread: a Welsh favourite, which like Marmite, you either love or hate. Laver is edible seaweed. For laverbread, the seaweed is boiled until it becomes a spinach-like flavoursome purée and it's then fried coated in oatmeal. It goes well with dry-cured bacon, and is served with many a Welsh fry-up.

Glamorgan sausages: a meat-free mixture of cheese, leeks and breadcrumbs that you can enjoy all round the country, not just in Wales.

Full English breakfast
Paul Merrett
TV Celebrity chef

"Rightly or not we are sometimes viewed as poor relations when it comes to culinary matters but no country starts the day as well as this. Eggs, bacon, potato, tomato, sausage, mushroom, fried bread, black pudding – not the way to start every day but just now and then… I always think of early morning fishing trips, returning cold and tired and hungry – croissant and jam – not likely!"

Jellied eels: originally an East London staple, as they were once so plentiful and cheap. You're guaranteed to find them in London eel and pie shops.
Kedgeree: this exceedingly British dish from the days of the Raj includes rice, smoked haddock and egg with spicy additions of saffron and nutmeg. It's a rich breakfast or brunch dish that is part-baked in the oven.
Mulligatawny soup: a peppery soup that's a legacy from the Raj. Its name comes from the Tamil words for 'pepper' and 'water'.

Beef and Yorkshire pudding
Colin Spencer
Author of several books on food and drink

"The point is the pudding, it has to be baked beneath the beef, so that the middle of it absorbs all the beef juices. The rim of the pudding puffs up and should be crispy and brown, but the middle – ah, what poems of sensual and extravagant delight should be written about this. At the end of roasting the beef must still be pink in the middle. I'd shove a 3lb piece of sirloin into a hot oven for 20 minutes, then place a rack beneath the beef and pour in the batter, made with three eggs and leave for another 20-15 minutes. Bliss."

Omelette Arnold Bennett: a classic mixture of smoked haddock, eggs and cheese invented for the novelist Arnold Bennett by Savoy chef Baptiste Virlogeux, who was the inspiration for Roho, a character in Bennett's novel *Imperial Palace*.

Fruit cakes
Mitzie Wilson

Editor of delicious. magazine

"My favourite British recipe is rich fruit cake. My mother used to make wedding cakes as a business from home, so I've grown up eating cake. I adore fruit cakes of every kind and still make my own with any combination of dried fruits, especially the newer exotic fruits like dried cranberries, mango, figs, etc. I often add chunks of marzipan to the mixture too because I'm greedy (saves icing it later). A rich fruit cake is something you just can't buy in any other country. Our Christmas cakes are unique, our tea breads divine and Dundee cake is perfect with a cup of tea. Even the not so nice pre-wrapped fruit cake sold at train stations will do – I just can't get enough of it."

Pease pudding: it won't set the world alight, but if you love dried or mushy peas, you'll love this pea pudding mainly found in restaurants up north. Look for puddings with herbs or bacon added. **Parkin:** the northern version of gingerbread and traditionally eaten on Guy Fawkes' night. The recipe varies from county to county, and it can be cakey or biscuity.

Fish pie,
Lorna Wing

Food consultant and caterer to the stars

"Fish pie stuffed to the gills with smoked haddock in a creamy parsley sauce, topped with a fluffy mound of buttery mash potato. It's British comfort food at its best, very soothing and something we do so well, up and down the country."

Queen of puddings: a naughty concoction of jam, bread and custard, all topped with meringue.

Scotch broth: also known as barley soup, this is a filling mix of lamb, barley and vegetables. Great for cold winter's days.

Scotch pancakes: small, thick round drop scones that cry out for butter and golden or maple syrup.

Scotch woodcock: an after-dinner savoury that's really fancy scrambled eggs and anchovies on toast.

Shepherd's and cottage pies: no pastry but a fluffy mash topping for either a rich lamb mince and gravy sauce (shepherd's), or beef (cottage). They were traditionally made from leftovers from the Sunday roast, but these days are more likely to be made from mince. The shepherd's pie recipe is thought to have originated in Cumbria and the Lake District.

Spotted Dick: sweet suet pudding studded with raisins and served with thick creamy custard.

Summer pudding: a cold pudding of summer berries encased by syrup-soaked white bread.

British cheeses

Silvana Franco

TV chef and author of several cookery books

"I think British cheeses are the best in the world, so I have to go for something simple but incredibly British like a Cheddar cheese scone, warm from the oven, split and spread with salted butter. Alternatively, Cheshire cheese melted on thick toast with a smudge of Fruity HP is pretty hard to beat – I could eat it for tea every night!"

Toad in the hole: a batter pudding with sausages baked in the oven. Years ago it would have been made with pieces of leftover meat or more expensive cuts like fillet.

Treacle tart: if you want a quick sugar hit, make it this pastry-based sugar, eggs and treacle-filled treat. The prettiest tarts have lattice pastry tops.

Apples

Henrietta Green

Food writer and founder of the Food Lovers' Fair, who also runs the regional and seasonal website www.foodloversbritain.com

"They really are glorious examples of the range and diversity of British produce. No other country grows them as well because our climate is ideal. In all, we grow 3,000 different varieties, and they have wonderful complex flavours. My favourite way to cook them is in a cider and apple soufflé with apple crisps."

Welsh rarebit: cheese is melted with egg and Worcestershire sauce for a creamy topping for toasted bread. A popular lunchtime, or anytime, snack.

'Even wine writers can **dread** being handed the wine list'

Julie Arkell recounts common mistakes when ordering wine, advises on how to avoid plonk and overpriced bins, and stay within drink and drive limits.

One of the things I dread when going out to dinner with friends is being handed the wine list. Surprised? Well, as a wine professional, it is true that I can claim a bit of a headstart, but in its wake run alarmingly high expectations from my fellow diners. Believe you me, I can struggle with a wine list just like everybody else!

I have also had my fair share of restaurant wine disasters; the most memorable being the bottle that arrived at the table (already opened) that in no way contained the wine it purported to be on the label. My date did not take kindly to the fuss I kicked up (and he never asked me out again!). >

Paris goblets and a wine list bearing no producer names, no vintages and no wine descriptions signal a lackadaisical attitude towards wine. You are unlikely to experience any earth-moving wine-drinking moments here! Conversely, a sea of glasses and a thick, leather-bound list sporting 200-plus wines can be equally daunting and unsatisfactory.

Under these circumstances, do not be afraid to ask the sommelier for help – he (or, increasingly, she) is your friend and ally. Given an indication of the style you prefer, the amount of money you wish to spend and some hints about what you are going to eat, a sommelier should be familiar enough with the wines to guide you to a suitable recommendation. A selection of half bottles may be proposed or, if you are lucky, you may be able to buy a number of different wines by the glass, the perfect solution if a variety of dishes is being ordered from the menu. Wine by the glass is also an excellent way of exploring new tastes and trends – Pinot Grigio instead of Chardonnay, or Malbec instead of Merlot.

If the restaurant does not have a sommelier, then ordering can be harder. One tip is to forget all about what you are planning to eat and to concentrate on picking a wine style that you know you will enjoy. It really does not matter if you end up drinking Australian Shiraz with salmon. If you want to be more adventurous, however, then select a wine made from your favourite grape and go to a different country. For example, if you like southern French Merlot, try a Chilean Merlot instead. Indeed, wines from the new world (countries such as Australia and South Africa) are usually the most reliable. Having said that, if you are eating Italian, it makes sense to drink Italian wine. Ditto Spain. Ditto France. Ditto any classic wine-producing country. >

Top five tips for ordering wine

1 It may not represent the best value, but try a glass of house wine to see if you like it (you may even be offered a free taste, if you ask). Good restaurants take their flagship wines seriously, choosing them with care. House champagne can also be a brilliant alternative to more expensive brands. English sparkling wine is also very fashionable – and is very tasty.

2 If in doubt, stick to a brand. Brands become brands because they are popular. And they become popular because they taste good.

3 Food-friendly wines that go with just about everything include Australian Riesling, Alsace Pinot Blanc, Pinot Grigio, Sauvignon Blanc, Pinot Noir and new world Chardonnays, Semillons, Merlots and Cabernet Sauvignons.

4 Traditional wine and food matching rules were made to be broken. But there are some combinations that never work. Avoid artichoke, blue cheese dressing, capers, English mustard, fried egg, horseradish/wasabi, kippers, mint sauce, oily fish, over-ripe brie/camembert, pickles, raw onion, salsa, salted anchovies, salted peanuts, smoked cheese, spinach, very hot chillies, vinaigrette dressing and vinegar.

5 Always check that you have been given the wine you ordered and make sure that the bottle is opened at the table.

But what about value for money? Obviously, one pays far more for restaurant wine than it would cost in the shops, and it can be difficult to determine if you are being charged fairly. Unfortunately, unless you can make a direct comparison to a retail price, you will never really know. Furthermore, each restaurant calculates its mark-up according to the profits required to cover overheads – and, naturally, these vary from establishment to establishment. It is nevertheless worth noting that most restaurants employ a sliding scale of mark-ups, making relatively little profit on the finest wines while filling their cash registers with fat profits from sales of house wine.

Whatever you choose, remember that it is your money paying for it. If you cannot drink it all, take it home! >

Wine in pubs and bars

Restaurant rules apply to pubs and bars as well – although you are unlikely to find a sommelier in a pub. The biggest pitfall is bottles that have been open for too long. If your glass of wine seems tired, send it back and ask for a new bottle to be uncorked. Trendy airline-sized bottles guarantee freshness on one level, but how old is the stock? Wine ages really quickly in tiny bottles.

Corked wine and when to complain

Most wine bottles are sealed with a natural cork. Trouble arises, however, when the cork has been contaminated by a nasty compound called 2,4,6-trichloroanisole (TCA), which causes a smell and taste of rotting mushrooms, dirty bird cages, sweaty rugby socks and every kind of musty thing you can think of. 'Corked' wine should very firmly be rejected and you should ask for another bottle. Don't be shy. Even if the sommelier disagrees, insist on another bottle for comparison. Be assertive in the nicest of ways.

A corked wine is not the same as a heavily oaked wine, even if you do not like it. A good oaked wine will smell and taste of vanilla and buttered toast. A bad one will make you feel that you have swallowed a floorboard! Unfortunately, the latter is not considered a fault. Reject it, but offer to pay for it with good grace.

Know your limits

Drink-driving is a major issue — and quite rightly so. Each year, 15 per cent of all deaths on our roads involve drivers who are over the legal drink-drive limit.

The limit currently stands at 80 milligrammes of alcohol contained in 100 millilitres of blood, but there is no fail-safe rule to determine how much you can drink and stay under it. The amount and type of alcoholic drink, your gender, weight, age, metabolism and whether or not you have eaten all play their part.

As a general guide, a man weighing 12 to 13 stone should consume no more than four units of alcohol, equivalent to two pints of standard bitter at 3.5 per cent alcohol by volume (ABV). For an average woman (nine to ten stone), the maximum level drops to three units.

Given that women often drink wine when they are out, this can mean that she is 'allowed' just one 175ml glass of wine — generally described as 'standard size' — with an ABV of 14 per cent, a strength not unusual for modern-day wines. This equates to 2.45 units, so it is clear that a second (or larger) glass would put a woman well over the limit. Incidentally, you can work out the exact number of alcohol units in a drink by multiplying its volume in millilitres by its ABV and dividing the sum by 1000.

It takes about an hour for a unit of alcohol to be neutralized by the liver. But always keep in mind that even the tiniest amount of alcohol in your bloodstream will affect your judgement and will impair your reaction time, making you a worse driver as a result. Perhaps the sensible message here is not to drink and drive at all.

Julie Arkell is author of several books on wine and writes for national newspapers and magazines on the subject.

Coralie Dorman is a
freelance food writer. She
was formerly features
editor of *BBC Good Food*
and is now contributing
editor of *delicious.* magazine.

"Ling, winkle, gurnard and smelt,
pomfret, weever and dab. How
many other species, trawled
from ancient deep oceans or
clear freshwater streams, are
as colourful in name, texture
and taste? Fish is also health-
enhancing, offering low-fat
protein and oily varieities are
high in Omega-3 fatty acids."

fishing
for the facts

*To help you get the most from the most popular fish and
shellfish, follow Coralie Dorman's buying and cooking guide
plus get a taste of some of the exciting dishes and flavour
combinations that you'll see featured on Les Routiers
members' menus up and down the country.*

Cod

Buying and cooking
Over-fished it might be, but cod is still the UK's favourite fish. Mostly available in fillets, but if you're buying steaks, get them from the meaty shoulder end. Roast, fry, grill but only poach if the fish is flapping fresh as it can taste bland.

Eating out
Best in winter when icy seas firm it up, cod is ubiquitous and goes well with almost any flavouring a chef cares to introduce it to, from cheesy sauces and soft mash toppings to crisp, lively chilli and lime dressings.

Lobster

Buying and cooking
Buy big is the maxim, as the older lobsters are, the more meat they'll contain. If they're live, put them in the freezer for a couple of hours, then slowly bring to the boil in lots of water and they won't feel a thing. The males have larger claws, but females taste better.

Eating out
Old-fashioned, rich and over the top yes, but Lobster Thermidor stands the test of time. Here's why: the boiled meat is mixed with cheesy mornay sauce flavoured with mustard, piled back into the shell, sprinkled with breadcrumbs and grilled.

Crab

Buying and cooking
Live crabs should be energetic wavers, and arguably approached as recreational cooking. Even ready-boiled ones too, what with all the picking and the patience of a saint required to enveigle flesh from the shell. Cock crabs have bigger claws, but hens taste sweeter.

Eating out
The south-east coastal waters of England produce some of the finest crabs, in particular the sweet-tasting Cromer, from Norfolk. Savour soft-shell crabs in summer, and for the rest of the year, nothing could be finer than a dressed crab. Good in fishcakes and goes particularly well with avocado.

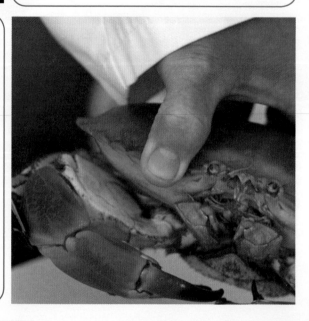

Squid

Buying and cooking
Best to get the fishmonger to clean this unweildy mollusc. If you've ever seen a Greek fisherman giving a squid a damn good thrashing by beating it on the rocks, it's not because of any Basil Fawltyesque frustrations, but rather to tenderise it for, as everyone knows, it's a fine line between soft flesh and chewing on rubber bands. Cooking too makes a difference – the rules are fast and furious or long and slow.

Eating out
Calamari, once derided as the preferred fare of the average idiot Briton abroad, is once again on top. The tender rings and perky sprouting tentacles coated in crisp batter, deep-fried and served with a squeeze of fresh lemon and perhaps a lemony avgolemono sauce for dipping says all that needs to be said really.

Oysters

Buying and cooking
Always buy live with shells clamped shut, and aim to eat them *au natural* as soon as humanly possible after you've got them home, as they lose their liquor rapidly. Grill in their shells topped with a white sauce, or egg and breadcrumb the meat and deep fry. Natives are the flatish type, Pacifics the frilly-shelled, more cup-shaped variety.

Eating out
The ancient oyster beds of Colchester and Whitstable have made oysters part of our culinary heritage. Sexually ambivalent, oysters can change from male to female and back again on a whim. Natives are best in winter when there's an 'R' in the month, although Pacifics are eaten all year round.

Prawns and langoustines

Buying and cooking
The warmer the water, the bigger the prawn, although prawns do survive in cold seas too. Without exception, buy them raw as cooked prawns more often than not taste woolly. Run the point of a knife under the black intestinal vein that runs along the back. Fried they take just minutes to turn from inky blue to baby pink.

Eating out
A well-excecuted prawn cocktail is a thing of beauty, and potted shrimps under a blanket of clarified butter a real treat. Langoustines or Dublin Bay prawns aka Sixties' scampi just need a swift roasting in the oven and some handmade mayonnaise to dip the prized flesh into.

Salmon

Buying and cooking

Farmed salmon can be good but wild salmon is
best, simple as that, and it's much better to eat
less of a better quality. Poach whole, or as fillets or
steaks, or fry gently in butter and oil. It's okay too
to leave the centres just slightly pink.

Eating out

The stalwart of the cold buffet, a whole salmon
is hard to beat. The chef's way of fast-frying the
oily skin until it's crisp adds another contrasting
dimension to the soft, pink flesh, and fishcakes
made with more salmon than mash and served
with a sweet chilli sauce are brilliant.

Sea bass

Buying and cooking

Anyone who cooks appreciates the white flesh
and fine, clean taste of bass – and the skin also
tastes especially good although it needs to be
scrupulously descaled. Look for dazzling silver
skin and rock-hard flesh. Don't serve it with bold
flavourings, just a bit of oil or butter and some
fresh fishy herbs like fennel, dill or parsley.

Eating out

A holiday fish if ever there was one, sea bass is
best throughout the spring and summer months,
but pricewise, this is top end stuff although worth
every penny. You'll find it on every menu too from
Chinese to swanky British.

Trout

Buying and cooking

You're more likely to get farmed trout now than
any caught in some freshwater babbling brook.
Still, farmed means fresh and this midweek supper
fish is cheap and wholesome. Shower it with
butter-fried almonds or simply roast it in foil
with a knob of best butter.

Eating out

The classic *truite au bleu* relies on the fish being
caught and cooked within the hour if it's to be
any good. Odd as it sounds, the natural slime
that denotes freshness gives the cooked fish a
blueish tinge.

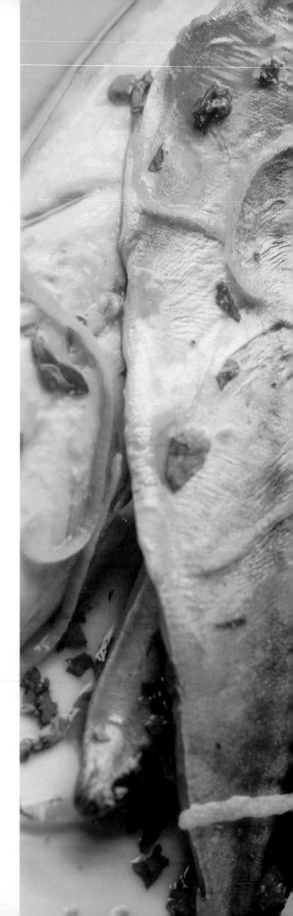

Skate

Buying and cooking
A lazy fish that prefers to sit on the sea bed and wait for its dinner, it's the wings you'll buy to eat, but if there's the slightest whiff of ammonia, don't even get your purse out. Skate are cartilaginous rather than skeletal, so the flesh scrapes off the bendy 'bones' really easily. Dip wings in seasoned flour spiked with cayenne and shallow fry in butter.

Eating out
Skate with black butter, or *raie au beurre noir* is superb, as is the addition of a few piquant capers or caperberries to this dark buttery sauce. Poached skate wings, their stringy flesh harvested then gathered into balls, battered, deep-fried and served with chips, puts an elevated spin on the nation's favourite Friday night supper.

Halibut

Buying and cooking
A giant among flat fish, which can grow up to 200kg, halibut is cut up and bought as steaks. Because it tends to be on the dry side, it responds well to braising or poaching in wine or a simple court bouillon.

Eating out
Farmed all year round, if you happen to spot it on a menu in early summer, chances are it will be wild halibut which is not to be missed. Like other white fish, it's an excellent canvas for a whole host of flavourings.

Monkfish

Buying and cooking
An ugly brute in anyone's book. The head makes up half its body weight and has little use except for stock. It's the tail that's the prize – meaty, almost prawn-like in texture, and excellent roasted as a whole, or chopped large as generous kebabs and grilled. Don't forget to peel the skin off before you cook.

Eating out
Also called angler fish because of the strange little 'fishing rod' which comes out of it's head. *Lotte en gigot* means a whole tail will arrive on your plate, and don't pass on any dish which includes monkfish livers, which although rare are uncommonly good.

Who's cooking what at Les Routiers restaurants?

Sarah Holgate and Margaret Morgan of Hive on the Quay in Aberaeron, West Wales (page 230) get their lobster live and kicking from nearby Cardigan Bay. They also make a flavoursome piquant monkfish and skate stew with leeks, tomatoes, olives and a sprinkle of gremolata – parsley, lemon and garlic – on top.

At Mussel and Crab in Newark, Nottinghamshire (page 142), owners Bruce and Allison Elliot-Bateman and their chef Philip Wright bring in their Cromer crab live.

"We only use the cock crabs as there is more meat on them. We mix the meat with a bit of black pepper and lemon juice, and that's it. Simple."

Philip also does a crab bisque enriched with local cream, serves his oysters with a chilli relish and bakes sea bass with roasted vegetables to bring out their sweetness.

At Bryces in Ockley, near Dorking in Surrey (page 154), the fish gets delivered six days a week, and in the bar, cod comes in a crisp beer batter and in the restaurant, it's roasted with a chorizo and Parmesan crust. Oysters from Loch Fyne arrive at your table poached in their own liquor and served with a bacon hollandaise sauce flavoured with fresh chervil, chives and parsley.

"Fish doesn't need complicated sauces,"
Bill Bryce asserts, *"It just has to be the freshest it can."*

Catch the best of British

There are so many fabulous fish and shellfish available in Britain, that we should be making the most of what's on offer, says Seafish.

In Britain, we could dine out on a different species of fish or shellfish caught from around the world almost every day of the year. But according to the Sea Fish Industry Authority (Seafish) the nation's favourite three choices remain virtually unchanged.

Cod, salmon and haddock, and in that order, remain Britain's top three fish. But says Seafish, there are around 100 varieties of fish caught around our coastline that are readily available to try at restaurants and buy from fishmongers and fish markets. We just need to become more adventurous when it comes to netting some winners.

Celebrity chef Rick Stein has long been leading the trend for local seafood at his Seafood Restaurant in Padstow. There, 95 per cent of the seafood on the menu is locally caught. And he is setting new standards of fish and chips at his new chippie in Padstow. There you can enjoy the delights of Cornish gurnard or megrim with chips. Les Routiers' members are also at the forefront of this trend for serving locally caught fish, which is very often line-caught and bought fresh off the boat.

Surprisingly 90 per cent of our cod is imported and we have excellent stocks of other seafood around to tempt us. In winter, try alternatives to cod such as pollack, gurnard and ling; in summer there's amazing flatfish such as lemon or Dover sole, turbot and brill, and in winter mackerel and sardines. All year-round, we can tuck into marvellous monkfish and in Scotland they have redfish, that is similar to red snapper. Just a few to look out for on menus and at fishmongers around the country.

Seafish was set up in 1981 and works to help consumers find out about all types of fish, convey the health benefits of eating fish regularly, as well as help all sectors of the industry raise their standards, improve efficiency and ensure fish stocks remain sustainable for the future.

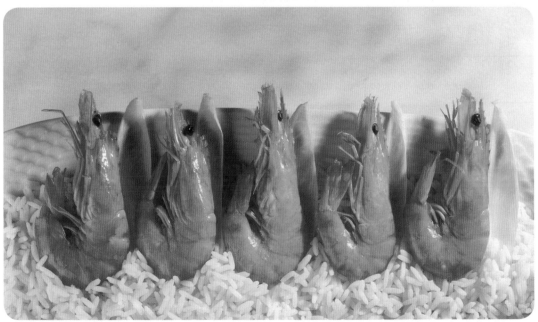

A key date in the Seafish calendar is the annual Seafood Week, which in 2004 runs from 1-8 October. And the date is no coincidence, as it's this time of year when we have the best stocks of many different fish available. During the week, Seafish will be advising on buying and cooking fish and shellfish. It will be running special promotions with restaurants and retailers, including a selection of Les Routiers establishments. For information about events for Seafood Week and a wealth of related information check out the Seafish website at www.seafish.org.uk.

Restored
in the Best Possible Taste

How three makeovers resulted in three new Les Routiers members

It took £1.5m and several determined organisations to restore the attractive timber-framed Ballater Station Restaurant to its former glory. A feat of funding coordination by Scottish Enterprises, Scottish Heritage, Aberdeenshire Council and the European Union saved this historic station from being demolished. "It was a case of burn it down or restore it to some purposeful use that would help pay towards its maintenance," said David Young the project manager for Aberdeenshire Council. The station was built for Queen Victoria in the 1860s, and this was the end of the line for the Royal Train when the Queen visited Balmoral. The station was going to be nearer the Castle, but Queen Victoria was a staunch member of the not in my own back yard group, and didn't want a line running through her 10,000-acre estate. So like other visiting royalty, she would arrive at the 600ft-long Ballater Station, which has one of the longest platforms in the country. The station housed the Queen's waiting room, with toilet, although there was no running water in those days. For those curious about its former life, this waiting room is now an exhibition area, outlining the station's history. Tsar Nicolas was one visitor and it continued to be used until the 1960s.

"It was a case of burn it down or restore it to some purposeful use that would help pay towards its maintenance"

The restoration project involved more than just the station, as the square outside had to be reconfigured for parking. And the project took one and a half years to complete. First, the building was completely gutted.

According to David Young: "The building was fine from one metre upwards, but banks of snow had damaged the foundations, so they had to be replaced. We also had to take off and insulate the roof as it gets very cold here in winter." He now likens the station to a vintage car, "All the bits are original, but there are a few new bits which are identical to the original parts." And it's all in great working order. The station's stained glass windows, smart mahogany panelling and a glass-ceilinged roof were in excellent condition and are the star attractions of the restaurant today. The station is also a focal point for the small community of Ballater, which has just 2,000 inhabitants. Like many small places that attract visitors and tourists, royalty among them, there are excellent quality shops and, of course, thanks to its restoration, fine dining at the Station Restaurant.

Corsewall Lighthouse, Corsewall

The rectangular hotel block next to Corsewall Lighthouse tower was once home to the principal lighthouse keeper and his two lighthouse assistants and their families. New owner Gordon Ward, who took over in 2000, says before electricity, lighthouse keeping was labour intensive, with a pendulum mechanism and pull chain being manually operated and reset every 40 minutes to provide the light.

The main block was bought from the Lighthouse Board in 1994, and was renovated in one year into a smart hotel with stylish bedrooms. Apart from reconfiguring the rooms, the main work involved removing the outside staircase that led to the top section and building an attractive spiral staircase inside instead, which is quite a stunning feature. Corsewall, originally built in 1815, is still a working lighthouse and, like all lighthouses, it has its own individual signal. It gives five flashes, three blanks, five flashes and three blanks – 16 lens in all in one minute, so passing ships can track their position before heading out across the Atlantic. Luckily, for hotel guests the flashing lights are only seen out at sea and in front of the lighthouse they shine as five solid fingers of light. There are now plans to make the lighthouse itself into a visitor attraction.

"Luckily, for hotel guests the flashing lights are only seen out at sea and in front of the lighthouse they shine as five solid fingers of light"

"From Turkey, we ordered 20 tons of marble for the bathrooms, solid oak four-poster beds and lavish chandeliers for the two conference rooms"

Stone Court Hotel and Chambers

Renovating this former judges' residence has been the hardest project Musa Kivrak has undertaken in his 30 years as hotelier.

British builders and planning applications were the main stumbling blocks as he worked to turn this listed building into a smart hotel and restaurant. One year and £1m later, his project was achieved, but not without setbacks.

The main problem was having his grant application being turned down. You are not allowed to start any work if you are changing the purpose of the building, and as he had already started some work on the condemned and crumbling building before he sent in his application no money was forthcoming.

The work needed to be carried out was extensive: "Walls, the roof, ceilings, windows, rewiring and heating all had to done," he says. "We also had to build a car park and sort out access."

And Musa didn't stint on materials. "From Turkey, we ordered 20 tons of marble for the bathrooms, solid oak four-poster beds and lavish chandeliers for the two conference rooms." Nice touches remain of the former occupants. Room keys are attached to judges' gavels and their portrait prints adorn the walls in the bedrooms. The restaurant has the original wood panelling. The renovations involved 26 months of hard work for Musa, but it has paid off as Stone Court is a real treat for residents and restaurant goers.

Eat your way
through the seasons

Eating British foods in season means you are opting for foods when they are at their flavoursome best. Okay, there are a few dull months when root vegetables seem to be all that's available, but for most of the year, we can enjoy varied supplies of home-grown produce. Some seasons may be incredibly short, such as asparagus in late May or runner beans in June, but each month brings something different to tempt. Check our calendar and use it as a guide when you're deciding what to order in our members' restaurants. The majority of Les Routiers' members are dedicated followers of the seasons, rather than what's fashionable. They source some of the best local produce (see food maps), and use their ingredients inventively.

January

- Carrots, turnips, squash, celeriac, shallots, cabbage, leeks, parsnips, Brussels sprouts, garlic, Jersey cauliflowers
- Forced rhubarb, pears
- Goose, venison, hare
- Lobster, scallops

March

- Beetroot, Jerusalem artichokes, leeks, purple sprouting broccoli, spring greens, white cabbage, leeks, radishes
- Early rhubarb
- Shin of beef
- Brill, halibut, John Dory, mackerel, sardines, lobster

February

- Chicory, leeks, squash, cabbage, parsnips, most root vegetables, shallots, red cabbage, Jerusalem artichokes
- Forced rhubarb
- Chicken, guinea fowl, Welsh mountain lamb
- Lemon and Dover sole, wild salmon, brill, cod, crab oysters, mackerel, skate, turbot

April

- Purple sprouting broccoli, spring greens, carrots, watercress
- Rhubarb
- Spring lamb, beef
- Sea trout, prawns, crab, monkfish, halibut

May

- Asparagus, Swiss chard, radishes, watercress, spring greens
- Strawberries
- Duck
- Sea bass, monkfish, turbot

June

- Aubergines, courgettes, broad beans, peas, lettuce, peppers
- Gooseberries, tayberries, elderflowers, redcurrants, cherries, strawberries
- Welsh lamb
- Grey mullet, crab

July

- Tomatoes, cauliflower, sage, watercress, fennel, runner beans, peas
- Strawberries, raspberries, loganberries, cherries, currants, gooseberries
- Veal
- Trout, pike, clams, haddock, lobster, shellfish

September

- Cucumber, spinach, onions, sweetcorn
- Damsons, blackberries, figs
- Partridge, wood pigeon, duck, venison
- Oysters, mussels, sea bass

August

- Peas, lettuce, aubergines, courgettes, peppers, sweetcorn
- Greengages, strawberries
- Hare
- Skate, John Dory, crayfish

October

- Pumpkins and squash, celeriac, red cabbage, kale, courgettes, mushrooms, beetroot, marrow
- Apples, pears
- Pheasant, guinea fowl, woodcock, partridge
- Eels, oysters, mussels

November

- Broccoli, Brussels sprouts, cabbage, cauliflowers, leeks, onions, potatoes, root vegetables
- Apples, pears
- Beef, pheasant
- Haddock, cod, halibut, turbot, Dover sole, plaice, huss, eel, grey mullet

December

- Celery, red cabbage, root vegetables, Brussels sprouts, pumpkin, beetroot
- Pears
- Turkey, goose, duck
- Sea bass, cod

"Eating in season is the logical and sensible thing to do. When we eat food in season, we're eating it at its flavoursome best, and it's ludicrous not to make full use of it"
Henrietta Green, food writer and founder of the Food Lovers' Fair

London

Eating out in London has never been so appetising and the hotel scene is just as vibrant, with somewhere to suit all pockets. You'll find Les Routiers' members offer comfort and style at prices that will leave you plenty left over to splash out on some fine dining, writes Melanie Leyshon.

The capital's restaurants come and go, but there are those that stay the course, consistently offering authenically good cooking. Not only do they cater for hungry tourists, who are here one minute and gone the next, but they are popular neighhourhood haunts in their own right.

The majority of Les Routiers' London members fall into this category: Food for Thought, Caffé Mamma and Le Truc Vert, for example, have been cooking up a storm for years. Their philosophy of offering authentic cuisine instead of following fashionable food whims has paid off, and they have built up a loyal band of customers.

If you visited Food for Thought five years ago, then returned today, you'd still find it much as it was – queues on the stairs and a satisfying range of hearty vegetarian fare. It may have added new recipes to its line-up of soups, stews and dishes, but the quality, and the portions, are no way diminished. Our selection of pubs and bars are also a delectable and dependable selection, from the refurbished Alma to the comfortable familiarity of the Swag and Tails or the Ebury Wine Bar.

And you can expect the same high standards and comfort at Les Routiers' hotels and guest houses. The number of anonymous chains in the capital has mushroomed, offering rooms decorated to the same spec whether they're in London, Paris or Madrid, but our members have maintained their individuality.

Check into the Harlingford or Mayflower, for instance, and you'll find the style and service, plus all the extras, that you'd enjoy at a top hotel. Among our new members this year are the Langorf Apartments, which are ideal for those who want to sample the foods from London's many farmers' markets and top food halls.

And with all our properties close to transport, the capital's main attractions are all just a stop or two away…

Central

10 Manchester Street

10 Manchester Street, London W1V 4DG
Telephone: +44(0)870 4016477
+44(0)20 7486 6669
stay@10manchesterstreet.fsnet.co.uk
www.10manchesterstreet.com

Stay at this central London hotel and you'll be spoilt for choice of things to do within walking distance. Marylebone High Street, Oxford Street and Bond Street shops are close by, and you have the Wallace Collection and Madame Tussaud's on the doorstep. The hotel will appeal to those looking for a stylish hotel without having to pay over the top prices. It is furnished with understated elegant antique furniture and provides affordable accommodation and a friendly, no-frills service. There are special rates at weekends. The fine, early 20th century building was completely refurbished in the late 1990s. The spacious ground-floor sitting room sets the tone with its comfortable sofas, soft lamps and laid-back air. Double rooms are generously proportioned and have high ceilings. They are well kitted out too, with fluffy bathrobes, mini-sound systems, mini-fridges, satellite TV, tea trays and trouser press. The single bedrooms are compact but well designed. There are also nine suites with separate sitting rooms. The bed and breakfast rates include continental breakfast, but you can have a full English breakfast for a surcharge. They don't serve dinner, but there are plenty of lunch and dinner options available at nearby cafés, bars and restaurants.

Rooms: 46. Double room £120, single £95.
Closed: Rarely.
Other points: Residents only. No-smoking area.
Children welcome.
Directions: 5 minutes walk from Baker Street tube station, off Dorset Street. (Map 2, B5)

Central

Café in the Crypt

Crypt of St Martin-in-the-Fields, Duncannon Street, London WC2N 4JJ
Telephone: +44(0)870 4016485
+44(0)207 839 4342
www.stmartin-in-the-fields.org

Its brilliant location, just a step away from Trafalgar Square and the theatre district, make this terrific-value café a welcome escape from the West End crowds. This landmark church crypt with its brick-vaulted ceilings, pillars, and gravestones on the floor make for a dramatic and airy setting. It's the ideal stop-off for a quick, inexpensive meal pre or post theatre, or before catching a train from Charing Cross. The extensive self-service offers an appealing array of pick-and-mix salads, soup and daily-changing meat and fish dishes. Popular choices include avocado and tuna mayonnaise or papaya filled with salt beef, peach and buffalo mozzarella salads, and stuffed peppers. For something more substantial look to mains of roast leg of lamb steak with a rosemary sauce and minted apricots with fresh vegetables or wild mushroom pasta bake with a Stilton glaze. But you can also just relax with a hearty sandwich and pot of tea. Generous portions and the fact tables are spaced well apart are other plus points. The short, well-chosen wine list is clearly annotated and reasonably priced. After eating, you could explore the Gallery in the vault or book for one of the many classical concerts.

Prices: Main course from £6.75. House wine £10.50.
Last orders: Food: Monday-Wednesday 20.00 (Thursday-Saturday 23.00, Sunday 20.00).
Closed: Rarely.
Food: Traditional English.
Other points: No-smoking area. Children welcome.
Credit cards not accepted.
Directions: Nearest Tubes: Charing Cross, Leicester Square.
(Map 2, C7)

www.routiers.co.uk

Central

Ebury Wine Bar and Restaurant

139 Ebury Street, London SW1W 9QU
Telephone: +44(0)870 4016481
+44 (0)20 7730 5447
nigel@eburywinebar.co.uk

A London classic that reassuringly doesn't change. The décor is French in style, but the service and atmosphere is traditional British to the core. There are two bars, both with close-packed wooden tables backed up by waiter service, and seats at the bars for eating and drinking. If you wine and dine alone, the many prints on the walls will keep you entertained. The wine list is tremendous, and is one of the reasons for its ongoing success. It's globally diversified, very accessible, and there is a great house selection at keen prices with a good range by the glass. Two or three sittings per table for lunch, crowded in the early evening, is all par for the course. There's an excellent value set lunch, and bar snacks, which take in bread, houmous and roasted garlic to spicy fishcakes with an oriental dip; and they're available all day. The carte of contemporary brasserie fare updates some traditional comfort food: pan-fried skate with samphire and tomato salad, for example, or grilled calf's liver, cold potato and roasted pepper salad, and pork and leek sausages with pomegranate and onion jus. Enterprising puddings include assiette of lemon, and chocolate blancmange with cappuccino sauce.

Prices: Set menu £13.50 (2 course). Main course from £9.50. House wine £12.
Last orders: Food: lunch 14.45 (Sunday 15.00); dinner 22.30 (Sunday 22.00).
Closed: Christmas-New Year.
Food: Modern European.
Other points: Children welcome.
Directions: Ten minutes walk from Victoria British Rail and Victoria tube, or Sloane Square tube. (Map 2, E5)

Central

Food for Thought

31 Neal Street, Covent Garden, London WC2H 9PR
Telephone: +44(0)870 4016483/6484
+44(0)20 7836 9072/0239

Once a banana ripening warehouse, this compact basement vegetarian restaurant is a legend in its own lunchtimes. Every day customers queue from the dining area, eager to partake in this ever-changing vegetarian extravganza. Takeaways are dispatched upstairs. Vanessa Garrett has clocked up 24 years at the restaurant and her high standards and seasonal, homemade dishes at reasonable prices means she continues to attract new fans. You may have to share a table, but for a more sedate meal come around 3-4pm. All the food is made with fruit and vegetables selected from Borough and New Covent Garden markets. The soups, like summer mushroom and leek, are hearty and delicious, and can be enjoyed with great hunks of freshly baked bread or the biggest, crumbliest scones. Mains include a Venetian feast of roasted Mediterranean vegetables in a light tomato and basil sauce, topped with a fresh herb polenta. Long-time favourites include vegetable stir-fry in a tamarind and ginger sauce served with brown rice, and there are wonderful cakes and puddings such as sugar-free carrot cake with apple glaze. It's unlicensed, but you can bring your own wine and there's no corkage charge, or drink from the free jugs of water infused with orange.

Prices: Set lunch and dinner £9.90. Main course from £4.
Unlicenced, BYO's welcome, no corkage charged.
Last orders: Food: 20.30 (Sunday 17.00).
Closed: Easter Sunday.
Food: Vegetarian.
Other points: Totally no smoking.
Directions: Covent Garden tube. Head due north form exit, approximately three minutes walk down Neal Street on the left hand side. (Map 2, C7)

Individual charm and warmth

Central

Fung Shing

15 Lisle Street, London WC2H 7BE
Telephone: +44(0)870 4016476
+44(0)20 7437 1539
www.fungshing.com

It's often hard to decide between one Chinese restaurant and the next in London's Chinatown, but be rest assured this venerable old timer is among the best Cantonese restaurants in the area. The extensive menu caters for all budgets. Starters range from the modestly priced vegetarian spring rolls to the more lavish and adventurous braised sharks fin. The same applies to the main courses, with the more unusual ingredients available at a price. But you can keep within a moderate budget by choosing sweet and sour prawns or chicken, or go some way to blowing it with the lobster with black bean sauce or braised fresh carp with ginger and spring onion. Other interesting dishes include stewed belly pork with yam in hot pot: the yams have that required perfumed flavour and truly soft, mushy texture that comes from long cooking, and belly pork is as tender as could be. Set menus offer a reassuringly familiar version of Cantonese cooking, but careful choosing amongst the separate chef specials will deliver a more ambitious, rewarding meal at a similar price. The wine list covers most bases, and includes a fine wine selection.

Prices: Set menu £17. Main course from £8. House wine £14.50.
Last orders: Food: 23.00.
Closed: Rarely.
Food: Traditional Cantonese.
Other points: Children welcome. Two private rooms avaiable.
Directions: Nearest tube: Leicester Square. Behind the Empire cinema. (Map 2, C4)

Central

Harlingford

61-63 Cartwright Gardens, London WC1H 9EL
Telephone: +44(0)870 4016474
+44(0)20 7387 1551
book@harlingfordhotel.com
www.harlingfordhotel.com

Revamped by interiors specialist Nathalie O'Donohoe, the Harlingford retains the elegance of a Georgian town house, but captures a contemporary mood with tasteful and vibrant furnishing and colour schemes. The standard of refurbishment is incredibly high, and for a centrally located hotel, the Harlingford offers outstanding value. The areas for relaxation have been given much thought. After taking in the sights, you can chill out in the smart lilac-themed sitting room that shows off Victorian paintings in a setting of modern fabrics and textures, or ask for the key to the hotel's pretty private garden. Like many well-priced, tasteful central London hotels, the rooms are not huge but they are all perfectly formed. The all-white foyer creates a sense of calm and coolness. The breakfast room is dominated by an art deco illuminated stained glass mural, while modern flower vases form centrepieces on each table and these splashes of colour complement the clean lines of the light white and cream design. The 43 bedrooms are decorated in five different themes, and several can accomodate three or a family of four. The rooms are spread over five floors, so older or infirm guests should request ground floor accommodation. It has a sister hotel, the Mabledon Hotel, in nearby Mabledon Court.

Rooms: 43. Double room from £95, single from £75, family room from £105.
Closed: Never.
Other points: Children welcome. NCP car park nearby. Access to tennis courts and garden.
Directions: Few minutes walk from Kings Cross, Euston and St Pancras stations. Turn into Mabledon Place which turns into Cartwright Gardens. The hotel is at the bottom of the crescent. (Map 2, B7)

The Royal Borough of Kensington and Chelsea

PORTOBELLO ROAD, W. 11.

The Royal Borough of Kensington and Chelsea

WESTBOURN GROVE W.11

Central

Swag and Tails

10-11 Fairholt Street, London SW7 1EG
Telephone: +44(0)870 4016244
+44(0)20 7584 6926
theswag@swagandtails.com
www.swagandtails.com

After a busy shopping stint in Harrods and Harvey Nicks, step into the haven of calm that is Knightsbridge village. And a choice place to recharge is at the quaint Swag and Tails. Outside, it's prettily flower-clad, inside you'll find a civilised yet informal bar, with original panelling, stripped wooden floors and open fires. There's a cosy quieter dining area at the rear. Suits, shoppers and well-heeled locals quickly fill the bar at lunchtime, attracted by the welcoming atmosphere and the modern, Mediterranean-style dishes listed on a constantly changing blackboard menu. Opt for a pint and a classic burger, or linger longer over something more sophisticated. Start with Bayonne ham salad with pickled mushrooms and a lentil and parsley vinaigrette and move on to lime and coriander marinaded chicken breast with a warm salad of tandoori potatoes and onion bahji. The good selection of fish comes from Billingsgate and meats from Smithfield. Puds are a real treat too. Choose Eton mess tart with lemon sorbet and mint syrup or date sponge pudding with caramel sauce and ice cream, or there's its popular plate of Irish cheeses with a delicious pear and date chutney. The interesting list of wines comes with useful tasting notes, and 11 are offered by the glass, including decent house champagne. Note the hard-working licensees, Annemaria and Stuart Boomer-Davies, close the pub at weekends.

Prices: Main course from £10.95. Bar/snack from £7.50. House wine £11.50.
Last orders: Bar: 23.00. Food: lunch 15.00; dinner 22.00.
Closed: Saturday, Sunday, all Bank Holidays and 10 days over the Christmas period.
Food: Modern British.
Other points: No-smoking area. Dogs welcome in the bar in the evening. Children welcome in the restaurant.
Directions: Harrods is the nearest reference point. On the opposite side of the road turn into Montpelier Street and take the first left into Cheval Place and then the second right and first left. (Map 1, E4)

Central

The Tate Britain Restaurant

Millbank, London SW1P 4RG
Telephone: +44(0)870 4016486
+44(0)20 7887 8825
www.tate.org.uk

Dining here is a satisfying experience, and that's before you even get to the food. There is the stunning 1926 Rex Whistler mural that forms a backdrop to admire, and exploring the legendary Tate wine list is also a joy, as it offers some of the best value wines in London. After a few years adrift, the list has returned to its former glory thanks to young sommelier Hamish Anderson. It's comprehensive and each wine comes with the sommelier's recommendations. There's also a good selection of half bottles. Décor-wise, the restaurant may initally seem sombre and formal, but the atmosphere is lifted by the noisy lunchtime crowd and the chic white-clothed tables and black leather banquettes. The menu runs along modern British/European lines and majors in sophisticated, light dishes. The short carte menu has seven choices per course. You could start with dressed Cornish crab and lemon mayonnaise or cream of Jerusalem artichoke and nutmeg soup, then follow with a main of baked cod fillet with Scottish rope-grown mussel stew, or breast of chicken wrapped in prosciutto with minted pasta wheat 'risotto'. The smaller set lunch is good value, and doesn't stint on flavour. It may offer roasted plum tomato soup with garlic toast, followed by confit roasted pork belly with a cassoulet of white beans and chocolate truffle tart with marinated golden raisins.

Prices: Set lunch £20.50. Restaurant main course from £10.75. House wine from £15.50.
Last orders: Food: lunch 15.00 (Sunday 16.00).
Closed: 24-27 December.
Food: Modern British.
Other points: No-smoking area. Children welcome.
Directions: Nearest tube: Pimlico. 77a bus. (Map 2, E7)

www.routiers.co.uk

Central

Le Truc Vert

42 North Audley Street, London W1K 6ZR
Telephone: +44(0)870 4016478
+44(0)20 7491 9988
trucvert@madasafish.com

Refined and relaxing, this Mayfair version of a village shop, complete with restaurant, is a haven of civility, just moments from Oxford Street. Home-baked croissants, Danish pastries, quiche, savoury vegetarian pasties, muffins and cakes can be ordered throughout the day, and early risers take note, breakfast kicks off at 7.30am, including Saturdays. For a snack or lunch, you can order from the conventional menu, or make up your own selection from the goodies in the shop. In the early evening, the restaurant atmosphere really kicks in. And it's a slick and seamless transformation. Wooden tables are covered with crisp white linen and the lighting pitched accordingly. You can eat well for less than £20. The menu delivers the likes of seafood and sausage gumbo to start, followed by chargrilled veal escalope with roast broccoli, roast fig, watercress and blue cheese dressing, with raspberry crème brûlée to finish. There's a good range of French wines to accompany your meal. The shop is a veritable Aladdin's cave of ingredients and you're bound to be tempted by the shelves of goodies, including stacks of pestos, salsas, sun-dried tomatoes, and delicacies such as artichoke cream, as well as a range of French honey, and top-quality cheeses. Free-range organic eggs and natural yogurts are also for sale, as are pâtés, an astonishing range of fruit juices, and the vegetable display, which brings a bright splash of colour.

Prices: House wine £8.
Last orders: Food: 21.00 (Sunday 16.00).
Closed: Public holidays.
Food: Modern European.
Other points: Totally no smoking. Children welcome.
Directions: Between Oxford Street and Grosvenor Square.
Nearest tube: Bond Street. (Map 2, C5)

East

Hanoi Café

98 Kingsland Road, London E2 8DP
Telephone: +44(0)870 4016480
+44(0)20 7729 5610
hanoicafe@hotmail.com

It looks basic and unassuming, but don't be fooled by the understated décor inside and out. They serve exceptionally good, authentic Vietnamese food here. The interiors may not be fancy, but nice touches like fresh flowers on each of the wooden tables and oriental pictures on the walls help create a pleasant vibe. Hai Nguyen has built this business into a friendly neighbourhood restaurant whose welcome extends to children. The menu is a comprehensive collection of Vietnamese favourites and some less well-known dishes. New and interesting recipes are added periodically. The noodles are much noted, especially the Vietnamese wonton noodle and chicken glass noodle soups. Among the most well-known dishes are stir fries, such as beef with oyster sauce, cashew chicken and ginger and spring onion chicken. The more adventurous might opt for the roll-your-own summer rolls of grilled pork belly, the crispy aromatic lamb, or the enticing choice of claypot dishes, which includes pineapple fish, tofu and aubergine, or spicy orange duck. Among the list of light bites, the spareribs are excellent, and there is much else to tempt such as crisp wrap prawns, fried crab claws and vegetable tempura. Towards the end of the evening, it gets quite buzzy as a livelier crowd makes the most of the late opening, so come earlier for a quieter meal.

Prices: Set lunch £3.80 and dinner £10. Main course from £4.60. House wine £8.90.
Last orders: Food: 23.30 (Friday and Saturday 24.00).
Closed: Rarely.
Food: Vietnamese.
Other points: Children welcome.
Directions: 15 minutes walk towards Shoreditch from Liverpool Street Station or a short walk from Old Street station.
(Map 1, see inset)

Regional produce

North

The Alma

59 Newington Green Road, London N1 4QU
Telephone: +44(0)870 4016471
+44(0)207 359 4536
thealma@tiscali.co.uk
www.the-alma.co.uk

It's a traditional London pub that's been refurbished to smart standards, but its stylish makeover doesn't get in the way of relaxed dining. Deep red and aubergine walls, stripped wood floors and mismatched tables and chairs combine to create a Bohemian feel; an atmosphere which is enhanced in the evening by soft candlelight. In winter, make a beeline for the sofas and low chairs around the roaring fire. In the summer, the small garden area with wrought iron tables and chairs is the perfect peaceful place for al fresco dining. You can eat at large tables dotted throughout the bar or in the more formal restaurant area. The new owners, Caroline Hamlin and Kirsty Valentine, come with much experience, having worked in various leading gastropubs in London before striking out on their own. This has clearly served them well, especially when it comes to the food. A wonderfully eclectic modern British menu changes twice daily and could start with mackerel escabeche and potato salad or a ham and parsley terrine with chutney and pickled red cabbage. This may be followed by braised salt cod with courgettes, tomato, basil and chickpeas or grilled rib-eye steak with sautéed potatoes, onions, beetroot and horseradish. The generous portions leave little room for puddings but the homemade ice creams and tarts must be tried. There is a well-chosen wine list.

Prices: Set lunch (1 course) £6 includes drink (Tuesday-Friday). Main course restaurant from £8.50. Tapas from £2.00 every Friday and Saturday. House wine £10.50.
Last orders: Bar: 23.00 (24.00 Friday and Saturday). Food: lunch 15.00 (Sunday 16.00); dinner 22.30 (Sunday 22.00).
Closed: 25-27 December and 1-2 January.
Food: Modern British.
Other points: Dogs welcome. Garden. Children welcome. Available for private functions.
Directions: At the end of Essex Road. 73 bus from Angel, 277 or 30 bus from Highbury and Islington station. Canonbury overland station. (Map 1, see inset)

North

Almeida Restaurant and Bar

30 Almeida Street, Islington, London N1 1AE
Telephone: +44(0)870 4016470
+44(0)20 7354 4777
oliviere@conran-restaurants.co.uk
www.almeida-restaurant.co.uk

Conran owned and designed, the Almeida may be one of his smaller restaurants but it's all the nicer for that. Its cool spaciousness is offset by a cosy authentic French feel that brings warmth to the stylishy elegant setting. The gleaming state-of-the-art steel and chrome open-plan kitchen is headed by Ian Wood whose take on classic French cooking is assured and gutsey. His brasserie menu pursues the route of French cookery honestly, builds on simplicity and is very strong as a result, as starters of boudin blanc aux pommes, and salade lyonnaise reveal. Main courses are equally appealing, with scallops provençal, steak au poivre, or pot roast monkfish being spot on. The trolley of charcuterie remains a popular favourite, as is the fabulous desserts trolley that comes laden with tarts, from which one can choose a selection for a tasting plate. The largely French wines, which run to 150-plus choices, offer a generous number by the glass. Simple tapas-style dishes are available in the low-slung, rich red bar. Prices throughout are not greedy, though stray away from the good value set lunch or pre-theatre menu and costs can climb – the value lies in excellent quality and superb execution of French favourites.

Prices: Lunch and pre-theatre set menu £17.50 and £14.50 (2 course). Main course from £11.50. House wine £12.50.
Last orders: Food: lunch 14.30 (Sunday 15.00); dinner 23.00.
Closed: Good Friday.
Food: Traditional French.
Other points: No-smoking area. Children welcome.
Directions: Between Angel and Highbury and Islington underground stations, off Upper Street Islington. (Map 1, see inset)

www.routiers.co.uk

North West

Langorf Hotel & Apartments

20 Frognal, Hampstead, London NW3 6AG
Telephone: +44(0)870 4016482
+44(0)20 7794 4483
langorf@aol.com
www.langorfhotel.com

Housed in a beautiful redbrick Edwardian building and located in fashionable Hampstead, the Langorf is the perfect location for exploring the village as well as for getting into the West End in no time. Finchley Road tube is a 5-minute walk away and offers a fast tube link into central London in around 10 minutes. The hotel fits into the boutique category, being chic and friendly at the same time. Continental breakfast is included and is served in the airy breakfast room that overlooks the pretty walled garden. Another bonus is that the hotel has a licensed bar and offers 24-hour room service, providing soups and light snacks. There are 31 en suite bedrooms, all furnished to high standards, and apartments, which are either studios, one and two bedrooms, and available for a minimum of three nights and a maximum of three month stays. Bedrooms are well equipped and come with TV, satellite, hairdryers and coffee and tea-making facilities. Studios and apartments are spacious and have small kitchens, and DVD players. This level of comfort and space at these prices would be hard to find elsewhere.

Rooms: 31 plus 5 apartments and 10 studios. Double/twin room from £80, single from £70. Studios from £100, apartments from £115 (1 bedroom) and £130 (2 bedrooms).
Closed: Never.
Directions: Three miles north of Oxford Street. Three miles south of junction 1/M1. Off the A41 Finchley Road. (Map 1, see inset)

North West

No 77 Wine Bar

77 Mill Lane, West Hampstead, London NW6 1NB
Telephone: +44(0)870 4016475
+44(0)20 7435 7787

Opened in 1982, this friendly neighhourhood wine bar may not have changed its unpretentious décor much, but continues to ring the changes on its wine list and menu. New wines are added to its already comprehensive list every two months, and new recipes pop up on the menu just as often. Regulars will be glad to know that its ever-popular, proper beefburger that comes with a melted smoked cheese and a homemade relish of braised onions and capsicums, is still a feature. There's also a daily fish special, such as roast salmon with sautéed potatoes and French beans, plus a small selection of meat dishes such as chicken schnitzel. Lighter lunches include Spanish tapas and Mediterranean snacks such as houmous and flatbreads. Dine al fresco in summer, or cosy up inside around one of the small polished pine tables scattered throughout a maze of tiny quarry-tiled rooms. A good degree of intimacy is guaranteed, though do beware, the atmosphere can become quite smoky unless you happen on a section devoid of puffers. What keeps this place in the popularity stakes is simple but wholesome food and its wide choice of good value wines.

Prices: Main course from £7.95. House wine £11.45.
Last orders: Food: lunch 15.00; dinner 23.30.
Closed: Rarely.
Food: Modern British/pan Pacific.
Other points: No-smoking area. Children welcome. Dogs welcome in the bar. Al fresco seating.
Directions: Nearest tube: West Hampstead. Ten minutes drive from the foot of the M1. (Map 1, see inset)

Down-to-earth, friendly service

Specialist suppliers

at The Alma

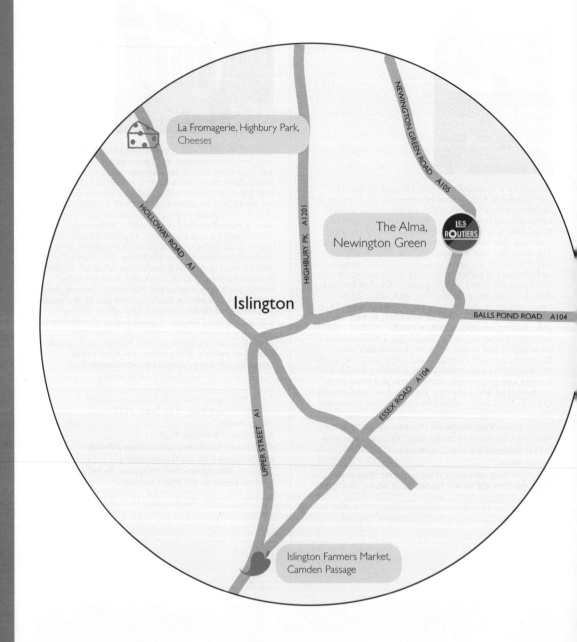

La Fromagerie, Highbury Park, Cheeses

NEWINGTON GREEN ROAD A105

HOLLOWAY ROAD A1

HIGHBURY PK A1201

The Alma, Newington Green

LES ROUTIERS

Islington

BALLS POND ROAD A104

ESSEX ROAD A104

UPPER STREET A1

Islington Farmers Market, Camden Passage

Chef Caroline Hamlin insists on using the best ingredients for her modern European menu. Practically on her doorstep is the Sunday Islington Farmers' market, which brings together around 40 suppliers. Norfolk honey, Harvest Moon watercress, Brighton fish, Quality Herbs and Artisan cakes are just a taster of what's on offer. It's here that Caroline selects her asparagus, tomatoes, and mixed salad leaves. She gets the freshest cheese for her cheeseboard from La Fromagerie, a specialist cheese shop run by Patricia Michelson, with branches in Highbury and Marylebone. Here you can buy the best of continental and British cheese, from the freshest mozzarella di bufula to the best of British such as Appleby's Cheshire, Colston Bassett and Cornish Yarg. Caroline calls to find out what's good, so she can offer a changing selection of delectable cheeses and is working her way through their extensive list. The quality meats on the menu come from Kentwell Farm in Suffolk, which uses traditional farming methods to rear its Tamworth pigs, Norfolk Horn sheep and Longhorn cows.

La Fromagerie: 30 Highbury Park, London; 0207 3597440
Kentwell Farm: Long Melford, Suffolk; 01787310207
Islington Farmers Market: Essex Road, opposite Islington Green, Islington, London. Sundays 10am-2pm

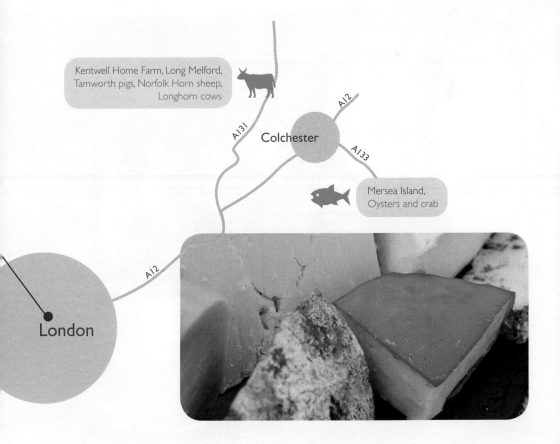

Kentwell Home Farm, Long Melford,
Tamworth pigs, Norfolk Horn sheep,
Longhorn cows

A131

A12

Colchester

A133

Mersea Island,
Oysters and crab

A12

London

The Alma, London N1, see page 50

South West

Caffé Mamma

24 Hill Street, Richmond, London TW9 1TW
Telephone: +44(0)870 4016487
+44(0)20 8940 1625
caffemamma@hotmail.com
www.caffemamma.co.uk

Twenty years down the line and Caffé Mamma remains a bright spot on central Richmond's culinary map. True to its Italian roots, it's a buzzy, friendly, family restaurant that serves good-value Italian favourites in a lively setting. Its most unusual claim to fame is its trompe l'oeil of a Neopolitan street with an actual washing line of clothes that runs across the rear of the restaurant. Don't worry if this setting isn't to your taste, there is plenty of other seating upfront, which is non smoking, and where you can dine at stylish café-style tables, with a backdrop of cheery purple and yellow walls and blond wood floors. The menu covers traditional favourites, and charts its course via antipasti, insalate, pasta, pizza and dolci, backed up by a special of the day such as calf's liver and fresh herbs. The sliced aubergine with cheese, and bresaola with rocket and olives are fabulous starting points. You could then follow with pasta of fresh seafood with mussels, prawns, calamari and clams, or trenette al pesto made with proper pesto sauce using fresh basil, garlic, pine nuts and pecorino. The house red is light and fruity, and as well as wines they also serve cocktails. Leave room for the excellent made-to-order zabaglione or Italian ice creams.

Prices: Main course from £5.45. House wine £11.65.
Last orders: Food: 24.00 (Sunday 23.30).
Closed: Rarely.
Food: Italian/Pizza and Pasta.
Other points: No-smoking area. Children welcome.
Directions: In the centre of Richmond, heading towards Kingston and Twickenham, near river bridge. (Map 1, see inset)

South West

Justin James Hotel

43 Worple Road, Wimbledon, London SW19 4JZ
Telephone: +44(0)870 4016488
+44(0)20 8947 4271
info@justinjameshotel.com
www.justinjameshotel.com

This attractive late-Victorian house, originally built in the 1890s as a doctor's surgery, is conveniently located to make the most of Wimbledon's highlights. It's close to the town centre shops and the railway station for trains into central London, and just a leisurely uphill stroll away from pretty Wimbledon Village and the many shopping and eating and drinking opportunites that it has to offer. It is an excellent base for tennis fans, as the All England Tennis Club is just over a mile away, and during the two-week tournament buses run from the town centre to the Club. The house is smart, homely and friendly, and efficiently run. All the well-maintained bedrooms are en suite and have cable TV, tea and coffee-making facilities, as well as the extra perks of a hairdryer, phone and IT connection. There is no lounge or bar, but there is a neat, small ground-floor breakfast room where you can enjoy a good traditional English breakfast. This hotel makes a welcome change from the impersonal middle-market chains and compares very favourably on price. It'll come as no surprise to learn that this hotel has many returning guests, so if you're thinking of staying here you will need to book at least a month in advance.

Rooms: 20, 1 not en suite. Double room from £80, single from £45, family room from £95.
Closed: Rarely.
Other points: No-smoking area. Garden. Children welcome. Car park.
Directions: Follow the A219 to Wimbledon. The hotel is a few minutes walk from Wimbledon Station. (Map 1, see inset)

Good food and wine

South West

The Mayflower Hotel

26-28 Trebovir Road, Earl's Court, London SW5 9NJ
Telephone: +44(0)870 4016473
+44(0)20 7370 4934
info@mayflower-group.co.uk
www.mayflowerhotel.co.uk

Two white-stuccoed Edwardian houses make up this recently renovated town house hotel. It's on a typically leafy street leading off Earls Court Road, and it's an ideal base if you're planning to visit the Exhibition Halls. Earls Court tube is only a minute's walk away and provides direct access to Heathrow Airport, the City and West End, while the shopping areas of Knightsbridge and Chelsea, and the museums at South Kensington are all within easy reach. The hotel's interiors fuse eastern influences with spacious modern lines and have been carried out with some flair. Light bedrooms with high ceilings and ceiling fans are enhanced by Indian and oriental antiques, beautiful hand-carved wardrobes and bedside tables, richly ornate beds are covered in rich, vibrant, luxurious Andrew Martin fabrics, a perfect foil to the neutral effect of pale stone and wood floors. All rooms have state-of-the-art technology with internet access, wide-screen TVs, CD players and personal safes; lighting is soft and subtle. En suite bathrooms are stylish and sparkling in marble and chrome with superb walk-in showers and contemporary white bowl sinks. Those on a lower floor are in an exotic dark green marble, but the fittings and general feel are the same. Breakfast is buffet-style.

Rooms: 48. Double room from £79, single from £59.
Closed: Never.
Other points: Children welcome.
Directions: From Earls Court Road tube station exit left; go pass McDonald's and take the first left into Trebovir Road. The Mayflower is 40 yards along on the left hand side. (Map 1, E2)

South West

Murano

110 Kew Road, Richmond, London TW9 2PQ
Telephone: +44(0)870 4016489
+44(0)20 89488330
www.muranorestaurant.co.uk

It's moved to new premises nearer Kew Gardens, but this popular Italian is still only a 10-minute walk from Richmond train station. Its authentically good Italian food is quite a draw. The new location offers the benefits of al fresco dining under an awning at the front, as well as a minimalist setting and airy dining inside. As always, the most pleasing aspect of this restaurant is its emphasis on quality seasonal ingredients. The antipasti line-up is strong with proper buffalo mozzarella and cured smoked ham with Sardinian pecorino or warmed goats' cheese salad on ciabatta with roasted mixed vegetables. The pastas are a class apart too and come with fresh lobster or crab or a superb vegetable recipe, plus there's fresh tomato or seafood-filled ravioli. Main courses cover the spectrum and offer fresh scallops, lamb with artichokes, John Dory, venison and whole sea bass served with fresh vegetables. It's hard to resist the desserts, especially the traditional panna cotta and the delicious orange crème brulée. A good wine entry point is a glass of prosecco, then you can take a tour of the all-Italian list, which is strong on classics from the regions and islands.

Prices: Main course from £9.25. House wine £12.55.
Last orders: Food: lunch 15.00; dinner 23.30.
Closed: Never.
Food: Italian.
Other points: No-smoking area. Children welcome.
Directions: In Richmond town centre, near Kew Gardens and Richmond station. (Map 1, see inset)

South West

Twenty Nevern Square Hotel

20 Nevern Square, Earl's Court, London SW5 9PD
Telephone: +44(0)870 4016472
+44(0)20 7370 4934
hotel@twentynevernsquare.co.uk
www.twentynevernsquare.co.uk

East meets west luxury best describes this west London hotel. Nowhere is this more apparent than in the 19 en suite bedrooms. Each luxurious room has been individually co-ordinated on a Far East theme, with much of the furniture specially commissioned from Indonesia. Four-poster beds have been designed and carved separately, and small spaces work to maximum advantage. Unifying factors are in the use of wooden Venetian blinds and rich natural textiles such as cotton, linen, velvet and wool. Thoughtfulness is also apparent throughout the hotel, from the ornate birdcage, commissioned in Indonesia, set in a splendid 'lobby', down to the evening menu served in the little airy conservatory, Café Twenty. Here you can dine on deliciously light Mediterranean dishes made with fresh ingredients that are quick to prepare, such as Caesar salad, spaghetti carbonara, or chicken musa – fried chicken with fresh carrots and broccoli in a herb and butter sauce. In the morning, the aroma of freshly baked rolls and croissants is enough to raise any reluctant riser. Continental breakfast is served in the conservatory restaurant and a full English breakfast can be ordered on request. There is no extra charge for room service.

Rooms: 20. Double/twin from £110, single from £90.
Last orders: Food: 23.00.
Closed: Never.
Other points: No-smoking area. Car park.
Directions: From Earls Court tube station take Warwick road exit, turn right. The second street on the right is Nevern Square. (Map 1, E2)

West

Adria Hotel

44 Glenthorne Road, Hammersmith, London W6 0LS
Telephone: +44(0)870 4016479
+44(0)20 7602 6386
info@adria-hotel.co.uk
www.adria-hotel.co.uk

Convenience and good value and the fact it's set in a large, handsome house give this family-run hotel in Hammersmith the edge over an impersonal chain. It's only a few minutes walk from Hammersmith tube and opposite a multistorey car park; although it does have some limited parking of its own. You are also just a short stroll from Hammersmith's main shopping street and near the concert venue Hammersmith Apollo. It's an attractive house with much kerb appeal: smart wrought-iron gates that open into a tidy paved front courtyard and polished stone steps that lead up to an entrance porch surrounded by coloured marble tiles set into which is a video-entry intercom. The interiors are just as neat and well looked after. Up-to-date bright, modern bedrooms, some with three beds are available, each have compact, modern shower rooms. Tea and coffee-making facilities and TVs are also provided. You breakfast in the south-facing basement room, and this is where you can also relax at other times of the day on sofas to watch TV. Cold drinks are available from a vending machine in the hall.

Rooms: 16. Double room from £69, single from £49.
Closed: Rarely.
Other points: No-smoking area. Children welcome. Garden.
Directions: 120 yards from Hammersmith Tube, exit North. (Map 1, see inset)

Affordable good value

England

Locally sourced produce is the latest sexy thing on menus, from Land's End to John O'Groats. The regions are so well stocked with the finest and freshest ingredients, that eating outside of London has become a veritable feast, says Lorna Wing

Culinary hotspots are popping up all around the country as chefs who've worked their way to the top of the capital's foodie scene have moved to the country, where they are making their mark, and encouraging the trend for family friendly, buzzy, casual restaurants and gastropubs, where the food is simple, quick and slick.

But only a few years ago, eating out of London was all too often about artifice and instant eye appeal. But, the balance has shifted and we have come to appreciate good quality local food. Chefs have a treasure-trove of foods to cook with: locally slaughtered rare-breed meats, traditionally hung game, spankingly fresh fish, artisan breads and seasonal fruit and vegetables. Specialities such as these give individuality to menus, as do award-winning cheeses, divinely calorific locally made ice creams and hand-patted butters. There no longer a place for frozen meals pinged to within an inch of their lives, or processed pap with a history as dodgy as a dictator.

Our appetite for good food has also been helped by the explosion of TV food programmes, a feast of cookery books and new food magazines. And chefs and cooks such as Hugh Fearnley-Whittingstall, Delia Smith, Rick Stein and Nigel Slater, among others, all deserve accolades for the way they've radically influenced how we shop, cook and eat, as do farmers' markets, rural farm shops and imaginative box schemes.

Food is increasingly a source of tremendous pleasure all around Britain, whether it's our good old-fashioned favourites such as the freshest fish and chips or more unusual combinations using exotic spices and ingredients. That's one thing that Les Routiers'' members and diners agree on. And, thankfully, we can now eat as well out of London as we can in. Long may that continue!

Bath

Eastern Eye

8a Quite Street, Bath BA1 2JS
Telephone: +44(0)870 4016287
+44(0)1225 422323
inf@easterneye.co.uk
www.easterneye.com

Light floods into the huge, wide-open Georgian room through each of the three glass domes and the large windows set at each end. In addition, there's lovely Georgian plasterwork and mouldings, columns and fanlights. This is a stunning setting for this Indian restaurant, which specialises in the cuisine of northern India and Bengal. Start with the obligatory poppadoms and chutney tray, accompanied by cold Indian lagers (Bangla comes highly recommended), while checking out the menu. But be prepared to tear yourself away from the usual jalfrezi or dansak. In Bath, Eastern Eye is renowned for the quality of its food. As well as the familiar favourites, there's an interesting range of chef's recommendations including seafood and vegetarian dishes. For example, butty kebabs from Bengal are small slices of delicately spiced and tender lamb cooked in a tandoori oven, a perfect partner to another Bengali dish of channa bhaji, which is fried chickpeas in a spicy sauce. Main courses such as Karali lamb and garlic chilli masala chicken are clearly produced with panache and pilau rice is served fresh and fluffy. The combination of freshly cooked food, reasonable prices and swift, friendly service fills the Eastern Eye; you may even have to book for a Monday night.

Prices: Main course from £7.50. House wine £11.95.
Last orders: Food: lunch 14.30; dinner 23.30.
Closed: Rarely.
Food: Indian.
Other points: No-smoking area. Children welcome.
Directions: Exit 18/M4. (Map 4, B7)

Bath

Rajpoot

Rajpoot House, 4 Argyle Street, Bath BA2 4BA
Telephone: +44(0)870 4016288
+44(0)1225 466833
www.rajpoot.com

The lovely aroma of fragrant spices welcomes you as you step down into this popular basement restaurant close to Pulteney Bridge. It has won many accolades for its exquisite food. The cellar restaurant is divided into three snug, but cool, air-conditioned rooms, each with its individual theme: Old India, Indian Cottage and Kamra. The authentic feel is created by the traditionally decorated bar and richly coloured ceilings, while exposed brick walls and crisp white clothes provide contemporary touches. The wide-ranging menu features the ever-popular dansak, birianyi, rogan josh and sag, and is supplemented by a comprehensive selection of vegetable side dishes, known as bahjees, and breads. The stars of the show though are the Bangladeshi dishes, such as chicken tikka massala and tandoori murg, and the unusual Rajpoot salmon. If you prefer set meals, then the all-encompassing tandoori thali of tandoori murg, chicken tikka, shish kebab, nan and pilau rice is a good choice. The wine list includes a red and a white from India and a good choice of wines by the half bottle.

Prices: Set lunch £6.95 and dinner £25. House wine £12.50.
Last orders: Food: lunch 14.30; dinner 23.00 (Friday and Saturday 23.30).
Closed: Rarely.
Food: Indian.
Other points: No-smoking area. Children welcome.
Directions: Junction 18/M4. City centre, on Pulteney Bridge.
(Map 4, B7)

Bath

Tilley's Bistro

3 North Parade Passage, Bath BA1 1NX
Telephone: +44(0)870 4016289
+44(0)1225 484200
dmott@tilleysbistro.co.uk
www.tilleysbistro.co.uk

Good food and good prices mean that David and Dawn Mott's bistro is one of the most popular places to eat in Bath. The couple have run the bistro for over 12 years and built up an excellent reputation. To avoid disappointment, it's best to book, especially at weekends. Set over three floors in one of Bath's oldest houses, you'll find Tilley's has bags of character. The main beamed dining room with an original stone fireplace at either end has a cosy wine bar atmosphere. Above, up some windy stairs, is a comfortable lounge with sofas, a small bar and a private dining room. The set lunches are very good value, with substantial portions of, say, grilled mushroom stuffed with mussels and garlic and herb butter, then escalope of pork milanaise with spaghetti in a tomato sauce and melted mozzarella. In the evening, they don't differentiate between starters and main courses, simply offering a choice of medium-sized dishes of which diners choose two or more from the range of cold, warm and hot selection. These include crab à la Saint Malo, woodcutter's salad that comes topped with pan-fried strips of smoked chicken and melted Gruyère, and fillet steak au poivre. The pudding list includes fabulous Salcombe dairy ice cream from Devon as well as champagne summer fruit jelly. There's a global selection of wines, nearly all under £20, with about nine available by the glass.

Prices: Set lunch £11.50 and dinner £20 and £25.
Main course from £10. House wine £13.
Last orders: Food: lunch 14.30; dinner 23.00.
Closed: Sunday.
Food: French and English.
Other points: No-smoking area. Children welcome.
Directions: M4/Junction 18. In the centre of Bath near to the Abbey. (Map 4, B7)

Chillcompton

Court Hotel

Linch Hill, Emborough, Chillcompton, Bath BA3 4SA
Telephone: +44(0)870 4016428
+44(0)1761 232237
reception@courthotel.co.uk
www.courthotel.co.uk

This hotel is so well-placed, near Bath and Bristol and close to the attractions of Cheddar Gorge and Glastonbury, that it's perennially popular with both business and tourist travellers. It's a country hotel set in three and a half acres of grounds with lovely views to the Mendip Hills. As well as the tranquillity this offers, the friendly and efficient staff will ensure you have a relaxing and comfortable stay. Bedrooms in the main house are traditionally decorated. There are further ground floor rooms in an adjacent wing and bedrooms in the separate lodge. But it's the rooms in the coach house in the grounds that are the most up-to-date. However, all rooms are well equipped with extras such as hairdryers and trouser presses. Traditional sums up the cooking at Browne's restaurant, which offers a wide range of meat, fish and vegetarian options. Chicken Grand Marnier, grilled lamb cutlets glazed with honey and rosemary, and beef stroganoff are among the meat choices, while from the fish line-up there are sea bass and halibut, while vegetarians can indulge in a creamy mushroom stroganoff. Less formal meals are served in the bar and conservatory. The wide-ranging wine list is very reasonably priced.

Rooms: 18. Double room from £65, single from £45.
Prices: Sunday lunch £11.50. Main course from £12.
House wine £9.50.
Last orders: Food: lunch 14.30; dinner 22.00. No food on Bank Holidays.
Closed: Rarely.
Food: Traditional English/Continental.
Other points: No-smoking area. Children welcome. Garden. Car park.
Directions: Take the A367 from Bath to Radstock, then Wells Road to Chilcompton. Take A37 from Bristol. (Map 4, C7)

An alternative Britain

Ivinghoe

The Kings Head

Station Road, Ivinghoe, Leighton Buzzard,
Bedfordshire LU7 9EB
Telephone: +44(0)870 4016310/6311
+44(0)1296 668388/668264
info@kingsheadivinghoe.co.uk
www.kingsheadivinghoe.co.uk

The Kings Head more than holds its own in the charm
and character stakes in the exceedingly pretty village
of Ivinghoe. It is an attractive ivy-clad 16th century
building that impressively takes up one side of the village green. Its original features of low beams, oak panelling, antique furniture and period portraits create a
lovely old-fashioned ambience. And the traditional feel
runs throughout, from the bars to the restaurant and
up to the banqueting suite. None more so than in the
wonderful restaurant, which oozes old English character and elegance. The food by chef Jonathan O'Keefe
is equally impressive. Choose from the good-value
Bon Appetit menu (excludes Sunday lunch and Bank
holidays) or the carte. Starters include slow-cooked
belly of pork with couscous or smoked salmon and
lambs lettuce, followed by mains of fillet of Buccleuch
beef or the restaurant speciality of roasted Aylesbury
duckling. The apple sauce with calvados and sage and
onion dressing perfectly complement the succulent,
rich meat making this a real treat. In the smaller bar
area, the huge open fireplace creates a cosy atmosphere
that is ideal for a post-supper coffee or drink in those
colder months, while the larger bar is the perfect place
to relax comfortably, perhaps for an aperitif before the
culinary delights. The banqueting suite, with interesting art from Woburn Fine Arts adorning the walls, is
available for business or pleasure and is an excellent
setting for a private function.

Prices: Set lunch £16.50. Restaurant main course from £16.50.
House wine £18.95.
Last orders: Food: lunch 14.15; dinner 21.30.
Closed: Sunday evening, 27-29 December.
Food: Modern British.
Other points: No-smoking in the restaurant. Children welcome.
Car park. Prviate banqueting.
Directions: M25. Take the A41 to Tring, turn right onto the
B488 to Ivinghoe. Restaurant is on the right at the junction with
the B489. (Map 5, 4B)

www.routiers.co.uk

Newbury

The Yew Tree Inn

Hollington Cross, Andover Road, Highclere, Newbury,
Berkshire RG20 9SE
Telephone: +44(0)870 4016004
+44(0)1635 253360
eric.norberg@theyewtree.net

This former 16th century coaching inn on the edge of the Hampshire Downs has stacks of charm and character. Ancient beams, huge logs smouldering in the inglenook fireplace are complemented by light wood furnishings and smart wooden floors that lend a contemporary feel to this stylishly refurbished dining pub. Several interconnecting rooms provide a choice of dining areas, which all have linen-draped tables and whitewashed walls. Head chef Eamon Moore freshly prepares a wonderfully executed short 'bill of fare' that's modern and imaginative in style and revolves around local produce. Dishes include a starter or main course portion of crayfish and herb risotto with Parmesan cheese, or corn beef hash browns or traditional Swedish gravadlax served with a dill and mustard sauce. Alternatively, order game and pork terrine, move on to duck confit with bubble-and-squeak and honey and orange jus, calf's liver with bacon, horseradish mash and onion gravy, or steamed sea bass with stir-fried bok choi, spring onion and ginger and a chilli and red pepper salsa. Finish, perhaps, with frosted berries with hot white chocolate sauce. Upstairs are six charming en suite rooms, all tastefully furnished and equipped to a high standard. The inn is a good spot for lunch if you are visiting Highclere Castle.

Rooms: 6. Double from £60, prices include breakfast.
Prices: Restaurant main course from £8.95. House wine £9.95.
Last orders: Bar: 23.00. Food: lunch 15.00 (Sunday 16.00);
dinner 22.00 (Sunday 21.00).
Closed: Rarely.
Food: International.
Other points: No-smoking in restaurant. Dogs welcome. Garden.
Car park.
Directions: Exit 13/M4. Take the A34 to Highclere and then the
A343 to Andover, the Yew Tree Inn is after you have gone through
the village of Highclere. (Map 5, C3)

Reading

London Street Brasserie

2-4 London Street, Riverside, Reading, Berkshire RG1 4SE
Telephone: +44(0)870 4016283
+44(0)1189 505036
www.londonstbrasserie.co.uk

Its contemporary good looks coupled with modern menu certainly draw the crowds. The bright restaurant has clean lines with white walls, polished wooden floors, wooden tables, high-backed mauve-dressed chairs and pictures for sale. In fine weather, the ground-floor dining room opens out onto a small decked area. The carte hits a modern European note with plenty of nods to the Mediterranean, Orient and Asia. Spoil yourself with Sevruga caviar, six smoked salmon blinis and a miniature frozen Smirnoff, or cruise straight into the main starters of, say, seared peppered tuna loin with oriental pickled vegetables, lemon oil, sesame, soy and oyster dressing and crispy wonton. Classic brasserie dishes such as entrecôte with béarnaise sauce and chips, sit along side more distinctly modern teamings, namely pink-roasted venison fillet and McSween's haggis, figs, baby spinach, port, redcurrant and juniper sauce. Bread is from the Degustibus bakery, and there are excellent local cheeses. Puddings are richly indulgent, none more so than hot chocolate fondant with Baileys ice cream. The 40-bin globetrotting wine list offers eight varieties by the glass. Under the same ownership as the Crooked Billet, Stoke Row (see entry).

Prices: Set lunch £13.50 (2 course, 12.00-19.00 daily).
Main course from £11. House wine £13.50.
Last orders: Food: 22.30 (Friday and Saturday 23.00).
Closed: Rarely.
Food: Modern British.
Other points: Riverside terrace (heated).
Directions: Exit 10 or 11/M4. Follow signs to 'Oracle' park
in 'Oracle' multi-storey car park. (Map 5, C4)

Individual charm and warmth

Bristol

Ganges

368 Gloucester Road, Bristol BS7 8TP
Telephone: +44(0)870 4016282
+44(0)117 9245234

This long-established Indian is vividly decorated, and its large glittering chandeliers give it the edge in the glamour stakes. The food is equally vibrant. True to its name, the cooking focuses on the three main regions through which the River Ganges flows; it rises in Tibet, flows through India and reaches the sea at Bangladesh. The major influence though comes from North India and so you'll find the most popular curries, from mild lamb pasanda to a fiery vindaloo king prawn, alongside biryanis on the menu. If you tend to stick to your favourite dish, this is the place to branch out as the chef has half a dozen well thought out and well-priced set menus, plus there's an all-encompassing thali of tandoori murg, lamb tikka, shish kebab, naan, pilau rice, and chicken tikka. Vegetarian dishes, including a vegetarian thali, are a high point, as the vegetables are always fresh, never frozen. The wine list is a cut above too, and includes classics such as Sancerre and Barolo. There's a refreshing selection of bottled and draught beers, including Cobra, Kingfisher and Lal Toofan.

Prices: **Set lunch and dinner from £14.50. House wine £8.95.**
Last orders: **Food: lunch 14.30; dinner 23.30.**
Closed: **Rarely.**
Food: **Indian and Bangladeshi.**
Other points: **No-smoking area. Children welcome.**
Directions: **On the A38 Gloucester Road. (Map 4, B6)**

Bristol

San Carlo Restaurant

44 Corn Street, Bristol BS1 1HQ
Telephone: +44(0)870 4016281
+44(0)117 922 6586

The seating here is plentiful, and it needs to be as its authentic Italian cooking and city-centre location means it's always busy. The tall Victorian building stands in an attractive pedestrianised area. Inside, it's one long, narrow room that's light, bright and airy. The atmosphere is unmistakably Mediterranean, an ambience that is common to all four restaurants in this small, stylish group. It's adopted a contemporary theme: mirrored walls, white-tiled floor, with colour in the form of potted plants and trees of different shapes and sizes. It serves all the popular favourites at reasonable prices, and the cooking is a cut above the norm for a city-centre eaterie majoring in pizzas and pastas. The lengthy menu lists familiar trattoria dishes: fritto misto; buffalo mozzarella with tomato, basil and avocado; saltimboca all romana; piccata al limone; and suprema di pollo genovese. Blackboard specials extend the choice with a range of seafood that could include dressed crab, grilled Dover sole and mixed grill of fish. There's a selection of well-priced Italian wines, with a good selection by the glass and France and the new world bringing up the rear. Its buzzy atmosphere and friendly service are bound to raise your spirits.

Prices: **Main course from £11. House wine £11.20.**
Last orders: **Food: 23.00.**
Closed: **Rarely.**
Food: **Italian.**
Other points: **Children welcome.**
Directions: **In Bristol city centre. (Map 4, B6)**

Chalfont St Giles

The Ivy House

London Road, Chalfont St Giles,
Buckinghamshire HP8 4RS
Telephone: +44(0)870 4016007
+44(0)1494 872184
www.theivyhouse-bucks.co.uk

The attractive Ivy House has become even more visitor friendly since its major revamp, which saw the addition of five en suite rooms, a bigger dining room, an al fresco patio and toilet facilities for baby changing and for people with disabilities. But the modernisation hasn't altered the charm of this impressive 17th-century brick-and-flint free house set in the heart of the Chiltern Hills with wonderful views across the Misbourne Valley. The charming ambience is retained in the wood and slate-floored bar, with its old beams, cosy armchairs, wood-burning fires and fine old pictures. It offers five changing real ales and a select list of wines; 20 by the glass. A menu of modern British dishes prepared by chef/proprietor Jane Mears and her team reveals a confidence to experiment with ingredients and produce unusual dishes – look to the blackboard for the day's specials. Starter choices range from homemade soups, to ragoût of artichoke hearts, basil, sun-dried tomatoes and garlic. Main courses extend to roast salmon with pesto and Parmesan, chargrilled sirloin steak with creamy pepper sauce, and loin of lamb with redcurrant and mint sauce, plus winter casseroles, summer salads, pasta meals and homemade puddings, perhaps hot chocolate pudding and chocolate fudge sauce. Retire to one of the individually furnished bedrooms and wake up to lovely Chiltern valley views and a hearty breakfast.

Rooms: 5. Double room £95, single occupancy £75.
Prices: Main course from £8.50. House wine £10.95.
Last orders: Bar: lunch 15.00; dinner 23.00 (open all day at the week-end). Food: lunch 14.30; dinner 21.30
(all day at the week-end).
Closed: Never.
Food: Modern British/global.
Other points: No-smoking area. Children welcome.
Dogs welcome in the bar. Garden and courtyard. Car park.
Directions: Exit2/M40. Situated directly between Amersham and Gerrards Cross on the A413. (Map 5, B4)

Chalfont St Peter

The Greyhound Inn

High Street, Chalfont St Peter, Buckinghamshire SL9 9RA
Telephone: +4490)870 4016008
+44(0)1753 883404
reception@thegreyhoundinn.net
www.thegreyhoundinn.net

Following its major refurbishment, The Greyhound cleverly combines contemporary elegance with the traditional character of such an old building. It's a comfortable country inn in a pretty village on the edge of the Chiltern Hills, and within easy reach of the M40 and London. Escape the capital to stay in one of the 12 beautifully appointed bedrooms, where exposed beams and solid oak beds blend well with en suite marble bathrooms, rain-drench showers and Molton Brown toiletries. Feeling pampered, head downstairs and sink into one of the deep sofas by the roaring fire in the low-beamed bar for a pre-dinner drink. The wood-panelled dining room has a light and airy feel, with chunky furnishings and access to a neat terrace kitted out with upmarket teak tables and chairs. Food successfully combines traditional English dishes with contemporary and Mediterranean influences, with starters such as terrine of the week or Serrano ham, dressed salad and poached egg. The style continues in the mains of whole sea bass with a chive and lemon sauce and chargrilled vegetables or pan-fried calf's liver with red wine and pancetta. Puddings are a delight, especially the lemon tart with stem ginger ice cream. The bar menu includes hearty mains of battered fish and chips, moules, sandwiches and snacks, plus of course, good ale and a wine list that offers many by the glass.

Rooms: 12. Double from £100, single from £90, family from £120.
Prices: Set lunch and dinner £12.50. Restaurant and bar main course from £8.50. House wine £12.50.
Last orders: Bar: 23.00. Food: lunch 15.00; dinner 22.00 (Sunday 21.30).
Closed: Rarely.
Food: Modern British.
Other points: No-smoking area. Dogs welcome in the bar.
Garden. Children welcome. Car park.
Directions: Exit1/M40 and Exit16/M25. Take the A40 towards Gerrards Cross, turn right on to the A413 towards Amersham, second roundabout on the left. (Map 5, B4)

Regional produce

Double chocolate chip ice cream *at the Ivy House*

Jane Mears of the Ivy House in Chalfont St Giles is pretty sure double chocolate chip is the winning flavour with her customers, though pistachio comes a close second. She is also quick to point out that this isn't just any old ice cream, this is Beechdeans – an ice cream company that takes care of every step from 'cow to customer'. This involves milking a pedigree herd of 120 Jersey and 270 Fresian cows twice a day on the 600-acre family farm and producing 1.5 million litres of ice cream every year.

Beechdean Ice Cream,
Upper North Dean

A413

A4128

A404

High Wycombe

Beaconsfield

Based in the heart of Buckinghamshire's Chiltern Hills, Beechdean Ice Cream started in 1989 after Susie Howard took part in a one-day ice cream making course, with a small machine and a van. Nowadays their ice cream can be found in all sorts of places ranging from the Albert Hall and Buckingham Palace to the Les Routiers listed Ivy House. This picturesque 17th century brick and flint free house is well known for its fabulous food and sourcing of local produce. There are homemade soups on the blackboard and meats sourced from nearby butchers Goddens and Tom Robertsons as well as vegetables from D H Aldridge and eggs from Lower Bottom Farm, and for dessert, of course, three scoops of Beechdeans double chocolate chip.

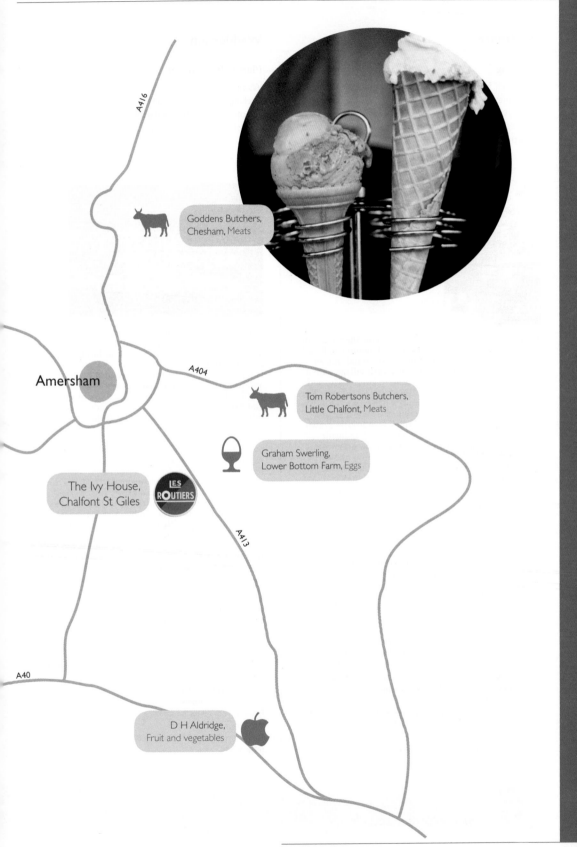

A416

Goddens Butchers,
Chesham, Meats

Amersham

A404

Tom Robertsons Butchers,
Little Chalfont, Meats

Graham Swerling,
Lower Bottom Farm, Eggs

The Ivy House,
Chalfont St Giles

LES
ROUTIERS

A413

A40

D H Aldridge,
Fruit and vegetables

Mentmore

The Stag

The Green, Mentmore, Buckinghamshire LU7 0QF
Telephone: +44(0)870 4016011
+44(0)1296 668423
reservations@thestagmentmore.com
www.thestagmentmore.com

Mike and Jenny Tuckwood have brought their years of catering experience to this traditional country pub and have turned its flagging fortunes right round. It's an attractive building in a picture-postcard village with a lovely garden overlooking Mentmore House. The addition of good food has boosted its business no end. The classic bar is the place to sample Charles Wells ales and interesting bar food. Snack meals run to hearty sandwiches of Mexican chilli steak or butterfly prawn Mentmore salad, and one-dish meals of handmade local spicy sausages with mash and onion gravy, or an evening dish like Moroccan braised lamb with vegetable couscous are just as satisfying. Imaginative, seasonally changing evening menus are served in the stylishly modernised two-tiered restaurant, which has direct access to the garden. Parma ham-wrapped fresh peach stuffed with mascarpone cheese makes for an unusual and tasty starter, or there's grilled aubergine and pepper with mozzarella or pork rillettes with crab apple jelly. Thoughtful attention to flavours produces main courses such as roasted loin of lamb with honey and wholegrain mustard on spicy couscous, and venison T-bone steak on creamed potatoes with wild mushrooms and pink peppercorn sauce. Finish with a traditional bread and butter pudding with vanilla ice cream or a plate of British cheeses. All the wines on the global list are offered by the glass.

Prices: Restaurant set lunch and dinner £28, main course £16.
Bar lunch £4 or £6 and dinner £6 or £8. All wines by the glass.
Last orders: Bar: 23.00. Food: lunch 14.00 (bar food 15.30);
dinner 21.00 (bar food 21.30); Sunday 20.30 (bar food 21.00).
Closed: Restaurant closed Monday lunch and evening.
Food: Modern British.
Other points: No-smoking area. Children welcome at lunch and over 12 years old in the evening. Dogs welcome in the bar.
Large garden with seating. Limited car park.
Directions: Five miles north east of Aylesbury off A418 towards Leighton Buzzard. (Map 5, B4)

Waddesdon

Manor Restaurant

Waddesdon Manor, Waddesdon, Aylesbury,
Buckinghamshire HP18 0JH
Telephone: +44(0)870 4016309
+44(0)1296 653242

The last remaining complete example of 'le style Rothschild' in Europe, Waddesdon Manor must rank as one of the finest places to visit in Britain. Built in the style of a 16th century French château, the Manor is set in acres of parkland, surrounded by mature trees and has a fine Victorian garden. It's now run by the National Trust, which charges for tours of the grounds and Manor. To get a taste of the grandeur, book a table in the relaxed surroundings of the ground-floor servants' hall where you will find one of the most original restaurants. With its core clientele firmly in mind, the kitchen mixes National Trust tearoom classics with a lunch menu that is an inspired juxtaposition of traditional dishes from the Rothschild menu books and modern dishes. Simple menu descriptions translate into equally straightforward dishes such as smoked haddock chowder with curry oil, or braised ham hock with mustard mash. The kindly priced wine list, with its full range of Rothschild family wines, will appeal to serious oenophiles, and the advice of the young sommelier should be heeded. In the grounds is the Stables Restaurant with a casual air and gingham tablecloths indicating a choice of simpler dishes such as soups, sandwiches, filled jackets, popular cakes and pastries. Also in the grounds, is the old Victorian Dairy, elegantly restored and fully equipped for weddings and private dinners. A number of guides have a policy of not including restaurants where you have to pay an entry fee, but we make an exception as food and wine here are well worth the £4 fee.

Prices: Restaurant main course from £9.50. House wine £12.
Last orders: Food: lunch 15.00.
Closed: Monday, Tuesday, Christmas until the end of February.
Food: Modern European.
Other points: Totally no smoking. Garden. Children welcome.
Car park.
Directions: Off the A41 between Bicester and Aylesbury.
(Map 5, B4)

www.routiers.co.uk

Huntingdon

Old Bridge Hotel

1 High Street, Huntingdon, Cambridgeshire PE29 3TQ
Telephone: +44(0)870 4016371
+44(0)1480 424300
oldbridge@huntsbridge.co.uk
www.huntsbridge.com

Contemporary design has transformed this 18th century town house into a slick hotel for the 21st century. Modern touches such as sea grass and wicker work well alongside the antiques. The 24 bedrooms make up an eclectic range of individually styled rooms, some are quite traditional, while others have striking design statements. In the main dining room, the look is restrained elegance: light panelled walls, lots of white linen and red high-back chairs. The menu also leans heavily towards the contemporary. Indulge in sushi and sashimi with wasabi, pickled ginger, soy, coriander and cress salad, followed by roast breast of corn-fed Goosnargh duck with stir-fried Chinese vegetables and sticky rice cake or roast fillet of Aberdeenshire beef with fondant potato, spinach and fricasée of wild mushrooms. The terrace restaurant is boldly designed, dominated by huge Julia Rushbury murals and big windows, giving a real orangery feel. Chef/patron Martin Lee interprets the Huntsbridge Group philosophy of sourcing quality ingredients and turning them into imaginative yet restrained dishes. Ideas range from salad of white beans with wild garlic, spinach and oregano and pancetta to chargrilled leg of Cornish lamb steak with couscous and roast red peppers. The range of outstanding wines is a top-class, winning selection – the classics are the best of their kind – and very good value, with a brilliant selection of over 20 wines by the glass.

Rooms: 24. Double room from £120, single from £80.
Prices: Set lunch £15.50. Main course from £12.75.
House wine £12.
Last orders: Food: lunch 14.30; dinner 22.00.
Closed: Rarely.
Food: Modern British.
Other points: No-smoking area. Children welcome. Garden.
Car park.
Directions: At the intersection of the A1 (north-south) and the A14 (east-west). (Map 10, D5)

Keyston

Pheasant Inn

Keyston, Huntingdon, Cambridgeshire PE18 0RE
Telephone: +44(0)870 4016017
+44(0)1832 710241
pheasant.keyston@btopenworld.com

The Pheasant is picture-postcard pretty, made up of 16th century cottages with a thatched roof, set beneath a huge sycamore tree, in the heart of the village. Outside, it's a mass of floral planters and tubs with tables and chairs for you to dine al fresco and enjoy the idyllic, time-stopped-still scene. The quintessentially olde England continues inside with the hunting and shooting prints, old horse-drawn implements suspended from the ceiling, a mass of blackened beams, brick inglenooks, flagstone floor and stripped boards. The cooking however is anything but olde worlde and offers an interesting array of dishes using a combination of British and Mediterranean ingredients. Starters include salad of artichokes, soft herbs, pine nuts and aged balsamic vinegar or Cornish crab with sorrel, shaved fennel and lemon. These could be followed by mains of pan-fried Western Isles salmon with tomato and fennel compote, pot-roasted guinea fowl or Aberdeenshire steak. Puddings of honey and hazelnut tart with thick Jersey cream or warm chocolate tart with pistachio ice cream are fabulously indulgent. The delights of the wine list are also a joy to behold, with around 40 of the 100 well-chosen bins priced under £20. The higher-priced bottles benefit from a straight cash mark-up that means this is the place to experiment – sheer hedonism at fair prices.

Prices: Set lunch £14.95. House wine £11.50.
Last orders: Food: lunch 14.00; dinner 21.00 (Sunday 21.00).
Closed: Rarely.
Food: Modern British.
Other points: No-smoking areas. Dogs welcome daytime only.
Children welcome. Car park.
Directions: Village signed off A14 west of Huntingdon. (Map 9, D4)

Down-to-earth, friendly service

Three Horseshoes, Madingley

Madingley

Three Horseshoes

High Street, Madingley, Cambridge,
Cambridgeshire CB3 8AB
Telephone: +44(0)870 4016018
+44(0)1954 210221

Within this picturesque thatched inn, the quintessentially rural look gives way to country chic and a lively cosmopolitan atmosphere. The Victorian orangery look does justice to the original architecture. It mixes a light Mediterranean feel with period elegance through pastel-coloured waxed wood, stripped floor boards, old-style foodie prints, brick fireplaces, leather-topped bar stools and banquettes. Moving through to the conservatory restaurant, though similar in design and with an identical menu to the bar area, white linen, wicker chairs, lots of shrubs and indoor plants growing up trellis create a relaxed mood. Richard Stokes's confident cooking is a sound interpretation of the Huntsbridge Group's policy of using seasonal food and prime raw materials. Meals don't stint on bringing together bags of fresh flavours in starters such as smoked buffalo mozzarella with vine tomatoes, rocket, black olives and basil or pea and mint soup with crème fraîche and pancetta. Mains include chargrilled breast of chicken with green and yellow courgettes, new potatoes and salsa verde and other flavoursome creations feature centrepieces of pan-fried salmon fillet, Cumbrian rump steak and roast monkfish. As with all Huntsbridge places, there is a superb choice of wines, offering the great and godly as well as the unusual, with 34 halves listed.

Prices: Bar main course from £9.50. House wine £11.50.
Last orders: Bar: lunch 14.00; dinner 21.00. Food: lunch 14.00
(Sunday 14.30); dinner 20.30.
Closed: Rarely.
Food: Italian.
Other points: No-smoking area. Restaurant no smoking.
Children welcome. Garden. Car park.
Directions: Two miles west of Cambridge. From London leave the
M11 at the A1303 exit. From the north take the A14 then A1307.
(Map 10, D5)

Werrington

Cherry House Restaurant

125 Church Street, Werrington, Peterborough,
Cambridgeshire PE4 6QF
Telephone: +44(0)870 4016420
+44(0)1733 571721

The quaint thatched cottage that's home to the Cherry House Restaurant comes with a manicured lawn and a pond. The interiors are olde worlde and feature beams, exposed-stone and an open-fireplace in the dining room. The time-honoured style follows through to the kitchen, where regional ingredients figure and cream and butter sauces are popular. French-trained Andrew Corrick is passionate about food and has created a loyal following for his cooking, both the set-price lunch and dinner menus. He's conceived an exciting menu that includes many French and British classics, including timbale of fresh salmon mousse wrapped in Scottish smoked salmon with locally grown asparagus tips and French onion soup to start. Mains offer roast breast of Gressingham duck with a raspberry vinegar and pink peppercorn sauce or tournedos of Scottish beef fillet, served with a creamy Stilton and port sauce and a julienne of celeriac. Alternatively, tuck into medallions of Grasmere Farm pork with a creamy tarragon mustard sauce, or supreme of chicken with a rich red wine and oyster mushroom sauce. For simpler tastes, and at a supplement, there is a selection of grilled steaks. The wine list, helpfully organised by style, offers a comprehensive selection that aims mostly for everyday drinking at reasonable prices.

Prices: Set menu £20.95. House wine £10.95.
Last orders: Food: lunch 14.00 (Sunday 14.30);
dinner 21.30 (Saturday 22.30).
Closed: Monday.
Food: Modern British with French influence.
Other points: No-smoking area. Garden. Children welcome.
Car park.
Directions: North of Peterborough, The Cherry House is
signposted off the A15. (Map 10, D5)

Good food and wine

Warmingham

The Bear's Paw Hotel

School Lane, Warmingham, Sandbach,
Cheshire CW11 3QN
Telephone: +44(0)870 4016303
+44(0)1270 526317
enquiries@thebearspaw.co.uk
www.thebearspaw.co.uk

This late-Victorian brick-built hotel beside the River
Weaver overlooks willow-dappled watermeadows
and Warmingham's pretty parish church. If you put a
premium on spacious bedrooms and bathrooms, then
you've come to the right place. Seven new large en
suite bedrooms have recently been added to the exist-
ing line-up of six. Overall, the public room décor leans
towards the old-fashioned, but this is part of its down-
to-earth charm. The open-plan lounge surrounds a
spacious central bar and there are log fires and plenty
of traditional style wood panelling and seating to make
it feel cosy. The bar menu offers light bites such as
club sandwiches or a good-value, weekly changing set
lunch menu. Real ale fans will be delighted to learn
that there are micro-brewery ales on handpump, perhaps Slater's Premium or Khean's Fine Leg Bitter. In
the restaurant, the carte menu offers a range of British
classics, but beware, portions are not for the faint-
hearted. Start with goats' cheese tartlets with red
pepper and fennel compote and salad or bacon and
black pudding salad with a herb dressing, before
tucking into breast of chicken stuffed with spinach
and brie, poached monkfish or rack of lamb.

Rooms: 12. Double room from £60, single from £50,
family from £70.
Prices: Set lunch £12.95. Restaurant main course from £11.95.
Bar main course from £7.95. House wine £9.95.
Last orders: Bar: 23.00 (weekends). Food: dinner 21.00
(21.30 weekends).
Closed: Monday to Friday daytime.
Food: Modern British.
Other points: No-smoking area. Children welcome. Garden.
Car park.
Directions: M6/Exit 16,17,18. (Map 8, B6)

West Auckland

The Manor House Hotel and Country Club

The Green, West Auckland, Co Durham DL14 9HW
Telephone: +44(0)870 4016342
+44(0)1388 834834
enquiries@manorhousehotel.net
www.manorhousehotel.net

Built on foundations that date back to the 12th
century, the manor is now home to a traditional hotel
with leisure facilities galore. Guests have a large pool,
sauna et al at their disposal. The refurbishment has
been sympathetic and has focused on the casual and
comfortable. Individually decorated bedrooms have
four posters and lovely period furnishings and details.
Many of the en suite bathrooms are spacious, and
in keeping with the style of the rooms. An ongoing
programme of upgrading ensures high standards of
appearance are maintained. You can wine and dine
in three areas. The Beehive Bar is the most informal
and has an immense and glorious stone fireplace that
incorporates the original beehive oven as its centrepiece. Log fires roar here in winter and you can enjoy
a good-value bar meal and tapas in the evening. The
Juniper Brasserie is smart but less formal than the restaurant. Here you can tuck into duck with an orange
or port sauce, seared rump of lamb, or baked fillet
of cod. At the Juniper Restaurant you can dine like a
king on sea bass fillets with a Pernod cream sauce and
crispy leeks or ostrich steak with braised red cabbage,
pears and cassis gravy. Good value seems to be the priority, not least on a wine list that offers plenty of good
choices by the glass.

Rooms: 35. Double from £84, single from £42.
Family room from £104.
Prices: Sunday lunch from £7.95. Set dinner £19.95.
Main course restaurant from £12. Main course brasserie from £7.
House wine £11.95.
Last orders: Food: lunch 14.00; dinner 21.30.
Closed: Never.
Food: Eclectic.
Other points: No-smoking area. Children welcome.
Dogs welcome overnight. Garden. Car park. Licence for
Civil Weddings.
Directions: Exit 58 off the A1 (M). Take the A68 and follow it to
West Auckland. (Map 12, C6)

www.routiers.co.uk

Lostwithiel

Trewithen Restaurant

3 Fore Street, Lostwithiel, Cornwall PL22 0BP
Telephone: +44(0)870 4016285
+44(0)1208 872373
brianrolls1@supanet.com
www.trewithenrestaurant.supanet.com

During his 23 years at the helm of this restaurant, Brian Rolls and his co-chef Kathryn Rowe have built up a loyal local clientele. While the setting is slightly old-fashioned and on the cramped side of cosy, this is more than made up for by friendly staff, the hearty cooking and good use of local ingredients. The emphasis is on homemade, from breads to the ice creams and even the afterdinner chocolates. You will be treated to West Country specialities. Locally reared meats, such as venison served with a juniper berry sauce and pork from Tywardreath with a mushroom and basil sauce, are perennial favourites. The daily fish catch is also used creatively and may include sea bass coated in oat crumbs with a citrus and caper sauce. In summer, there is a short lobster menu that features lobster Newburg, the classic recipe with a creamy, sherry sauce. The restaurant is part of Cornish heritage too: the original walls date from the 16th century when it was part of the Duchy Palace Complex. The Duchy Palace next door, which is now a Masonic lodge, was the seat of the Cornish Parliament in the 13th century. Booking in advance is recommended.

Prices: **Set dinner £26. Main course from £15. House wine £11.50.**
Last orders: **Food: dinner 21.30.**
Closed: **Sunday and Monday except for Bank Holiday weekends and Mondays during the Summer.**
Food: **Modern British with international influences.**
Other points: **No-smoking area. Children welcome.**
Directions: **M5. A390, halfway between Liskeard and St Austell, five miles south Bodmin (A30) and five miles east of the Eden Project. (Map 3, E3)**

Newquay

Great Western Hotel

Cliff Road, Newquay, Cornwall TR7 2NE
Telephone: +44(0)870 4016028
+44(0)1637 872010
bookings@great-western.fsnet.co.uk
www.chycor.co.uk/greatwestern/

If you find uninterrupted ocean views appealing, then you'll love the panoramic views of the Atlantic from this smart beachside hotel. The public rooms and bedrooms overlooking the Great Western Beach certainly make the most of it. The hotel was originally built as a superior boarding house in 1875 in anticipation of the coming of the railway in 1876, and it has zoomed up the style and standards stakes over the years. Light and airy en suite bedrooms are very well maintained and equipped. And they have thought of all possible requirements for a successful family holiday. Amenities include an indoor swimming pool with a jacuzzi, a 10-hole mini golf course, pool table and Sky TV in the bar, as well as a children's area in the Belle bar. In the evenings, relax and enjoy an aperitif and the views in one of the elegant bars before dining in the restaurant. The changing set menu will please traditionalists and features classics such as roast beef, chicken chasseur and a daily fish choice such as salmon, cod and plaice. Dishes incorporate a range of local meats and vegetables and, of course, not forgetting that key Cornish treat – clotted cream.

Rooms: **72, 2 not en suite. Double room from £45 per person, single from £50 dinner, bed & breakfast.**
Prices: **Set dinner £17.50. Bar main course from £4. House wine £8.**
Last orders: **Bar: 23.00.**
Closed: **Rarely.**
Food: **Modern British.**
Other points: **No-smoking area. All bedrooms are non-smoking. Children welcome. Dogs welcome overnight. Garden. Car park. Indoor heated pool.**
Directions: **From Indian Queens (A30) to Quintrell Downs, right at roundabout to seafront. Hotel on right. (Map 3, E3)**

Affordable good value

Padstow

Molesworth Manor

Little Petherick, Padstow, Wadebridge,
Cornwall PL27 7QT
Telephone: +44(0)870 4016447
+44 (0)1841 540292
molesworthmanor@aol.com
www.molesworthmanor.co.uk

This handsome former rectory that dates from the
17th century is Grade II listed and is set in lovely
mature gardens. It's in the centre of the village of Little
Petherick, just two miles from the bustling seafood
Mecca of Padstow, but it's a veritable haven from the
seaside summer crowds. Jessica Clarke has taken over
the running of this unconventional country guesthouse
from her parents, together with her partner, Geoff
French. It's a genteel house, with spacious hallways,
sitting rooms with antique furniture, open fires, rugs
on the floors; the décor is completely in keeping with
the age of the house. Eleven bedrooms present vary-
ing degrees of grandness and their names are evocative
of the house in its heyday: Her Ladyship's and His
Lordship's Rooms on the first floor, for example, and
the Cook's Room and the Butler's Room on the second.
Open fireplaces, wrought-iron or brass bedsteads, and
good Victorian furniture complement the house style.
Six bedrooms have en suite bathrooms; the rest have
their own private facilities. Breakfast is a splendid cold
buffet served in the light and airy conservatory. They
don't serve dinner, but you'll find plenty of pubs,
restaurants and bistros nearby, with Padstow having
more than its fair share thanks to Mr Stein. Note that
no credit cards are taken.

Rooms: 11, 2 with private facilities. Double room £32-£42 per
person, single from £30.
Closed: November-January.
Other points: Totally no smoking. Garden. Children welcome.
Car park.
Directions: Situated off the A389 from Wadebridge to Padstow in
village of Little Petherick. The manor is signposted and halfway
up/down the hill. (Map 3, D3)

Polperro

Nelsons Restaurant

Big Green, Saxon Bridge, Polperro, Cornwall PL13 2QT
Telephone: +44(0)870 4016376
+44(0)1503 272366
nelsons@polperro.co.uk
www.polperro.co.uk

Near the harbour, this striking, ivy-covered restaurant
more than fits a maritime bill with its strong nautical theme. Admiring mariners' memorabilia, much of
which is related to Admiral Nelson, is an interesting
distraction. Peter Nelson, no relation, has been running Nelsons for 30 years, but time has not diminished
his enthusiasm for fresh fish and shellfish menu that
changes daily, depending on the catch. Fish specials are
chalked up on a board. Lobster fans will be pleased to
learn that lobster Thermidor and lobster Nelson, which
comes with Madeira and cream, are permanent fix-
tures on the printed menus. Regulars and tourists are
drawn by Peter's sound cooking that goes well beyond
fish to include meat, game and poultry. He is also
happy to cook customers' favourite dishes on request.
Highlights of the menu include baked Polperro crab
mornay and fillet of sole caprice. The selection of meat
dishes includes plain grilled steaks, tournedos Rossini
and Gressingham duck with blackcurrants. Downstairs
in Captain Nemo's bar-brasserie a simpler menu is on
offer, which includes, for example, crab salad, garlic
mussels, seafood pancake filled with Polperro crab and
prawns, steak and kidney pudding and seafood linguine with seafood and Parmesan sauce. Wines run to
around 500 choices, and there's also a wide choice of
beers and lagers available.

Prices: Set menu £12.75 (2 courses). Main course from £11.95.
Last orders: Food: lunch 14.00; dinner 21.45. No food Tuesday and
Wednesday lunch.
Closed: Monday.
Food: Seafood/French.
Other points: Children welcome.
Directions: 25 miles from Plymouth (A38) and five miles from
Looe (A387). On the Saxon Bridge in Polperro. (Map 3, E3)

St Austell

Anchorage House

Nettles Corner, Boscundle, Tregrehan Mills, St Austell, Cornwall PL25 3RH
Telephone: +44(0)870 4016418
+44(0)1726 814071
stay@anchoragehouse.co.uk
www.anchoragehouse.co.uk

Immaculately kept and extended, this Georgian-style lodge has an added bonus: a 15-metre-long lap pool in its beautifully landscaped gardens. Inside, the decoration has been executed with verve, passion and with comfort in mind. The lounge is spacious and comfortable, with abundant reading matter and complimentary tray of sherries, leading to the grand but informal plant-filled conservatory where breakfast and dinner is served on one large table. Breakfasts are a feast of yogurts, berries, fruits, cereals and English fry-ups. Newspapers are included. They don't have a license, but you can bring your own wine for dinner, which is served Wednesday, Friday and Sunday, and other days by arrangement. Jane and Steve Epperson are welcoming, and refreshingly laid back hosts. They've spent over 10 years constantly improving the property to deluxe standards. Bedrooms are a real star attraction. There are only three, but each is elegant and individually styled. The two-storey loft suite is spotlessly maintained with every luxury you could wish for: chocolates, biscuits, fresh flowers, a turn-down service, king and super king-size beds. Magnificent bathrooms have large baths and separate power showers, and lots of luxury lotions and potions. There's also a jacuzzi, with bathrobes provided for those wishing to use it.

Rooms: 3. Double room from £45 per person, single from £70.
Prices: 4 course dinner by prior arrangement from £29.
Unlicensed.
Closed: December-February.
Other points: Totally no smoking. Garden. Car park. Jacuzzi and outdoor swimming pool.
Directions: A30/A391. Two miles east of St Austell on the A390; take the turning for Tregrehan across from the St Austell Garden Centre. Then immediately turn left into the driveway leading into the courtyard of the lodge. (Map 3, E3)

St Austell

Auberge Asterisk

Mount Pleasant, Roche, St Austell, Cornwall PL26 8LH
Telephone: +44(0)870 4016419
+44(0)1726 890863
ferzan@l'auberge.freeserve.co.uk
www.auberge-asterisk.co.uk

Viewed from the A30 this cream-coloured, squarely solid old house looks like a rural French Relais Routiers. Its large, slightly faded plaque is prominently displayed on high. This is a very simple restaurant-with-rooms, run with dedicated enthusiasm by Ferzan Zola, almost as a one-man operation. Food is the star turn here, with fresh produce delivered daily and translated into an eclectic menu that delights as much in old classics as in interpretations of modern ideas. Expect fish terrine served with saffron or mustard sauce, or a fresh, scintillating seafood salad of prawns, baby octopus and shellfish. Main courses run to fillet of local beef with ginger and black beans, venison steak with Calvados and cream, or monkfish with a saffron sauce. Puddings are a speciality, with meringue roulade, Grand Marnier soufflé, profiteroles and even a homemade Black Forest gateau. The wine list is short but wide ranging and prices are, well, a steal. Upstairs are five en suite bedrooms: neat, well-maintained rooms with pretty views, offering very good value in an area that is becoming increasingly short of bed space with the runaway success of the Eden Project. It is advisable to book for both rooms and the restaurant.

Rooms: 3. Double room from £49.50, single from £34.75.
Prices: Main course from £12. House wine £8.
Last orders: Food: dinner 21.00
(Wednesday-Saturday for non-residents).
Closed: Rarely.
Food: Modern European.
Other points: Children welcome. Garden. Car park.
Directions: On the A30. two miles west after Innisdown roundabout (Bodmin By-Pass). About five miles from the Eden project. (Map 3, E3)

An alternative Britain

A taste of Cornwall

at Anchorage House

You can tuck into some prize produce at Anchorage House, as owners Jane and Steve Epperson pride themselves on serving the best regional speciality foods. Their meats come from long-established family butcher Charles Harris Butchers at Tywardreath. As well as selling local pork, lamb and beef, the shop specialises in sausages. Charles's daughter Sue makes the 40 plus varieties available, including the award-winning pork and garlic and lamb and mint. Over at Lobbs Farm Shop, based adjacent to the Lost Gardens of Heligan, Jane gets many of her vegetables and picks up other grocery lines such as the wonderfully flavoursome Helford Creek apple juice and Trenance Chocolates that she serves with after-dinner coffee. The shop has been open since September 2003 and 70 per cent of its lines are Cornish. For smoked fish and meats, Jane visits the renowned Cornish Smoked Fish Co., at Charlestown, which cold smokes mackerel, smoked salmon and hot smokes kippers, salmon and the duck breast to name just a few lines. The smoking is all done to traditional methods and mainly with hardwood oak. Jane uses smoked duck in one of her salad starters and smoked mackerel for her homemade pâté. She also buys their fabulous Smoked Cheddar for her cheeseboard.

Charles Harris: 41 Church Street, Tywardreath, Par, Cornwall; 01726 812051
Cornish Smoked Fish Co: Charlestown, St Austell, Cornwall; 01726 72356
Lobbs Farm Shop: Heligan, St Austell, Cornwall; 01726 844411

A30

A390

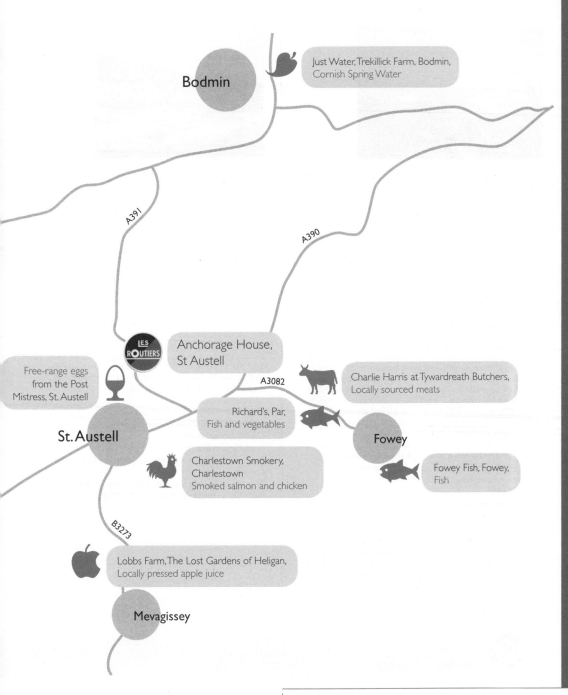

Bodmin

Just Water, Trekillick Farm, Bodmin, Cornish Spring Water

A391

A390

Anchorage House, St Austell

Free-range eggs from the Post Mistress, St. Austell

A3082

Charlie Harris at Tywardreath Butchers, Locally sourced meats

Richard's, Par, Fish and vegetables

St. Austell

Fowey

Charlestown Smokery, Charlestown Smoked salmon and chicken

Fowey Fish, Fowey, Fish

B3273

Lobbs Farm, The Lost Gardens of Heligan, Locally pressed apple juice

Mevagissey

St Ives

The Garrack Hotel and Restaurant

Burthallan Lane, St Ives, Cornwall TR26 3AA
Telephone: +44(0)870 4016421
+44(0)1736 796199
garrack@accuk.co.uk
www.garrack.com

Set on a hilltop with views of Porthmeor Beach and 30 miles of coastline, the Garrack Hotel has an enviable position above St Ives. It's been run by the Kilby family for 36 years and they ensure it's consistently well run, from its facilities to the food. It's got a homely feel but has all the amenities you'd expect of a good hotel. There is a separate sun terrace and leisure centre with indoor pool, sauna, solarium and gym plus it's surrounded by two acres of gardens. Bedrooms in the main house are decorated in an unfussy country fashion, while rooms in the sea-facing, lower-ground-floor wing are more contemporary. Some rooms have four-posters and spa baths. The restaurant is a well-matched addition to the main building. Here, Phil Thomas adopts a classic modern English approach. Seasonal and local ingredients, especially seafood are a strength. The roll call takes in a starter of pan-fried south coast scallops with smoked paprika, oyster mushrooms and a lime and coriander oil, followed by pan-fried Cornish monkfish with courgettes and red onions roasted in pumpkin oil with a poppy seed cream. There is a separate menu for lobster. The wine list is carefully selected from various suppliers to offer a global choice. Fair wine prices are achieved by applying fixed mark-ups, rather than the traditional percentage.

Rooms: 18. Double room from £114, single from £68.
Prices: Set dinner £25.50 (four course). House wine £9.05.
Last orders: Food: dinner 21.00.
Closed: Rarely.
Food: Modern English.
Other points: No-smoking area. Garden. Children welcome. Car park.
Directions: Leave the A30 and follow the signposts to St Ives, A3074. At the second mini roundabout take the first left, B3311, signposted St Ives. In St Ives at the first mini roundabout take the first left and follow the signs for the Garrack Hotel. (Map 3, E2)

Tolverne

Smugglers Cottage of Tolverne

Tolverne, Philleigh, Truro, Cornwall TR2 5NG
Telephone: +44(0)870 4016453
+44(0)1872 580309
tolverne@btconnect.com
www.tolverneriverfal.co.uk

Good home cooking and hospitality are the bywords here. The Newman family has been running this thatched 15th century cottage on the banks of the River Fal since 1934, and have gained quite a reputation for their Cornish specialities. It's a truly unique place, full of history with nautical memorabilia filling the interior. Most notably, the Americans used the cottage and slipway as an embarkation point for the D-Day landings, and General Eisenhower visited the troops here. One of the dining rooms is devoted entirely to the SS Uganda. Commitment to good food includes four different varieties of authentic Cornish pasties that are considered something of a speciality, plus there are excellent chicken and ham pies, fish pies, and filled baguettes and ciabatta. But leave space for the fabulous puddings and cakes, or treat yourself to their very good cream teas. There are non-smoking dining rooms and the bar has a collection of more than 100 malt whiskies. When planning your route here, try and arrive by boat as this is much more fun and picturesque than coming by car.

Prices: Main course from £5. House wine £9.
Last orders: Food: 17.30 (Summer 20.30).
Closed: November-May.
Food: Modern British.
Other points: No-smoking area. Children welcome. Garden. Car park.
Directions: Near the King Harry Car Ferry, on the Roseland Peninsula, on the banks of the river Fal. (Map 3, E3)

www.routiers.co.uk

Wadebridge

Buskers

Polmorla Mews, Wadebridge, Cornwall PL27 7LR
Telephone: +44(0)870 4016284
+44(0)1208 814332
www.buskers-wadebridge.com

Former stables and a courtyard have been transformed into a pretty café that serves everything from breakfast to supper. It's a pleasing setting with the enclosed walled courtyard decked out with marble tables and pretty metal chairs. This small cobbled area is where locals and visitors take coffee, brunch or come to dine beneath hanging flower baskets. Inside, it's all rustic charm with rough plastered mustard walls downstairs and aubergine walls upstairs adorned with guitars, accordians, drumkits and wonderful music posters covering all eras, and reminders of proprietor Mike Holloway's passion for music. By day, choose from the Fully Monty fried English breakfast or light snacks of homemade soup, houmous or jerk chicken skewers as well as sandwiches and filled baguettes. The evening menu kicks off at 7pm when the mood changes to dining by soft candlelight. Food also steps up a gear. Start with fresh mussels with a creamy, wine sauce or chargrilled scallops. Mains include fresh crab with tagliatelle or lamb moussaka plus there's plenty to tempt on an ever-changing specials boards courtesy of Maggie Holloway who runs the kitchen. She promotes Cornish produce wherever possible, and the café is a member of the Campaign for Real Food. Scallops are sourced from Looe, mussels from Fowey, and they serve Cornish cheese and wines. Roskilly's homemade ice cream is as an alternative to just as tempting homemade apricot and almond tart or pineapple and ginger roulade. You can also order thin crust pizzas to eat in or takeaway.

Prices: Main course from £10. House wine £9.95.
Last orders: Bar: lunch 15.00; dinner: until late.
Closed: Closed Sunday. During the winter also closed Monday.
Food: Eclectic, specialising in fresh fish and shellfish.
Other points: No-smoking area. Children welcome. Courtyard.
Directions: In the centre of Wadebridge off Polmorla Road and Polmorla Walk. (Map 3, D3)

Alston

Lovelady Shield

Alston, Cumbria CA9 3LF
Telephone: +44(0)870 4016354
+44(0)1434 381203
enquiries@lovelady.co.uk
www.lovelady.co.uk

Elegance with ease best describes this classical Georgian house that has been tastefully turned into a hotel. Built on the site of the 13th century Love of Our Lady convent, it is approached by a tree-lined drive and stands in a wonderfully secluded spot by the River Nent. The interior exudes an air of relaxation, admirably maintained by owner Peter Haynes and his wife Marie, who are natural and experienced hosts and run everything with total enthusiasm. Smart bedrooms each have their own distinctive character, but are all charming and decorated in soothing creams and white, and come with CD players and Scrabble. Dinner is well worth the asking price and after 15 years at the stove, there is agreement that the formula of a four-course, short-choice dinner has not stifled Barrie Garton's sense of adventure. He produces classic country house-style dishes with modern touches where appropriate. A June dinner could deliver warmed fresh asparagus spears with a fine herb butter sauce, followed by spicy parsnip and creamy apple soup, then a tournedos 'en croute' of prime Aberdeen Angus beef fillet, cooked in a light puff pastry parcel with red wine and wild mushroom sauce. Fresh peaches, flamed in brandy and honey and served with banana ice cream make for a great finale. A seriously thoughtful list of more than 100 bins will inspire wine lovers.

Rooms: 10. Rooms from £60 per person, dinner, bed and breakfast.
Prices: Set dinner £32.50 (4 courses). House wine £12.95.
Last orders: Food: dinner 21.00.
Closed: Lunch, except first Sunday of every month.
Food: Modern British.
Other points: No-smoking area. Children welcome over 7 years old. Garden. Car park. Licence for Civil Weddings.
Directions: On the Durham Road (A689) just outside Alston. (Map 11, C4)

Individual charm and warmth

Appleby-in-Westmorland

Tufton Arms Hotel

Market Square, Appleby-in-Westmorland,
Cumbria CA16 6XA
Telephone: +44(0)870 4016034
+44(0)17683 51593
info@tuftonarmshotel.co.uk
www.tuftonarmshotel.co.uk

This former 16th century coaching inn was given a
Victorian-style makeover by the Milsom family in
1989. The refurbishment has been beautifully executed
and reflects the ambience of that period through
attractive wallpapers, heavy drapes, old fireplaces and
large porcelain table lamps. The heavily balustraded
main staircase is a magnificent feature. On the food
front, they serve light lunch and supper menus in the
clubby bar, with a more formal menu available in
the stylish restaurant with its conservatory extension
overlooking a cobbled courtyard. Cooking is of a high
standard, be it rack of Cumbrian fell-bred lamb, or
game from the local Dalemain Estate, where Nigel
Milsom regularly arranges shooting parties, along with
fishing, a major attraction for many guests. Fish is
delivered from Fleetwood, to create, perhaps, paupiette
of lemon sole stuffed with smoked salmon with a dill
white wine sauce. There is a French accent to the carefully selected, well-annotated wine list of 160 bins,
although other parts of Europe and the new world get
a look in, too. The 21 bedrooms vary from suites with
period fireplaces, antique furnishings and large old-
style bathrooms to more conventional well-equipped
rooms with good proportions, and there are some
compact and simply furnished rooms to the rear.

Rooms: 21. Double/twin from £95.
Prices: Set dinner £24.50. Restaurant main course from £9.75.
Bar main course from £6.95. House wine £9.50.
Last orders: Bar: 23.00. Food: lunch 14.00; dinner 21.00.
Closed: Rarely.
Food: Traditional English and French.
Other points: Children welcome. Dogs welcome overnight.
Car park. Licence for Civil Weddings.
Directions: Exit38/M6. Take the B6260 to Appleby via Orton.
(Map 11, D4)

Bassenthwaite Lake

Ouse Bridge Hotel

Bassenthwaite Lake, Dubwath, Cockermouth,
Cumbria CA13 9YD
Telephone: +44(0)870 4016429
+44(0)17687 76322
enquiries@ousebridge.com
www.ousebridge.com

Once a prestigious Lakeland home, this hotel enjoys
wonderful views over Bassenthwaite Lake and
Skiddaw. Apart from its lovely location, the great
attraction of staying here is the very personal care of
owners Kathy and Andrew Woods. They are gradually
refurbishing and already their fresh, modern interiors
are lifting the look and feel of this hotel. The lounge
and small bar now has pale leather sofas, and is the
ideal spot for relaxing after walking and for admiring the views. Bedrooms and en suite bathrooms are
pristine, uncluttered and comfortable, and many have
lake views. Andrew is passionate about good food and
he spends much time sourcing good local produce. The
daily changing menu is limited but reflects the best of
what's available, and does not stint on flavour. Start
with fresh asparagus with Parmesan and prosciutto
on dressed leaves. Mains include breast of chicken
with lemon and herbs or pork loin steaks stuffed with
mozzarella and mushrooms accompanied with fresh
vegetables. There is always a good vegetarian option.
A simple good value wine list should satisfy all tastes.
Breakfast is also something quite special and includes
local meats and free-range eggs.

Rooms: 10, 2 with private bathroom. Double from £31, single from
£23. Prices are per person per night and include breakfast.
Prices: Set dinner £16. House wine £9.50.
Last orders: Dinner served between 19.00 and 20.00.
Closed: From Christmas to the end of January.
Food: Modern British.
Other points: No-smoking area. Children welcome over
10 years old. Car park.
Directions: Exit40.M6. Take the A66 towards Keswick for 25 miles.
Turn right onto the B5291 and Ouse Bridge is 50 yards along on
the left hand side. (Map 11, C3)

Borrowdale

Seatoller House

Borrowdale, Keswick, Cumbria CA12 5XN
Telephone: +44(0)870 4016430
+44(0)17687 77218
seatollerhouse@btconnect.com
www.seatollerhouse.co.uk

It's been a guest house for over a century, so Seatoller House visitors' book, which dates back to the 19th century, makes for interesting reading. The house has only recently come under the new ownership of Lynne Moorehouse and Daniel Potts, who are continuing to maintain the same high standards and relaxed atmosphere. It's an informal hotel, where friendliness and tranquillity are enduring appeals. The gardens are particularly interesting, as some of the plants and trees date back over 100 years. The prettily decorated bedrooms are being gradually updated in a cottage style. All have stunning views of either the garden or surrounding fells. The dinner menu might be short, but it offers full traceability of meats and uses seasonal produce, organic flour from the Watermill at Little Salkeld for homebaked bread, Cumberland organic mustard, fresh fish from Fleetwood and locally brewed Jennings ale. Slow roasting in the Aga produces some wonderfully tender meat dishes. A typical dinner menu might be homemade spicy lentil soup and homemade sun-dried tomato loaf, followed by Aga slow-roasted pork loin filled with apple and prune stuffing with a red wine gravy and vegetables, rounded off with bread and butter pudding. The cheeseboard includes many local favourites. The range of wines offers plenty of well-priced classics. Seatoller is also famous for its annual invite-only man hunts – of hares and hounds – that are run over the central Lakeland fells, inspired by the great manhunt in Robert Louis Stevenson's *Kidnapped*.

Rooms: 10, 6 with private bathrooms. Double room from £81, single from £42.50, family room from £100.
Prices: Set dinner £15. House wine £9.00.
Last orders: Dinner served at 19.00.
Closed: 28 November to 10 March.
Food: Traditional British.
Other points: No-smoking area. Dogs welcome. Children welcome. Garden. Car park.
Directions: Junction 40/M6. Seatoller is eight miles from Keswick along the B5289 past the shores of Derwent Water. (Map 11, D3)

Cartmel

Aynsome Manor Hotel

Cartmel, Grange-over-Sands, Cumbria LA11 6HH
Telephone: +44(0)870 4016386
+44(0)15395 36653
info@aynsomemanorhotel.co.uk
www.aynsomemanorhotel.co.uk

Now the home of the Varley family, this manor conveys the genuine feeling of a lived in, and loved, country house. Cartmel and the surrounding south Lakes area enjoys a mild climate, apparently down to its proximity to Morecambe Bay. For centuries it has been a favoured area – Cartmel Priory dates from 1188 – and Aynsome Manor expresses this feeling of peace and tranquillity well. The home comforts start in the combined entrance hall-small lounge, which has an open fire and comfortable seating. There's a small separate bar and dining room with polished tables, ornate ceiling, cut glass, linen, candles, and old pictures, which make it feel comfortably grand. En suite bedrooms are spacious and tastefully appointed with craftsman-fitted furniture and fabrics and wall coverings adding light and colour. In the kitchen, care is taken in sourcing local ingredients for the generally contemporary dishes on offer. Three options per course appear on the set dinner menu. To start, there's Aynsome's smoked haddock and fresh salmon fishcake with dill cucumber linguine and toasted coconut and lemon beurre, perhaps followed by pan-fried tenderloin of British beef on sweet potato ragoût and a Bordelaise sauce. Service is charming and the wine list is well chosen and favourably priced.

Rooms: 12. Double/twin room from £58, single from £68. Prices include dinner and breakfast.
Prices: Set lunch £15 and dinner £20. House wine £12.50.
Last orders: Food: 20.30. Residents only Sunday lunch and dinner.
Closed: First three weeks in January.
Food: Modern British.
Other points: No-smoking area. Dogs welcome overnight. Garden. Children welcome. Car park.
Directions: Exit 36/M6. Follow the A590 to Barrow. At the top of Lindale Hill turn left and follow the signs to Cartmel. (Map 11, D4)

Regional produce

Cockermouth

Quince and Medlar

13 Castlegate, Cockermouth, Cumbria CA13 9EU
Telephone: +44(0)870 4016456
+44(0)1900 823579

This is a vegetarian restaurant in the modern sense. At the Quince and Medlar you may order mung beans, but they will arrive stuffed into mangetout with ginger cheese and dressed leaves. And the dark, heavy floral wallpaper, deep-blue window dressings and lacy tablecloths lend an air of informal elegance to the two small, intimate dining rooms and sitting room. Colin and Louisa Le Voi have owned this landmark vegetarian restaurant for 15 years, winning many awards from the Vegetarian Society for their innovative take on meatless cooking. Menus centre on appetising combinations. A starter of asparagus crown comes on dressed green leaves and with lemon-scented croûtons, while beetroot and horseradish fill a sweet potato tuile. Mains of red pepper roulade, and nutty bundles of chopped cashew nuts and grated parsnip testify to the imagination at work here and local produce is firmly to the fore. The wine list is totally organic with a French focus but offers up interest from elsewhere too, including a clutch of English country wines.

Prices: Main course from £12.75. House wine £10.75.
Last orders: Food: dinner 21.30.
Closed: Sunday, Monday and one week in mid January.
Food: Vegetarian.
Other points: Totally no smoking.
Children welcome over 5 years old.
Directions: Exit 40/M6, take the A66 to Cockermouth. Once in town the restaurant is next to Cockermouth Castle, opposite Castlegate Art Gallery. (Map 11, C3)

Cockermouth

Winder Hall Country House

Low Lorton, Cockermouth, Cumbria CA13 9UP
Telephone: +44(0)870 4016277
+44(0)1900 85107
nick@winderhall.co.uk
www.winderhall.co.uk

This 15th century manor house has all the comforts of a small country house hotel. Since taking over three years ago, Nick and Ann Lawler have worked at improving the quality of the décor and ambience. The small lounge with sink-into-me sofas and open fire is warm and inviting, while each of the lovely five en suite bedrooms are spacious and individually decorated in tasteful colours and fabrics, and are roomy enough for armchairs and antique furniture. And the couple pay as much attention to the restaurant and the food as they do to the rest of the house. Dinner is served in the striking oak-panelled room with log fire and grand piano. The menu incorporates local ingredients and visits the Orient for spices and the Mediterranean for fresh flavours. Choose your starter from say mushroom tart or grilled asparagus with a lemon dressing and Parmesan, then follow with a main of Lakeland lamb cooked in red wine, rosemary and balsamic vinegar or seared salmon with a lime dressing on a bed of stir-fried vegetables. And don't overlook the desserts as they include delightful individual rhubarb tarts or crispy apple tart with apple or cider sorbet. The wine list offers value and character.

Rooms: 7. Double room from £45, single room from £65.
Prices: Set dinner £27.50 (4 course). House wine £10.50.
Last orders: Food: dinner served at 19.30.
Closed: Occasional family holiday.
Food: Modern British.
Other points: Totally no smoking. Children welcome. Garden. Car park. Licence for Civil Weddings. Fishing rights.
Directions: Exit 40/M6. From Keswick take the A66 west to Braithwaite, then the B5292 Whinlatter Pass to Lorton. Take a sharp left at the B5289 signed to Low Lorton. (Map 11, C3)

www.routiers.co.uk

Grange-over-Sands

The Hazelmere Café and Bakery

1 Yewbarrow Terrace, Grange-over-Sands,
Cumbria LA11 6ED
Telephone: +44(0)870 4016385
+44(0)15395 32972
hazelmeregrange@yahoo.co.uk

Ian and Dorothy Stubley's long-established, incredibly good café and bakery in the pretty seaside town of Grange-over-Sands has just about everything going for it. The bakery alone bakes 30-40 different breads and morning goods, from Lakeland plum bread and vanilla slices and strawberry tarts to authentic French sticks and ciabatta. Next door in the café, tuck into an array of these homemade goodies and other local produce, not forgetting the spectacular selection of speciality teas. Dorothy is passionate about good tea and sources the 30 or so listed from single estates in India, China, Japan, Sri Lanka, to name just a few places. Staff are happy to help you choose. For something you won't get elsewhere try the fabulous Cumbrian rum nicky, a sweet pastry case filled with a sweet mix of cherries, dates, rum butter, spices and stem ginger, served with créme fraîche. The Stubleys have put together an eclectic menu of other tempting dishes besides cakes that uses many local ingredients. Thus, you will find Penrith goats' cheese and salmon smoked in Cartmel alongside the usual tuna sandwiches and scones. They also have amazing homemade preserves and chutneys too. Especially good are the pickled damsons served with smoked duck, as the local damsons from Lyth Valley are considered the best in the country. Children are very welcome and have their mini menu of adult dishes such as the Cumbrian lamb tattie pot made from either Herdwick or Salt Marsh lamb, and beer-battered haddock and big chips.

Prices: Set lunch £6.95. Main course from £6.45.
House wine £2.05 for a glass.
Last orders: Food: 14.30 (Winter 16.00).
Closed: Rarely.
Food: Traditional English.
Other points: Totally no smoking. Children welcome.
Dogs welcome.
Directions: Exit 36/M6 take the A590 then the B5277, signposted Grange-over-Sands. Pass Grange Station and at the mini roundabout take the first exit, 25 yards on the right. (Map 11, D4)

Grange-over-Sands

Netherwood Hotel

Lindale Road, Grange-over-Sands, Cumbria LA11 6ET
Telephone: +44(0)870 4016384
+44(0)15395 32552
blawith@aol.com
www.netherwood-hotel.co.uk

Everything about this family-run mansion is impressive. Its elevated position, the sweeping views of Morecambe Bay sands, its attractive woodland backdrop and terraced formal gardens to the front. The atmosphere is relaxed family country house, but the amenities are top-notch: a well-equipped gym, pool and business and function facilities. It's a family-run establishment and prides itself on a high level of service. The Fallowfield brothers are also constantly working to make improvements to the décor. The lounges have been updated for comfort and the spacious bedrooms are being refurbished continuously and they have elegant, quality furniture and immaculate bathrooms. The dining room offers stunning views over the gardens to Morecambe Bay. There's plenty of choice on the set menus, and you couldn't accuse the chef of serving run-of-the-mill dishes, as many have an exotic touch. Start with peaches stuffed with mascarpone or skewers of black tiger prawns and snapper, then move on to medallions of wild boar with a Brazilian sauce or supreme of guinea fowl with a mango glaze. Finish with a luscious classic like chocolate and Grand Marnier torte or strawberry sablé.

Rooms: 32. Rooms from £70 per person, family room from £150.
Prices: Set lunch £16 and dinner £30. Bar lunches available.
House wine £13.
Last orders: Food: lunch 14.00; dinner 20.30.
Closed: Never.
Food: Global.
Other points: No-smoking area. Children welcome.
Dogs welcome overnight (in chosen rooms). Garden. Car park.
Licence for Civil Weddings.
Directions: Exit 36/M6, then A590 for Barrow-in-Furness. Left at the roundabout onto the B5277, then left again at Lindale roundabout; hotel on the right before the train station. (Map 11, D4)

Down-to-earth, friendly service

Grasmere

The Jumble Room

Langdale Road, Grasmere, Cumbria LA22 9SU
Telephone: +44(0)870 4016383
+44(0)15394 35188
thejumbleroom@which.net
www.thejumbleroom.co.uk

This small contemporary café-restaurant is a wonderful find in traditional Lakeland. The Jumble Room has been in Andy and Chrissy Hills' family for more than 50 years. It started life at the beginning of the 18th century as Grasmere's first shop where, among other things, Grasmere Rushbearing Gingerbread was made. The menu offers a colourful range of exciting dishes that will brighten any jaded palate. During the day the café serves a whole range of snacks, sandwiches and light meals with the emphasis firmly on local and organic produce. All show flair, imagination and could include aubergine and goats cheese stacks, Thai chicken, Szechuan chilli beef with stir-fried noodle or home-made lamb sausages with sticky onion marmalade. It is the evening, however, when the Jumble Room really comes into its own: vinyl tablecloths are replaced with crisp linen, the handmade velvet cushions plumped, and out come the candles. The menu has influences from Troutbeck to Thailand, with starters of Moroccan spiced lamb kofta made with local Herdwick lamb, fresh coriander, cumin, preserved lemons, tarragon, or there's muscat chicken served with buttered, minted new potatoes and organic greens. Jumble Room fish and chips is always available. The delicious puddings change so often they are difficult to list. The good-value wine list is an eclectic mix from around the world with six European organics.

Prices: Restaurant main course from £9. Bar main course from £5. House wine £9.95.
Last orders: Food: lunch 16.30; dinner 22.30.
Closed: Monday, Tuesday, 23 -27 December, lunchtimes during the winter.
Food: Global.
Other points: Totally no smoking. Children welcome.
Directions: From Ambleside take the A590 and turn left into Grasmere. Turn left again at the church and take the first right opposite the tourist information. The Jumble Room is 200 yards along on the right hand side. (Map 11, D4)

Hawkshead

Queen's Head Hotel

Main Street, Hawkshead, Ambleside, Cumbria LA22 0NS
Telephone: +44(0)870 4016041
+44(0)15394 36271 / +44(0)800 137263
enquiries@queensheadhotel.co.uk
www.queensheadhotel.co.uk

The period features of this attractive 16th century inn-cum-hotel are a real draw for visitors to the Lakeland District. The bar has beamed ceilings with open fires and is the perfect place for a sip of ale after a long walk, be it Robsinsons Bitter or the aptly named Cumbria Way. The dining room oozes character too with its wooden panelling and beams. But while it may look traditional, it serves exciting modern dishes, and features plenty of quality fish and local meats. Choose from whole mussels pan fried with herbs, served with rye bread and garlic aïoli to start and follow with Esthwaite Lake organic trout, baked with olives, tomato and fresh basil or the more exotic orange tilapia roasted with ginger and served with an orange and lemon butter. Local meat includes Herdwick lamb oven roasted and served with a fresh tarragon, chervil and shallot sauce or there's beer-braised local pheasant with leeks, potatoes, prunes and bacon. Vegetarians are well looked after too with a comprehensive salad bar and imaginative meals that include white risotto scented with lemon thyme and topped with crumbled feta. There are 14 bedrooms, which are prettily decorated in a rural-chic style with either brass, canopied or four-poster beds. Rooms at the front have the best views over the village.

Rooms: 14, 2 not en suite, two with private bathroom. 2 four-poster beds and 2 family rooms. Double room from £34 per person, single from £47.50.
Prices: Main course lunch from £7.25. House wine £10.95.
Last orders: Bar: 23.00. Food: lunch 14.30; dinner 21.30.
Closed: Rarely.
Food: Modern British.
Other points: No-smoking area. Children welcome.
Directions: Exit 36/M6 and follow the A590 to Newby Bridge. Take the second right and follow the road for eight miles into the centre of Hawkshead. (Map 11, D4)

www.routiers.co.uk

Orton

New Village Tea Rooms

Orton, Penrith, Cumbria CA10 3RH
Telephone: +44(0)870 4016387
+44(0)1539 624886

If you're looking for a friendly and much more appetising alternative to motorway services on the M6, exit at junction 38 and head for the pretty village of Orton. There you'll find Christine Evans's treat of a traditional tearoom, which she has run for over a decade. Christine has built up a regular clientele who break long journeys to eat here, plus a loyal local clientele who pop in for lunch or tea, or come to buy one of her special homemade ready meals. The tearooms were originally four separate rooms for farm labourers. They have been converted in this Lakeland-style café. Cream walls, open fire, wooden tables with dark green and lace cloths, a dresser stocked with homemade cakes and biscuits and an open-plan kitchen all add to its homely charm. There are six tables downstairs and five up, plus seating in the small garden. Homemade scones, sandwiches, toasties, jacket potatoes and Lakeland ice cream dominate the printed menu, with a blackboard detailing the day's specials. These run to soups of lentil and bacon, or curried parsnip, bakes such as chicken and broccoli, or broad bean, onion and tomato, and homemade desserts of sticky toffee pudding or chocolate and orange crumble. Cakes are available to take away plus there's a large selection of takeaway frozen ready-made meals, such as beef cobbler, which knock spots off the supermarket offerings.

Prices: Lunchtime special from £5.50.
Last orders: Food: 17.00 (Winter 16.30).
Closed: Sunday before 25 December to 2 January.
Food: Teashop.
Other points: Totally no smoking. Garden. Car park.
No credit cards accepted. No licence.
Directions: Exit 38/M6 take the road signposted to Appleby. In Orton take the Shap Road in front of the George Hotel. New Village Tea Room located straight ahead opposite the post office. (Map 11, D4)

Penrith

Alan's Cafe Restaurant

Poets Walk, Penrith, Cumbria CA11 7HJ
Telephone: +44(0)870 4016431
+44(0)1768 867474
alanschef@btinternet.com

This is a café by weekdays serving cakes and light lunches and a stylish restaurant on Friday and Saturday evenings. Owner-chef Alan Potter pulls off both of these guises with aplomb. The modern décor – light colours and whitewashed wood furniture – is an inviting setting in which to enjoy the fine selection of teas, coffees, freshly baked breads, cakes and scones, or you can opt for one of the lunchtime specials, such as breast of chicken on a bed of tagliatelle with bacon and button onions or pan-fried salmon with a lemon and lime dressing. At weekends the mood changes, with soft lighting and subtle background music creating the right ambience for special occasions. The fixed price evening menu offers four choices per course and covers meat, fish and vegetarian options, and includes coffee. Cream of carrot, orange and coriander soup and pan-fried fillet of sea bass with provençal vegetables and balsamic reduction feature among the starters, while rib-eye of British beef with a green peppercorn sauce and roasted vegetable tagliatelle with a spiced tomato sauce tempt in the main course section. Round off with a wicked traditional dessert such as bread and butter pudding or sticky toffee pud.

Prices: Set dinner £20 (4 course). Restaurant main course from £11.50. Bar main course from £7. House wine £11.50.
Last orders: Lunch 14.30; dinner served from 19.00 (Friday and Saturday only).
Closed: Monday to Thursday evenings and all day Sunday.
Food: Modern British.
Other points: No-smoking area. Children welcome.
Directions: Exit40/M6. Just off the Market Square in the town centre. (Map 11, C4)

Good food and wine

Penrith

Watermill

Little Salkeld, Penrith, Cumbria CA10 1NN
Telephone: +44(0)870 4016432
+44(0)1768 881523
organicflour@aol.com
www.organicmill.co.uk

Here you can combine sightseeing with a stop-off for snacks. The mill is set in quite breathtaking scenery off the Alston road. In pink-painted buildings, it is tucked away at the bottom of the village beside Sunnygill Beck and its waters are channelled down the mill race to turn the wheels. The mill was restored by Nick and Ana Jones in 1975, and they are committed to producing flour from grain grown to bio-dynamic organic standards by English farmers. Take a tour of the water-powered corn mill, one of the few in the country, before treating yourself to delicious homemade goodies in the tearoom. All the food they serve is organic and vegetarian. The Joneses were granted a Soil Association licence in 2002. Come in the morning and you can enjoy a late breakfast of porridge with maple syrup and toast with Watermill marmalade; at teatime, it's tea and scones with homemade jam, or organic arabica coffee with a flapjack or irresistible chocolate brownie. In between, you can have a miller's lunch of Loch Arthur cheese and homemade chutney, quiche with salads or homemade soup with a selection of different breads. Budding bakers will be pleased to learn that the Joneses also run breadmaking courses.

Prices: Main course lunch from £5.50.
Last orders: Food: 16.45.
Closed: 24 December-30 January.
Food: Totally Organic.
Other points: Totally no smoking. Children welcome. Car park.
Directions: Six miles from exit 40/M6. Take the A686 for five miles to Langwathby, left at the village green, then two miles to the mill. (Map 11, C4)

Ullswater

Brackenrigg Inn

Watermillock, Lake Ullswater, Penrith, Cumbria CA11 0LP
Telephone: +44(0)870 4016046
+44(0)17684 86206
enquiries@brackenrigginn.co.uk
www.brackenrigginn.co.uk

This white-washed inn dating from the 18th century is pretty in its own right, but factor in a long outdoor terrace overlooking Ullswater and it moves into the premier league. Inside, its homely and friendly and offers great value dining. Where you eat depends on the décor you prefer. There's a traditonal and attractive bar with wood panelling and polished wood floors, open fire and views over the surrounding countryside, or the lounge dining room, which is carpeted and furnished with polished mahogany pieces. A separate restaurant is also traditionally appointed and has splendid views. The owners have built up a good reputation for well-executed, contemporary food over the years. The bar menu offers good value, no-nonsense meals such as traditional smoked salmon or grilled goats' cheese salad and mains of Cumberland sausages, pasta bake or fish and chips. A sophisticated five-course dinner incorporates Mediterranean and British flavours. You could start with halloumi cheese baked with tomatoes and oregano, served with garlic bruschetta and drizzled with pesto, then move on to roast rump of lamb marinated in red wine, rosemary, orange and garlic, then round off with one of the homemade desserts or cheese. The location is a great base for walking, and all the en suite and modern bedrooms have fine views.

Rooms: 17. Double from £27 per person. Single from £32. Superior rooms and suites also available.
Prices: Set Sunday lunch £9.95. Set dinner £18.95. Restaurant main course from £10.50. Bar main course from £8.25. House wine £10.95.
Last orders: Bar: 23.00. Food: lunch 14.30; dinner 21.00.
Closed: Never.
Food: Modern British.
Other points: No-smoking area. Dogs welcome overnight (some rooms). Garden. Children welcome. Car park.
Directions: On A592 south west of Penrith; 6 miles from Exit40/M6, overlooking Ullswater. (Map 11, C4)

www.routiers.co.uk

Wasdale

Wasdale Head Inn

Wasdale, Gosforth, Cumbria CA20 1EX
Telephone: +44(0)870 4016047
+44(0)19467 26229
wasdaleheadinn@msn.com
www.wasdale.com

This area is a magnet for walkers and climbers and visitors who come to admire rather than tackle the Great Gable or Scafell. The inn, with its backdrop of the steep fells, has plenty attractions of its own. Ritson's bar, named after its first landlord and the world's biggest liar, has high ceilings, a polished slate floor, wood panelling, climbing memorabilia and stunning photos of the surrounding countryside. It dispenses top-notch homebrewed Great Gable beers on handpump and substantial food in the form of thick soups, Cumbrian sausages and ham, and Borrowdale trout, served from a hot counter. By contrast, the residents-only part of the building is imposing. The bar has large Tudoresque furniture and the lounge is elegantly furnished. The restaurant, open to non residents, offers a four-course, traditional British dinner along the lines of air-dried Cumbrian ham, local farm-reared Herdwick lamb or fillet steak, and classic puddings. The pick of the 14 bedrooms is the garden room, with its muslin-draped four-poster. Four suites in a separate building have kitchen units, and dinner can be served for you to reheat. The Christmas package is legendary. No turkey or telly? Then the Baa Humbug! Stuff the Bloody Turkey! break is for you.

Rooms: 14. Room from £49 per person.
Prices: Bar meal from £6. Set dinner (4 course) £25. House wine £11.90.
Last orders: Bar: 23.00. Food: 21.00.
Closed: Rarely.
Food: Traditional British.
Other points: Totally no smoking. Children welcome. Dogs welcome overnight. Garden. Car park.
Directions: Wasdale Head is signed off A595 between Egremont and Ravenglass. (Map 11, D3)

Affordable good value

Air-cured ham and bacon
at the Brackenrigg Inn

Richard Woodall is an extraordinary company. Based in the small village of Waberthwaite, it is one of the oldest family businesses in the world. It's in its 7th and 8th generation of family members and is famous for its traditionally cured hams, bacon and sausages. Using the same recipes and techniques as the Woodall's of more than 170 years ago and with the expertise of many generations' knowledge in refining it has resulted in a fantastic product. Indeed, the Royal Family has awarded their sausage with a Royal Warrant. It helps that from start to finish the pigs are reared by Richard Woodall, the company farming their own herd of around 180 sows in large straw-filled barns with natural light and fresh air and in a completely chemical and preservative-free environment. There is a real feeling of tradition at Richard Woodall's, the business is even in the original premises. Further inland, the Brackenrigg Inn, in the small hamlet of Watermillock near Ullswater keeps a constant supply of Woodall's air-cured ham and bacon whilst sourcing their Cumberland sausage (that they might serve with delicious apple mash) from Adam Jackson and his farm a stone's throw away.

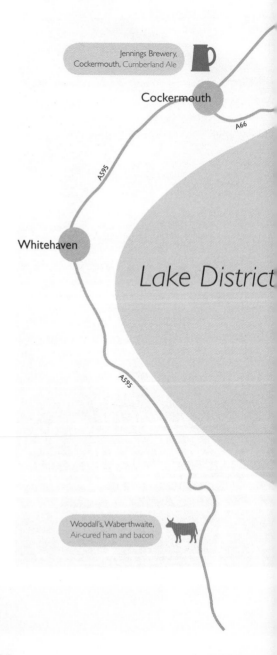

Jennings Brewery, Cockermouth, Cumberland Ale

Cockermouth

A66

A595

Whitehaven

Lake District

A595

Woodall's, Waberthwaite, Air-cured ham and bacon

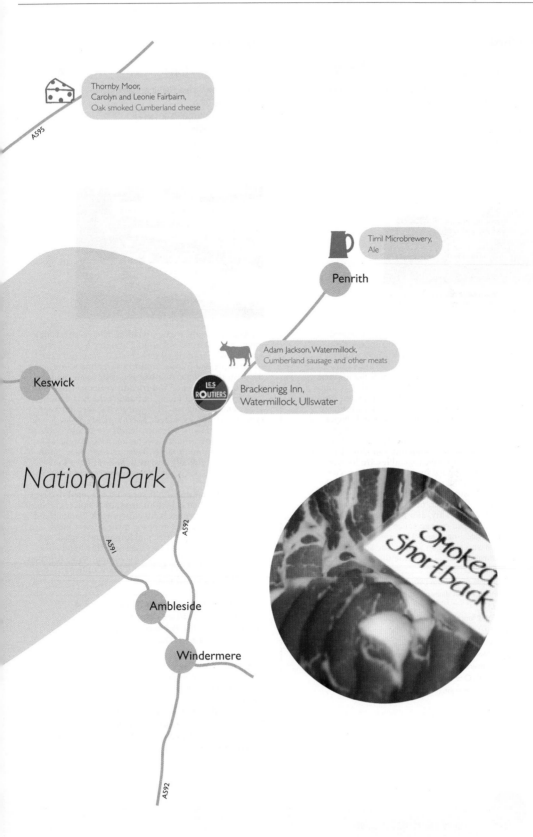

Thornby Moor,
Carolyn and Leonie Fairbairn,
Oak smoked Cumberland cheese

A595

Tirril Microbrewery,
Ale

Penrith

Adam Jackson, Watermillock,
Cumberland sausage and other meats

Keswick

LES ROUTIERS

Brackenrigg Inn,
Watermillock, Ullswater

NationalPark

A592

A591

Ambleside

Windermere

A592

Bideford

Riversford Hotel

Limers Lane, Northam, Bideford, Devon EX39 2RG
Telephone: +44(0)870 4016291
+44(0)1237 474239
riversford@aol.com
www.riversford.co.uk

The Jarrard family run their hotel with style and
simplicity, drawing on strong, loyal support that
has built up over the last 30 years. Their winning
combination is quality coupled with good value. All
15 bedrooms are en suite, are very well maintained
and individually decorated in light, relaxing colours;
the best rooms have four-poster beds. Pleasant public
rooms include the light, airy restaurant with lovely
garden views to the River Torridge beyond. Nigel
Jarrard presides over the kitchen and is to be praised
for his emphasis on buying local ingredients. Game
comes from local shoots, Somerset and Dorset cheeses
are from Hawkridge Farm, vegetables are locally
grown and meat supplied by a local butcher. The
menu is strong on the traditional with dishes such
as tournedos Rossini, and Devon lamb chops with
mustard and brown sugar, but there are modern touches too. Fish is a speciality, and local sea bass could be
teamed with dill and orange sauce or king scallops
sautéed in garlic, ginger and Thai spices and served
with a lemon and tarragon sauce. The short selection
of wines continues the good value theme.

Rooms: 15. Double room from £80, single from £50.
Prices: Set lunch £14, set dinner £18. Main course from £8.
House wine £12.
Last orders: Food: lunch 14.00; dinner 21.30.
Closed: Never.
Food: Specialises in local seafood.
Other points: No-smoking area. Children welcome.
Dogs welcome overnight. Garden. Car park.
Directions: J27/M5. One mile north of Bideford on the A386,
Limers Lane is on the right. (Map 3, C4)

Dartmouth

Stoke Lodge Hotel

Cinders Lane, Stoke Fleming, Dartmouth,
Devon TQ6 0RA
Telephone: +44(0)870 4016441
+44(0)1803 770523
mail@stokelodge.co.uk
www.stokelodge.co.uk

Tucked alongside a steep, winding village street high
above Start Bay, this charming country house hotel
has an away-from-it-all feel about it. You can't fail
to be impressed by the comfortable country house
décor in the lounge-cum-bar and restaurant, and by
the relaxed ambience and friendly welcome that goes
with it. The south-facing building, which is mainly
17th century with an 18th century façade, has been
sympathetically extended. There's plenty to keep you
entertained: lawns, terraces, tennis court and outdoor
swimming pool, indoor swimming pool, sauna, spa
bath and a snooker table. Bedrooms are bang up to
date and individually designed. Several have four-
poster beds. Cooking is based around good quality
local ingredients. The daily changing set menu offers
a choice of traditional but superbly executed dishes,
including smoked eel with horseradish sauce, cream of
leek soup, and grilled lamb cutlets with Cumberland
sauce. Old favourites appear on the dessert menu,
notably bread and butter pudding with custard, and
sherry trifle. Stephen Mayer ensures this hotel runs
smoothly through his hands-on commitment. It makes
a tremendous holiday base, and there's plenty to keep
the children amused too.

Rooms: 25. Double room from £89, single from £56.
Prices: Set lunch £14.50 and dinner £19.95.
Main course from £11.95. House wine £9.95.
Last orders: Food: lunch 13.30; dinner 21.00.
Closed: Rarely.
Food: Modern British.
Other points: No-smoking area. Children welcome.
Dogs welcome overnight. Garden. Car park. Indoor and outdoor
swimming pools.
Directions: M5/A38. From the M5 at Exeter take the A38 towards
Plymouth. Turn off at Buckfastleigh and follow the signs to Totnes
and then Dartmouth (A381 or A3122). Turn right to Stoke
Fleming. (Map 4, E5)

www.routiers.co.uk

Exeter

The Twisted Oak

Little John's Cross Hill, Ide, Exeter, Devon EX2 9RG
Telephone: +44(0)870 4016055
+44(0)1392 273666
info@thetwistedoak.co.uk
www.thetwistedoak.co.uk

Following major refurbisment, Martin Bullock's pub-restaurant combines rustic charm with contemporary minimalism. The red brick, clematis and ivy-clad Twisted Oak stands beside a picturesque Saxon bridge in rural isolation close to the village of Ide, just a few miles from Exeter. The wooden-floored bar has a cosy, snug feel with its rich russet walls, leather sofas and polished wooden tables. In addition, there's a carpeted lounge into the new conservatory dining room; the latter enjoying views across the secluded garden. The menu is built around good traditional food with a modern twist using seasonal and local ingredients. Alongside the traditional classics such as local sausages with creamy mash and shallot gravy or rump steak with chunky chips and red onion confit, you'll find roast cod with tomato and cardamom sauce and noodles, and grilled mussels with sauce Romesco and fries. For pudding, try the baked cheesecake with caramelised strawberries. Chalkboards list the day's delivery from Looe fish market. Alternatively, tuck into lunchtime salads and filled baguettes and enjoy some real ales including locally brewed O'Hanlon's Firefly. Families are made most welcome with a good children's menu and a large play area.

Prices: Restaurant main course from £9.95.
Bar main course from £6.95. House wine £9.95.
Last orders: Bar: lunch 15.00; dinner 23.00. Food: lunch 14.30; dinner 21.30.
Closed: Never.
Food: Modern British.
Other points: No-smoking area. Dogs welcome in garden only. Car park.
Directions: Exit31/M5. Travel towards Ide village just off the A30 to Oakhampton, Twisted Oak is just outside the village. (Map 4, D5)

Holsworthy

Blagdon Manor

Ashwater, Beaworthy, Holsworthy, Devon EX21 5DF
Telephone: +44(0)870 4016345
+44(0)1409 211224
stay@blagdon.com
www.blagdon.com

Steve and Elizabeth Morey pay as much attention to the little details as they do to the overall décor and dining. The Manor is luxurious to the core and ultimately relaxing. The Grade II listed building was built in two sections, one dating from the 16th century, the other from the 17th, and it has been cleverly integrated with a bar/lounge and library in the oldest part, which is reached through a covered cobbled courtyard. The seven bedrooms are all charming, individually decorated and supremely appointed, with views over the gardens. The dining room leads to the newly built conservatory and is a lovely setting for cooking that mixes imagination with sound combinations. The starting point is prime raw ingredients such as new season lamb, superior local seafood and regional cheeses, plus they use their home-grown produce. Dishes in the short three-course menus might offer warm salad of ham hock with lentils, shallot and English mustard vinaigrette, and confit of Gressingham duck with wild mushrooms and balsamic vinegar jus. Fish dishes are enticing, perhaps a main of pan-fried Cornish cod fillet with a fricasée of potato, or smoked haddock, tomatoes, coarsegrain mustard and chives. Desserts may include the irresistible hot banana pancake soufflé with toasted coconut ice cream.

Rooms: 7. Double/twin from £100. Single from £72.
Prices: Set lunch £17 and dinner £30. Sunday Lunch £19.50. House wine £10.
Last orders: Food: lunch 14.00; dinner 21.00.
Closed: Monday and Tuesday lunch and Sunday and Monday dinner to non-residents. Two weeks at the end of January and two weeks in early November.
Food: Modern British.
Other points: Dogs welcome overnight. Garden. Car park.
Directions: Signed from the A388 at Blagdon Cross, 10 miles north of Launceston and at Swingate Cross four miles south of Holsworthy. Follow hotel signs down the lanes for approximately one mile. (Map 3, D4)

An alternative Britain

Plymouth

Browns Hotel & Brasserie

80 West Street, Tavistock, Plymouth, Devon PL19 8AQ
Telephone: +44(0)870 4016443
+44(0)1822 618686
enquiries@brownsdevon.co.uk
www.brownsdevon.co.uk

This former coaching inn has recently been refurbished along chic and contemporary lines throughout the hotel-restaurant and bar. Set in Tavistock, it makes an ideal base for touring Devon, and provides all-day eating opportunities for non-residents, from morning coffee through to a fine dinner. It is the oldest hostelry in the town, and water from the Tavistock spring has been served here as far back as Roman times. In fact, guests today can still enjoy Dartmoor Spring bottled water from the Roman well in the hotel's atrium. The 20 en suite rooms are all beautifully appointed and come with the added extras, including satellite TV, data port and coffee-tea making facilities. For lunch head to the Wine Bar with its comfortable sofas and open log fire or to the light and airy Conservatory. Dinner is served in the Brasserie and head chef John McGeever puts local ingredients such as fresh fish from Brixham and organic meats to superb use in his well thought out menu. Begin with baked goats' cheese Charlotte or paupiette of organic smoked salmon and trout. Mains include roasted local venison, grilled Devon duckling and roasted organic chicken breast, which all come with interesting accompaniments. The wine list is impressive, and it's worth ordering some of the Camel Valley sparkling wine, which is as good as champagne. Brown's offers a warm and friendly atmosphere and to slick, professional standards.

Rooms: 20. Double/twin from £90, single from £65, family from £140.
Prices: Restaurant main course from £10.50. Bar snack from £7.50. House wine £14.50.
Last orders: Food: lunch 14.30; dinner 21.15.
Closed: Never.
Food: Modern British.
Other points: No-smoking area. Garden. Children welcome. Car park. Gym and indoor swimming pool.
Directions: M5 joining the A30. (Map 3, D4)

Salcombe

Victoria Inn

Fore Street, Salcombe, Devon TQ8 8BU
Telephone: +44(0)870 4016058
+44(0)1548 842604
ajcannon@aol.com

Andrew Cannon has made a stylish statement inside this typical seaside town pub, both through the interiors and on the menu. Step inside and you'll find swish, modern décor, the result of a year-long refurbishment programme. Flagstones, heavy beams, chunky wooden tables and chairs, open log fire and pictures of old Salcombe feature in the cool bar area. Wind your way upstairs to a comfortable lounge bar and more formal dining area, both with stunning views across Salcombe harbour. Menus state that everything is freshly prepared from Devon produce, so look out for local butcher meats, fresh fish landed along the coast, locally made cheeses and ice cream, and hand-cut chips from Devon potatoes. For lunch, you could tuck into thick and creamy shellfish chowder, honey-roasted Devon ham with free-range eggs and chips, and chicken and ham pie with suet-crust pastry. The evening meals step up in sophistication and the views get even better at sunset. Start with Salcombe scallops with garlic and parsley butter, move on to John Dory on buttered tagliatelle and chervil and white wine cream sauce, and finish with a rich dark chocolate and whisky mousse. You're bound to find a good wine match for your meal with eight wines offered by the glass, or sip some West Country ale.

Prices: Set lunch £12.95, set dinner £19.95. Restaurant main course from £9.95. Bar main course from £4.95. House wine £10.75.
Last orders: Bar: 23.00 (Sunday 22.30). Food: lunch 14.30; dinner 21.00.
Closed: Rarely.
Food: Modern British.
Other points: No-smoking area. Dogs welcome. Garden. Children welcome.
Directions: (Map 4, E5)

Slapton

The Tower Inn

Church Road, Slapton, Kingsbridge, Devon TQ7 2PN
Telephone: +44(0)870 4016059
+44(0)1548 580216
towerinn@slapton.org
www.thetowerinn.com

The 14th century Tower Inn is tucked away in a sleepy village just inland from Slapton. It takes its name from the ancient ruins of a tower it stands beside, all that remains of a monastic college. The inn was built in 1374 to accommodate the artisans building the college and 600 years on guests continue to be warmly welcomed, more recently by Annette and Andrew Hammett who bought the pub in December 2003. You will be served good modern pub food from lunch and dinner menus that include much local fish and meat. At lunch, there are generously filled sandwiches, starters of platter of locally smoked fish or homemade soup of the day, with mains of trio of local sausages with wholegrain mustard mash or smoked cod fillet and mash. From the evening menu, begin with a hearty starter of crab and prawn tower with basil oil or sautéed scallops and prawns with chilli noodles, followed by pheasant supreme, lamb shank or roast sea bass. Stone walls, open fires, low beams, scrubbed oak tables and flagstone floors characterise the interior, and the atmosphere is enhanced at night with candlelit tables. There are three cottage-style en suite bedrooms and a super large rear garden.

Rooms: 2. Room from £55.
Prices: Restaurant main course from £9. House wine from £10.
Last orders: Bar: lunch 14.30 (Sunday 15.00); dinner 23.00.
Food: lunch 14.15 (Sunday 14.30); dinner 21.30.
Closed: Rarely.
Food: Modern British.
Other points: No-smoking area. Garden and courtyard.
Children welcome. Car park.
Directions: Off the A379 between Dartmouth and Kingsbridge, or off the A381 between Totnes and Kingsbridge. (Map 4, E5)

Stokenham

The Tradesmans Arms

Stokenham, Kingsbridge, Devon TQ7 2SZ
Telephone: +44(0)870 4016060
+44(0)1548 580313
nick@thetradesmansarms.com
www.thetradesmansarms.com

Named after the men who traded in Dartmouth and stopped off at the pub en route home to Kingsbridge, this 14th century part-thatched cottage is quite a find. It's tucked away in the centre of the picturesque old village. The simplicity of décor is what makes it so appealing. The low-key furnished main bar has a stone fireplace, wood-burning stove and heavy beams, and there's a rustic and equally informal dining room. Landlord Nick Abbot, who moved to Devon following years running a busy gastropub in the Chilterns, knows a thing or two about serving good food. Along with chef Tim Hoban, he offers quality food from locally sourced produce. Meats and fish are smoked on the premises, fish is from day boats at Brixham and Plymouth, scallops are dived for in Start Bay, vegetables are grown four miles away, and Sutton Plymouth Pride is brewed along the road. You can expect some of the freshest flavours on the daily changing menu, which includes pan-fried scallops with chorizo sausage, tagliatelle with clams, crabmeat and white wine, crab cakes with sweet chilli jus, braised lamb shank with mint and rosemary gravy, venison steak with roast root vegetables, and whole grilled lemon sole. Light lunches of hot sandwiches, daily curries as well as various omelettes are also available.

Prices: Set lunch and dinner £21.50. Restaurant main course from £7.95. Main course bar from £4.95. House wine £11.95.
Last orders: Bar: 23.00 (during summer months open all day at the weekend). Food: lunch 14.30; dinner 21.30.
Closed: Rarely.
Food: Modern British.
Other points: No-smoking areas. Dogs welcome. Garden.
Children welcome. Car park.
Directions: Just off the A379, behind the village green between Dartmouth and Kingsbridge, one mile inland from Torcross. (Map 4, E5)

Individual charm and warmth

Tavistock

Tor Cottage

Chillaton, Lifton, near Tavistock, Devon PL16 0JE
Telephone: +44(0)870 4016444
+44(0)1822 860248
info@torcottage.co.uk
www.torcottage.co.uk

A get-away-from it all location that offers a relaxing break in idyllic surroundings. The five rooms are set out in the extensive and beautiful grounds, but all are within close walking distance of the main house. If you want privacy and seclusion, then you've come to the right place. The most private rooms are at Laughing Waters, the latest addition next to the stream. All the rooms are en suite and come with private terraces and patio furniture, fridges, tea and coffee-making facilities plus other useful items such as torch, umbrella, magazines and a welcoming trug of champagne truffles, sparkling wine and fruits. Owner Maureen Rowlatt has created a wonderful, relaxed place to stay. If you want to be pampered you can enjoy a wonderful breakfast hamper in your room or take it in the bright and airy conservatory in the main house. The food is sourced locally and the Cornish smoked salmon and scrambled eggs is a great start to the day. No evening meals are served as such, but by arrangement, a picnic hamper can be delivered to your room. They come full of goodies, such as homemade sandwiches, chutneys, West Country cheese, salads and the most delectable home-made scones with Devonshire cream and strawberries. This is an excellent base for exploring Dartmoor or the Tamar Valley, but just as nice is losing yourself in these beautiful grounds and taking the odd dip in the very private outdoor heated pool.

Rooms: 5. Double from £130, single from £89.
Prices: Picnic platters for two, £28. BYO.
Closed: Mid December to mid January.
Food: Modern British.
Other points: Totally no smoking. Garden. Car park.
Directions: M5/A30. Keep Chillaton post office on your left. Go up the hill for 300m and veer off to the right down bridleway track. (Map 3, D4)

Torquay

Orestone Manor

Rockhouse Lane, Maidencombe, Torquay, Devon TQ1 4SX
Telephone: +44(0)870 4016440
+44(0)1803 328098
enquiries@orestone.co.uk
www.orestone.co.uk

The views from the hotel across to Lyme Bay are reason enough to book in. But add a stylishly furnished hotel, great food and attentive service and you can see why Orestone Manor Hotel is such a gem along the Torbay coastline. The elegant and relaxed surroundings have been created by Rose Ashton. There is a touch of the Raj throughout, not least in the refined drawing room, which has a distinct colonial feel. This is the perfect place to enjoy a pre-dinner drink and peruse the extensive dinner menu. The smart interiors continue through to the 12 individually furnished suites and bedrooms. All are en suite and have tremendous sea views. The most lavish rooms are the ground floor Garden Room with terrace and The Horsley, an open-plan suite with four-poster bed on the first floor. Dining is a real treat, as the menu offers contemporary dishes using the best local ingredients plus produce from the hotel's gardens. Start with crab consommé, then move on to West Country lamb or baked fillet of salmon with herb couscous and lobster velouté. Puds are sheer decadence and the local cheeses are excellent too. Snacks, lunches and teas can be enjoyed in the conservatory all day. Other facilities include an outdoor heated pool and indoor snooker table.

Rooms: 12. Double/twin from £119, single from £89.
Prices: Set lunch £17.95. Restaurant main course from £16.50 at dinner. Bar snack from £7.50. House wine £12.95.
Last orders: Food: lunch 14.00; dinner 21.00. Open for afternoon teas.
Closed: Rarely.
Food: Modern British.
Other points: No-smoking in restaurant. Garden. Dogs welcome. Children welcome. Car park.
Directions: From Torquay, follow the A379 (signposted Teignmouth) up Watcombe Hill. Then watch for Brunel Manor and turn right down Rockhouse Lane about 50 yards further on. There is a signpost to the hotel on the main A379 road at the top of Rockhouse Lane. (Map 4, D5)

Regional produce

Fontmell Magna

The Crown & Coach House

Fontmell Magna, Shaftesbury, Dorset SP7 0PA
Telephone: +44(0)870 4016066
+44(0)1747 811441
oldcoachho@msn.com

Liz Neilson has tranformed The Crown since she bought it two years ago. With her new chef Robin Davies, formerly at the Clarence Hotel, Dublin, they have turned an ordinary village local into a pub with a reputation for good food. Local produce and fresh food from small suppliers have helped them fulfil their culinary aims. And what they can't get locally, they make themselves. Fish is delivered daily from Poole, meat is sourced from local traceable herds, while farms in the Blackmore Vale supply dairy produce, and the cheeseboard features the local Ashmore Cheddar. Bread is baked on the premises. Robin's menu lists classic pub dishes all cooked to perfection, perhaps roast leg of Dorset lamb, rib-eye steak and chips, and fresh plaice with prawns and garlic butter. Alternatives may include cod fillet with a pesto crust and roast organic chicken with homemade bread sauce. Good puddings such as Dorset apple cake or treacle tart, Hall and Woodhouse beers, and good-value wines – eight available by the glass – contribute to an all-round culinary event. Bedrooms have an old-fashioned, Victorian style, but at the same time are light and airy. There's an en suite, while the other two share a large bathroom. They all have TV, and tea-making facilities.

Rooms: **3, 2 with private bathrooms. Double from £55.**
Prices: Restaurant main course from £8.95.
Bar main course from £6.95. House wine £7.
Last orders: Bar: open all day. Food: lunch 14.30 (Saturday and Sunday until 15.00); dinner 21.00 (Saturday 21.30).
Closed: Rarely.
Food: Classic British with traditional French influences.
Other points: No-smoking area. Dogs welcome. Garden.
Children welcome over 9 years old. Car park.
Directions: A303 Shaftesbury junction. From Shaftesbury take the A350 to Blandford Forum, pass through Compton Abbas and the Crown is in the centre of Fontmell Magna. (Map 5, D2)

Portland

Vaughans Bistro

93 Weston Road, Portland, Dorset DT5 2DA
Telephone: +44(0)870 4016315
+44(0)1305 822226
eat@vaughansbistro.co.uk
www.vaughansbistro.co.uk

Perched at the top of Portland Island is this delightful rustic bistro, which has become a culinary destination for locals and visitors to the island. The simple charm of the wood interiors creates a cosy atmosphere that belies the creativity of cooking that goes on behind the scenes. Mark Vaughan has put together an amazing collection of dishes – a printed menu and specials chalked up on the restaurant walls – and has achieved a much-deserved excellent reputation for his food that's all cooked to order. There is a wide choice of locally caught fish, such as red snapper with spicy fish sausage and tomato and basil sauce or paella with monkfish, scallops and tiger prawns. For starters, there's a light cherry tomato and gorgonzola tart or a terrine of scallops, langoustines and crab with courgette linguine tossed in truffle oil. As well as fish, there is plenty to tempt the carnivore. Leading the field is lamb wellington with an onion marmalade and spinach and mushrooms or fillet of local beef with fondant potato and a Stilton and peppercorn sauce, while vegetarians can tuck into a tasty nutty crumble of leek, parsnip and Stilton. A compact wine list is very well priced and offers much to complement the food.

Prices: Restaurant main course from £11.25. Sunday lunch £12.95.
House wine £8.95.
Last orders: Food: Lunch: 14.30 (Sunday only), dinner 22.00.
Closed: Lunchtimes and Sunday evening.
Food: Modern British.
Other points: Totally no smoking. Children welcome.
Directions: Follow the A354 on to Portland. Go to the top of the island and follow signs to Weston Road. (Map 5, E2)

Studland Bay

Manor House

Beach Road, Studland Bay, Dorset BH19 3AU
Telephone: +44(0)870 4016461
+44(0)1929 450288
themanorhousehotel@lineone.net
www.themanorhousehotel.com

Set in 20 acres of secluded grounds with delightful views over Studland Bay, this early 18th century Gothic manor house makes for an elegant and comfortable hotel. It retains an olde worlde feel, but comes with all the latest conveniences and good service. The baronial-feel, oak-panelled dining room with fireplace and dark-wood furniture, together with its adjoining bright conservatory, look out over the lawn to the sea, as does the comfortable, country-style lounge. Bedrooms are charming, light and spacious, with period furnishings. All are en suite with every convenience and many have sea or garden views. There's a four-poster suite in the Coach House annex and a further four posters in the main house. Facilities include a bar and outdoor tennis courts. Dinner is a meal to look forward too, with chef Giuseppe Singaguglia sourcing many ingredients locally. Venison comes from local estates, while shellfish is delivered from Weymouth, and regional cheeses include Dorset Blue Vinney, Stinking Bishop and Somerset brie. The evening menu may include tian of crab and avocado with a dill dressing or poached pear salad with Roquefort and toasted walnuts, followed by pan-fried skate wing with chargrilled vegetables and red pepper butter or seared local Studland venison with wild mushroom sauce and polenta. Around 40 affordable wines are bolstered by a few specials. English breakfasts are of the kind to set you up for the day.

Rooms: 21. Double room from £65 per person, single £85, including dinner.
Prices: Set dinner £30 (4 courses). House wine £12.
Last orders: Food: lunch 14.00; dinner 21.00.
Closed: Three weeks in January.
Food: Modern British/European.
Other points: No-smoking area. No children under 5 years. Garden. Car park.
Directions: 3 miles from Swanage, 3 miles from Sandbanks Ferry. (Map 4, D8)

Weymouth

The Roundhouse Restaurant

1 The Esplanade, Weymouth, Dorset DT4 8EA
Telephone: +44(0)870 4016314
+44(0)1305 761010
michael.clough@btopenworld.com
www.roundhouserestaurantltd.co.uk

Steeped in local history, the attractive Roundhouse has an enviable location overlooking the harbour, and has much to tempt on its menu. It's hard to believe that this elegant restaurant was once a tram ticket issuing office. It also housed American soldiers before the D-Day landings. The refurbishment is ongoing, but the interiors are already truly tasteful, down to the fact mobile phones aren't allowed, plus there are smoking and non-smoking restaurant rooms, and a bar for pre or post dinner drinks. Emphasis must be on the food though, as everything is homemade and freshly prepared, including the breads, sweets and sauces. Local delights feature prominently. Start with Weymouth Bay crab mushroom parcel. If it's a fish main course you want, then look to the specials board, which features the local fish of the day and a speciality of the restaurant. The other mains are just as delicious though: lamb's liver braised and served on colcannon mash with a bacon and shallot gravy, or carbonnade of venison served on a wild mushroom savoury bread and butter pudding and a Roundhouse favourite, shank of lamb with a mint and spiced chutney, glazed with a minted mash. The wide wine list means you'll easily find the ideal match for this fabulous food. Stunning views and food, a chef that's happy to show you around his kitchen and guest bedrooms are a combination that's hard to beat.

Rooms: 1. Double from £50.
Prices: Set lunch £15, set dinner £25. Restaurant main course from £14. Bar main course from £4. House wine £12.50.
Last orders: Lunch: 15.00; dinner: 22.30.
Closed: Not open for lunch out of season.
Food: Modern British.
Other points: No-smoking area. Dogs welcome. Children welcome. Car park.
Directions: M3. In Weymouth head towards the seafront and turn right. The Roundhouse is the last building before the pavilion. (Map 5, E1)

Down-to-earth, friendly service

Dorset cheeses
at The Crown & Coach House

You can sample local Dorset cheeses at The Crown & Coach House, as well as the more fancy French and Italian varieties. Liz Neilsen partners the two local star attractions Dorset Blue Vinney and Ashmore Cheddar plus they are available as Ploughman's throughout the day. She also serves her fillet steaks with Somerset Brie or the Ashmore Cheddar. Her main supplier is Roy Jenkins' The Circle of Cheese Company, which celebrates its 10th anniversary this year. Roy took over the ailing company with his wife Sara and they have grown the local cheese side of the business by 20 per cent. As a wholesaler, they supply cheese to the shops, restaurants and pubs in the Dorset area. Roy is a big fan of the Cheddar, which is a full-bodied, mature cheese, more for the table than for cooking with and also highly recommends the creamy, Blue Vinney, which he says is very popular in the area. As well as Dorset cheeses, look out for neighbouring county Somerset's Brie and Camembert, which give the French a run for their money.

The Circle of Cheese: Bedchester; 01747 811606

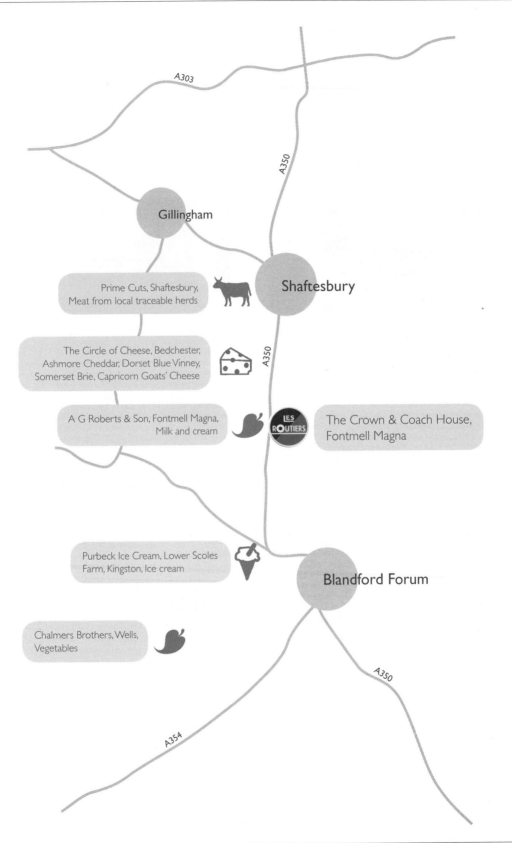

Chelmsford

Russells Restaurant

Bell Street, Great Baddow, Chelmsford, Essex CM2 7JR
Telephone: +44(0)870 4016292
+44(0)1245 478484
russellsrestaurant@hotmail.com
www.russellsrest.co.uk

It may look tiny from outside but Russells is Tardus-like and it can comfortably seat 70. The restaurant is in a Grade II listed tithed barn built in 1372, and it's one of the most magnificent buildings in Chelmsford. High ceilings give a sense of spaciousness and grandeur. Four dining rooms, one with a balcony overlooking the main room and bar, are smartly appointed. The old wooden beams add character, while chic lighting, crisp white tablecloths, and attractive place settings give a contemporary feel. The emphasis is on homecooking, right down to the freshly baked breads and creamy ice creams. Enthusiastic owner/chef Barry Watson is in charge of the English-French menu that centres around fresh, quality ingredients. The fixed price menus at lunch, dinner and Sunday lunch offer outstanding value. At lunch, start with a soup or marinated beef salad, before moving on to Mediterranean sole fillet or confit of duck leg. At dinner, salmon gravadlax kicks things off, and the mains line-up includes beef bourgignon and pan-fried grey mullet. There is a more extensive choice on the carte menu. Wine lovers will enjoy choosing from a 70-bin selection. And before dining, enjoy a drink and nibbles in Maximilian's bar or Joseph's Lounge. And for those looking for a gourmet treat, there is plenty to tempt in the next door deli, also under the same ownership.

Prices: Set lunch £12.95, set dinner £15.95. Restaurant main course from £12.95. House wine £10.95.
Last orders: Food: lunch 13.45 (Sunday 14.30); dinner 21.00 (Friday 21.30, Saturday 22.00).
Closed: Sunday evening and all day Monday. 2nd January for ten days.
Food: Modern French and English.
Other points: No-smoking area. Children welcome. Car park. Private functions.
Directions: A12 junction with A130. Follow the signs to Great Baddow and pass St Marys Church, take first right and second right at the Chase. (Map 6, B6)

Coggeshall

Water Lily Patisserie & Restaurant

3A Church Street, Coggeshall, Colchester,
Essex CO6 1TU
Telephone: +44(0)870 4016338
+44(0)1376 564464
paulfarmer5@aol.com
www.thewaterlily.co.uk

Paul Farmer's restaurant is charming, and blends in beautifully with the rest of this small historic village, which is primarily made up of 16th and 17th century buildings. The dark wood, beams and panelling create a cosy atmosphere. Front of house benefits enormously from the presence of Joanne Farmer. Friendly and smiling, she is just the sort of person to encourage a loyal following of local regulars. The cooking here is excellent and it comes as no surprise to learn that Paul was formerly head of banqueting at London's Grosvenor House, and has worked at the Ivy with Mark Hix. All this makes for a cooking style that takes its influences mainly from France and Italy, backed up by a lot of confidence and expertise. Much of the repertoire has a cosmopolitan feel to it, be it an intense wild mushroom cappuccino, or halibut provençal lightly seared on the griddle and served with savoy cabbage, fried vegetables and provençal sauce. Desserts are a highlight and they show a real skill for pastry work. Passion and white chocolate delice, triple chocolate brownies and tarte aux fraises are some of the delights. Set menus are good value, and a compact, well-chosen, helpfully priced wine list offers by the glass or bottle.

Prices: Set lunch from £10.95 and dinner £14.50. Restaurant main course from £11.95. Bar main course from £4.50. House wine £14.
Last orders: Bar: lunch 15.00 (Sunday 14.00); dinner 22.00. Food: lunch 14.00; dinner 22.00. Patisserie open until 15.00 daily.
Closed: Monday, Tuesday afternoon and all of January.
Food: French fusion and homemade patisserie.
Other points: No-smoking area. Garden. Children welcome.
Directions: From the M25 take the A12 exit for Kelvedon. Follow the signs to Coggeshall, approximately five miles from the Kelvedon turn off. (Map 6, B6)

Little Canfield

Lion and Lamb

Stortford Road, Little Canfield, Dunmow, Essex CM6 1SR
Telephone: +44(0)870 4016072
+44(0)1279 870257
info@lionandlamb.co.uk
www.lionandlamb.co.uk

This popular hostelry has all the charming elements you'd hope of quaint country pub. It's 200 years old in parts and the traditional furnishings have been chosen to set it off beautifully. Both the character bar and modern dining room extensions feature open brickwork, log fires, exposed pine, oak beams and a wealth of decorative memorabilia. Outside there's a large garden, with a children's play house that make it popular with families at weekends. A comprehensive bar menu offers lighter snacks such as paninis and sandwiches, beef salads, and also more substantial meals of Dunmow sausages with mash and onion beer gravy and fried fillet of beer battered cod and chips. The restaurant menu is again varied and a cut above. Start with grilled Portuguese sardines with lemon butter or fresh tortellini with peas, spinach and Parmesan flakes, then move on to mains of fillet of monkfish on Mediterranean vegetables with sun-dried tomato dressing or braised lamb shanks with a ragoût of white beans, parsley and streaky bacon. Much of the fish comes fresh from Billingsgate. On Sundays, they offer set courses and the roasted rib of Scottish beef served rare with all the trimmings is a real treat. The small family-owned Ridleys Brewery in Essex provide beers that are well worth sampling and there are six wines by the glass.

Rooms: 3. Double room from £65, single occupancy £60.
Prices: Sunday set lunch £16. Restaurant main course from £8.50.
Bar main course from £5. House wine £10.75.
Last orders: Bar: 23.00. Food: 22.00.
Closed: Never.
Food: Traditional/Modern British with an Australian influence.
Other points: No-smoking area. Children welcome. Garden.
Car park.
Directions: Exit 8/M11, and take the B1256 east to Takeley and Dunmow. Pub is on the left just after entering Little Canfield.
(Map 6, B6)

Cirencester

The Organic Farm Shop Café

Abbey Home Farm, Burford Road, Cirencester,
Gloucestershire GL7 5HF
Telephone: +44(0)870 4016307
+44(0)1285 640441
info@theorganicfarmshop.co.uk
www.theorganicfarmshop.co.uk

Hilary Chester-Master's expanding business is one of no more than a dozen Soil Association Certified organic cafés in the country. It is located on her organic farm north of Cirencester. The highly labour-intensive 15-acre vegetable growing area which surrounds the shop produces over 230 varieties of vegetable, herbs, soft fruits and cut flowers for the shop and café. The recently enlarged café, set adjacent to her well stocked organic shop and education centre the Green Room (where seminars and cooking demonstrations are held), offers a vegetarian menu inspired by the seasonal produce from the farm. Here, one can expect delicious fresh salads such as broad bean, feta and mint, homemade soups, quiches and pasties, alongside a good range of cakes and generously filled rolls and sandwiches; there's also a take-away menu. Hilary opened her Organic Farm Shop at Abbey Home Farm in June 1999. Her objective was to establish a market garden and to offer fresh local organic produce, including eggs, beef, lamb and pork from Abbey Home Farm, direct to the local community.

Prices: Main course £6.75.
Last orders: 16.00. Saturday until 15.30.
Closed: Rarely.
Food: Vegetarian and vegan/special diets.
Other points: No-smoking area. Children welcome. Terrace.
Car park.
Directions: Two miles north of Cirencester just off the A417.
(Map 4, A7)

Good food and wine

Cirencester

Wild Duck Inn

Ewen, Cirencester, Gloucestershire GL7 6BY
Telephone: +44(0)870 4016074
+44(0)1285 770310
wduckinn@aol.com
www.thewildduckinn.co.uk

First impressions of this quaint Elizabethan inn are excellent. The building, set in a sleepy rural backwater with well-tended gardens and a lovely lavender-lined entrance path, is instantly appealing. Inside, the cosy bar with rich burgundy walls decorated with old portraits creates just the right atmosphere for relaxation, especially if you bag one of the roomy armchairs. The restaurant's labyrinth of small rooms offers snug, informal dining. A printed menu is supplemented with daily-changing blackboard specials. At lunch you could choose a one-course meal of beer battered fish and chips, a Cheddar, brie, Stilton or ham ploughmans, or a classic fish pie. At dinner, there's more of an international slant with tuna carpaccio on tomato and red onion salad with a lemon and black pepper dressing, and popular favourites such as chargrilled sirloin steak, roast flat mushrooms, watercress salad and chips. The globetrotting wine list offers an impressive 30 by the glass, and the bar has five real ales. To make the most of your visit, stay in one of the individually decorated en suite bedrooms offering traditional comforts. But if it's a flying visit you're after, you can arrive by helicopter, as long as you give a week's notice and pay the landing fee.

Rooms: 11. Double room from £80, single from £60.
Prices: Main course from £6.95. House wine £9.95.
Last orders: Bar: 23.00. Food: lunch 14.00 (Sunday 14.30; dinner 22.00 (Sunday 21.30).
Closed: Rarely.
Food: Modern British.
Other points: Children welcome. Dogs welcome overnight. Garden. Car park.
Directions: Junction 15 or 17/M4. From Cirencester, take the A429 towards Malmesbury. On reaching Kemble turn left to Ewen. (Map 4, B7)

Clearwell

The Wyndham Arms

Clearwell, The Royal Forest of Dean,
Gloucestershire GL16 8JT
Telephone: +44(0)870 4016075
+44(0)1594 833666
nigel@thewyndhamhotel.co.uk
www.thewyndhamhotel.co.uk

Set in the wonderful 27,000-acre Forest of Dean, this hotel was at the head of the queue when it came to traditional features. In the main building it has got the lot: oak beams, flagstones and exposed original red brick. Right next door is ancient Clearwell Castle, which is now a wedding and function venue, so bedrooms are in high demand during the peak wedding season. Bedrooms are in an adjacent building and have been decorated along contemporary lines. They are spacious and well equipped with modern, en suite bathrooms. Owners Nigel and Pauline Stanley, and chef Ewan Jones make the most of local ingredients on their menu. These can include seasonal game from Lydney Park Estate, single herd meats, Gloucester Old Spot pork products, Brooks local ice cream, and real ales from Freewinners in the forest and Orchard Ciders from Brockweir in the Wye Valley. They are also active in the community cooperative for supplies of vegetables, salads and herbs, and local farmhouse cheeses. On the bar menu, there are some hearty dishes, including calf's liver, beef and ale pie, venison stew and wild mushroom and leek crêpes and with some fabulous puddings of lemon tart with a warm fruit coulis, or bread and butter pudding to finish.

Rooms: 18. Double room from £85, single from £45.
Prices: Restaurant main course from £8.95. House wine £10.95.
Last orders: Bar: 23.00. Food: lunch 14.00 (Sunday 14.30); dinner: 21.30 (Sunday 21.00).
Closed: First week in January.
Food: Modern British.
Other points: No-smoking area. Children welcome. Dogs welcome overnight. Garden. Car park. Licence for Civil Weddings.
Directions: Exit 2/M48. Via A48 and B4228 signed Forest of Dean, 12 miles from Chepstow. From the A48 at Monmouth via the A4176 and B4228, two miles from Coleford. (Map 4, A6)

Fairford

Allium ★

1 London Street, Market Place, Fairford,
Gloucestershire GL7 4AH
Telephone: +44(0)870 4016308
+44(0)1285 712200
restaurant@allium.uk.net
www.allium.uk.net

This stylish and elegant restaurant in the pretty Cotswold village of Fairford is a real treat. The new owners, formerly of Les Routiers award-winning restaurant, the Vineyard at Wickham, have created a contemporary establishment that has a light and airy feel; the white walls and modern art combining well with the linen-clad tables and interesting sculptures. An uncluttered yet sophisticated dining experience with attention to detail is of the utmost importance to James and Erica Graham and Nick Bartimote. Before going through to the dining area there is the option of relaxing for a pre-supper drink. Comfortable sofas are an inviting proposition before the culinary delights that await, especially with a fire roaring away in the winter months. The immaculate dining area lives up to their motto of 'relaxed fine dining' and it becomes obvious from the menu that the true focus is on the food. Everything is locally sourced where possible, apart from the fantastic array of cheeses, which are a British and continental selection. A twice-daily changing menu of mouthwatering dishes could feature a terrine of gammon hock and foie gras or ravioli of spider crab with sauce Jacqueline and chive oil to start followed by fillet of John Dory with saffron-poached fennel and sauce vierge or roasted venison with cauliflower purée. Puddings such as lemon and polenta cake with orange crème fraîche or warm chocolate fondant with white chocolate ice cream are highly recommended, especially as a specific wine is chosen to go with each. A good value gourmand menu is also available, all backed up by an extensive and well-chosen wine list.

Prices: Set lunch £17.50 and dinner £29.50 Gourmand meal £42.
Last orders: Food: 22.00.
Closed: 2 Weeks at the beginning January.
Food: Modern British/French.
Other points: No smoking in the restaurant. Children welcome.
Directions: M4/J15 and M5/J13. Between Cirencester and Lechlade on A417. On market place in Fairford. (Map 5, B3)

Frampton Mansell

White Horse

Cirencester Road, Frampton Mansell,
Gloucestershire GL6 8HZ
Telephone: +44(0)870 4016076
+44(0)1285 760960
www.cotswoldwhitehorse.com

It may look like any other unassuming country pub, but step inside the White Horse and it's a quite a different story. It has been stylishly updated by Shaun and Emma Davies who have transformed the fortunes of this once-ordinary pub. The interiors are now contemporary with olive-coloured walls and seagrass-style carpeting, all offset by unusual modern art, even in the loos, fashionable modern tables and colourful cushioned chairs. There's also a comfortable sofa area that seats six for pre-dinner drinks. Modern menus are built around fresh produce and quality local ingredients are superbly cooked. Meat comes from Chesterton Farm butchers near Cirencester, which specialises in rare and traceable breeds, and fish is delivered twice-weekly from Looe in Cornwall. Top-quality vegetables are used creatively, for example, carrot purée carries a hint of cumin; in addition, chips are handcut and bread is baked daily on the premises. Typical dishes include duck leg confit with chorizo sausage and balsamic, and black bream with braised fennel and a caper and chive cream. White and dark chocolate mousse is one of the popular pudding choices. Sourcing everything locally extends to real ale, so expect interesting brews from Hook Norton, Uley and Arkells breweries. The global selection of wines focuses on smaller growers with six by the glass or 50cl pot.

Prices: Restaurant main course from £8.95.
Bar main course from £4.95. House wine £11.75.
Last orders: Bar: lunch 15.00; dinner 23.00. Food: lunch 14.30; dinner 21.45 (Sunday 15.00).
Closed: Sunday evening.
Food: Modern British.
Other points: Children welcome. Garden. Car park.
Directions: J15/M4. J13/M5. Between Cirencester and Stroud on the A419. On the main road, not in the village of Frampton Mansell itself. (Map 4, A7)

Affordable good value

Farm house cider
at The Wyndham Arms

A formerly overgrown and disused farm in the picturesque Wye Valley is now producing top quality cider and perry. The 200-year-old farm was bought by the fortuitously named Keith Orchard, who discovered a host of cider apple and perry pear trees in his overgrown land. He now produces many varieties, winners of recent, prestigious awards and sells it throughout the West Country to various shops and top restaurants and pubs, namely Les Routiers member, the Wyndham Arms. Situated in the Forest of Dean, this historic 600-year-old hotel in the heart of cider and perry country is heavily involved in promoting local foodstuffs - you will find Orchards produce behind the bar and, perhaps, cropping up in dishes such as scrump pork – braised pork fillet cooked in cider and apples. Meanwhile, if you fancy sampling this wonderful stuff one must cover the basics – the simple Farm House Cider, the adventurous 'Dabinett' Cider which at a mind-blowing 8.3% ABV is the strongest and driest, and the unique 'Cannock' Perry, named after men that travelled from the Forest of Dean to work in the first Staffordshire foundries.

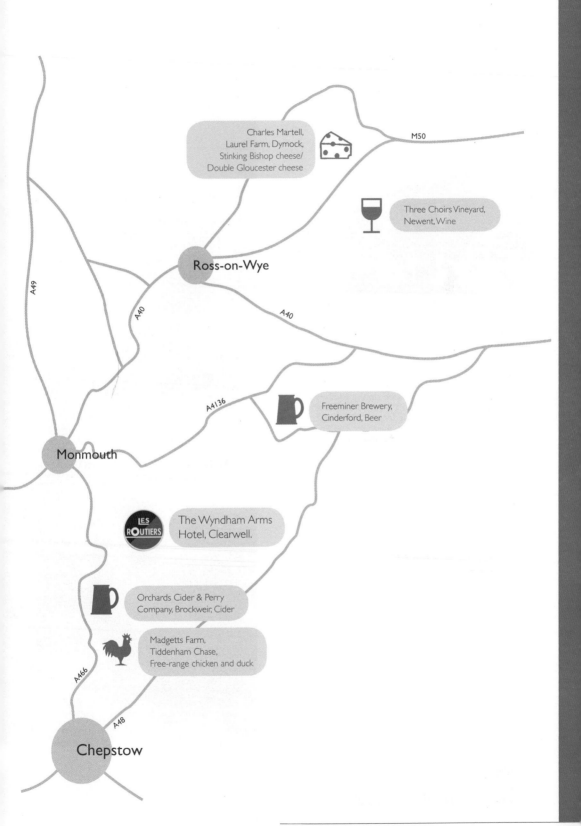

Charles Martell,
Laurel Farm, Dymock,
Stinking Bishop cheese/
Double Gloucester cheese

M50

Three Choirs Vineyard,
Newent, Wine

Ross-on-Wye

A49

A40

A40

A4136

Freeminer Brewery,
Cinderford, Beer

Monmouth

LES
ROUTIERS

The Wyndham Arms
Hotel, Clearwell.

Orchards Cider & Perry
Company, Brockweir, Cider

Madgetts Farm,
Tiddenham Chase,
Free-range chicken and duck

A466

A48

Chepstow

Northleach

The Wheatsheaf Inn

West End, Northleach, Gloucestershire GL54 3EZ
Telephone: +44(0)870 4016078
+44 (0)1451 860244
caspar@wheatsheafatnorthleach.com
www.wheatsheafatnorthleach.com

The setting of this stone-built former coaching inn is all you could wish for a rural spotover and good hearty meal. It's on the main street of an historic and pretty Cotswold wool town and is simply but tastefully furnished and looks something of a classic. The bars have flagstone floors, beams, log fires and lots of old wood. They offer well-maintained, cask-conditioned ales from small local breweries and a blackboard menu, whilst the classy, understated dining room is marginally more formal. Modern British favourites are inspired by what is available locally, warm pigeon salad with summer berries, and Gloucester Old Spot pork chop with apple mash, for example, or cod in beer batter and chips. Lemon posset or Eton mess are classic desserts, with local cheeses making a savoury alternative. Small blackboards include special wines of the moment, and the well-annotated list offers some impeccable choices on a globally inspired choices; 20 are offered by the glass. Eight en suite bedrooms are available, and though they currently lack the effortless rustic chic of the downstairs, size, character and comfortable furnishings are ample compensation.

Rooms: 8. Double/twin room from £60, single from £50, family room from £70.
Prices: Main course from £7. Bar/snack from £4. House wine £10.75.
Last orders: Bar 23.00. Food: lunch 15.00; dinner 22.00 (Sunday 21.00).
Closed: Never.
Food: Modern British.
Other points: No-smoking area. Children welcome. Dogs welcome in bar. Garden. Car park. Licence for Civil Weddings.
Directions: Village just off A429 between Stow-on-the-Wold and Cirencester. Exit 15/M4. (Map 4, A8)

Painswick

The Falcon Inn

New Street, Painswick, Gloucestershire GL6 6UN
Telephone: +44(0)870 4016080
+44(0)1452 814222
bleninns@clara.net
www.falconinn.com

The Falcon is the most attractive and popular watering hole for the many walkers and tourists that take to The Cotswold Way, which passes just outside. There's even a dedicated drying room for ramblers. Standing opposite the parish church, this stone-built inn's colourful history also takes in staging cockfights, the site of the first Masonic ceremony in Gloucestershire in 1794, and a period as the village courthouse. Interconnecting bar and dining areas are full of traditional character, the scene set by stone, tiled or carpeted floors, wood panelling, open log fires, and a mix of wooden benches and more formal furnishings. Jonny Johnston's careful sourcing of local produce, notably game from nearby shoots, locally grown vegetables, and butchers' meats, including belted Galloway beef from English Nature, is evident on the changing menus and the list of daily specials. Expect the likes of organic pork loin with cider, honey and apple sauce, braised venison with root vegetables, or best end of lamb with port and redcurrant sauce, and fish dishes such as organic Cockleford trout with red pesto. Twelve en suite bedrooms are split between the main building and the converted coach house. All are individually decorated with four-poster rooms in the inn and up-to-date colours, fabrics and furnishings in the coach house accommodation.

Rooms: 12. Double room from £68, single from £45.
Prices: Set lunch £12 and dinner £16. Restaurant main course £7.50. Bar snack from £4. House wine £8.95.
Last orders: Bar: 23.00. Food: lunch 14.30 (Sunday 15.00); dinner 21.30 (Saturday 22.00).
Closed: Never.
Food: Modern and Traditional British and European.
Other points: No-smoking area. Children welcome.
Dogs welcome overnight. Garden. Car park.
Directions: Junction 11a/M5. Painswick is on the A46 between Cheltenham and Stroud. (Map 4, A7)

Tewkesbury

Corse Lawn House Hotel

Corse Lawn, Tewkesbury, Gloucestershire GL19 4LZ
Telephone: +44(0)870 4016363
+44(0)1452 780771
enquiries@corselawn.com
www.corselawn.com

The attractive Queen Anne Grade II listed building, set in 12 acres of lush gardens and overlooking a glorious ornamental pond, has been further enchanced following refurbishment and extensions by the Hines. The family famous for its Cognac connections took ownership in 1978 and has upgraded all round, from the furnishings to the food. The ambience exudes the laid-back charm of a French auberge rather than down-to-earth English rustic hostelery. Expect quiet country good taste as seen in soft tones and country prints that is nowhere better exemplified than by the under-stated, carpeted bar and bistro that rubs along under the genial stewardship of 'Papa', Denis Hine. For use of residents and casual visitors alike, daily papers are available in the conservatory that leads to a sofa-lined lounge bar and the informally laid bistro. Baba Hine's kitchen matches the setting with admirable aplomb, skimping neither on quality nor finesse, whether you are lunching on a simple sandwich or a seriously good sirlion steak. Baba's enticing carte menus lean towards the sophisticated with baked queen scallops with provençal stuffing to start, followed by breast of duckling with pak choi, lemon grass and coriander or chargrilled salmon with crushed peas and chive beurre blanc. The choice of wines is also exquisite, but then you would expect no less of Cognac's noblest houses.

Rooms: 19. Single room from £85, double from £130.
Prices: Set lunch £19.50 and dinner £29.50.
Restaurant main course from £15. House wine £12.
Last orders: Bar: 23.00. Food: lunch 14.00; dinner 21.30.
Closed: Rarely.
Food: Anglo-French.
Other points: No-smoking area. Garden. Children welcome.
Dogs welcome. Car park. Licence for Civil Weddings.
Directions: Exit 1/2/M50. Five miles south-west of Tewkesbury on the B4211. (Map 4, A7)

An alternative Britain

Crondall

The Hampshire Arms

Pankridge Street, Crondall, Farnham,
Hampshire GU10 5QU
Telephone: +44(0)870 4016083
+44(0)1252 850418
paulychef@hantsarms.freeserve.co.uk
www.thehampshirearms.co.uk

Serious investment by chef-proprietor Paul Morgan
in early 2004 has seen big changes at his unpretentious pub secluded away in a Hampshire village. Paul's
energy and enthusiasm has been deflected away from
the kitchen into the fabric of the pub to complement
the style and quality of his food. So, the homely bar
has been smartened up, sofas now front the log fire in
the cosy lounge, the once tired-looking restaurant has
been remodelled and refurbished in modern style, toi-
lets are now rather swish, and a new extension houses
Paul's grill restaurant. His passion for fresh food and
quality ingredients extends to making everything on
the premises, including breads, ice creams and chocolate petits fours. Seasonally changing menus offer an
intelligent and well-balanced range of modern dishes.
This might translate as fennel and orange soup or
pan-fried scallops with celeriac purée and a fish and
chive butter sauce to start. Herb-crusted lamb on black
olive mash with a ratatouille of vegetables and lamb's
kidneys could follow, or monkfish wrapped in Parma
ham with pea risotto and a lobster and shallot sauce.
Alternatively, order a first-class steak from the grill
menu. Round off with baked rice pudding with rhubarb compote. Filled baguettes and lighter dishes are
also available at lunchtime.

Prices: Main course from £14.50. House wine £9.95.
Last orders: Bar: lunch 15.00; dinner 23.00. Food: lunch 14.00;
dinner 21.30. No food Sunday evening.
Closed: One week over Christmas.
Food: Modern British.
Other points: No-smoking in the restaurant. Garden.
Children welcome. Dogs welcome in bar area.
Directions: Exit 5/M3. Take the A287 for Farnham, turn off
at Crondall. (Map 5, C4)

Southampton

The White Star Tavern & Dining Rooms ★

28 Oxford Street, Southampton, Hampshire SO14 3DJ
Telephone: +44(0)870 4016087
+44(0)2380 821990
manager@whitestartavern.co.uk
www.whitestartavern.co.uk

Southampton's first gastropub, in up-and-coming
Oxford Street close to Ocean Village and West Quay,
has proved a great success, drawing both a lively
drinking crowd and discerning diners. Mark Dodd and
Matthew Boyle's dream of creating a stylish bar and
restaurant in what was a former seafarer's hotel in the
days of the Titanic, is well on track. Smart front bar
lounge areas have modern brown leather banqettes
and cream walls adorned with shipping photographs
and retro mirrors, yet retain the original flagstone
floors and the period open fireplaces. Beyond the large
wooden bar, lies the spacious, wood-floored and panelled dining rooms. Good use of fresh produce from
Hampshire suppliers can be seen in 'light bites' like
sautéed wild mushrooms in a cream sauce on toasted
brioche, salmon confit with gribiche or a classic BLT
baguette, and in the lunchtime carte with pan-fried
sea bream, shallot and sun-dried tomato mash and
roast pepper salad. In the evening, seared scallops with
spinach and blue cheese cream, and beef sirloin with
fondant potato and foie gras jus exemplify the style.
Breads and puddings such as the strawberry cheesecake
with balsamic and vanilla ice cream are all homemade.
There's an impressive list of cocktails, champagnes and
vodkas and eight wines by the glass.

Prices: Restaurant main course evening meal from £11.50,
lunch from £4. House wine £11.50.
Last orders: Bar: lunch 15.00; dinner 23.00 (Friday to Sunday open
all day, April to October open all day). Food: lunch 15.00; dinner
21.30 (Friday and Saturday 22.00, Sunday 21.00).
Closed: Rarely.
Food: Modern British.
Other points: No-smoking area. Children welcome week-ends
during the day. Outside seating.
Directions: Exit14/M3. Take the A33 to Southampton and head
towards the Ocean Village and Marina. (Map 5, D3)

Leominster

Lower Bache House

Kimbolton, near Leominster, Herefordshire HR6 0ER
Telephone: +44(0)870 4016394
+44 (0)1568 750304
leslie.wiles@care4free.net
www.smoothhound.co.uk/hotels/lowerbache.html

Rose and Leslie Wiles' homely 17th century farmhouse in a tiny hamlet, down a narrow country lane, more than fulfils the brief for a B&B. It is set in 14 acres of gardens and nature reserve and used to be a cider mill. This has been incorporated into the lovely, old-style dining-sitting room, with its high-vaulted ceiling, stone walls and flagstone floor. The two main house bedrooms are the top choices – large suites, with oak beams, separate sitting room and fresh milk with the hot drinks tray. There is also a cottage suite, which is a charming three-room complex. Local farm produce appears on a breakfast menu that spoils with its choice not just of bacon and eggs combinations, but the likes of kedgeree as well. Dinner is by arrangement with a small but good selection of wines. Raw ingredients are, as much as possible, organic and local, and often from their own kitchen garden. Start, perhaps, with home-smoked salmon with caviar, go on to lamb chops with courgette and garlic, sautéed potatoes and vegetables, and finish with classic tarte au pomme. Both Rose and Leslie are delightful, and work hard to make a stay at Lower Bache a memorable experience.

Rooms: **3.** Double room from £34.50 per person, single £44.50.
Prices: Set meal £21.50 (£17.50 2-courses, £25.50 4 courses).
Closed: **Rarely.**
Food: **Modern British.**
Other points: Totally no smoking. Garden. Children welcome over 8 years old. Nature Reserve. Car park.
Directions: Kimbolton village is two miles north of Leominster (which is off the A49). Lower Bache is signposted at the top of the hill on the Leysters road (A4112). Look out for the white butterfly sign. (Map 8, D5)

Individual charm and warmth

Walterstone

Allt-yr-Ynys Hotel

Walterstone, near Abergavenny, Herefordshire HR2 0DU
Telephone: +44(0)870 4016455
+44(0)1873 890307
allthotel@compuserve.com
www.allthotel.co.uk

Accommodation and food at Allt-yr-Ynys is top-class. The beautifully preserved 16th century manor house has en suite bedrooms, a fine restaurant, facilities such as indoor heated and spa pools and beautiful gardens. The house was once owned by William Cecil, chief minister to Elizabeth I, and many of its original features have been preserved. In the comfortable sitting room there is a fine moulded ceiling and oak panelling. The Jacobean suite still retains its original oak panelling and 16th century four-poster bed. The bedrooms are split between the main house and converted old stables and outbuildings; most have views over the mountains and woodlands. Strikingly decorated, they have canopied beds, tasteful fabrics and furnishings, and offer every modern convenience. The kitchen is loyal to regional and local produce, offering Welsh lamb, beef and cheeses in starters such as pan-fried whole Greenland Bay prawns with a lime butter and herb sauce. Mains could take in roasted rack of local lamb with a herb crust on a tomato and rosemary fondue with onion confit, or baked aubergine with courgette and pepper ratatouille topped with Welsh Cheddar. Equally appealing are puddings such as bread and butter pudding and vanilla crème brulée.

Rooms: 21. Double room from £85, single from £65.
Prices: Set lunch £16.95 and dinner £25. Main course from £11. House wine £14.75.
Last orders: Food: lunch 15.00; dinner 21.30.
Closed: Rarely.
Food: Modern British.
Other points: No-smoking area. Children welcome. Garden. Car park. Licence for Civil Weddings. Swimming pool, spa and sauna. Clay pigeon shooting.
Directions: A465 Abergavenny to Hereford road. Turn off five miles north of Abergavenny at Old Pandy Inn; 400 metres, turn right at Green Barn. (Map 8, E5)

Flaunden

The Bricklayers Arms

Hog Pits Bottom, Flaunden, Hertfordshire HP3 0PH
Telephone: +44(0)870 4016092
+44 (0)1442 833322
goodfood@bricklayersarms.com
www.bricklayersarms.com

Within minutes of leaving the M25 (J18), you are in rolling Hertfordshire countryside and encountering peaceful villages secluded away down winding lanes. Coated in Virginia creeper, Flaunden's low cottagey tiled pub dates from the 18th century and is a peaceful, inviting spot, especially in summer when its country-style garden becomes the perfect place to enjoy an al fresco pint of ale. On cooler days, the recently refurbished, timbered and low-ceilinged bar, replete with blazing log fires, old prints and comfortable traditional furnishings, are popular with both local diners and walkers for modern pub food. New owners Alvin and Sally Michaels have smartened up the place and introduced a good range of menus to suit all tastes. In the bar, follow a country stroll with thick-cut sandwiches, a steaming bowl of chilli, or tuck into a special of confit of duck with red wine jus. In the evening, come for starters of pan-fried foie gras and sherry jus, or fresh local asparagus with hollandaise, then follow with roast halibut with pink peppercorn sauce or best end of lamb served with red wine and shallot sauce. Finish with hot chocolate pudding. Also worth noting are the summer Sunday barbecues and live jazz in the garden.

Prices: Restaurant main course from £10.95. Bar snack from £5.95. House wine £10.95.
Last orders: Bar: 23.00.
Food: lunch 15.00 (Sunday 16.00); dinner 21.30 (Sunday 21.00).
Closed: Rarely.
Food: Modern British/French.
Other points: No-smoking area. Dogs welcome. Children welcome. Garden. Car park.
Directions: 10 minutes from Exit18/M25. Three miles south west of Hemel Hempstead. (Map 5, B4)

Regional produce

Biddenden

Claris's Tea Room

1/3 High Street, Biddenden, Kent TN27 8AL
Telephone: +44(0)870 4016397
+44(0)1580 291025
info@collectablegifts.net
www.collectablegifts.net.

The lovely 15th century, half-timbered brick building that's home to Claris's Tea Room is wonderfully chocolate boxy. It's got a traditional thatched roof and picture book looks outside, while inside it's just as charming with a small room with low beams, pretty white lace tablecloths, with everything served on white crockery. The unchanging menu is simple but scrumptious. Sandwiches of Scotch smoked salmon, cheese or ham on brown or white bread, homemade tomato soup served with thick slices of hot-buttered toast, creamed mushrooms, poached egg, or baked beans on toast are some of the snacks available. Then there are the lovely homebaked cakes, including cream-laden meringues, chocolate cake, fruit cake, lemon Madeira and Victoria sponge. Another popular choice are Claris's treat of a cream tea that consists of two homemade scones with a choice of Tiptree jams and fresh cream, and a pot of Indian or China tea. Tea is quite a speciality here, and there are world famous blends to choose from as well as herbal and fruit varieties.

Prices: Cream tea from £4.00.
Last orders: Food: 17.20.
Closed: Around three weeks in January.
Food: Traditional tea shop.
Other points: Totally no smoking. Children welcome. Garden. Car park. Credit cards not accepted.
Directions: Exit 8/M20, and take the B2163 to Sutton Valence, then the A274 to Biddenden. Or, exit 9/M20, then A28 towards Tenterden, then A262 to Biddenden. (Map 6, D6)

Dover

Wallett's Court Country House Hotel and Spa

Westcliffe, St Margaret's-at-Cliffe, Dover, Kent CT15 6EW
Telephone: +44(0)870 4016313
+44(0)1304 852424
stay@wallettscourt.com
www.wallettscourt.com

The Oakley family purchased what was a rundown Jacobean farmhouse over a quarter of a century ago, and have developed it over the years to its full potential. They have a good restaurant and more recently separate spa facilities in the grounds. The house retains many period features. The sitting room is filled with odd sofas, armchairs, coffee tables and candles, and service is relaxed, but professional and lacks pretention. Main house bedrooms range from small but comfortable standard rooms to vaulted beamed ceilings and antique four-poster beds. Other cosy rooms are in conversions in the grounds. Additional farm outbuildings now house a state-of-the-art gym, indoor swimming pool, sauna, mineral steam room, and hydrotherapy spa, plus there's an all-weather tennis court. Stephen Harvey delivers food with a broadly English character, derived mainly from carefully sourced ingredients, many of which are local and in seasonal. Brochettes of Rye Bay scallops and medallions of monkfish with a truffled balsamic reduction, and St Margaret's Bay lobster, Dover sole and Kentish asparagus and broad beans could make up a typical summer meal. Generous portions may put a stop on pudding for some, but a light finish is to be had with a timbale of summer fruits set in champagne jelly with fruit liqueur or iced lime parfait.

Rooms: 16. Double room from £90, single from £75.
Prices: Set lunch £17.50, set dinner £35. House wine £14.95.
Last orders: Food: lunch 14.00; dinner 21.00.
Closed: Monday and Saturday lunch.
Food: Modern British.
Other points: No-smoking area. Children welcome. Garden. Car park.
Directions: From Dover, follow the signs for A258 Deal. Once on the road, take the first right to St Margaret's at Cliffe; hotel is one mile on the right. (Map 6, C7)

Maidstone

Stone Court Hotel and Chambers Restaurant

28 Lower Stone Street, Maidstone, Kent ME15 6LX
Telephone: +44(0)870 4016406
+44(0)1622 769769
www.stonecourthotel.com

This house built in 1716 was once a residence for Crown Court judges and it will appeal to those looking for upmarket rooms and fine dining. It was saved from dereliction by restaurateur and hotelier, Musa Kivrak, and he has maintained a few legal touches. Not only are the bedrooms named after judges, but judges' gavels are used as key holders. Dedicated and enthusiastic, Musa has completed the makeover with good taste and it will appeal to a discerning clientele. The bar with original panelling and large inglenook is smart and intimate. There are 16 bedrooms that range in shape and size, the best being spacious with four-poster beds, solid wood furniture, muted colours and luxurious modern marble-tiled bathrooms. Appropriately, dinner is served in the Chambers Restaurant, an elegant, tastefully decorated room in pale yellow and rich deep blue with well-spaced tables and white cloths. The food is soundly prepared and classic in style with some more adventurous themes. The dinner carte menu offers starters of terrine of foie gras and duck confit with a truffle dressing or oriental seared tuna loin with Thai asparagus tempura, while mains may be medallions of venison with wild mushrooms or roast turbot fillet on herb mash. There is also a well-priced fixed menu with a more limited choice.

Rooms: 16. Double/twin room from £105. Single from £80.
Four-poster room from £175, room with jacuzzi £110.
Family room £145.
Prices: Set dinner £24.95. Restaurant main course from £19.50.
Bar main course from £4.50. House wine £15.50.
Last orders: Food: lunch 14.30; dinner 21.30.
Closed: Rarely.
Food: Modern British and French.
Other points: No-smoking area. Children welcome. Car park.
Licenced for Civil Weddings.
Directions: Exit 6/M20. Take the A229 Hastings Road to Palace Avenue. The entrance to the car park is on the right hand side of the road after the police station. (Map 6, C6)

Whitstable

Wheelers Oyster Bar

8 High Street, Whitstable, Kent CT5 1BQ
Telephone: +44(0)870 4016290
+44(0)1227 273311
www.whitstable-shellfish.co.uk

The striking pink and blue Victorian façade is a cheery and welcoming sight on the increasingly gentrified High Street. Originally a simple oyster bar, Wheelers has long branched out to become a mini seafood paradise, serving everything from cockles to crab and lobster, with plenty inbetween. It's best to book in advance as the old-fashioned dining room has few tables, but it's compact rather than cramped. The restaurant has been in the same family since it opened in 1856, and there's no connection with the London Wheelers. Chef Mark Stubbs arrived in 1997 and it became quickly apparent that here was a chef who had a talent for cooking seafood. What strikes most is the freshness and intensity of flavour. Dishes work because they have been carefully considered and the ingredients used are top notch, so a salad of pan-fried langoustines and queen scallops with baby leeks and local asparagus was subtly sensational. Classic combinations get an inventive twist as in pan-fried John Dory with prawns, coriander, butter beans and chorizo. But the simple native oysters unadorned are equally thrilling. A cold menu (to eat in or take away) is offered in the diminutive Victorian front oyster bar (four stools): delicate tarts of crab, prawns and butter sauce, hot smoked salmon fillets, crab sandwiches, oysters, eels, prawns, mussels, and baby octopus. There's no license, but no charge for corkage either.

Prices: Main course from £10. Unlicenced.
Last orders: Food: 19.30.
Closed: Wednesday, and the last two weeks of January.
Food: Seafood.
Other points: Children welcome. Credit cards not accepted.
Directions: Exit 7/M2. Turn off the Thanet Way at the roundabout to Whitstable and follow road through town. Restaurant at the end of the high street. (Map 6, C7)

Down-to-earth, friendly service

Thames estuary cockles

at Wheelers Oyster Bar

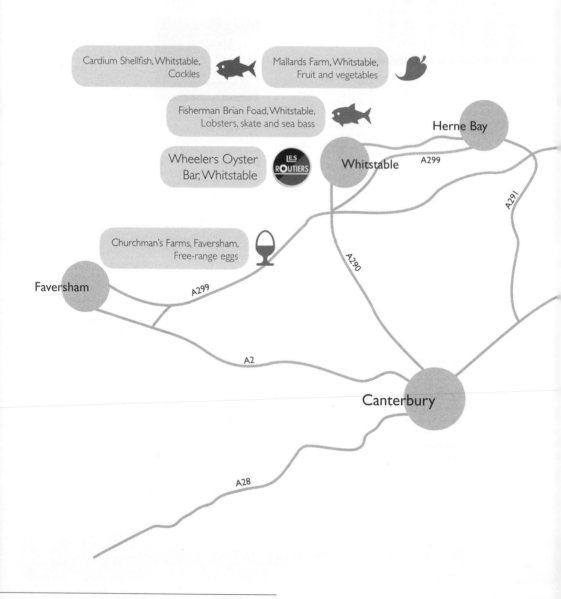

Cardium Shellfish, Whitstable,
Cockles

Mallards Farm, Whitstable,
Fruit and vegetables

Fisherman Brian Foad, Whitstable,
Lobsters, skate and sea bass

Wheelers Oyster
Bar, Whitstable

LES
ROUTIERS

Herne Bay

Whitstable

A299

A291

Churchman's Farms, Faversham,
Free-range eggs

A290

Faversham

A299

A2

Canterbury

A28

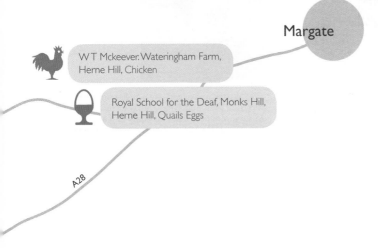

Mark Stubbs, head chef, at Wheelers can't get enough of Cardium Shellfish's cockles. 'They're the biggest, fattest, sweetest, high-quality cockle I've ever tasted.' Mark says that even if he bought them raw himself, he would never be able to cook them as well. Cardium, which has been in business for more than 30 years, has a large plant and has honed the skill of collecting and processing cockles. Its cockles come from beds along the Thames Estuary. The company is careful to rotate its dregging, so no beds are run down, and fine 18mm riddles don't pick up the baby cockles. The cockles we eat at Wheelers will have been three years old, and the best are picked from soft rather than hard ground. Mark says they're so good, you don't even need to serve them with malt vinegar as is the tradition. Just sip a crisp, fresh glass of Chablis instead. The cockle season runs from the second week in May to November. But while they taste wonderful, they don't have the same aphrodisiac qualities as oysters, says Cardium's John Gilson.

Cardium Shellfish: South Quay, Whitstable Harbour, Kent; 01227 264769

Blackpool

Raffles Hotel and Tea Rooms

73-77 Hornby Road, Blackpool, Lancashire FY1 4QJ
Telephone: +44(0)870 4016105
+44(0)1253 294713
enquiries@raffleshotelblackpool.fsworld.co.uk
www.raffleshotelblackpool.co.uk

If you're looking for home-from-home accommodation, then The Raffles is just the place. For a traditional seaside break, it offers very good value for money. The atmosphere is relaxed, and there's a comfortable lounge and bar for morning coffees or evening drinks. All bedrooms are compact, but not small, and meticulously decorated with some flair. There's a fabulous, oriental-themed room with Thai furniture, Chinese bedspread or rooms inspired by north Africa, Egypt and India. In addition, there are two bedrooms on the ground floor for guests who are not so nimble on their feet. Graham Poole and Ian Balmforth, the owners of this exceptional B&B-hotel, which is just minutes from Blackpool's Tower, have a real passion for their spick-and-span little gem. The standard of décor is high, housekeeping is exemplary and attention to detail spot on. On arrival you will be served freshly brewed tea or coffee in your room, despite the fact that do-it-yourself tea trays are standard issue in bedrooms, alongside the TV and quality towels. And, it is worth noting that the recently acquired premises next door have been converted into a tea room where meals as well as cakes and scones are served.

Rooms: 17. From £24 per person.
Prices: Main course from £4.95. Starters and sweets from £1.50.
Last orders: Food: 18.00.
Closed: Rarely.
Food: Traditional and Modern British.
Other points: No-smoking area. Children welcome. Car park.
Directions: Take the M55 towards Blackpool and follow the red signs for central car park. Leave the car park for the one-way system, Central Drive. Then turn left and Hornby Road will be the first immediate right. (Map 11, E4)

Bolton-le-Sands

Packet Bridge Village Fish and Chip Shop

30 Main Street, Bolton-le-Sands, Carnforth, Lancashire LA5 8DL
Telephone: +44(0)870 4016380
+44(0)1524 822791
john.wild@ukonline.co.uk
www.packetbridge.com

This takeaway is certainly worth going out of your way for. John and Hilary Wild have set their stall out to serve the best fish and chips and are proud to be counted in the top 100 of the Seafish Friers' Quality Award scheme. People travel miles for their traditional fare. Although you can't eat in, the Wilds are only too happy to point you in the direction of several local beauty spots where you can park up and enjoy stunning views over Morecambe Bay, while eating your lunch or supper. And they'll supply serviettes and wipes too. They serve good honest food cooked to perfection. Those with bigger appetites should order Moby Dick, a large cod. Apart from the fish selection, there is also a good range of Hollands pies or home-made chilli or beef curry, all with chips, of course. If you're popping in around Christmas, try John's famous battered Christmas pudding. Also worth looking out for are the shop's state-of-the-art frying range and the art deco Frank Ford range clock.

Prices: Fish and Chips from £3.20. Soft drinks from 60p.
Last orders: Food: lunch 13.00 (Saturday until 13.30); dinner 20.00 (on Friday until 21.00 in the summer).
Closed: Sunday and Monday.
Food: Fish and Chips.
Directions: Exit 35/M6. (Map 11, E4)

Hornby

The Castle Hotel

Main Street, Hornby, Lancashire LA2 8JT
Telephone: +44(0)870 4016107
+44(0)1524 221204
information@diningroomhornby.co.uk
www.diningroomhornby.co.uk

Close to Hornby Castle, a fine Victorian Folly, in the town's picturesque main street, the small and inti- mate Castle Hotel was restored and refurbished back to its former coaching inn glory in 2002. It now has 11 tastefully decorated en suite bedrooms. But the Castle is much more than a village inn, oozing luxury and style throughout the cosy lounge areas with deep sofas and crackling open fires, and elegant dining rooms with immaculately laid tables and fresh flowers. However, expect a friendly and informal atmosphere, and a great bar dispensing tip-top ales. Although bar food is served in the lounges when quiet, for an infor- mal meal head across the courtyard to the Castle Barns Bistro housed in well-converted outbuildings. Food is served throughout the day and from an impressive menu choice there may be starters of buttered brown shrimps, confit of duck with sweet orange dressing, or tomato and leek soup. Rustic and hearty main courses take in deep-fried bass with mushy peas and straw chips, linguine with hot smoked salmon and dill, wild mushroom and asparagus risotto, and lamb steak with spring onion mash and red wine jus. Good sandwiches and ploughman's lunches are available, and there's an excellent fixed-price dinner menu in The Dining Room.

Rooms: 11. Double room from £60, single from £50.
Prices include breakfast.
Prices: Bistro restaurant main course from £6.95. Fine Dining restaurant set dinner £39.95. House wine £10.95.
Last orders: Bar: 23.00. Food: Bistro 21.00.
Fine Dining Restaurant 20.30.
Closed: Never.
Food: Modern European in Bistro and Modern British in Fine Dining Room.
Other points: No-smoking area. Dogs welcome in certain areas. Patio. Children welcome. Two private dining rooms, Ballroom.
Directions: Exit34/M6. Travel towards Hornby and the Castle Hotel is on the A683. (Map 11, E4)

Poulton-le-Fylde

Monsieurs

12d Blackpool Old Road, Poulton-le-Fylde,
Lancashire FY6 7DH
Telephone: +44(0)870 4016296
+44(0)1253 896400

Monsieurs is a takeaway with a difference. By day it serves breakfasts and light snacks then in the evenings it switches over to fine French cooking. Residents of Poulton-le-Fylde can enjoy la crème de la crème of French dishes without picking up a sauté pan. The brainchild of Guy and Anita Jenkinson, Monsieurs is in the middle of town opposite the library. Even its entrance has the atmosphere of a Mediterranean café, but inside is simply the serving counter with the fully visible kitchen behind. Recline in comfortable chairs and flick through magazines while you wait for your order to be prepared. The daytime choice is simple, with breakfasts running to bacon and egg sandwiches and plates of scrambled egg on toast, while lunch takes in sandwiches, homemade soups and baked potatoes. However, come evening, the offerings are impres- sive. French-style cooking with coq au vin, chicken à la crème, navarin of lamb and beef bourguignon are always available, as well as side dishes of ratatouille, Vichy carrots and garlic sautéed potatoes. Lasagne, spaghetti bolognaise, and spicy chicken curry expand the range. Puddings are available too and it's hard to resist the good old British favourites of fruit crumbles, sticky toffee and bread and butter puds.

Prices: Main course from £8. Snack from £5.
Last orders: Food: lunch 14.00; dinner 21.00.
Closed: Sunday and Monday, last two weeks of July and first week of August.
Food: Traditional French and English/takeaway.
Other points: Totally no smoking. Children welcome. Car park. Credit cards not accepted.
Directions: Exit 3/M55, then A585 to Fleetwood. Left at first traffic lights, then left at the second lights onto the A586, and into Poulton one-way system. Situated opposite the library. (Map 11, E4)

Good food and wine

Preston

Thyme at The Sirloin

Station Road, Hoghton, Lancashire
Telephone: +44(0)870 4016297
+44(0)1254 852293

Not many people know this, but the name sirloin
originates from the 17th century when King James
anointed a loin of beef. Yes, it's true and it happened
here at this inn, hence the name. And to prove it, this
popular village inn has a plaque above its fireplace
commemorating the creation of Sir Loin. The big
attraction today is the upstairs restaurant, sister to
the original Thyme in Longbridge. The inn restaurant
shares the same philosophy and champions local,
seasonal produce. Rustic flavours and hearty flavours
are signatures of the cooking here, which is incredibly
inventive. Start with chicken livers in creamed cardamom and coriander sauce or crisp confit of duckling
with a salad of apple, vanilla and roasted hazelnuts.
Obviously, star of the menu has to be Thyme's famous
sirloin of beef pot roasted with a mousse of pancetta
and thyme with a galette potato and red wine jus. But
that doesn't eclipse dishes such as the very good breast
of Goosnargh chicken filled with a wild mushroom
and asparagus farce, straw potatoes and morel-scented
cream. The confident and accomplished cooking is
evident right through to the puddings with poached
pear and crumbly Lancashire upside down cake with
apple sorbet or hot chocolate fondant tart with white
chocolate ice cream proving irresistible. There is a
balanced list of sensibly priced wines.

Prices: Restaurant main course from £11.95.
Bar main course from £4.95. House wine £10.75.
Last orders: Bar: 23.00. Food: lunch 14.00 (no food Saturday
lunch); dinner 21.30 (Sunday 20.00)
Closed: All day Monday and first week in January.
Food: Traditional British.
Other points: No-smoking area. Dogs welcome. Garden. Car park.
Directions: M65. (Map 11, F4)

Preston

Thyme Restaurant

1-3 Inglewhite Road, Longridge, Preston,
Lancashire PR3 3JR
Telephone: +44(0)870 4016433
+44(0)1772 786888

After a complete refurbishment, Thyme has re-emerged
as a light and airy contemporary setting that's ideal
for wining and dining. You can eat or just drink informally in the bar area or move into the chic but relaxed
dining area for lunch or dinner. Much thought has
gone into making this a stylish, modern space. Smart
furniture, modern artwork and chic table settings are
all winners before you even get to the menu. And here
too, quality is to the forefront. Locally sourced ingredients mixed with international influences create an
interesting choice of dishes. There are good-value set
lunch and dinner menus. Start with tian of peppered
smoked mackerel, prawns and horseradish mayonnaise
on crisp leaves, then follow with spiced chicken noodle
salad with cashew nuts and a soy dressing, and finish
with lemon and lime sponge with stem ginger ice. The
full carte and specials menu widens the selection. Start
with say Lancashire cheese and chive fishcakes with
homemade tartar, then crisp, slowly roasted duckling,
black pudding mash and red wine jus, and a pudding
of orange and passion fruit crème brulée with orange
and Grand Marnier ice cream. The wine list tours the
world and if there isn't anything from the selection of
beers to your liking, you can pop next door to their
pub for further refreshment.

Prices: Set lunch £8.95, set dinner £9.95. Restaurant main course
from £11.95. Bar main course from £4.95. House wine £10.75.
Last orders: Bar: lunch 14.30; dinner 21.30 (Sunday 20.00). Food:
lunch 14.30; dinner 21.30 (Sunday 20.00).
Closed: All day Monday and one week at the beginning of January.
Food: Traditional British.
Other points: No-smoking area.
Directions: Exit31A/M6. (Map 11, E4)

www.routiers.co.uk

Whitewell

Inn at Whitewell

Forest of Bowland, Whitewell, Clitheroe,
Lancashire BB7 3AT
Telephone: +44(0)870 4016111
+44(0)1200 448222

Set amid the wild beauty of deepest north Lancashire,
this magnificent get-away-from-it-all inn enjoys fine
views over the River Hodder. In fact, it's so far from
the hussle and bustle, that the inn is the sum and the
parts of Whitewell. Despite its splendid isolation, there
is much to keep you entertained: fishing, a wine merchants, art gallery and a shop selling homemade foods.
The 17 individually decorated bedrooms are furnished
with antiques, have Victorian baths and peat fires.
The best and largest have the river views. It's easy
to feel immediately at home, as the atmosphere is so
laid back. The unique ambience is thanks to Richard
Bowman and his staff who imbue this hostelry with
warmth and a pleasing quirkiness plus there's the mildy
eccentric setting created by a haphazard arrangement
of furnishings, the open log fires and colourful rugs.
Food is unpretentiously good: at lunch it's salads and
substantial sandwiches; supper in the bar may be fish
pie, and pork medallions with mustard sauce, while the
evening carte menu may feature local estate venison
or Goosnargh duck. A superlative wine list completes
the picture. Brilliant extras include video recorders and
stereo systems in the bedrooms.

Rooms: 17. Double/twin room from £89.
Prices: Restaurant main course from £12.
Bar main course from £7.50. House wine £9.50.
Last orders: Bar: lunch 15.00; dinner 23.00. Food: lunch 14.00;
dinner 21.30.
Closed: Rarely.
Food: Modern British.
Other points: Children welcome. Dogs welcome overnight.
Garden. Car park. Licence for Civil Weddings. Fishing.
Directions: Exit 32/M6 to Longridge. Centre of Longridge follow
signs to Whitewell. (Map 11, E4)

Leicester

San Carlo Restaurant

38-40 Granby Street, Leicester, Leicestershire LE1 1DE
Telephone: +44(0)870 4016280
+44(0)116 251 9332

This small chain of city-centre eateries is a cut above
the norm and majors in good-value pizza and pasta.
The décor is contemporary, simple and the same across
the chain, which has outlets in Birmingham, Bristol
and Manchester. The light and airy feel is helped by
mirrors lining the walls and white-tiled floors that create a sleek Mediterranean look that's softened by lots
of potted plants and trees. This branch, ranging over
three floors, has a great atmosphere. The look inside
may be modern but the food is traditional, with an
extensive range of pizza and pasta, and classic trattoria dishes such as pollo sorpresa and saltimbocca
alla romana. Seafood is delivered once, sometimes
twice daily, and the seafood specials board is updated
accordingly. Sardines, dressed crab, lobster tagliolini,
grilled Dover sole, and king prawn and monkfish
kebab are typical examples. The wine list covers an
extensive selection of Italian and French wines, with
just a couple from the new world, and a dozen served
by the glass.

Prices: Main course from £9. House wine £11.20.
Last orders: Food: 23.00.
Closed: Rarely.
Food: Italian.
Other points: No-smoking area. Children welcome.
Directions: Situated in Leicester city centre just outside the busy
shopping area. (Map 9, C3)

Affordable good value

Nether Broughton

The Red House

23 Main Street, Nether Broughton, Melton Mowbray,
Leicestershire LE14 3HB
Telephone: +44(0)870 4016114
+44(0)1664 822429
bookings@the-redhouse.com
www.the-redhouse.com

It's a stylishly revamped early Victorian house with
all the hallmarks of a city boutique hotel. All eight en
suite bedrooms have a contemporary glamourous look
through simple designs executed with luxurious fabrics. You'll also find unexpected goodies in bedrooms:
DVDs, olives, pistachio nuts, mineral water and freshly
baked cookies. Much thought has been given to the
outdoors, where there is a smart decked courtyard,
for the over-14s only, and the Garden Bar and Grill
in the old stables. The bar has a more traditional feel
with dark wood furniture and smart leather seating.
Chalkboards offer the day's bar menu, which includes
a pasta and soup of the day, Bison burger with fat
chips and brown onions and fish and chips with minted mushy pies. Modern styling distinguishes the restaurant with, for example, a bar that consists of a pine
wood frame filled with old books. Or, for a change of
scene, step through an arched walkway to the adjoining dining room that's filled with light and looks over
the new rear terrace. From the winter menu, you can
choose spiced duck salad, green papaya and Thai herbs
with a chilli dressing; mains are equally appealing and
include braised salmon, scallops, mussels and prawns
with tarragon butter. Food is suitably matched by an
expansive and global wine list.

Rooms: 8. Twin/double room from £50 per person.
Prices: Restaurant main course from £9.95. Bar snacks from £5.
House wine £12.
Last orders: Bar: 23.00 (Sunday 22.30). Food: lunch 15.00 (Sunday
17.00); dinner 22.00 (Sunday 18.00).
Closed: Rarely.
Food: Modern British.
Other points: No-smoking in the restaurant. Children welcome.
Dogs welcome in the bar. Car park. Outside garden bar and open
kitchen. Meeting room. Marquee facility.
Directions: Exit 25/M1, the A52, then the A606 to Melton. Situated
on the A606 between Nottingham and Melton Mowbray, five miles
north of Melton. (Map 9, C4)

Stapleford

Stapleford Park

near Melton Mowbray, Leicestershire LE14 2EF
Telephone: +44(0)870 4016396
+44(0)1572 787522
reservations@stapleford.co.uk
www.staplefordpark.com

Down the ages its many owners have all added to the
splendour and grandeur of this wonderful country
house. But the good-taste additions look seamless. It
has been beautifully refurbished and now offers all
you could want for the perfect country escape. The
hall is a stunning feature as are the 52 individually
designed plush bedrooms, each sponsored by a business in their own style. Wedgwood, Mulberry and
Nina Campbell are just a few companies involved.
Downstairs the lounge and public rooms ooze luxury
and style, but instead of seeming formal the efficient
and helpful staff ensure there is homely feel to pro-
ceedings. Set in its 500 acres of parkland, originally
created by 'Capability' Brown, are tennis courts, a
fabulous golf course and gym, spa offering treatments
and a 22-metre pool. There are two options for dining: the elegant Grinling Gibbons dining room, where
acclaimed chef Wayne Vickerage serves fine traditional-
meets-European dishes, or the more informal Pavilion
Brasserie, which has stunning views over the golf
course and surrounding parkland. Here you can enjoy
an excellent good-value, two-course set lunch, as well
as the carte menu. In the Grinling Gibbons restaurant
manager and wine expert Laurent Bergmann is on
hand to help with your selection from the wine list.

Rooms: 52. Double/twin room from £198, single from £175,
family room from £240.
Prices: Set lunch £30 and dinner £44 (for 10 or more persons).
Restaurant main course from £10. Bar main course from £10.
House wine £28.
Last orders: Food: 21.00. (cold snacks 24 hours a day).
Closed: Never.
Food: Modern British.
Other points: No-smoking area. Children welcome.
Dogs welcome. Garden. Car park. Licence for Civil Weddings.
Directions: M1/J21a northbound. M1/26 southbound. From
Melton Mowbray follow signs to Stapleford, take the right turning
and Stapleford Park is two miles on the left. (Map 9, C4)

www.routiers.co.uk

Lincoln

Hillcrest Hotel

15 Lindum Terrace, Lincoln, Lincolnshire LN2 5RT
Telephone: +44(0)870 4016377
+44(0)1522 510182
reservations@hillcrest-hotel.com
www.hillcrest-hotel.com

As you relax in the quiet grounds of this town house, it's hard to believe it's bang in the middle of Lincoln. Formerly a rectory, this hotel is coveniently located on a secluded leafy avenue close to the cathedral, of course, and the arboretum. Host Jennifer Bennett and her team make you feel immediately at home. They can supply you with all the information you need about local events throughout the year, from racing to recitals. The 15 bedrooms are spread over four floors and all are individually designed; the best is a spacious, yet cosy, four-poster bedroom decked out in pretty lace and florals. In the public rooms, the décor is a mix of the bold and the traditional and beautifully sets off the ornate plasterwork and high ceilings. The food is hearty, good home cooking. Popular choices include pork with an apple and prune compote, and breast of chicken with a lemon sauce, both served with generous helpings of fresh vegetables. They barely leave room for a pudding but it's hard to resist the locally made ice cream. A short list of mainly new world wines provides good drinking at reasonable prices.

Rooms: 14. Double room from £85, single from £63.
Prices: Set dinner £19. Main course from £13.75.
House wine £11.50.
Last orders: Food: lunch 14.00; dinner 20.30. No food all day Sunday and Saturday lunch.
Closed: 21 December to 6 January.
Food: Modern European.
Other points: No-smoking area. Children welcome. Dogs welcome overnight. Garden. Car park. Internet.
Directions: From Wragby Road/Lindum Hill (A15), take very small road - Upper Lindum Street. Go to the bottom of the road, then turn left into Lindum Terrace; the hotel is 200 metres on right. (Map 9, B4)

Lincoln

The Lincoln Hotel

Eastgate, Lincoln, Lincolnshire LN2 1PN
Telephone: +44(0)870 4016378
+44(0)1522 520348
sales@thelincolnhotel.com
www.thelincolnhotel.com

Owned by Trust House Forte until two years ago, this 72-bedroom city centre hotel is now independently owned and has been stylish refurbished. Bedrooms come with all the creature comforts and are contemporary-chic in style, with an emphasis on quality beds and bed linen. The reception is spacious and nicely reappointed, and guests can unwind in the modern bar and lounge and enjoy fabulous locally sourced and well-priced food in the smart dining room. Dishes fit into the modern-European category, but have a distinct Italian slant. Start with cannellini bean and parsley soup or crab and prawn fritters with caviar salsa, followed by mains of wild mushroom risotto with slow-roasted garlic or something more traditional such as grilled prime Lincolnshire rump steak with thyme-roasted tomato and flat mushrooms. For less formal meals, you'll find plenty of choice in the bar, from filled baguettes of chargrilled steak or smoked salmon and cucumber with lemon and dill dressing to bruschetta and soup of the day. Other treats include traditional afternoon tea, desserts and cakes, coffees and teas. This is a great location for exploring Lincoln, in fact part of the Roman remains of Eastgate are in the front car park and gardens, and many rooms have views of the cathedral.

Rooms: 72. Double from £80.
Prices: Brasserie main course from £7.25. Main course bar/snack from £4.75. House wine £11.95.
Last orders: Food: 21.30.
Closed: Rarely.
Food: Modern European.
Other points: No-smoking area. Garden. Children welcome. Car park. Licensed for Civil Weddings. Conference facilities.
Directions: A46 follow signs for Lincoln North. At roundabout turn right onto Riseholme Road; continue to follow this road to junction, turn right and hotel is on the right. (Map 9, B4)

An alternative Britain

Manchester

Dimitris Tapas Bar and Taverna

Campfield Arcade, Tonman Street. Deansgate,
Manchester M3 4FN
Telephone: +44(0)870 4016405
+44 (0)161 839 3319
manchester@dimitris.co.uk
www.dimitris.co.uk

Stepping into Dimitris is like stepping into a
Mediterranean bar-restaurant. At weekends, the
atmosphere is lively and in the evenings, you really
feel you could be abroad. The concept of cheap dining
and cheery surroundings has been a winning formula
for owner Dimtris who has expanded the idea into a
chain. The restaurant is incredibly laid back and has
wooden floors and bright tablecloths. You can also
eat in the outside heated dining area, or the separate
bar and cellar bar. The menu also has something-for-
everyone appeal, which is good Mediterranean cooking
that includes Greek taverna favourites such as houmous and taramasalata plus guacamole and tapenade.
In the mains section, Loukanika pork sausages made
with wine and served with tzatsiki, or octopus slowly
cooked with onions in red wine, vie for attention with
salt and pepper spare ribs and chorizo sausage and
salsa, and so on through salads, vegetables, pasta and
couscous. What sets the cooking apart is the policy of
offering good food at affordable prices. Popular dishes
such as the kalamata platas and the mega mezzes are
set menus for two or more people and are exceptional
value, as is the Manchester soup and sandwich lunch
deal. The wine list takes a popular global view and
includes a few Greek wines that are worth trying.

Prices: Set lunch from £10.95, set dinner from £16.35.
House wine £10.95.
Last orders: Food: 23.30.
Closed: Rarely.
Food: Mediterranean.
Other points: Children welcome. Heated arcade.
Directions: At the end of Deansgate, near GMEX and Castlefield
just off the main road in the arcade. (Map 12, F5)

Manchester

San Carlo Restaurant

40-42 King Street West, Manchester M3 2WY
Telephone: +44(0)870 4016404
+44(0)161 834 6226
www.sancarlo.co.uk

With restaurants in Bristol, Leicester and Birmingham,
the expanding San Carlo chain is making quite a name
for itself. Each of the restaurants has its own individual menu and so they are not slaves to a formuliac
approach. This smart city-centre Manchester branch
majors in fish and it puts its fine catch to good use in
its specials and menu. The main menu focuses on popular Italian favourites using excellent ingredients, many
from Italy, mixed with quality fish. The chef has a
good eye, so everything from the antipasti to the mains
comes pleasingly presented and in generous portions.
Antipasti of carpaccio tascanoal porcini and fresh mussels in either a provençal or meurniére sauce are a cut
above the norm. Moving on to mains, you can choose
from a wide selection of pasta dishes, which are also
strong in the fish department. Tonna arrabbiata is nicely hot and the chilli marries well with the tuna, while
spaghetti shellfish is a veritable extravaganza. There
is much else besides fish to tempt, from mushroom
risotto to the Italian connoisseur's breast of chicken
with spicy Italian sausage, or the classic ham-wrapped
veal saltimbocco. It's worth dressing for dinner as the
contemporary dining room shouts smart, from the
table settings to the general décor.

Prices: Restaurant main course from £12. House wine £12.50.
Last orders: Food: 23.00.
Closed: Rarely.
Food: Italian.
Other points: No-smoking area. Children welcome.
Directions: Just off Deansgate. (Map 9, A2)

Ramsbottom

Ramsons

16-18 Market Place, Ramsbottom, Bury,
Greater Manchester BL0 9HT
Telephone: +44(0)870 4016412
+44(0)1706 825070
chris@ramsons.org.uk

Ramsons is perfectly formed, cosy and compact, and has a well-thought out menu. Its three small ground-floor rooms are decorated in a smart yet timeless style. Chris Johnson brings Italian flair and flavour to his menu, which is a model of flexibility. Come early in the day for Italian breakfast or brunch, or lunchtime for some tremendously good value dishes. At dinner, you can feast on wild boar salami with rocket and Parmesan shavings, and steamed fillet of salmon with roast fennel and champagne sauce. Dishes are built around prime raw ingredients, impeccably sourced and simply but superbly cooked, as can be seen in a classic roast sirloin of beef with baby potatoes and red wine sauce served for Sunday lunch. Seasonality is the key to the impressive repertoire, and flavours work well, whether it's a starter of wild nettle soup with basil infusion, or a pudding of rhubarb crumble and Jersey cream. The wine list is concise but inspiring, and is accompanied by excellent tasting notes. A retail discount for those wanting to take some home is a novel touch. You are also invited to check the cellar for the many wines that are stocked but not on the list. The basement café is modelled on an Italian enoteca and has a good menu of light dishes.

Prices: Set lunch and dinner £14.50. Main course from £13.50. House wine £10.
Last orders: Food: lunch 14.30 (Sunday 15.30); dinner 22.00.
Closed: All day Monday and Sunday evening.
Food: Italian Influenced.
Other points: Totally no smoking. Well-behaved children welcome (no special children menus).
Directions: From the M66 take exit 1 northbound. Turn right at the lights and left at the next lights. Take a right at the third lights, Ramsons is on the right hand side. (Map 12, F5)

Individual charm and warmth

Woodforde's Nelson's Revenge *at The Lord Nelson*

On the Norfolk Broads lies the famous Woodforde's Brewery. The quality of the beers brewed here is not in doubt as amongst many awards they have twice won the supreme accolade of CAMRA's 'Champion Beer of Britain'. Care and attention to detail are the watchwords; the barley is grown in the surrounding countryside and malted in Norfolk in the traditional style. A unique aspect is that the brewery has its very own borehole, this high quality water is low on nitrates and is considered very important in the production of the beer. Combine this with the finest bitter and aromatic hops and the brewery's own yeast and you have a winning combination.

Woodforde's is a relatively young company having started in 1981, one of a wave of brewers rebelling against the blandness of the large brewing companies. Well known regionally, they became nationally famous after their Norfolk Nog 'Old' Ale became Champion Beer of Britain. Since then awards have been coming thick and fast. As well as actually owning three pubs the beer can be found in numerous local pubs, one of these being the Lord Nelson. A pretty pub, named after Norfolk's favourite son, the pub has remained reassuringly unchanged for years. With its stoneflagged floors and original wooden settles, it is like stepping back in time and makes a lovely setting for a pint of Woodforde's Nelson's Revenge.

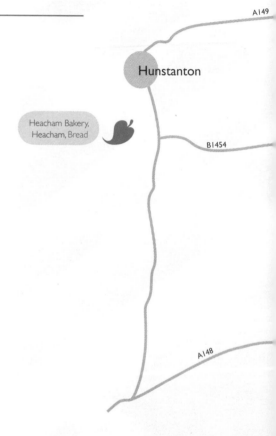

A149

Hunstanton

Heacham Bakery, Heacham, Bread

B1454

A148

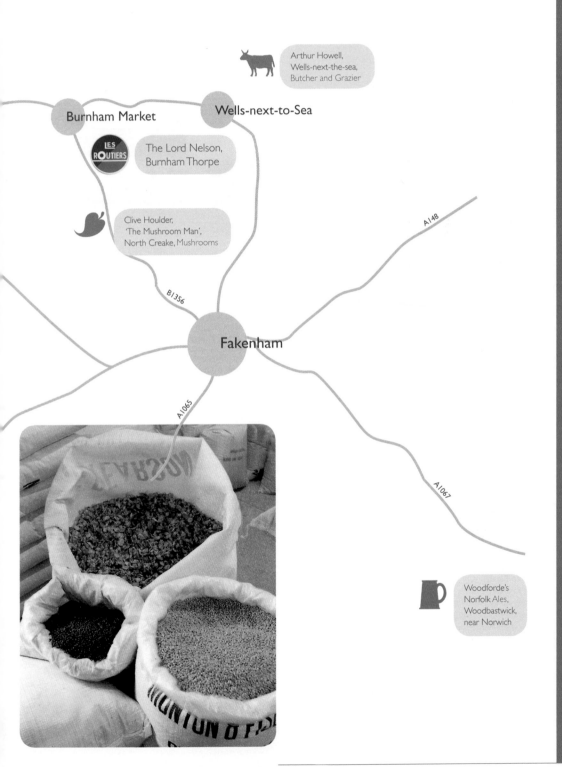

Arthur Howell,
Wells-next-the-sea,
Butcher and Grazier

Burnham Market

Wells-next-to-Sea

The Lord Nelson,
Burnham Thorpe

Clive Houlder,
'The Mushroom Man',
North Creake, Mushrooms

A148

B1356

Fakenham

A1065

A1067

Woodforde's
Norfolk Ales,
Woodbastwick,
near Norwich

Brancaster Staithe

The White Horse

Brancaster Staithe, King's Lynn, Norfolk PE31 8BY
Telephone: +44(0)870 4016118
+44(0)1485 210262
reception@whitehorsebrancaster.co.uk
www.whitehorsebrancaster.co.uk

Views from the large conservatory dining room are wonderful. In fact, many consider the picturesque sight of the tidal marshes to Scolt Head Island not only the best in Norfolk, but in England. Add good quality food into the mix and this is a great place to dine any time of the day. The dining room décor doesn't try to compete with the landscape. Simple natural objects from the beach and contemporary artwork are the only subtle adornments. In the evening, candles twinkle on the well-spaced out tables. The emphasis is on fresh fish and ingredients from local suppliers. Start with Thornham oysters, Letzer smoked salmon with caper berries or Brancaster Staithe Mussels with chilli, coriander and tomato or white white, cream or grilled with pesto. Mains offer whole roasted sea bass or Graves roast rump of English lamb with sweet onion tartlet. The wine list offers good value and 11 by the glass, while beers from East Anglian brewers are a popular choice in the bar. There are also stunning views from the bedrooms in the extension, which has been designed in the shape of a wave to give every spacious room a piece of terrace. New bedrooms upstairs are decorated in soft colours and have handsome modern furniture. The best views are from the two-tiered Room at the Top, which has its own telescope.

Rooms: 15. Double room from £84, single supplement £20 per night.
Prices: Main course from £9.50. House wine £10.80.
Last orders: Bar: 23.00. Food: lunch 14.00; dinner 21.15.
Closed: Rarely.
Food: Modern British.
Other points: No-smoking area. Children welcome.
Dogs welcome overnight. Garden. Sun deck terrace. Car park.
Directions: Midway between Hunstanton and Wells-next-Sea on the A149 coast road. (Map 10, C6)

Burnham Thorpe

The Lord Nelson

Walsingham Road, Burnham Thorpe, Norfolk PE31 8HL
Telephone: +44(0)870 4016120
+44(0)1328 738241
enquiries@nelsonslocal.co.uk
www.nelsonslocal.co.uk

The pub, originally called The Plough, pre-dates Nelson by over 100 years but was renamed in 1797 to honour his victory at the Battle of the Nile. England's most famous seafarer was born in the nearby rectory in 1758. The pub is in an unspoilt rural cottage in a sleepy village. A narrow, worn brick-floored corridor leads to a timeless, old-fashioned bar on the left which has some mighty high-backed settles and sturdy tables and plain chairs. Nelson memorabilia abounds in the form of prints and paintings. Owners David and Penny Thorley may have installed a hatchway bar but top-notch Greene King and Woodforde's ales are still drawn straight from the barrel in the adjoining tap room. The refurbished Victory Barn is a separate, cosy room with beams and open fire, and is available for functions. Outside, there's a rear garden that's perfect for families. Using fresh local produce, including game from Holkham Estate and seafood from coastal villages, daily menus range from smoked haddock mousse or tiger prawns with a sesame and chilli dipping sauce to mains of whole Dover sole oven baked with salsa verde or bangers on mash with onion gravy. There's also a separate children's menu. If you're feeling daring and not driving, don't leave without trying the secret and rather potent rum concoction, Nelson's Blood.

Prices: Restaurant main course from £8.95. Bar main course from £7.95. House wine £10.50.
Last orders: Bar: lunch 15.00 (14.30 during the winter); dinner 23.00. Food: lunch 14.00; dinner 21.00 (no food Sunday evening).
Closed: Monday during the winter.
Food: Traditional British/European.
Other points: No-smoking area. Children welcome.
Dogs welcome in the bar. Car park. Garden. Childrens play area in garden. BBQ in the summer.
Directions: One and three quarter miles from Burnham Market, just off the Burnham Market to Creakes/Fakenham Road. (Map 10, C7)

www.routiers.co.uk

Cley next the Sea

terroir

High Street, Cley next the Sea, Norfolk NR25 7RN
Telephone: +44(0)870 4016302
+44(0)1263 740336
whalebone.house@virgin.net
www.thecafe.org.uk

Kalba Meadows and John Curtis have created a contemporary restaurant that serves fantastic food first, which just happens to be vegetarian second. Dinner starts at 7.30pm and is intended to be enjoyed at a relaxed pace. They don't do sittings, and smokers take note, there's no smoking either. Freshness is the order of the day, and dinner is planned in the afternoon, once it's known what local, organic produce is available. The full list of suppliers is on the menu. Credentials are impeccable and include local organic farmers to Neal's Yard Dairy. Dishes change daily and have a strong Mediterranean influence. Set dinner menus are three or four courses. The first two courses are a similar size. Dishes show imagination and flair with recipes such as saffron and butterbean couscous with a watercress, parsley and pink grapefruit salad to start, followed by say celeriac and thyme cakes, cavalo nero cooked with puy lentils and peperoncino, and mushrooms roasted in seasoned breadcrumbs. Course three consists of fabulous cheese and four is a delicious dessert such as Corsican cheesecake with Wiveton strawberries. They also serve Sunday lunch. Two double rooms are available (minimum stay two nights). Bathrobes, slippers, binoculars, books, CD player, cafétière and hot waterbottles are included.

Rooms: 2. Single nights not accepted. Two nights for two people from £200 for dinner, bed and breakfast.
Prices: Set lunch £15.50 and dinner £22.50 (4 course). Wines from £13.
Last orders: Dinner served Tuesday to Sunday 19.30 for 20.00. Booking essential.
Closed: Sunday evening (except June to September and Bank Holidays) all day Monday, Tuesday to Saturday lunch, December and January and two weeks in September/October.
Food: Modern British Vegetarian.
Other points: Totally no smoking. Credit cards not accepted.
Directions: On the A149 coast road midway between Cromer and Wells-next-the-sea. (Map 10, C7)

Cromer

Richard and Julie Davies

7 Garden Street, Cromer, Norfolk NR27 9HN
Telephone: +44(0)870 4016301
+44(0)1263 512727

If you're on holiday in the seaside resort of Cromer, it's highly recommended you sample those eponymously named crabs. For the best, look no further than this small, glass-fronted retail unit. It might look like an other unassuming fishmongers from the outside, but Richard and Julie Davies who run it are the most famous retailer and wholesaler in these parts and they have a great reputation for good seafood. That's not surprising as they come from a prominent seafaring family that goes back eight generations, and they know their subject. The fish shop was opened 30 years ago and dressed Cromer crab remains a speciality. Cromer crabs are smaller than those from other parts of the country, but far sweeter and meatier. Richard Davies uses the most up-to-date equipment, including the use of catamarans (for speed) to work his 700 crab pots. Once landed, crabs are sorted, washed and boiled in 25 minutes, ensuring that they are sold in the best condition. They also catch their own lobsters and sell an abundance of wet fish from Lowestoft and shellfish, notably King's Lynn shrimps.

Prices: Fishmongers.
Last orders: Shop: 17.30.
Closed: Rarely.
Other points: Car park.
Directions: In the town centre of Cromer. (Map 10, C7)

Regional produce

Garboldisham organic flour

at terroir

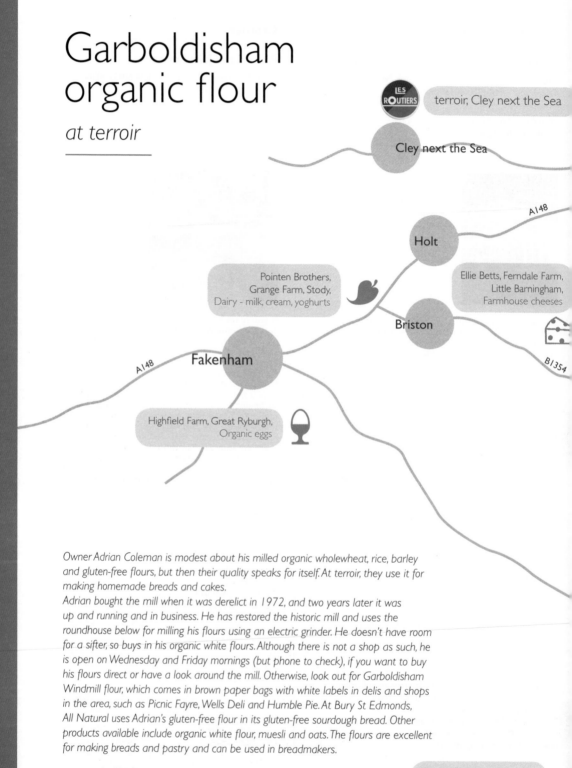

terroir, Cley next the Sea

Cley next the Sea

A148

Holt

Pointen Brothers,
Grange Farm, Stody,
Dairy - milk, cream, yoghurts

Ellie Betts, Ferndale Farm,
Little Barningham,
Farmhouse cheeses

Briston

B1354

A148

Fakenham

Highfield Farm, Great Ryburgh,
Organic eggs

Owner Adrian Coleman is modest about his milled organic wholewheat, rice, barley and gluten-free flours, but then their quality speaks for itself. At terroir, they use it for making homemade breads and cakes.

Adrian bought the mill when it was derelict in 1972, and two years later it was up and running and in business. He has restored the historic mill and uses the roundhouse below for milling his flours using an electric grinder. He doesn't have room for a sifter, so buys in his organic white flours. Although there is not a shop as such, he is open on Wednesday and Friday mornings (but phone to check), if you want to buy his flours direct or have a look around the mill. Otherwise, look out for Garboldisham Windmill flour, which comes in brown paper bags with white labels in delis and shops in the area, such as Picnic Fayre, Wells Deli and Humble Pie. At Bury St Edmonds, All Natural uses Adrian's gluten-free flour in its gluten-free sourdough bread. Other products available include organic white flour, muesli and oats. The flours are excellent for making breads and pastry and can be used in breadmakers.

Garboldisham Windmill: Diss, Norfolk; 01953 681 593

Garboldisham Windmill, Diss,
Organic flours and muesli

Cromer

A140

Groveland Fruit Farms,
Roughton,
Apple juice, vegetables

1am

A140

orwich

Strattons, Swaffham, see page 135

Norwich

The Wig and Pen

6 St Martins Palace Plain, Norwich, Norfolk NR3 1RN
Telephone: +44(0)870 4016125
+44(0)1603 625891
info@thewigandpen.com
www.wigandpen.com

Arrive early, bag a window seat, or a table on the sunny front terrace, and savour the fabulous cathedral views over lunch at this partly modernised old beamed pub opposite the cathedral close. Dishes range from the tried and tested on the printed menu – sandwiches, baked potatoes, beefburger, ham, egg and chips and all-day breakfasts – to homecooked daily specials like broccoli and Stilton soup, Hungarian beef goulash, a good steak and kidney pie with shortcrust pastry topping and rich gravy, and fresh fish supplied by Howards fishmongers along the road. Inside, log fires crackle in the original beamed bar, where legal related prints and pictures of the pub adorn the walls, and the welcoming atmosphere continues through to the modern dining extension. Expect to find lawyers and locals supping pints of ale at the bar, shoppers and tourists popping in for lunch and, in the evenings, a young, lively crowd who come for the beer and live sport on the TV. Real ale enthusiasts are spoilt for choice. Brewery badges on the six handpumps may feature Oulton Ales' Wet and Windy, Woodforde's Wherry and Adnams Old Ale – all kept in tip-top condition, great beer to wash down some hearty, traditional pub food.

Prices: Restaurant main course from £7.50. Bar main course from £3.00. House wine from £8.95.

Last orders: Bar: 23.00. Food: lunch 14.30; dinner 21.00.

Closed: Sunday evening. Christmas Day, New Years Day.

Food: Traditional and Modern British.

Other points: No-smoking area. Children welcome over 14 years old. Garen. Wheelchair access.

Directions: Adjacent to Norwich Cathedral. 100 years from Maids Head Hotel Tombland. Walking distance from the River Wensum. (Map 10, C7)

Old Buckenham

The Gamekeeper Freehouse

The Green, Old Buckenham, Attleborough, Norfolk NR17 1RE
Telephone: +44(0)870 4016467
+44(0)1953 860397
richardashwell@thegamekeeperfreehouse.com
www.thegamekeeperfreehouse.com

Set by the largest village green in East Anglia, this attractive inn fits perfectly into the picturesque village of Old Buckingham. American actor James Stewart drank here when he was posted to the village during the Second World War and it is also reputed to have two friendly ghosts, George and Angelina, who are also partial to a late drink or two. It's a traditional pub with a lovely rural feel in its different rooms, upstairs and downstairs. In the winter there's an open fire and in summer you can dine al fresco in the garden. The restaurant menu is comprehensive and includes many local ingredients in season. Appetisers include imaginative dishes such as warm salad of saffron-scented fish of the day or pasta with wild mushrooms, rocket and Parmesan. Mains include the traditional such as lamb shank and the more exotic pan-fried salmon with tiger prawns. In the bar, you can feast on hearty favourites such as fish and chips, chicken tandoori and steak burger. It's also renowned for its beers, most notably Adnams and brews from the nearby Wolf brewery. The wine list is a good mix of reasonably priced new and old world varieties. And if you want to extend your stay, there are three cosy, good value rooms upstairs, complete with DVD players, although the bathroom is shared.

Rooms: 3 with private bathrooms. Double room from £45, single from £30.

Prices: Restaurant main course from £8.95. Bar snack from £7.50. House wine £10.95.

Last orders: Bar: 23.00. Food: lunch 14.30 (Sunday 17.00); dinner 21.00 (Friday and Saturday 21.30. No food Sunday evening).

Closed: Never.

Food: Modern British.

Other points: No-smoking area. Dogs welcome. Garden. Children welcome over 3 years old. Car park.

Directions: Exit A11 at Attleborough then join the B1077 towards Diss. Continue for two and a half miles into the village of Old Buckenham, The Gamekeeper is on your right. (Map 10, D7)

Down-to-earth, friendly service

The Crown Hotel, Wells-next-to-Sea

Swaffham

Strattons

4 Ash Close, Swaffham, Norfolk PE37 7NH
Telephone: +44(0)870 4016427
+44(0)1760 723845
enquiries@strattonshotel.com
www.strattonshotel.co.uk

This Queen Anne Palladian villa has been transformed into a luxurious yet comfortably relaxed hotel-restaurant. Set in the heart of the Breckland countryside, Strattons is just minutes from the marketplace in Swaffham, but manages to transport you away from the mundanity of the every day. Owners Les and Vanessa Scott have restored the villa to its former glory, but treated each guestroom to an individual look, from a plush red bedroom to a grand blue and gilt Venetian room. And they pay as much attention to the food as they do to the furnishings. The couple pride themselves on using local, seasonal and, where possible organic, ingredients. The cooking style is modern European using the best local game, fish and meat. Starters include baked Cromer crab to a Normandy recipe for mushrooms in a port and béchamel sauce and a broad bean and lemon soup. Mains are also a delectable bunch and include organic salmon with arame served with watercress and new potatoes and fillet of corn-fed organic chicken braised in lavender with spring onion and bacon mash. Puddings are just as plush and the cheeseboard offers a great selection. There's a good range of fine wines at fair prices. Prepare to be pampered in all departments.

Rooms: 8. Double from £50, single from £85, family from £180. Prices per person.
Prices: Set dinner from £37.50.
Last orders: Food: 21.00. (Dinner only, closed Sunday).
Closed: Rarely.
Food: Modern British.
Other points: Totally no smoking. Dogs welcome. Garden. Children welcome. Car park.
Directions: At the north end of the market place, tucked behind the shop fronts. (Map 10, C6)

Wells-next-to-Sea

The Crown Hotel

The Buttlands, Wells-next-to-Sea, Norfolk NR23 1EX
Telephone: +44(0)870 4016128
+44(0)1328 710209
reception@thecrownhotelwells.co.uk
www.thecrownhotelwells.co.uk

In a striking position overlooking the green, known as The Buttlands, stands the fine building that's home to The Crown. This former coaching inn has been given a contemporary, uncluttered makeover by Jo and Chris Coubrough. Each of the 11 en suite bedrooms has a fresh white and blue theme and exudes a calm, uncluttered and stylish ambience. The understated elegance is quite refreshing in such traditional surroundings, and the décor makes unwinding easy. The room line-up includes two family suites with videos and baby-monitoring facilities. For an informal and relaxing meal, eat in the Crown bar, which has old beams and an open fire. Choose from lighter bites such as the Crown Black Slate – a tray of European and Asian appetisers, or houmous with bread, Caesar salad or heartier options such as paella with monkfish, crab claws, squid, clams and chorizo or The Crown beefburger. In the elegant restaurant, the food is more sophisticated modern British, with touches of the Pacific Rim. Starters include flash-fried squid with bacon and black pudding or terrine of lamb shank and sweetbreads with sauerkraut and mains offer steamed North Sea cod with ginger, lemon grass and lime or pan-fried fillet of beef, dauphinoise potato and duck liver parfait glaze. A well put together wine list complements the wide range of flavours in the food.

Rooms: 11. Double from £95.
Prices: Set dinner £29.95. Restaurant main course from £19.95. Main course bar from £7.95. House wine £10.90.
Last orders: Bar: 23.00. Food: lunch 14.00 (Saturday and Sunday and during peak season 14.30). Dinner: 21.30.
Closed: Never.
Food: Modern British.
Other points: No-smoking area. Dogs welcome in bar area only. Children welcome. Car park.
Directions: From Fakenham head along the B1105 until you reach Wells, turn right to the town centre and take the second right. (Map 10, C6)

Good food and wine

Oundle

Falcon Inn

Fotheringhay, Oundle, Northamptonshire PE8 5HZ
Telephone: +44(0)870 4016131
+44(0)1832 226254

It's a small village but it certainly packs in the history. Richard III was born and Mary Queen of Scots executed here. More information about royal connections are displayed at the local church, which itself merits a visit for its unusual octagonal lantern tower. The Falcon is also perfectly positioned at the heart of the village. It's run by Ray Smikle and John Hoskins of the Huntsbridge Group with an emphasis on quality food. You can eat in the bar, which has some has exposed stonework and is smartly decked out with Windsor and tapestry-covered chairs and nice touches such as of fresh flowers. A snack menu chalked up on a board, and the printed, monthly changing menu is offered in the bar as well as the dining room. The double conservatory dining room provides a slightly more formal setting, with a mix of green director chairs and green Lloyd Loom chairs complementing the pale-green walls. The dishes are thoroughly modern and definitely not run of the mill. A spring meal could start with a terrine of potato, aubergine and spinach with goats' cheese and a curry sauce, followed by a main course of spicy Thai duck breast, peanuts, noodles, coriander and lime dressing. Chocolate brownie gateau with clotted cream is a delicous way to round off a very enjoyable meal. There are few wine lists of 100 bins that could be so indulgent, and with such an eclectic, esoteric and stimulating selection.

Prices: Set lunch £15.50. Restaurant main course from £9.75. Bar main course from £8.95. House wine £12.
Last orders: Bar: lunch 15.00; dinner 23.00. Food: lunch 14.15; dinner 21.30.
Closed: Rarely.
Food: International.
Other points: No-smoking in the restaurant. Children welcome. Dogs welcome in the bar. Garden. Car park.
Directions: Village signposted off A605 between Oundle and Peterborough, one mile north of Oundle. (Map 9, D4)

Bellingham

Riverdale Hall Hotel

Bellingham, Northumberland NE48 2JT
Telephone: +44(0)870 4016353
+44(0)1434 220254
iben@riverdalehall.demon.co.uk
www.riverdalehall.demon.co.uk

This country house hotel with 20 simply decorated rooms has an excellent reputation for its sporting facilities as well as its fine food. The cricket field in the grounds explains much of the décor inside, as trophies and cricketing photos adorn many of the walls, clashing merrily with the rural-chic stencilling. The proximity and opportunity to fish from the River Tyne explains why the restaurant fish is so good and fresh. The kitchen draws on many top-notch local ingredients for its daily-changing menu. This may include succulent Northumbrian lamb, rich Kielder venison and tasty locally made pork and leek sausages. A selection of local cheeses is an alternative to more fancy puds such as white chocolate panna cotta. For a less formal experience, you can eat in the bar, where the menu consists of sandwiches, jacket potatoes and steaks, or there's an extremely good-value set menu that expands the choice to include slow-cooked lamb on root mash with wine gravy, Cajun-spiced sea bass or a simply cooked fillet steak with chips. Puddings are just as good, with garden-fresh rhubarb crumble or local Northumbrian cheeses completing the picture.

Rooms: 26. Double room from £78, single from £44.
Prices: Set lunch £11.95, set dinner £18.90. House wine £9.40.
Last orders: Food: lunch 14.30; dinner 21.30.
Closed: Rarely.
Food: Traditional English.
Other points: No-smoking area. Children welcome. Garden. Car park. Indoor swimming pool. Licence for Civil Weddings. Dogs welcome overnight.
Directions: From the A69 take the B6320 to Bellingham. After the bridge in Bellingham, turn left. The hotel is 150 yards on the left. (Map 12, B5)

Langley-on-Tyne

Langley Castle Hotel

Langley-on-Tyne, Hexham, Northumberland NE47 5LU
Telephone: +44(0)870 4016355
+44(0)1434 688888
manager@langleycastle.com
www.langleycastle.com

This handsome medieval fortified castle built in 1350 is a fairytale place to stay. Castellated towers, mullioned windows and seven-foot-thick stone walls, coupled with tasteful makeover, make it easy to step back in time. Bedrooms have been lavishly decorated and each has a canopied or four-poster bed, and a luxurious bathroom with swathes of cloth framing the baths. You can't fail but be won over by the romance of it all, especially as the medieval feel has been captured in the huge public rooms and in the Josephine restaurant. There can be few more evocative settings for a meal. The exposed stone and arched doorways provide the ideal setting for Andrew Smith's classic Anglo-French cooking. The set-price menus use locally and regionally sourced raw ingredients, and are complemented by a separate menu offering dishes at a supplement. From the main menu there could be ham hock and vegetable terrine with homemade apricot-scented pease pudding, loin of Langley lamb rolled with a venison and rosemary farce and served with port wine jus and parisienne of vegetables, and a tangy lemon cream tart with orange and lemon syrup and a lime sorbet for dessert. The wine list is well annotated with a good choice both inside and outside France.

Rooms: 18. Double rooms from £115, single from £99.50.
Family room supplement £20.
Prices: Set lunch £18.50. Set dinner £29.50. Restaurant main course from £12.50. Bar main course from £7.50.
House wine £12.75.
Last orders: Food: lunch 14.00; dinner 21.00.
Closed: Rarely.
Food: Modern British.
Other points: No-smoking area. Children welcome. Garden. Car park. Licence for Civil Weddings.
Directions: M6. Situated between Newcastle and Carlisle, two miles south on the A686 from Haydon Bridge. (Map 12, C5)

Longframlington

The Anglers Arms

Weldon Bridge, Longframlington, Morpeth, Northumberland NE65 8AX
Telephone: +44(0)870 4016135
+44(0)1665 570271
johnyoung@anglersarms.fsnet.co.uk
www.anglersarms.com

This grand 18th century coaching inn is set beside an old stone bridge over the River Coquet just off the A697 north of Morpeth. With a mile of private fishing, wonderful walking in the Cheviot Hills, which rise up behind the inn, and Northumberland's famous coast and castles just a short drive away, the Anglers provides the perfect base from which to explore this unspoilt area. Traditionally furnished bar and lounges are spacious and immaculately maintained, with log fires, plenty of wood panelling, fine old pictures and polished ornaments setting the appealing scene for supping pints of ale and enjoying the popular bar food. Food is well sourced from quality suppliers, with meats from local butchers and fish from the North Sea coast. From the traditional bar menu, start with pork and chicken liver paté with Cumberland sauce, or tomato and feta salad, then move on to grilled local trout, Border lamb cutlets on root mash with mint and rosemary sauce, or homemade steak and ale pie. More formal dining is in a refurbished Pullman railway carriage, where you can sample smoked breast of guinea fowl with pesto sauce or lemon sole stuffed with spinach and prawns. En suite rooms have brass or pine beds and peaceful rural views.

Rooms: 5. Double room from £60, single from £40, family from £90.
Prices: Restaurant main course from £14.95. Bar main course from £7.95. Set menu on request. House wine £12.50.
Last orders: Bar: lunch 14.00 (Sunday 14.30); dinner 21.30 (Sunday 21.00). Food: lunch 14.30; dinner 21.30.
Closed: Rarely.
Food: Traditional British.
Other points: No-smoking area. Dogs welcome in accommodation rooms. Children welcome. Garden. Car park. Licenced for Civil Weddings.
Directions: From the A1 take the A697 to Wollder & Coldstream, carry on to Weldon Bridge and follow signposts. (Map 12, B5)

Affordable good value

Otterburn

Otterburn Tower

Otterburn, Northumberland NE19 1NS
Telephone: +44(0)870 4016445
+44(0)1830 520620
reservations@otterburntower.com
www.otterburntower.com

Close to the Scottish Border, Otterburn Tower has seen many turbulent times, not least when it was beseiged following the Battle of Otterburn in 1388. This remote part of Northumberland is as rich in history as it is in fine food products, which are used to great effect in the Tower's menu. Set in extensive grounds, the historic Tower has a fantastic atmosphere inside and out. Thick walls, large fireplaces and oak panelling provide cosy protection from the outside world. The bedrooms are also comfortably appointed and have many period features. Among the most distinctive is The Library Room with a fireplace with log fire and four-poster bed. The food should also be singled out for a distinction. The farm and Tower kitchen garden provide the vegetables and herbs, while local ingredients from River Rede wild trout to Doddington luxury ice creams make for an exquisite dinner, whether that's the good value Fireside set menu or the carte. The tender and succulent pan-fried calf's liver with a creamy mash, caramelised silverskin onions and crispy bacon is excellent. And there is much else besides to tempt from local game, lamb and pork to Northumbrian cheese such Elsdon goats' cheese. Even the mineral water comes from the Tower's own well. After dinner, head to the small and elegant cosy bar or retire to the Drawing Room with its magnificent marble fireplace.

Rooms: 18. Double room from £120, single from £75. Children £30 each.
Prices: Set dinner £25. Restaurant main course from £14.50. Bar snack from £6. House wine £12.50.
Last orders: Food: 21.00.
Closed: Never.
Food: Modern British with Northumbrian values.
Other points: No-smoking area. Dogs welcome. Garden. Children welcome. Car park. License for Civil Weddings.
Directions: A1, Newcastle airport exit. Take the A696 until you reach Otterburn. (Map 12, B5)

Warkworth

Jackdaw Restaurant

34 Castle Street, Warkworth,
Northumberland NE65 0UN
Telephone: +44(0)870 4016409
+44(0)1665 711488

This family-run restaurant-cum-craft shop serves this picturesque Northumbrian village exceedingly well throughout the day with hearty lunches, cream teas and more sophisticated evening meals. It's a small operation run in a relaxed manner by husband and wife team Rupert and Gillian Bell: she cooks, he runs front-of-house. Set in a semi-detached stone picturesque house which dates from 1717, it's on a steep hill that leads to the castle. A cosy, cared for setting is created by the polished antique tables and a roaring fire in colder months. The menu blends traditional British styles with a modern twist. The couple use good local ingredients to good effect, such as meat from butcher, R Turnbull, who buys from local farms. Lunchtime mains have a satisfyingly traditional flavour too, say, sausages with colcannon and rich onion gravy. In the evening, the dishes are more adventurous, such as braised beef olives with black pudding, button onions and mushrooms. Starters take in smoked Tweed salmon, or fresh asparagus with hollandaise sauce, with puddings of brown sugar meringues with raspberry purée, and rhubarb crème brûlée or a selection of local cheese. The wine list is short but thoughtful and covers the old and new worlds. Altenatively, come for afternoon tea when you can tuck into homemade scones, fresh lemon sponge, or ham or cheese sandwiches.

Prices: Sunday set lunch £12.95. Main course from £8.95. House wine £10.75 and £12.75.
Last orders: Food: lunch 14.00; dinner 21.00.
Closed: Sunday and Thursday evening, all day Monday and January to mid February.
Food: Traditional English.
Other points: Totally no smoking. Children welcome.
Directions: 7 miles south of Alnwick on the A1068 coast road. (Map 12, B6)

www.routiers.co.uk

Langar

Langar Hall

Langar, Nottingham, Nottinghamshire NG13 9HG
Telephone: +44(0)870 4016466
+44(0)1949 860559
imogen@langarhall.co.uk
www.langarhall.com

Thanks to the efforts of Imogen Skirving, this 170-year-old house retains its classical English country charm but with a twist. The house is full of antiques and artefacts but conveys a relaxed, family feel: next to large ancestral paintings you'll find a table of local honey for sale. Public rooms have a lived-in style, full of books, comfortable sofas, open fires and fantastic country views. Bedrooms in the main house vary in size, but come with all extras such as big towels, and dressing gowns. Courtyard rooms, known as the Church Wing, are more up-to-date, but match the main house in their appeal. The restaurant is set in what was an inner hall. Its bottle-green marble pillars, huge fireplace topped with a large antique mirror and silver candelabra make it a grand setting, and the tables have nice touches such as fine crystal and fresh flowers. The food reflects the house and its situation. Chef Toby Garratt's cooking is unpretentious, strictly seasonal with the emphasis on local quality ingredients reared or grown within 50 miles of Langar. On the menus, you'll find home-reared lamb, Stilton whey-fed pork, game, local meat, fish from Brixham, and langoustines from Scotland. No less than three Stiltons grace the cheeseboard, Colston Bassett, Long Clawson and Cropwell Bishop, alongside with some French classics. The wine list is particularly good value.

Rooms: 11. Double room from £130, single from £65.
Prices: Set lunch from £15 and dinner from £35.
Last orders: Food: lunch 14.30; dinner 21.30.
Closed: Rarely.
Food: English.
Other points: No-smoking area. Children welcome.
Dogs welcome overnight by prior arrangment. Car park.
Licence for Civil Weddings. Garden.
Directions: 15 miles from Nottingham on the A52. (Map 9, C4)

Nottingham

World Service

Newdigate House, Castle Gate, Nottingham,
Nottinghamshire NG1 6AE
Telephone: +44(0)870 4016279
+44(0)115 847 5587
enquiries@worldservicerestaurant.com
www.worldservicerestaurant.com

Newdigate House, the 17th century Georgian building that houses World Service, is fairly hidden and a real find. It's tucked away down a narrow lane that leads up to the castle. The elegant exterior is matched by a contemporary elegance inside. And looks can be deceptive, as behind a high boundary wall is a delightful private courtyard, oriental-style garden and a pleasant south-facing terrace. The Marshall Room is a modern addition to the building and this cosy, panelled bar with a lighter section overlooking the garden is a relaxing place to enjoy a pre-dinner cocktail. The dining area is raised and has a chic-oriental look. Walls are lined with rectangular-framed mirrors, horizontal panels of oriental patterned fabrics hang down from the ceiling and pan-Asian artefacts add to the chilled vibe. As its name suggests, food is international-fusion without being fussy – but you can also enjoy more simply made dishes such as sea bass or lamb shank. The flavours are vibrant, especially through the use of colourful relishes and accompaniments such as orange salad and beetroot caper salsa with fillet of halibut and spiced rice. If you're looking for good value, come for lunch, as the short set menu is excellent. Start with chicken liver parfait with spiced apricot, followed by pan-fried salmon with Mediterranean vegetables and couscous and chocolate patterned pudding with pistachio ice cream. This restaurant is popular with locals, especially for business lunches and special occasions, and the evening carte menu offers equally exquisite choices.

Prices: Set lunch £14. House wine £10.90.
Last orders: Food: lunch 14.15 (Sunday 15.00); dinner 22.00
(Sunday 21.00).
Closed: 1-8 January.
Food: Modern European.
Other points: No-smoking area. Children welcome.
Directions: Park at the top of the town in the NCP car park.
Turn right up the side of Broad Marsh shopping centre. Continue up Castle Gate and cross the main road. World Service is in the first large house on the right hand side. (Map 9, C3)

An alternative Britain

Belvoir Castle game
at Langar Hall

Nottingham

A52

LES ROUTIERS

Langar Hall, Langar,
Lamb and stilton whey
fed pork from the park

Cropwell Bishop and Colston
Bassett Dairies, Stilton

Blackberry Farm,
near Langar, Beef
and chicken

Long Clawson Dairy,
Blue stilton

A606

A46

Melton Mowbray

Chef-consultant Toby Garratt is luckier than most in sourcing game, as his vegetable gardener is also his game agent. During the season, Bill doubles as a ferret man working with gamekeepers on the Duke of Rutland's Belvoir Estate, which is just six miles away. This means Toby gets a good choice from the shoots. The speciality at Langar Hall is partridge, and they get the French red-legged variety from Belvoir when they're in season from around mid-September. Langar Hall's head chef Gary Booth cooks it simply: roasted with bacon, foie gras and with a Madeira or port wine sauce. Also available from the Belvoir are pheasants, rabbits and hares, and woodcocks around November. All Langar Hall's meat is local. In fact, it keeps its own lamb which graze on the grass at the front of the hall. Beef, stilton whey-fed pork and free-range chicken are also on the menu.

A1

A52

Grantham

A607

Belvoir Castle, Rabbit, pigeon, partridge, pheasant and pike

A1

GAME PIE
Venison, Pheasant, Rabbit, Pigeon
Min Meat 40%

£5.50

KING'S ENGLISH PORK PIES Since 1853

Cookoo Farm, near Stamford, Ducks and guinea fowl

Tuxford

Mussel and Crab

Sibthorpe Hill, Tuxford, Newark,
Nottinghamshire NG22 0PJ
Telephone: +44(0)870 4016138
+44(0)1777 870491
musselandcrab1@hotmail.com
www.musselandcrab.com

If you've a hankering for fish then this restaurant, just a short drive from the A1, is the place to indulge a passion for all things piscine. Supplementing a basic menu are no less than 22 blackboards full of specials, mainly fish and shellfish, plus meat and game options. The braised lamb shank comes highly recommended. Stars among the starters are simply prepared oysters, crab bisque and top-of-the-range Beluga caviar, but check the latter's price tag before diving in, or stick with the more sensibly priced Avruga. Bruce Elliot-Bateman and chef Philip net the freshest fish, whether native or exotic, with much of it delivered daily from Brixham, in Devon. Marinated swordfish, Cromer crab and Witch (Torbay sole), steamed mussels and Indonesian escolar give just a small flavour of what's on offer. The good quality food draws the crowds, but knowlegeable staff manage the service efficiently. As well as the wide food choice, there are various eating areas to choose from. The two distinct restaurant areas are a traditional oak-beamed dining room and a terracotta and ochre painted Mediterranean themed room. There are also several bar areas. Wines are displayed on boards, and if you want a soft drink don't miss out on a glass of the popular homemade lemonade, which comes highly recommended.

Prices: Main course from £11. House wine £10.25.
Last orders: Bar: lunch 14.30 (Sunday 14.45); dinner 22.00 (Sunday 21.30). Food: lunch 14.30 (Sunday 14.45); dinner 22.00 (Sunday 21.00).
Closed: Rarely.
Food: Modern British.
Other points: No-smoking area. Dogs welcome in the bar. Garden. Car park.
Directions: From junction A57/A1 (Markham Moor), take B1164 to Ollerton/Tuxford; pub 800 yards on right. (Map 9, B4)

Oxford

Cotswold Lodge Hotel

66A Banbury Road, Oxford OX2 6JP
Telephone: +44(0)870 4016451
+44(0)1865 512121
info@cotswoldlodgehotel.co.uk
www.cotswoldlodgehotel.co.uk

The hotel setting, a few minutes drive from the town centre on the way to the well-heeled North Oxford corridor, offers the best of both worlds: accessibility to Oxford city centre and the tranquillity that's more akin to a country hotel. Step into the entrance hall with the elegant drawing room to the left and the clubby bar to the right, and you immediately know this is not your average anonymous business traveller stopover. Much attention has been paid to the detail. The comfortable bedrooms come in many shapes and sizes, so there's something for every visitor in style and price bracket. If you want to splash out, the richly coloured Merton suite right under the eaves (one of 10 highly individual suites) is recommended. Cheaper, but very desirable alternatives are the light but cosy rooms overlooking the suntrap of a courtyard, and they come with balconies on the upper floor. The restaurant serves a broadly based classic French-British set-price menu, complemented by a more extensive carte. Fresh ingredients are part of the appeal of dishes such as warm chicken liver salad with herb oil and balsamic vinegar, and mignons of beef with a red wine and shallot sauce. An excellent choice of French wines and champagne is supplemented with a new world selection.

Rooms: 49. Double room from £175, single from £125.
Prices: Restaurant main course from £9.50. House wine £17.50.
Last orders: Food: lunch 14.30; dinner 22.00.
Closed: Rarely.
Food: Modern British.
Other points: No-smoking area. Children welcome. Car park.
Directions: Half a mile north of the city centre. (Map 5, B3)

www.routiers.co.uk

Witney

The Fleece

11 Church Green, Witney, Oxfordshire OX28 4AZ
Telephone: +44(0)870 4016151
+44(0)1993 892270
fleece@peachpubs.com
www.peachpubs.com

The Peach Pub Company run by Victoria Moon and Lee Cash has grown from one pub to three. Immediately after buying the One Elm in Stratford-upon-Avon, they acquired the lease on the Fleece, a stylish 10-bedroomed inn overlooking the church green in upmarket Witney. The bedrooms have all been revamped in warm, vibrant colours and come with funky mirrors, fabrics and furnishing and useful extras such as hairdryers. Smart, modern refurbishment has also been carried out in the bar and dining areas. The Peach Pub Company trademark leather sofas around low tables, individual mirrors and modern artwork on warm, earthy coloured walls creates a laid-back atmosphere. And a continental-style opening time of 8am for coffee and breakfast sandwiches appears to have found favour among Witney residents. Equally popular is the all-day sandwich, salad and deli-board menu, the latter offering starters or nibbles with drinks of charcuterie, cheese, fish and unusual antipasti. Modern main menu dishes range from sausage of the week with mash and red onion marmalade to whole sea bass with tarragon and lemon crushed new potatoes, and 35-day dry-aged rump steak served with béarnaise sauce.

Rooms: 10. Double/twin from £75, single from £65 and family from £85.
Prices: Restaurant main course from £7.50.
Bar main course from £1.35. House wine £10.50.
Last orders: Bar: 23.00.
Closed: Rarely
Food: Modern European.
Other points: Dogs welcome. Garden. Children welcome. Car park.
Directions: In the town-centre. Witney is just off the A40 Oxford to Cheltenham road. (Map 5, B3)

Witney

Greens Restaurant

Witney Lakes Resort, Downs Road, Witney,
Oxfordshire OX29 0SY
Telephone: +44(0)870 4016469
+44(0)1993 893012
resort@witney-lakes.co.uk
www.witney-lakes.co.uk

To find Greens Restaurant follow signs to the Witney Lakes Resort on the western edge of the town. This combines an 18-hole golf course and a Scandinavian chalet-style building, which houses a private health club and business conference centre and restaurant. The latter comes with a peaceful lakeside setting with views across neat fairways to the 18th hole. Light and airy with a central bar area and a splendid summer dining terrace, it offers good quality brasserie-style cooking. Sean Parker is passionate about local produce, sourcing all meats, free-range eggs and soft fruits from local farms as well as using quality small suppliers associated with the Oxfordshire Food Group. Commendably, everything is freshly made on the premises, including bread made from flour milled at nearby Shipton. The menu has an international flavour. Start with roast asparagus and Parma ham on bruschetta, tomato confit, red pepper and sweet soy dressing, and follow with Oxfordshire loin of pork saltimbocca with celeriac mash and sticky Madeira and sage jus. Other dishes might include pan-fried fillet of red mullet or teriyaki marinated Oxfordshire ribeye steak. And there's much to tempt on the puddings menu too: bitter chocolate tart, chocolate ice cream and strawberry compote or there is a selection of handmade British farmhouse cheeses.

Prices: Restaurant main course from £9.50.
Bar main course from £6. House wine £10.95.
Last orders: Food: lunch 15.00; dinner 22.00.
Closed: Saturday lunch, Sunday evening.
Food: Modern British.
Other points: Totally no smoking. Garden and Terrace. Children welcome. Car park. Private dining. Golf course. Business centre.
Directions: Exit9/M40. From Oxford A40 take the second turning for Witney and turn right at the roundabout following the signs to Witney Lakes Resort. From Cheltenham or Burford take the A40 follow the signs to Oxford and then as above. (Map 5, B3)

Individual charm and warmth

Oakham

The Old Plough

2 Church Street, Braunston, Oakham, Rutland LE5 7DH
Telephone: +44(0)870 4016395
+44 (0)1572 722714
info@theoldplough.co.uk
www.theoldplough.co.uk

Majoring in good home-cooked food and offering some superb ales, this welcoming inn is perfect for lunch or dinner. The extensive menu runs to bar meals, grills, table d'hote, carte and chefs specials, all of which are very well priced. Just as extensive is the choice of areas to dine. Depending on your mood and the weather, there's the bar with an open fire, the light and airy conservatory, or the garden patio. At lunch and on certain evenings, there's a good value plat du jour set menu, offering either two or three courses. Start with soup or pâté and move on to lamb's liver and mash, steak and ale pie or vegetable kebab. The chef's specials such as Barnsley lamb chop or salmon fillet also hit the spot, as do the selection of steaks and other meats from the grill. The wine list maybe short but offers some popular brands from around the world, and well-priced bottles from Chile and Australia. If you like beers, you've come to the right place, as they offer excellent ales from The Grainstore Brewery. You're also guaranteed a warm welcome from proprietors Claire and David Cox, who also ensure everything runs like clockwork.

Rooms: 5.
Prices: Set lunch £13.95 and dinner £14.95.
Restaurant main course £7.95-£16. Bar main course £4.95-£6.50.
Last orders: Bar: 23.00. Food: 21.30.
Closed: Never.
Food: Traditional English.
Other points: No-smoking area. Children welcome.
Dogs welcome. Garden. Car park.
Directions: From Oakham High Street, go over level crossing and bear left. Take 2nd left towards Braunston driving for 2 miles. (Map 9, C4)

Clungunford

Bird on the Rock Tearoom

Abcott, Clungunford, Shropshire SY7 OPX
Telephone: +44(0)870 4016401
+44(0)1588 660631
www.birdontherock.com

Taking tea, and there are 50 to choose from, at this classic tearoom is quite an occasion. You feel as if you're stepping back in time. Set in a 17th century magpie-timbered country cottage, the café-tearooms are run by a couple of enthusiasts who've brought their design and stage skills to an ever-growing, appreciative clientele. Started over five years ago, Douglas and Annabel Hawkes came from the movie industry; Annabel was couturier to Madonna's Evita. Everything is in period, from Douglas's black and white waiter's uniform with ankle-length apron to the Spode-Italian designed china and the cotton doilies that cover the sugar. Soft background music is from the 1930s. Bread, cakes, herb scones, and the like, are from Mrs Beeton's original recipes and they are perfect; the Victoria sponge is a must. From the Gamekeeper's lunch with cheese and homemade chutney, progress to Classic Cream Tea, or Poirot's Sleuths Tea, with The Complete Jeeves served on a silver cake stand (advance booking only) as a special treat. All produce is sourced from the best suppliers. There's single herd cream from a Herefordshire farm, for instance, organic smoked salmon and their own smoked tea, which is accredited by the Tea Council, from a smokery in nearby Clunbury.

Prices: Lunch from £5.25. Afternoon tea from £5.25.
Seasonal variation.
Last orders: Food: 17.30 (Winter 16.30).
Closed: Monday and Tuesday. Check for seasonal variations.
Food: Specialises in Teas. Traditional English.
Other points: Totally no smoking. Children welcome. Garden.
Car park.
Directions: Eight miles north west of Ludlow on the B4367 to Knighton. (Map 8, C5)

Regional produce

Ludlow

The Clive Restaurant with Rooms

Bromfield, Ludlow, Shropshire SY8 2JR
Telephone: +44(0)870 4016398
+44(0)1584 856565
info@theclive.co.uk
www.theclive.co.uk

In a former life, The Clive was a farmhouse. It's named after Clive of India, who once lived here. The building dates from the 17th century and the façade is classic Georgian, but inside it's a mixture of modern and traditional designs. The Lounge Bar, where Clive's original coat of arms hangs, is a hugely atmospheric beamed room, and is approached via a modern bar serving local ales such as Hobsons Bitter and Town Crier, and wines by the glass. Next door, the simply designed Café Bar provides informal lunches of say chargrilled vegetables with couscous and pesto, followed by fillet of Cornish ling with a basil and sun-dried tomato crust with salad and new potatoes, which make for a keenly priced set two-course meal at lunch or dinner. More sophisticated, and pricier, cooking in the restaurant next door delivers more modern and ambitious British dishes along the lines of scallops wrapped in bacon with mixed salad and a lemon dressing, and roast fillet of Shropshire beef or noisette of Shropshire lamb served with coq d'or potatoes. The wine list offers a wide selection at good prices. The en suite bedrooms are particularly light, airy and modern and are excellently appointed. They come with TV, internet point, tea-making facilities and hairdryers.

Rooms: 15. Double room from £60, single from £40.
Prices: Set lunch £15.45. Restaurant main course from £12.95.
Cafe/bar main course from £7.95. House wine from £10.75.
Last orders: Bar: 23.00. Food: lunch 15.00; dinner 22.00
(Sunday 21.00).
Closed: Rarely.
Food: Modern British.
Other points: No smoking area. Children welcome. Garden.
Car park.
Directions: Two miles north of Ludlow on the A49. (Map 8, C5)

Ludlow

De Greys

5-6 Broad Street, Ludlow, Shropshire SY8 1NG
Telephone: +44(0)870 4016399
+44(0)1584 872764
degreys@btopenworld.com
www.degreys.co.uk

The classic black and white timbered building in the centre of town is a fitting setting for this classic tearoom, a Ludlow landmark. Staff look the part dressed in their their neat black and white outfits with frilly aprons. French chef Jean Bourdeau is now in charge of the tearoom/restaurant, which is behind the small bakery-cake shop. It's a striking room, heavy with beams and timbers, some lovely stained-glass windows, and is traditionally styled with red carpets and matching tablecloths and curtains. De Greys is open all day serving tearoom traditionals such as hearty breakfasts that include quality local bacon and pork sausages and good cafétière coffee, Welsh rarebit, toasted teacakes, pastries and afternoon teas. By 10am the place is bustling with mid-morning shoppers. In addition, there is a printed menu that takes popular dishes and gives them a twist, such as duo of fresh duck and goose breast with a sweet and sour orange sauce and confit of celeriac or fillet of sea bass with baby vegetables and a white wine sauce. In the evenings, the dinner menu includes even more delectable dishes with mains of fillet of Herefordshire beef wellington and chargrilled lobster with a langoustine bisque. Complementing this exquisite food is a well-annotated wine list that's a keenly priced global selection. At weekends, they often have a pianist tinkling away, which adds to the atmosphere.

Prices: Set dinner £15.95-£20. Main course from £8.95.
Lunch main course from £5.95. House wine £8.50.
Last orders: Food: lunch 17.00 (Friday and Saturday 17.30);
dinner 21.00.
Closed: Monday-Thursday and Sunday evening.
Food: Modern British and Traditional French.
Other points: No-smoking area. Garden. Children welcome.
Bakery shop.
Directions: Take the A49 to Ludlow. De Greys is found in the centre of Ludlow, just below the Buttercross clock tower.
(Map 8, D5)

www.routiers.co.uk

Ludlow

The Feathers Hotel

Bull Ring, Ludlow, Shropshire SY8 1AA
Telephone: +44(0)870 4016400
+44(0)1584 875261
feathers.ludlow@btconnect.com
www.feathersatludlow.co.uk

It's one of Ludlow's best known and most photo-graphed buildings and has won much acclaim for its striking looks. This stunning 17th century black and white landmark has been described as 'that prodigy of timber-framed houses and the most handsome inn in the world' by the *New York Times*. Under new owner-ship, it has shaken off its former corporate image. The public rooms have become more welcoming and the 40 bedrooms come with more creature comforts. Rooms are divided into standard and four-poster rooms plus there's a luxury four-poster suite. Improvements have also been made in the kitchen. The chef uses ingredi-ents that are sourced locally such as rare-breed beef. Dishes are best categorised as modern-traditional, and include pan-roast Clun Valley lamb with petit rata-touille, minted new potatoes, garlic confit and red wine sauce, and peppered Gressingham duck served with spiced Puy lentils, celeriac fondant, roast pickled pear and walnut jus. The sensibly short dinner menu can be two or three courses and may include delights such as pan-fried wild turbot with horseradish gnocchi, pur-ple sprouting broccoli and béarnaise sauce, followed by Valrhona chocolate fondant, almond milk ice and chilled Irish coffee. An astute selection of wines offers good drinking from around the world.

Rooms: 40. Double room from £90, single from £70, luxury from £140.
Prices: Set lunch £16.50 and dinner £27.50. Main course from £12. House wine £12.
Last orders: Food: lunch 14.30; dinner 21.30 (Friday and Saturday 22.00).
Closed: Rarely.
Food: Modern British.
Other points: No-smoking area. Children welcome. Dogs welcome overnight. Car park. Licence for Civil Weddings.
Directions: From Hereford take the A49 towards Leominster and on to Ludlow. (Map 8, D5)

Highbridge

Battleborough Grange Country Hotel

Bristol Road, Brent Knoll, Highbridge, Somerset TA9 4HJ
Telephone: +44(0)870 4016306
+44(0)1278 760208
info@battleboroughgrangehotel.co.uk
www.battleboroughgrangehotel.co.uk

The owners have made quite an impact with the Battleborough Grange Hotel and the facilities here are in great demand. It is certainly a marvellous place for relaxing holidays, conferences, wedding ceremonies and receptions, lunch and evening meals, and caterng for special occasions. The beautiful countryside around is steeped in ancient history. On one side, Brent Knoll, an Iron-Age fort, towers in the background, and on the other, there are clear views over the Somerset Levels to Glastonbury Tor in the distance. Set in attractive landscaped gardens, the former farmhouse has been sympathetically extended and brought up to date over the years. There are 14 prettily decorated bedrooms, some with four posters and spa baths, and with gleam-ing and luxurious modern bathrooms. The lively bar and a conservatory restaurant are a focal point in the evenings. The menu offers hearty traditional country cooking that relies on local lines of supply. Start with avocado and crab salad or eggs Benedict, before mov-ing on to mains of duck with an orange and Grand Marnier sauce, or beef medallions with a mushroom, onion and red wine sauce. The global wine list is sensi-bly priced. Its attractive location makes Battleborough Grange not only popular for weddings, but the loca-tion, just one mile from the M5, is certainly handy for those looking to break their journey, either for a meal or overnight. More rooms will be available in 2005.

Rooms: 15. Double room from £72, single from £57. Honeymoon suite available.
Prices: Set menu £18. House wine from £9.95.
Last orders: Bar: 23.30. Food: 21.00.
Closed: 25th December evening - 2nd January.
Food: Modern British.
Other points: No-smoking area. Children welcome. Garden. Car park. Licence for Civil Weddings.
Directions: Exit 22/M5, turn right at the roundabout towards Weston-super-Mare, A38. Hotel is one mile on the left of the A38 just past Sanders Garden World (on the right). (Map 4, C6)

Down-to-earth, friendly service

Langport

Brown and Forrest
Smokery Restaurant

Bowden Farms, Hambridge, Langport, Somerset TA10 0BP
Telephone: +44(0)870 4016366
+44(0)1458 250875
brownforrest@btinternet.com
www.smokedeel.co.uk

It may be a small family business but it's big on experience when it comes to smoking fish and meat. Michael Brown started his smokery in a converted cider barn in the early 1980s after learning how to smoke eels in Germany, and he has combined selling fine smoked products with serving them in his fairly spacious café. As this is a small smokery, producing low volumes, more time and effort are spent on the smoking process. Salmon, for example, is hung in the traditional way and oak-smoked for 16 to 18 hours, eels are hot-smoked over beech and applewood to give a strong smokey flavour. And if you simply can't wait until you get home to try the wares, then head for the neat café, with its red-chequered tablecloths. Start with smoked eel on rye, then order a plate of smoked chicken salad and new potatoes with homemade chutney, and finish with smoked Cheddar, or golden syrup bread and butter pudding, and you will come to the conclusion that Brown and Forrest is one of those great little finds. This is the kind of place where the friendly owner and staff, not to mention the food, will have you detouring back for more. It is worth noting that staff are happy to give interested visitors a brief tour of the smokery to explain the smoking process. And if you can't get there, you can order their products online.

Prices: Set lunch £13.50. Main course from £6.75. House wine £9.
Last orders: Food: 16.00.
Closed: Sunday, Bank Holidays.
Food: Modern British.
Other points: Totally no smoking. Children welcome. Car park.
Directions: Exit25/M5. From Taunton follow signs for Langport. At the Bell Inn in Curry Rivel, turn right and follow the signposts to Hambridge and Ilminster. After one and a half miles see Smokery sign on the left. (Map 4, C6)

Montacute

The Kings Arms Inn

Montacute, Somerset TA15 6UU
Telephone: +44(0)870 4016159
+44(0)1935 822513
kingsarmsinn@realemail.co.uk
www.greenekinginns.co.uk

This 17th century hamstone inn is located in an excellent spot, opposite the church and the National Trust's Montacute House in a very picturesque and unspoilt village. It was once an ale house owned by the abbey, and later it became a coaching inn on the Plymouth-London route, where horses were changed before the gruelling climb up Ham Hill. Today's comfortable inn offers characterful accommodation in 15 en suite bedrooms, all of which are spacious and well equipped; some have comfortable four-poster beds. Downstairs, the Windsor Room is a relaxing lounge, but it's the Pickwick Bar that remains the centre of village life. Here, Greene King ales are served, alongside popular bar meals that range from homecooked ham sandwiches to steak and kidney pie with shortcrust pastry. The daily-changing set-price menu and evening carte is served in the Cottage Restaurant. Start, perhaps, with smoked duck and mango salad or roasted red pepper soup topped with a fresh crab cake, then move onto a salmon, prawn and clam pot, guinea fowl or fillet of beef Rossini. Follow a relaxing night with a decent breakfast and a walk on the National Trust's wooded St Michael's Hill behind the inn.

Rooms: 15. Double room from £80, single room £65.
Prices: Set lunch from £12.95 and dinner from £21.95.
Main course from £11.95. Main course bar meal from £7.95.
House wine from £9.95.
Last orders: Bar: 23.00. Food: lunch 14.30; dinner 21.00.
Closed: Rarely.
Food: Modern British.
Other points: No-smoking area. Children welcome.
Dogs welcome overnight. Garden. Car park.
Directions: Take A3088 at Cartgate roundabout on A303, signed Montacute House. Exit 25/M5. (Map 4, C6)

Shepton Mallet

Bowlish House

Wells Road, Shepton Mallet, Somerset BA4 5JD
Telephone: +44(0)870 4016160
+44(0)1749 342022
enquiries@bowlishhouse.com
www.bowlishhouse.com

This stunning mid 17th century Palladian fronted house has been sympathically and thoughtfully updated by Jason Goy and Darren Carter who took over in 2000. They are continuing the tradition of running Bowlish House as a restaurant with rooms. And there is much to admire; the ceilings are high, wood panelling is a big feature, and there's a stained glass window halfway up the stairs, all offset by soft lighting from picture lights above paintings supplied by the local art gallery. The intimate restaurant leads through to a large conservatory, which, in turn, overlooks the well-maintained walled garden. Lighting is soft, and tables are laid with white linen, candles and fresh flowers – a vast antique mirror on one wall reflects the scene. Darren Carter delivers a simple, short menu that could open with chicken liver and wild mushroom parfait accompanied by red onion marmalade and aged balsamic vinegar, or tiger prawns in a rich sun-dried tomato and soured cream dressing. Main courses bring a classic steak and Guinness pie, or baked fillet of salmon with wholegrain mustard and cream sauce, and there could be chocolate tart with vanilla ice cream to finish. Bedrooms are spacious, enhanced by large windows, good beds, comfortable chairs, quality furniture, and thoughtful extras such as good quality lotions and potions.

Rooms: 3. Double room from £80, single occupancy £65.
Prices: Set dinner £29.95. House wine £12.50.
Last orders: Food: lunch 14.30; dinner 21.30 (Sunday 19.00)
Closed: Rarely.
Food: Modern British.
Other points: No-smoking area. Garden. Children welcome. Car park.
Directions: On the A371 Wells to Bath road. (Map 4, C7)

Wells

The Crown at Wells and Anton's Bistrot

Market Place, Wells, Somerset BA5 2RP
Telephone: +44(0)870 4016161
+44(0)1749 673457
eat@crownatwells.co.uk
www.crownatwells.co.uk

In 1695 Quaker William Penn, the founder of Philadelphia, preached to a crowded marketplace from an upper window of the historic Crown. It was built in 1450 and is within sight of the Gothic cathedral and Bishop's Palace. The traditional, pubby Penn Bar is very popular and serves good pub grub. This is complemented by Anton's, a contemporary wine-bar-meets-bistro, offering informal dining at lunch and dinner. Its dark-wood beams are offset by half pitch-pine walls hung with cartoons, which are originals by a well-known local cartoonist after whom the bistro is named. Anton's generously portioned dishes continue the contemporary theme with the likes of crab, prawn and salmon fishcakes with chilli and basil relish, followed, perhaps, by braised Moroccan-style lamb shank with couscous. Baked almond tart with praline ice cream or West Country cheeses make a good finish. A special and good value Les Routiers menu is available at lunchtimes and early evenings; the choice changes fortnightly. A 30-plus wine list offers 12 by the glass. Bedrooms are all en suite and are decorated in keeping with the old traditional inn. Some of the larger rooms at the front have four-poster beds.

Rooms: 15. Double room from £85, single from £50. Family room from £100.
Prices: Set lunch from £10.95. House wine £11.50.
Last orders: Bar: lunch 15.00; dinner 23.00. Food: lunch 14.30; dinner 21.30 (Sunday 21.00).
Closed: Never.
Food: Mediterranean.
Other points: No-smoking area. Children welcome. Dogs welcome overnight. Car park.
Directions: Centre of Wells, in the Market Place. Follow signs for hotels and deliveries to take you into the Market Place. (Map 4, C6)

Good food and wine

Leek

Number 64

64 St Edward Street, Leek, Staffordshire ST13 5DL
Telephone: +44(0)870 4016382
+44(0)1538 381900

Number 64 is an elegant Grade II listed Georgian town house set right in the centre of Leek. It was built in 1747 along clean, classic lines. Tasteful refurbishment of the interiors has achieved a transformation that sets apart your average hotel and restaurant. And it is quite a hive of activity. Incorporated into the building is a speciality food shop and patisserie selling breads baked on the premises, plus cakes, local cheeses and hand-finished chocolates. There is also a coffee lounge with an all-day menu, a vaulted, exposed-stone basement wine bar that's good for a simple snack and a glass of wine, a small, pretty restaurant and three well-appointed bedrooms. In the kitchen, they are committed to cooking with regional produce and delivering straightforward, modern British cooking. Lunch is a well put together selection of local and British ingredients, and includes stroganoff of Aberdeenshire beef and escalope of Cornish cod with a puy lentil and bacon ragoût. For a truly gastronomic experience, we recommend you try the evening Signature menu of four courses. This starts with tian of hot-roasted west coast salmon, then moves on to confied pavé of Devon lamb with a creamed leek, apple and baby spinach suet pudding. The chocolate delight 64 is just as its name suggests, deliciously delightful. Finish with coffee and a chocolate ballotin. The wine list opens with two pages of global house wines; prices, even at the finer end are reasonable, with bottles rarely going over £20.

Rooms: 3. From £65 per night.
Prices: Cooked breakfast £5. Sunday lunch from £15 (2 course). Main course lunch from £6.25. Main course dinner from £14.50. House wine £9.95.
Last orders: Food: snacks 17.00; lunch 15.00; dinner 21.00.
Closed: Sunday evening and all day Monday.
Food: Modern British.
Other points: Restaurant no-smoking. Children welcome. Garden. Street parking available.
Directions: In the centre of Leek. (Map 9, B2)

Stafford

The Swan Hotel

46-46a Greengate Street, Stafford, Staffordshire ST16 2JA
Telephone: +44(0)870 4016435
+44(0)1785 258142
info@theswanstafford.co.uk
www.theswanstafford.co.uk

The ancient Swan is steeped in history: Charles I slept here at the time of the Civil War and Charles Dickens recorded a miserable night during the inn's dip in fortune in late Victorian times. Total refurbishment has brought The Swan firmly back as a focal point in this pleasant county town. Public areas extend to a contemporary café filled with stylish wicker chairs and comfy soft sofas, a smart brasserie with marble-topped tables, and a bar looking out onto a rear courtyard with wooden tables and chairs. In addition, all 27 bedrooms have a comfortable, contemporary look and are decorated in soft colours, some with a soothing coffee and cream theme, and a mix of bath or shower rooms. Sizes vary and some rooms have original features, which were uncovered during renovations. Food in the brasserie uses good local and regional produce. An expansive menu offers starters of confit duck salad with peppered oranges and walnut vinaigrette, mains of seared sea bass with pak choi, artichoke crème fraîche and lemon oil, and with chocolate steamed pudding with chocolate sauce and caramel ice cream to finish. The wine list is impressively set out and categorised by flavour and offers a wide, evenly global selection at very reasonable prices.

Rooms: 27. Double/twin from £85.
Prices: Set lunch £8.95 (2 course). Restaurant main course from £7.95. Main course (coffee shop) from £4. House wine £9.85.
Last orders: Food: lunch 14.30; dinner 22.00 (Sunday 21.00).
Closed: Rarely.
Food: Modern British.
Other points: No-smoking area. Garden. Children welcome. Car park.
Directions: Exit 13 and 14/M6. Situated on the High Street in Stafford town centre. (Map 9, C2)

www.routiers.co.uk

Bungay

Earsham Street Café

11-13 Earsham Street, Bungay, Suffolk NR35 1AE
Telephone: +44(0)870 4016468
+44(0)1986 893103

Now in its fifth year, Rebecca Mackenzie and Stephen David's stylish café has expanded to become more fully fledged restaurant. Its deli section has moved to other premises along the same street, freeing up more dining space. Set in a bright yellow 17th century terrace, the three-storey restaurant has that unfussy, rustic-chic makeover that's in keeping with the age of the building. Much effort has been put into the menus. The lunchtime menu is extensive, offering inspired Mediterranean-style dishes such as fricasee of monkfish and shellfish, saffron, fennel and linguine to the more local, venison sausage with olive mash, honey roast parsnips and onion gravy. In the mornings and afternoons, life glides along with pots of tea, cakes and snacks. The restaurant also opens on the last Friday and Saturday of every month, offering a more sophisticated set menu. You could start with a crayfish cocktail with caviar, crème fraîche and chargrilled bread or chicken liver parfait with brioche toast and onion chutney, then move on to mains of tortellini with ricotta and walnuts, sautéed oyster mushrooms and sprouting broccoli or magret of duck with pan-fried foie gras, wilted spinach, dates and fondant potato. Puds are also a treat, from warm chocolate brownie with clotted cream to pear and frangipane tart with vanilla ice cream. The expanded wine list offers a good choice and good value, and 10 half bottles.

Prices: Restaurant main course from £7.95. Snack from £3. House wine £11.50.
Last orders: Food: lunch 14.00; dinner 21.00.
Closed: Sunday and evenings except for the last Friday and Saturday of every month.
Food: Modern British/Mediterranean.
Other points: Totally no smoking. Children welcome. Garden.
Directions: (Map 10, D7)

Cavendish

The George

The Green, Cavendish, Sudbury, Suffolk CO10 8BA
Telephone: +44(0)870 4016169
+44(0)1787 280248
reservations@georgecavendish.co.uk
www.georgecavendish.co.uk

Jonathan and Charlotte Nicholson saw the potential and had the vision to restore this 600-year-old timber-framed building that was down and out. Since they took it on in 2002, it has risen to great new heights, culinary and décor wise. It is now a smart and stylish pub-restaurant, replete with eye-catching mustard and green facade. Inside, everything has been stripped back, so that wood, exposed brick and standing timbers create a modern space offset by neutral colours. That this is a dining pub is obvious, tables laid up for eating fill every space, though don't be put off popping in for a drink as there's a small bar area for those just wanting a pint of Woodforde's Wherry or a glass of wine from a short, well-composed global wine list. Former Conran head chef Jonathan uses fresh local seasonal produce and his inventive daily menus include a keenly priced two or three course lunch menu and a carte that may deliver starters of six rock oysters on ice with shallot dressing and lemon or foie gras and goose roulade with grape chutney and brioche. For main course, there may be roast sea bass with asparagus and lemon and thyme velouté or risotto of wild mushrooms with black truffle and Gruyère. Charlotte has created five bright and airy, simple but stylish en suite bedrooms upstairs, all with charming village views.

Rooms: 5. From £37.50 per person.
Prices: Restaurant main course from £12.75.
Bar snack/light lunch from £4.95. House wine £10.25.
Last orders: Bar: 23.00. Food: lunch 15.00; dinner 22.00.
Closed: Sunday evening and all day Monday.
Food: Modern British
Other points: No-smoking area. Garden and terrace with heated canopies.
Directions: On A1092 between Haverhill and Long Melford. (Map 10, E6)

Affordable good value

Thornham Hall & Restaurant, Thornham Magna

Eye

The Fox and Goose Inn

Church Road, Fressingfield, Eye, Suffolk IP21 5PB
Telephone: +44(0)870 4016339
+44(0)1379 586247
foxandgoose@uk2.net
www.foxandgoose.net

Built first as a Guildhall around 1500, this magnificent timber-framed building is now home to The Fox and Goose. It backs on to the churchyard and faces the village pond. The dip in its fine culinary fortunes has been turned around by Paul Yaxley, a bold young chef. A comfortable lounge with new carpets and deep sofas replace the drab bar, and vibrant colours, modern works of art and an eclectic mix of dining tables have brightened up the two heavily beamed dining areas. It is still very much a restaurant, but with Adnams tapped from the barrel and excellent value light and set lunch menus, casual diners are made very welcome. Lunch on breast of partridge with artichoke purée, crushed new potatoes and a shallot jus or seafood gratin with spinach and Gruyère cheese to start, before mains of fillet of salmon with spinach risotto or calf's liver with celeriac and mushrooms. Dinner from the carte is equally upmarket and includes fillet of sea bream cooked in citrus fruit, with a chorizo and chervil risotto, followed by chicken breast stuffed with morel boudin, on rösti potato, oyster mushrooms and shallot purée. Finish with an exotic pineapple tarte Tatin with lemon grass ice cream and a pineapple crisp.

Prices: Set lunch £12.95. Restaurant main course from £10.95.
Bar main course from £6.50. House wine £11.95.
Last orders: Bar: lunch 14.00; Dinner 21.00 (Friday and Saturday 21.30, Sunday 20.30). Food: lunch 14.00; dinner 21.00.
Closed: Monday.
Food: Modern British with French influences.
Other points: No-smoking area.
Children welcome (over eight years old at dinner). Car park.
Directions: Take the A143 Diss to Bungay road; turn off to take the B1116 to Fressingfield, situated by the church. (Map 10, D7)

Thornham Magna

Thornham Hall & Restaurant

Thornham Magna, Eye, Suffolk IP23 8HA
Telephone: +44(0)870 4016340/6341
+44(0)1379 783314/788136
lhenniker@aol.com
www.thornhamhallandrestaurant.com

A traditional English country house has been given a welcome quirky twist by its current owner Lady Lesley Henniker-Major. The property has been in her family since the 1750s, and she has brought her own sense of individual style to the newer building that replaces the house that burnt down in the 1940s. All that remains of the original building is the clock tower. If you love gardens, you'll find much to admire in the magnificent parkland and formal and kitchen gardens plus you can enjoy walks in the ancient surrounding woodlands. The spacious restaurant is housed in the Old Coach House, which also has extensive outside space for dining. The menu focuses on traditional favourites such as whitebait with tartar sauce and roast pork and apple sauce, as well as more offbeat dishes ranging from ostrich steak with creamed leeks and toasted cashew nuts to kangeroo casserole with chick peas. Puddings such as stem ginger ice cream and toffee sauce and raspberry cheesecake will hit the sweet spot. The wine list has much to offer without breaking the budget and takes you on a well thought out tour of the new and old worlds.

Rooms: 3. Double room from £85, single from £55.
Prices include breakfast.
Prices: Set lunch £15. Restaurant main course from £10.
House wine £12.95.
Last orders: Food: lunch 14.00: dinner 21.30.
Closed: Rarely.
Food: Traditional and Modern British.
Other points: Totally no smoking in the bar. Dogs welcome overnight. Garden. Children welcome. Car park.
Licence for Civil Weddings.
Directions: Half way between Ipswich and Norwich. From the A140 turn left at Stoke Ash White Horse Pub. Turn right at Thornham Magna, past the church and turn in at Hall Drive. (Map 10, D7)

An alternative Britain

Ockley

Bryce's

The Old School House, Ockley, Dorking,
Surrey RH5 5TH
Telephone: +44(0)870 4016175
+44(0)1306 627430
bryces.fish@virgin.net
www.bryces.co.uk

Formerly a boy's boarding academy, Bill Bryce has truly made his mark in his eponymous pub-restaurant in the 13 years he has been here. The restaurant majors on fish, which is delivered fresh every day from London, and it's the mainstay on the printed menus and ever-changing blackboards. Add oysters, mussels and scallops from Loch Fyne and the Pure Oyster Company at nearby Faygate, and crab from Portland and the Old School House becomes a seafood lovers' paradise. You can eat in the beamed bar or in the more formal restaurant. Bill understands that simplicity in preparation and presentation ensures that delicate flavours are allowed to shine. In the bar, simpler fare includes seafood lasagne, fishcakes and deep-fried Cornish cod fillet. The main fish event, however, is reserved for the set-price lunch and dinner menus, where imaginative specials may include fillets of red mullet on steamed bok choi and spring onions with sweet sesame and lime dressing, or chargrilled loin of swordfish with sautéed forest mushrooms, lime and cardamom jus. The wine list includes a good show of 14 by the glass, although there's also 'Bryce's Special Cellar' if you want a classic vintage. Beer lovers can choose between Fuller's London Pride and Gale's Butser Bitter.

Prices: Set lunch £22 (two course) and dinner £27.50.
Bar main course from £7.50. House wine £12.50.
Last orders: Bar: lunch 15.00, dinner 23.00. Food: lunch 14.30;
dinner 21.30.
Closed: Closed Sunday evenings in November, January
and February.
Food: Seafood.
Other points: No-smoking in the restaurant. Children welcome.
Dogs welcome in the bar. Patio. Car park.
Directions: J9/M25. Eight miles south of Dorking on the A29.
(Map 6, D5)

West End

The Inn @ West End

42 Guildford Road, West End, Surrey GU24 9PW
Telephone: +44(0)870 4016176
+44(0)1276 858652
greatfood@the-inn.co.uk
www.the-inn.co.uk

Gerry and Ann Price have truly made their mark on this refurbished pub-restaurant. It may have been through various incarnations, originally called the Butcher's Arms, it then became the Wheatsheaf in the 1950s, but it is now fair and squarely on the Surrey culinary map. Its latest name change has inspired locals to refer to it fondly as the 'dot com'. The subtle inn sign depicting a scene from Othello extolling the virtues of drinking with an Englishman, gives an indication of what lies beyond the ordinary exterior: a stylish, yet informal place, noted for its good wine list and great food. Light, modern and airy throughout, there are wooden floors, creamy yellow walls and crisp linen-clothed tables in the dining area and a warming wood-burner in the bar that creates a cosy relaxed atmosphere. Imaginative monthly menus, enhanced by daily specials, list an eclectic range of modern British dishes. There are good lunchtime light bites, and a sandwich menu to go with a pint of London Pride or Courage Best, or a glass of wine; there are seven by the glass from an enthusiasts' list. Alternatively, follow soup of the day with homemade breads or smoked salmon, feta and roasted pepper salad and citrus crème fraîche with pan-fried calf's liver with crispy pancetta, garlic and herb mash and a sage cream. Round off with pecan and rum fridge cake topped with chocolate mousse, or a plate of cheese.

Prices: Set lunch £18. Main course from £12.50.
Bar main course from £6. House wine £11.95.
Last orders: Bar: lunch 15.00 (Saturday 16.00); dinner 23.00.
Food: lunch 14.30; dinner 21.30.
Closed: Rarely.
Food: Modern British.
Other points: No-smoking area. Garden. Boules pitch. Dining
patio. Car park.
Directions: On the A322 Guildford to M3 road, two miles south
of J3/M3. (Map 5, C4)

Battle

Pilgrim's Restaurant

1 High Street, Battle, East Sussex TN33 OAE
Telephone: +44(0)870 4016352
+44(0)1424 772314
www.thepilgrimsrestaurant.co.uk

If you're a fan of old buildings with bags of atmosphere, you'll be won over by this Grade II listed built in 1444, and one of the earliest examples of a timber-framed Wealden hall house. After bending through the low door, you enter an impressive timbered entrance hall where you can enjoy a drink before moving into the low-beamed dining room. The stunning look is created by the combination of period features, open fires and contrasting modern art. And the food certainly lives up to the setting. Director Toby Peters is committed to using locally grown produce with the emphasis on fresh, natural and seasonal. Taste and flavour are paramount, evident in such dishes as double-baked Golden Cross cheese soufflé with a sweet pepper coulis, or ceviche of local plaice, lime juice, coriander, chilli potato and red onion salad. For mains, there may be best end of spring lamb, marinated artichoke, red onion potato cake and Marsala jus. The equally indulgent puddings include a white chocolate and vanilla parfait with Marsala syrup.

Prices: Set dinner £20.50 and £15.95 (2 course).
Restaurant main course from £11.20. House wine £10.95.
Last orders: Food: lunch 15.00; dinner 21.30. Open all day for lighter dishes.
Closed: Sunday evening.
Food: Modern British.
Other points: No-smoking area. Garden. Children welcome.
Directions: A21, follow the signs for Battle and Pilgrim's is located next to Battle Abbey. Public parking available behind the Abbey. (Map 6, D6)

Brighton

Nineteen

19 Broad Street, Brighton, East Sussex BN2 1TJ
Telephone: +44(0)870 4016304
+44(0)1273 675529
info@hotelnineteen.co.uk
www.hotelnineteen.co.uk

A smart urban hideaway in Kemp Town that is so cool that it offers many appealing extras such as late breakfast in bed to 11am, pampering room service from massage and facials to hair styling plus free entry to The Ocean Rooms, a trendy Brighton nightspot. The décor majors on white – duvets, walls, baths or shower rooms – and is incredibly tasteful. Owner Mark Whiting also has a great eye for modern art. Lovely touches in bedrooms include sweeties by the bed, plasma screen TVs, stunning glass tables, CD and video players, and burners for aromatherapy oils. Everything has been thought through, from the lighting to the beds – three of which are built on glass bricks. Carefully bought breakfast ingredients show attention to detail and quality: free-range eggs accompany smoked salmon, and there are BLTs, salads, yogurts, juices and smoothies. Complimentary bloody Marys and champagne ('not cava', insists Mark), is offered at weekends, and breakfast hours are incredibly civilised. If the weather is fine, there's a bijou flower and plant-filled patio, which is just off the breakfast room. The kitchen next door is available to guests to make their own tea, coffee and snacks. The massages, manicures, pedicures, and yoga sessions with a qualified instructor are part of a package that can be booked on arrival. The philosophy of Nineteen is total relaxation.

Rooms: 7. Rooms from £95 to £150 including breakfast.
Champagne breakfast on Sundays.
Closed: Rarely.
Other points: No smoking. Garden.
Directions: M23 onto A23 and head for Brighton town centre. Travel past the Pavilion on the right hand side. Keep left, turn left at the roundabout onto Marine Parade. Keep left again to turn left into Manchester Street, turn right into St James Street and the second right into Broad Street, Hotel Nineteen is the petrol green building on the left. (Map 6, D5)

Individual charm and warmth

Fresh vegetables
at Pilgrim's Restaurant

Deciding which fruit and vegetables to put on the menu at Pilgrim's is the most delicious dilemma. They are delivered from Netherfield Place Kitchen Gardens, and the chefs only decide what to incorporate into their dishes once they peer into their mystery box every day. The gardens only send what is ripe and at its best on the day. This 365-day-a-year working Victorian kitchen garden is part of a hotel acquired by the Rudland family. Grandfather Les and his small team have worked tirelessly to make this a year-round production centre for vegetables, fruits, salads and herbs, and classic Victorian produce. Since reopening one of the original glass houses, they now even grow melons, which have been added to Pilgrim's menu. During the summer, Netherfield also supplies flowers as well as fresh Moroccan mint and camomile for infusions to the restaurant.

Netherfield Place Kitchen Gardens: Netherfield, East Sussex; 01424 775287

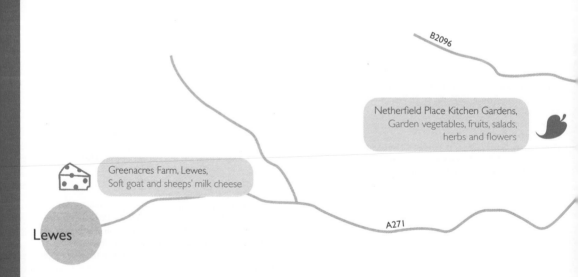

Netherfield Place Kitchen Gardens,
Garden vegetables, fruits, salads,
herbs and flowers

Greenacres Farm, Lewes,
Soft goat and sheeps' milk cheese

Lewes

B2096

A271

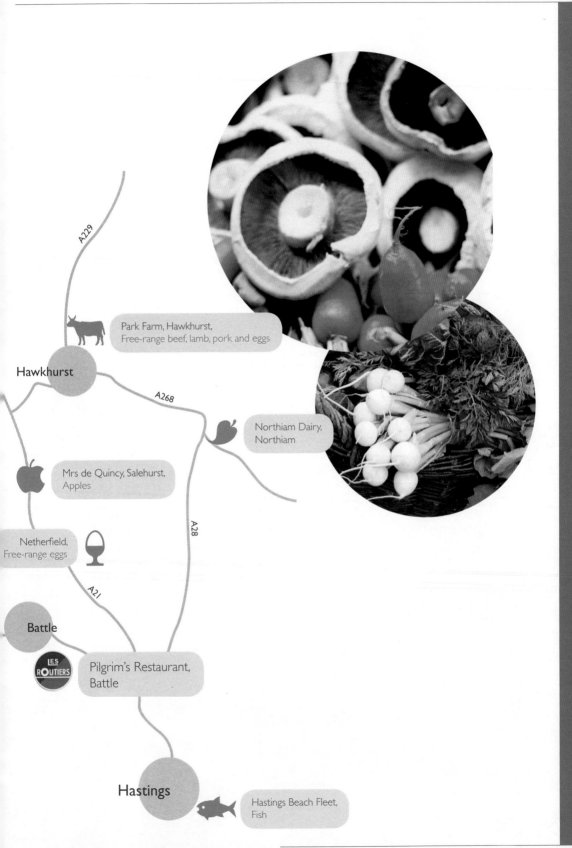

A229

Park Farm, Hawkhurst,
Free-range beef, lamb, pork and eggs

Hawkhurst

A268

Northiam Dairy,
Northiam

Mrs de Quincy, Salehurst,
Apples

A28

Netherfield,
Free-range eggs

A21

Battle

LES ROUTIERS

Pilgrim's Restaurant,
Battle

Hastings

Hastings Beach Fleet,
Fish

Brighton

Terre à Terre

71 East Street, Brighton, East Sussex BN1 1HQ
Telephone: +44(0)870 4016305
+44(0)1273 729051
mail@terreaterre.co.uk

Philip Taylor and Amanda Powley's groundbreaking vegetarian restaurant remains cutting edge even a decade or so since it opened. It's truly a one-off that thinks about food in a way that other restaurants don't. The cooking style is totally eclectic, with ideas drawn right across the Mediterranean to Central and Eastern Europe, the Far East and America, backed up by a kitchen confident enough to break culinary boundaries. Thus, a pâté brik is filled with minted cracked wheat, pressed sheep's cheese and preserved lemon and served with saffron-scented fennel, buttered string beans, and pickled apricots finished with tiger nut pesto. The house tapas plate is a great introduction to this unusual style – a starter for two to share or a satisfying lunch dish where a myriad of textures and culinary styles gives each mouthful an unpredictability that keeps interest buoyant. Right from the word go you notice the flavours, picking up on mint, cardamom, coriander, wasabi and tamarind. Other ingredients bolster strength: roast Jerusalem artichoke risotto served with truffled seasons mushrooms, a Madeira and balsamic reduction and sage and rootie chippers. The enthusiasts' wine list is totally organic; it is worth checking the board for the week's recommendations.

Prices: Restaurant main course from £11.95.
Organic wine list from £15.
Last orders: Food: 22.30.
Closed: Monday.
Food: Modern British and Vegetarian.
Other points: No-smoking area. Patio. Children welcome.
Directions: Just off the seafront, close to Palace Pier. (Map 6, D5)

Rye

Jeake's House Hotel

Mermaid Street, Rye, East Sussex TN31 7ET
Telephone: +44(0)870 4016438
+44(0)1797 222828
stay@jeakeshouse.com
www.jeakeshouse.com

The elegant late 17th century building – built originally by merchant Samuel Jeake as a storehouse – exudes a real sense of history. Jenny Hadfield has decorated each room individually using lots of deft personal touches to create an elegant look that mixes bold floral prints and striking colours with beams and standing timbers, period pieces such as a grandfather clock and a piano with highly polished antiques. An open fire may greet you (as well as Jenny's cats), as you come down to breakfast in the galleried hall of what was once a meeting house used by the Quakers. Tuck into local award-winning sausages, natural oak-smoked kippers and haddock from Rye Harbour, devilled kidneys, scrambled free-range egg with smoked salmon, and bread and croissants from the High Street baker, served with homemade preserves from the local Women's Institute. An honesty bar operates in the book-lined library; there are no evening meals served, but reservations can be made for nearby restaurants. Bedrooms are splendid with brass mahogany beds or four posters, drapes, cushions, and flowers. Sparkling bathrooms are equipped with luxurious towels. If you really want to spoil yourself stay at the Aiken Suite, which has lovely views to the sea. Outside, at the rear is a pretty courtyard. There's a private car park, a real boon as parking in Rye can be difficult.

Rooms: 11, 1 not en suite. Double room from £42 per person, single from £37.
Prices: Bar/snack from £4.50. House wine £12.
Closed: Rarely.
Other points: Children welcome over 12 years old.
Dogs welcome overnight. Car park.
Directions: Exit 10/M20 and follow signs for Brenzett, then directions for Hastings and Rye. Parking in Rye is restricted, but Jeake's House has its own private car park. (Map 6, D6)

Regional produce

Rye

Olde Moat House

Ivychurch, Rye, East Sussex TN29 0AZ
Telephone: +44(0)870 4016439
+44(0)1797 344700
oldemoathouse@hotmail.com
www.oldemoathouse.co.uk

This beautiful 15th century building is as good as its name and for a lot of the year has a ring of water running around the house and the lovely gardens that surround it. A truly picture postcard bed and breakfast, this is the perfect place to get away from it all. Walking into the house is like stepping back in time. Sloping floors upstairs remind you how ancient the house is, as do the exposed oak beams and antique furniture, comfortable sofas and a huge inglenook fireplace, which gives the sitting room a huge amount of character. The green dining room has a grand country house feel to it and this is where breakfast is served. Everything is on offer from cereal and fruit to pancakes and a full English breakfast. Evening meals are available on request. Hearty country dishes of smoked cod fish pie or Aga-cooked beef are typical of the food served. The three rooms are all individually decorated to the highest standard. Luxurious bedding and curtains create a cosy atmosphere that is sympathetic to the traditional nature and history of the house. All en suite, it is the small touches which will really delight; huge fluffy towels, the startling pink bathroom and bath, quality toiletries, four-poster beds and homemade cakes are just a few examples.

Rooms: 3. Double from £35, single from £40.
Prices are per person.
Other points: Totally no smoking. Garden. Children welcome over 14 years old.
Directions: Exit10/M20. Take the A2070 towards Brenzett. After approximately nine and three quarter miles turn left to Ivy church. the house is three quarters of a mile on the left hand side. (Map 6, D6)

Chichester

The George & Dragon

51 North Street, Chichester, West Sussex PO19 1NQ
Telephone: +44(0)870 4016181
+44(0)1243 785660
enquiries@gdchi.co.uk
www.georgeanddragoninn.co.uk

A favourite lunchtime stop-off, this lovely little pub is well positioned in the bustling centre of Chicester. In March 2004, new owners Don Hoare and Jen Day took over and they have retained its cosy, appealing atmosphere, and its reputation for good food. Wooden floors, scrubbed pine tables, roaring log fires in winter, and simple glass lanterns all make an inviting place to enjoy a break. Around the central bar, you will find a refreshing cross-section of visitors – shoppers, local businessmen, friends meeting for lunch, and tourists. Good traditional bar meals range from fresh Selsey crab sandwiches to a starter of chicken, mango and avocado salad drizzled in sweet chilli sauce, and a main course of hearty steak and kidney pudding, chips or new potatoes and fresh vegetables of the day. Beyond the bar is the light and airy conservatory restaurant, with a small patio. This suntrap is transformed into a barbecue area in summer. Seasonal menus revolve around fresh local produce, including vegetables and herbs from an organic garden. On the evening menu, there may be a starter of Mediterranean prawns in garlic butter, served with a mixed leaf salad and croûtons, a main course of lamb shank served in a rosemary and redcurrant gravy, followed by homemade puddings. The pub's old flint and brick stable block has been beautifully renovated and contains 10 stylish en suite bedrooms, all painted in warm yellow with contemporary lighting and heavy pine beds.

Rooms: 10. Double room from £75, single from £50.
Prices: Restaurant main course from £6.95. Bar snack from £3.50. House wine £10.50.
Last orders: Bar: 23.00. Food: lunch 14.30; dinner 21.15 (Sunday 21.30).
Closed: Rarely.
Food: Traditional and Modern British.
Other points: No-smoking area. Dogs welcome. Patio/courtyard. Children welcome.
Directions: Off A27 into Chichester, follow ring road to north of the city and top end of North Street. (Map 5, D4)

Chichester

The Royal Oak

Pook Lane, East Lavant, Chichester,
West Sussex PO18 0AX
Telephone: +44(0)870 4016183
+44(0)1243 527434
nickroyaloak@aol.com
www.sussexlive.co.uk/royaloakinn

Within a year of acquiring this tiny 200-year-old village inn Nick Sutherland had extended the dining area and converted the rear barn and cottage into bedrooms, thanks to a thriving dining trade and demand for accommodation due to its proximity to Chichester, Goodwood and the new Rolls Royce factory. Flint-built and accessed via a pretty raised terrace, this pretty cottage comprises an open-plan bar and dining area with open log fires, leather sofas, fat cream candles on scrubbed tables, and ales tapped from the cask. The food is modern British in style, with the main menu and daily blackboard additions featuring quality fish and meats from London markets and vegetables from local organic farms. Typically, a meal may begin with crispy crab cakes with sweet chilli, followed by Sussex pork and herb sausages, mash and balsamic onion jus, lamb steak with rosemary mash, or whole grilled lemon sole with chive butter. Lunchtime brings sandwiches and there are good homemade puddings. Very stylish bedrooms feature pastel décor, smart furnishings, flat-screen televisions, CD players and quality tiled bathrooms with power showers. Summer al fresco dining is on the sheltered front terrace.

Rooms: 6. Double/twin from £70.
Prices: Restaurant main course from £11. House wine £9.95.
Last orders: Bar: 23.00. Food: lunch 14.30; dinner 21.30.
Closed: Rarely.
Food: Traditional English and Mediterranean.
Other points: No smoking in the bedrooms. Garden and terrace.
Car park.
Directions: Village signposted off A286 Midhurst road a mile north of Chichester. (Map 5, D4)

Rusper

Ghyll Manor

High Street, Rusper, Horsham, West Sussex RH12 4PX
Telephone: +44(0)870 4016491
+44(0)845 3453426

In its 45 acres of parkland, you feel away from it all, but the manor's main entrance is in fact just off Rusper's High Street with its pubs and shops. It's easy to lose yourself in the tranquillity of this 17th century manor house with its nine acres of formal gardens, but it's just as easy to visit the local amenities, from golf courses to museums, and the pub. The house retains a classic feel in public rooms that are divided into a series of comfortable, traditionally styled lounges, including a relaxed, bright, airy conservatory, and a charming small bar. Bedrooms in the main house are individual, and come with fine period details and antiques; those in a converted stable mews set around a courtyard are spacious and modern with neat bathrooms. The old beamed restaurant serves modern British dishes. The menu is a mix of old favourites such as terrine of chicken and vegetables, and grilled Dover sole and up-to-the-minute dishes, attractively presented. You might start with devilled veal sweetbreads, sautéed with garlic, fresh chillies and ginger served with asparagus and sauce vierge. Main courses of grilled free-range chicken breast with a leek and truffle salad, or chump of South Down lamb, lead on to glazed coconut risotto or terrine of autumn fruits.

Rooms: 29. Double room from £159, single from £79.50.
Prices: Set lunch £17.80, set dinner £25.15. House wine £14.
Last orders: Food: lunch 14.00; dinner 21.30.
Closed: Rarely.
Food: Modern British.
Other points: No-smoking area. Children welcome.
Dogs welcome overnight. Garden. Car park.
Directions: Exit11/M23. Between Horsham and Crawley on the A264. (Map 6, D5)

Down-to-earth, friendly service

Steyning

Old Tollgate Restaurant and Hotel

The Street, Bramber, Steyning, West Sussex BN44 3WE
Telephone: +44(0)870 4016458
+44(0)1903 879494
info@oldtollgatehotel.com
www.oldtollgatehotel.com

You will find up-to-date and spacious accommodation at this hotel built on the site of a much older tollhouse. It's an extremely comfortably appointed roadside hotel just a hundred yards or so off the A283 and close to the village centre. Rooms are either upstairs in the main building, or in a separate block just across the courtyard from the main entrance. Public areas include an attractive lounge, as well as a split-level bar and carvery restaurant. Both have a very traditional air, with dark oak panelling a prominent feature. There's also a good emphasis on local produce in the carvery, with game from local shoots, locally smoked salmon and shellfish, and bread from a nearby baker. Bedrooms are all a good size, but are even larger in the main building, where sofa beds provide additional sleeping options. These rooms are especially suitable for families, with children under 14 accommodated free when sharing with their parents. All rooms have mini-bars and well-equipped bathrooms. The degree of comfort provided is more akin to hotels rated higher than three stars. Those on business will appreciate the ample desk space provided.

Rooms: 31. Rooms from £76.
Prices: Set lunch from £17.45, set dinner £23.95.
House wine £11.25.
Last orders: Food: lunch 13.45; dinner 21.30.
Closed: Rarely.
Food: Traditional English.
Other points: No-smoking area. Children welcome. Garden. Car park. Licence for Civil Weddings.
Directions: On A283; in Bramber village, four miles from Shoreham-by-sea. (Map 6, D5)

Steyning

Springwells Bed and Breakfast Hotel

9 High Street, Steyning, West Sussex BN44 3GG
Telephone: +44(0)870 4016457
+44(0)1903 812446
contact@springwells.co.uk
www.springwells.co.uk

This imposing creeper-clad Georgian merchant's house stands at the very eastern end of the High Street. The reception is at the end of the narrow entrance hall and to reach it you pass a homely and comfortable lounge and the attractive breakfast room. To the rear of the ground floor is the bar that incorporates a further lounge-cum-conservatory area, which looks out over a neat walled garden. The whole place has a very traditional and well-maintained air; the owner obviously takes great pride in the place. Bedrooms, whether they be on the first or second floor, are well appointed and of good size, those on the first being somewhat larger, and with higher ceilings. Furnishings are of good quality and are in keeping with the building's character – two rooms have four-posters. Bedrooms at the back enjoy views over the garden, are quieter, and have a sunnier aspect too. On the top floor, a couple of rooms have to share a bathroom. As well as tea/coffee-making facilities and biscuits, a bowl of fresh fruit stands at the bottom of the stairs, and there's a fridge with fresh milk and beers at the end of the first-floor corridor.

Rooms: 11, 2 not en suite. Double room from £79, single from £35.
Closed: Two weeks over Christmas and New Year.
Other points: Children welcome. Garden. Car park.
Directions: Off the A283. (Map 6, D5)

Turners Hill

Tulley's Farm

Turners Hill Road, Turners Hill, Crawley,
West Sussex RH10 4PE
Telephone: +44(0)870 4016335
+44(0)1342 718472
shop@tulleysfarm.com
www.tulleysfarm.com

Farms have never been such fun. With so much to see and do you could turn a trip to Tulley's into a day out. The Beare family started the farm more than 60 years ago with a small dairy herd, but have now expanded it to include a farm shop, an Animal Patch of farm animals for children, a PYO business and a maze design that changes each year, plus there's a courtyard full of other amusements. The extensive pick-your-own opens in April with rhubarb, and moves on to soft fruits from July to September, finishing with pumpkins in October. The farm shop is stocked with wholesome produce, including local and regional cheeses, while gardeners will appreciate the selection of spring and summer bedding plants and containers. During school holidays, from July to September, there's also the Amazing Maize Maze. The maize is planted in May and by July is three to four foot high when the grids are cut out. When you've found your way out, head for refreshments in the attractive Farmhouse, a large Victorian stable block conversion that serves hearty cakes and scones. Alongside the sweet offerings, there are also savoury bites such as filled jacket potatoes, sandwiches and a variety of different quiche.

Prices: Main course from £5.25.
Last orders: Food: 17.00 (Winter 16.30).
Closed: PYO closed October-June, otherwise open 09.00-18.00.
Food: Traditional English.
Other points: No-smoking area. Children welcome. Play area. Garden. Car park. Seasonal activities.
Directions: Exit 10/M23. Take the A264, then the B2028 to Turners Hill. (Map 6, D5)

Sunderland

Throwingstones Restaurant

National Glass Centre, Liberty Way, Sunderland,
Tyne and Wear SR6 0GL
Telephone: +44(0)870 4016460
+44(0)191 565 3939
info@nationalglasscentre.com
www.nationalglasscentre.com

Sunderland's National Glass Centre, an homage to glass, is housed in a striking building constructed of glass and steel, naturally. You can find out all about the history of glass, see demonstrations and artists at work and buy their wares. Resident restaurant, Throwing Stones, is set within this marvellous structure. Its views over the quayside make for quite a stunning setting to enjoy light bites and lunches, and evening meals on Fridays and Saturdays. Snacks include toasted muffins with various toppings such as chargrilled bacon with Cheddar, rolled tortillas with say piri-piri chicken with soured cream and open sandwiches, as well as tempting pastries. The lunch menu offers an international selection of tempting dishes from seafood antipasti or mozzarella and beef tomato with a basil dressing to start and mains of monkfish kebab, tandoori lamb kofta or lemon chicken, each of which come with imaginative accompaniments. As well as the comprehensive list of dishes, you can have meats from the grill. Puddings cater for more traditional tastes with old favourites such as rice pudding with sultanas and nutmeg. The wine list is compact but offers good value, especially from the new world.

Prices: Restaurant starter from 3.25 and main course from £6.50. House wine £9.95.
Last orders: Food: 14.45 (20.45 Friday, Saturday).
Closed: Monday-Thursday evenings.
Food: Modern British.
Other points: Totally no smoking. Children welcome. Car park. Licenced for Civil Weddings.
Directions: Off the A183 in Sunderland, signposted from all major roads. (Map 12, C6)

Good food and wine

Coventry

Turmeric Gold

166 Medieval Spon Street, Coventry,
Warwickshire CV1 1BB
Telephone: +4(0)870 4016490
+44(0)2476 226603
info@turmericgold.co.uk
www.turmericgold.co.uk

Turmeric Gold is quite a shining light on what is
otherwise the less-than-attractive Coventry Inner Ring.
The restaurant is set on a wonderful medieval street
and none of the building's original charm and features
have been lost to modernisation. There are still the
exposed brick, beams and timber framework, which
have been enhanced by vibrant eastern colours and
oriental antiques. The upstairs dining room has a particularly romantic feel with lots of hidden features and
private dining areas. The menu has the familiar line-up
of baltis and tandoori dishes alongside stalwarts such
as chicken jalfrazi and various dhansak and bhuna
dishes. Fluffy naans, a selection of vegetarian dishes
and a price range of set menus are also offered. What
distinguishes the cooking, however, are the fresh-tast-
ing flavours and lightness of touch to the dishes. There
is an option is to be treated like a Maharaja for £55.
This enables you to have as much food and drink as
you like in a private lounging area, which is covered in
silk and can be draped over for privacy.

Prices: Set lunch £6.95 and dinner £15-£20.
Restaurant main course from £10. House wine £9.25.
Last orders: Food: lunch 14.00; dinner 23.30.
Closed: Sunday lunch.
Food: Modern Indian.
Other points: No-smoking area. Children welcome. Car park.
Large private room.
Directions: Situated off the city ring road on junction 9, going
towards Upper Well Street. Turn right at the second traffic lights
onto Corporation Street. At the top of the street, turn right at
the roundabout onto Medieval Spon Street. Turmeric Gold is
found opposite Bonds night spot. (Map 9, D3)

Knowle

Cafe Saffron

1679 High Street, Knowle, Solihull,
Warwickshire B98 0RL
Telephone: +44(0)870 4016393
+44(0)1564 772190

Just one-mile from junction 5 of the M42, this evening-
only Indian in well-heeled Knowle is a cut above your
average curry house. Its bright outside lights and High
Street location make it easy to find and it's well worth
the short detour. The minimalist contemporary décor
with modern prints and warm orange-plastered walls
are a refreshing change from more traditional curry
houses. It also sets itself apart in the food department,
as the kitchen pays much attention to detail, preparation, and the look of the dishes. Good quality meat
and poultry are sourced from local butchers, and many
herbs and spices imported directly from Calcutta and
then freshly ground on site. All the favourites recipes
from India, Pakistan and Bangladesh are here. Start
with a classic chicken shashlick or prawn pathia puri,
for example, and move on to tandoori grills, and curries such as bhuna, korma, dopiaza, passanda, jalfrezi
and rogan josh. The wide menu provides a comforting,
something-for-everyone choice, but look to the list of
specialities for a more varied selection.

Prices: Main course from £8. House wine £7.95.
Last orders: Food: 23.30.
Closed: Lunch.
Food: Indian.
Other points: Children welcome. Car park.
Directions: Two miles south east of Solihull. Exit5/M42.
(Map 9, D3)

Birmingham

San Carlo

4 Temple Street, Birmingham, West Midlands B2 5BN
Telephone: +44(0)870 4016286
+44(0)121 633 0251

Busy and buzzy, San Carlo is a real gem down a narrow back street just off the city centre. This small Italian restaurant was the first in what is now a small chain, with three other branches. It has a pleasing modern Mediterranean look with a façade of marble and glass, and a spacious light and bright dining area with mirrors decorating the walls, white ceramic floor tiles, and potted plants and small trees creating a fresh contemporary look. The focus is on simple, flavoursome food, and prices are very fair for cooking that's above the norm for a city-centre eaterie majoring in pizzas and pasta. There's plenty to tempt in the way of soups, salads and risottos, as well as trattoria classic mains such as pollo sorpresa, scallopa milanese, and saltimboca alla romana. Blackboard specials extend an already wide choice, offering some very good fresh fish dishes; look out for excellent lobster Thermidor, crevettes in garlic butter, and spaghetti shellfish. There's a selection of well-priced Italian wines, with a good selection by the glass, but with France and the new world wines also making a splash.

Prices: Main course from £11. House wine £11.20.
Last orders: Food: 23.00.
Closed: Rarely.
Food: Italian.
Other points: No-smoking area. Children welcome.
Directions: In the centre of the city. (Map 9, D2)

Chippenham

Revolutions Cafe Bar and Restaurant

66 New Road, Chippenham, Wiltshire SN15 1ES
Telephone: +44(0)870 4016293
+44(0)1249 447500
sanddwebb@aol.com

Contemporary and in the town centre, this brasserie-style restaurant oozes good looks and serves good seasonal food. Sandie and Doug Webb take their policy of buying produce from local suppliers seriously, so much so that menus give credit to their beef and organic egg producers. And despite using quality ingredients, prices are incredibly reasonable. Lunch dishes, such as a Wiltshire ham and eggs with sauté potatoes and salad or roasted green pepper, mushroom and pimento risotto, are all under £5. There's also a good choice of salad and jacket potato options. The evening menu offers a selection of imaginative starters such as pan-fried duck breast with an almond and apricot sauce and mushrooms with a creamed garlic and Marsala sauce. The mains include a strong line-up of steaks plus other meat and vegetarian meals. Although licensed, a bring-your-own wine policy with a small corkage charge has proved popular and is encouraged, but if you forget, there's always the house Australian, and a selection of lagers, beers and spirits.

Prices: Lunch time menu from £2.95. Set dinner £14.95.
House wine £7.95.
Last orders: Open and food served from 09.00.
Closed: Sunday, Monday evening.
Food: Modern British.
Other points: No-smoking area. Children welcome.
Directions: Exit17/M4. Take the dual carriageway towards Chippenham and follow the signs to the town centre. Turn left through the railway arches and just before the first crossing Revolutions is on the right hand side. (Map 5, C2)

Affordable good value

Teffont Evias

Howard's House Hotel

Teffont Evias, Salisbury, Wiltshire SP3 5RJ
Telephone: +44(0)870 4016413/6414
+44(0)1722 716392 or 716821
enq@howardshousehotel.com
www.howardshousehotel.com

Howard's House Hotel dates back to 1623 and it has been in the same family since 1992. Maybe that explains why it has been lovingly looked after all these years and has been so tastefully and elegantly decorated. The beautiful gardens with large well-tended lawns and cottage garden flowers are a perfect setting for this charming house. In the sitting room you can relax on the large comfortable sofas where, in winter, the large stone fireplace blazes with logs. Upstairs, nine en suite bedrooms are luxuriously decorated, some have four-poster beds, all have bathrobes, and are spacious and comfortable with good views of either the garden or the surrounding countryside. Boyd McIntosh heads the kitchen and delivers his brand of sophisticated, ambitious cooking. He insists on quality, fresh local ingredients backed up by home-grown vegetables and herbs from the garden. The dinner carte menu offers starters such as wild mushroom and truffle risotto or roasted wood pigeon, followed by roasted halibut with caper and parsley mash or braised belly and roasted fillet of Wiltshire pork with a mustard mash. The table d'hote has equally enticing choices. Prices reflect the pedigree of the wine list, but the house wines offer fair drinking and some very good value.

Rooms: 9. Double room from £145, single from £95. Four poster £165.
Prices: Set lunch £22.50 and dinner £23.95.
Main course from £19.95. House wine £13.25.
Last orders: Food: lunch 14.00; dinner 21.30. Reservations only.
Closed: Closed Friday lunch.
Food: Modern British.
Other points: No-smoking in restaurant. Children welcome. Garden. Car park.
Directions: Due west from Salisbury towards Wilton and Chilmark, off the B3089 towards Hindon and the A303. (Map 5, D2)

Tenbury Wells

The Fountain Inn

Oldwood, St Michaels, Tenbury Wells, Worcestershire WR15 8TB
Telephone: +44(0)870 4016202
+44 (0)1584 810701
enquiries@fountain-hotel.co.uk
www.fountain-hotel.co.uk

Since its total refurbishment, this traditional black and white 17th century inn has gone from strength to strength. Not content with enhancing the olde English look of the low-beamed bar, Russell Allen has added an unusual centrepiece – a 1,000 gallon shark tank, with just that, 'Dancer' a leopard shark and some exotic fish to keep him company. There are also 11 smart en suite bedrooms. Seafood is, of course, big business here, with fish bought direct from Birmingham market on a daily basis, but other produce is sourced more locally, notably Herefordshire beef and game from Bowket's of Tenbury, home-grown organic herbs and vegetables, and handmade local cheeses from Hereford. With food served all day, the menu caters for all tastes, and that ranges from Worcestershire ploughmans and pork, apple and calvados paté or traditional beef and ale pie to the more exotic seafood roulade, or sea bass steak grilled with cajun spices served with a crevette. Excellent real ales include their award-winning Fountain Ale, and in the summer you can move outdoors to enjoy your pint and a pie. The pub also sets itself apart by serving food all day, from breakfast straight through to lunch and dinner.

Rooms: 11. Double/twin room from £39.50. Disabled suite available.
Prices: Main course from £6.95. Sunday lunch £12.95. House wine £9.95.
Last orders: Bar: 23.00. Food: 21.00 (later for bookings).
Closed: Never.
Food: Traditional British with Continental influences.
Other points: No-smoking in the restaurant. Children welcome. Large garden. Car park. Shark aquarium.
Directions: Junction 5/M5. One mile from Tenbury Wells on the A4112 Leominster road. (Map 8, D5)

www.routiers.co.uk

Bridlington

Georgian Tea Rooms

56 High Street, Old Town, Bridlington,
East Yorkshire YO16 4QA
Telephone: +44(0)870 4016300
+44(0)1262 608600

Diane Davison's old-fashioned tearoom, the Georgian Tea Rooms, is set on one of the most complete Georgian High Streets in Britain. The area is a source of pride and tourism for the old town of Bridlington, which is tucked away a mile inland from the better-known bustling seaside resort. The street has become even more recognisable since part of the series *The Royal*, a spin off of *Heartbeat*, was filmed here. The tea rooms are on the ground floor of a fine Grade II listed building, forming part of a three-floored antique emporium. The spacious rooms are painted in striking yellows and greens and filled with highly polished wooden tables. There's a separate room for smokers, plus a fantastic big garden dominated by a central fountain. Breakfast starts the day, a full English perhaps, or a breakfast bap filled with sausage or bacon, then the menu moves onto snacks of filled jacket potatoes, salads, toasted sandwiches and creamed mushrooms on toast as well as those teashop stalwarts of toasted teacakes and wonderful homemade cakes and pastries.

Prices: Main course from £3.45. House wine £8.99.
Last orders: Food: 17.00 (Sunday 15.00).
Closed: Closed for two weeks over Christmas and New Year.
Food: Traditional English.
Other points: No-smoking area. Children welcome.
Patio and garden.
Directions: In Bridlington's Old Town. (Map 12, E8)

Bridlington

Marton Grange

Flamborough Road, Sewerby, Bridlington,
East Yorkshire YO15 1DU
Telephone: +44(0)870 4016299
+44(0)1262 602034
www.marton-grange.co.uk

First impressions of this Grade II listed Georgian house are of an immaculate, well-maintained hotel. And the neatness and attention paid to the lawns and borders continues inside to the first-rate and attractively decorated and stylish rooms. Since he took over a few years ago, Stuart Nelson has transformed the house. There are 11 en suite with shower rooms with contemporary, restful décor and sparkling bathrooms: one bedroom is designed for people with disabilities. The public rooms are equally as attractive. Two comfortable drawing rooms are traditionally furnished and have lovely views to the gardens. Guests dine in two interconnecting dining rooms which are decorated in a soothing lemon with tables set with crisp cloths. Set menu dinners are well thought out and attractively presented. The daily-changing choice includes dishes using local produce. Starters may consist of cream of asparagus soup or egg mayonnaise with prawns, with Yorkshire pudding or mushroom stroganoff to follow. Bread and butter pudding or fresh lime tart with raspberry coulis round off a good home-cooked meal. Their full English breakfasts are also quite an occasion. Nearby is Flamborough Head, an outstanding stretch of coastline, which is famed for its colonies of nesting seabirds.

Rooms: 11. Double from £30 per person, single from £35.
Prices: Set dinner £14.50. House wine £9.
Last orders: Dinner served from at 18.00.
Closed: December, January and February.
Food: Traditional British.
Other points: Totally no smoking. Garden.
Children welcome over 12 years old. Car park.
Directions: Exit37/M62. Take the B1255 Bridlington to Flamborough road and Marton Grange is on the left, last drive-way off the lay-by. (Map 12, E8)

An alternative Britain

Wye Valley Fountain Ale

at The Fountain Inn

The Fountain Inn in Tenbury Wells serve
their very own personalised real ale.
Brewed down the road at Wye Valley
Brewery, you'll get a pint of unfiltered,
unpasteurised pure cask-conditioned
ale, fermented malted barley, hops,
yeast and water, just the way it
should be. Founded in 1985, the Wye
Valley Brewery is committed to using
old traditional methods while using
only the best quality raw materials.
This philosophy has brought huge
success and rapid expansion, indeed,
it is now recognised as the leading
cask ale brewery in the county. The
awards are impressive and include
'Supreme Champion' at the 2002
CAMRA National Winter Beer Festival
for the wonderfully named 'Dorothy
Goodbody's Wholesome Stout' and four
major awards, three of them again
from CAMRA at the Great Welsh Beer
Festival for Butty Bach (meaning 'my
little friend' - a very appropriate name
for some beer fanatics!). Les Routiers
urges you not to stop there but also to
sample their classic chestnut coloured
Wye Valley Bitter or their smooth
Hereford Pale Ale. Besides Fountain Ale
the Fountain Inn features a selection of
Wye Valley ales as does the Butchers
Arms in Painswick, Gloucestershire (see
Les Routiers Pubs and Inns Guide 2005).

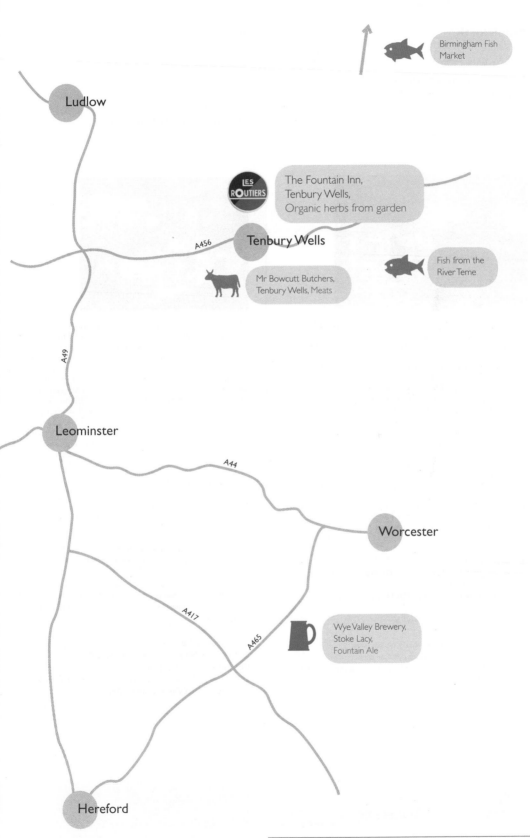

Birmingham Fish Market

Ludlow

LES ROUTIERS

The Fountain Inn,
Tenbury Wells,
Organic herbs from garden

A456   Tenbury Wells

Fish from the
River Teme

Mr Bowcutt Butchers,
Tenbury Wells, Meats

A49

Leominster

A44

Worcester

A417

A465

Wye Valley Brewery,
Stoke Lacy,
Fountain Ale

Hereford

Ampleforth

Shallowdale House

Ampleforth, Helmsley, North Yorkshire YO62 4DY
Telephone: +44(0)870 4016360
+44(0)1439 788325
stay@shallowdalehouse.co.uk
www.shallowdalehouse.co.uk

The rural setting of this house is quite lovely. It is surrounded by mature gardens that overlook the peaceful Howardian Hills, all in a designated area of natural beauty. Built in the 1960s, this light and airy house has large windows that provide the perfect frame for admiring the views. Hospitality is high on the list of owners Anton and Phillip who have created a relaxed, welcoming atmosphere. All the rooms are tastefully furnished in a contemporary style with period touches. Spacious, immaculate bathrooms add to the sense of luxury. You will dine well, as your hosts are keen to provide beautifully presented meals using local produce. A set dinner may include aubergine and red pepper roulade to start, a main course of braised Ryedale lamb shanks, followed by caramelised apple tart with home-made cinnamon and maple syrup ice cream. Breakfast is also a bit of an occasion. The location is a great base for visiting York, just 20 miles south, and nearby Castle Howard. And when you're not exploring the North Yorkshire Moors, take a trip to the attractive village of Ampleforth, which is renowned for its active priory and school.

Rooms: 3 (1 with private bathroom). Double room £77.50-£95, single from £57.50-£67.50.
Prices: Set dinner (4 course) £29.50. House wine £15.
Last orders: Dinner 19.30.
Closed: Over Christmas and New Year.
Food: Modern British.
Other points: Residents only. Totally no smoking.
Children welcome over 12 years old. Car park.
Directions: At the western end of Ampleforth on the turning to Hambleton. (Map 12, D6)

Ampleforth

The White Swan

East End, Ampleforth, York, North Yorkshire YO62 4DA
Telephone: +44(0)870 4016204
+44(0)1439 788239
www.whiteswanampleforth.co.uk

This comfortably modernised stone inn lies at the heart of Ampleforth on the edge of the Hambleton Hills and is just a short walk from the famous Catholic college that dominates the area. Following five years as head chef at the now closed Ryedale Country Lodge in Nunnington, Robert Thompson (and wife Gillian) took over The White Swan in April 2003. The past year has seen the food improve dramatically. The day's chalk-board menu now draws locals and well-heeled parents in for interesting, freshly prepared dishes. The country bar at the front has a quarry-tiled floor and an open log fire and is where the locals congregate. Diners head for the more modern rear dining area, where comfortable wall bench seating and a mix of tables and chairs create a relaxed and informal atmosphere. From lunchtime sandwiches, the menu may list warm crab, cheese and chive tartlet with cucumber and chilli salsa, or local black pudding on cherry tomato and herb mash with shallot gravy for starters. Mains take in classics like battered Whitby haddock and an excellent steak and ale pie with shortcrust pastry, and the more inventive, perhaps beef fillet with mushroom, brandy and mustard sauce. There's a lovely sheltered rear patio with views across the Vale of York.

Prices: Restaurant main course from £6.95. House wine £10.50.
Last orders: Bar: lunch 14.30; dinner 23.00. Food: lunch 14.00; dinner 21.00.
Closed: Rarely.
Food: Traditional British.
Other points: No smoking in dining room. Patio.
Children welcome. Car park.
Directions: In the centre of Ampleforth on the main street opposite the Post Office. (Map 12, D6)

Austwick

The Austwick Traddock

Yorkshire Dales National Park, via Lancaster,
North Yorkshire LA2 8BY
Telephone: +44(0)870 4016379
+44(0)15242 51224
info@austwicktraddock.co.uk
www.austwicktraddock.co.uk

Exquisitely tasteful, this elegant Georgian country
house nestles in the unspoilt village of Austwick,
with the added bonus of having the Yorkshire Dales
National Park as a backdrop. The Traddock was built
in the 18th century for the Ingilby family who contrib-
uted much to the development of this area of North
Yorkshire and Cumbria. New owners Bruce and Jane
Reynolds have kept many original features, but added
their own stylish touches. The hotel is comfortably
furnished with traditional antiques, plump sofas and
log fires. Eleven individual and classically decorated
bedrooms have modern en suite bathrooms and many
thoughtful touches such as flowers, fruit, shortbread,
and sherry. Careful, unpretentious cooking is built
around notably fresh, often seasonal, ingredients
– local and organic where possible – and runs to cream
of wild mushroom soup, for example, or Dales-breed
fillet steak with daupinhoise potatoes, caramelised
banana shallots and Madeira sauce or roasted fillet
of sea bass with sauce vierge. Puddings also hit the
spot such as the light raspberry shortcake sable with
whipped cream and raspberry coulis. All the set menus
also come with coffee and chocolate truffles.

Rooms: 11. Double/twin room £100-£140, single £50-£75.
Prices: Set dinner £25. House wine from £12.
Last orders: Food: dinner 21.00; Sunday 19.00.
Closed: Lunch (except Sunday), and Sunday-Tuesday evenings.
Food: Modern and Traditional British.
Other points: No-smoking area. Dogs welcome. Garden.
Children welcome. Car park.
Directions: Exit34/M6. From the M6 or M1, take the A65.
Austwick is located midway between Skipton and Kirkby
Lonsdale, two and a half miles north-west of Settle. (Map 12, E5)

Filey

The Downcliffe House Hotel

The Beach, Filey, North Yorkshire YO14 9LA
Telephone: +44(0)870 4016416
+44(0)1723 513310
info@downcliffehouse.co.uk
www.downcliffehouse.co.uk

As it's right on the beach most of the rooms at The
Downcliffe Hotel have fabulous views of Filey's six
miles of golden sands, taking in Flamborough Head
to the tip of Filey Brigg. Filey is a charming, unspoilt
coastal town and the Downcliffe is the ideal place to
enjoy a relaxed and peaceful break. The hotel is run by
Nick and Caroline Hunt who have created a homely
yet stylish hotel. A real fire roars in the bar and the
restaurant in the winter. All the bedrooms are en suite
and generously proportioned, some have four-poster
beds, and all are decorated in the Victorian style that
runs through the house. Sitting in the restaurant overlooking the beach, you feel like you're really on holiday. True to its location, the menu includes fresh fish,
but also acknowledges the farms that surround Filey.
The strongly modern British menu may offer smoked
salmon or lardons of pan-fried liver with bacon and
mushrooms with salad to start, followed by its popular
grand platter of fruits de mer or Downcliffe shoulder
of lamb with minted gravy sauce. A suitably indulgent
finish would be hot fudgy chocolate gateau and cream.

Rooms: 11. Double room from £88, single from £44,
family room from £132.
Prices: Set dinner £20. Main course from £10. House wine £10.
Last orders: Food: lunch 14.00; dinner 19.00.
No food Sunday and Monday evening.
Closed: December-February.
Food: Seafood/British.
Other points: No-smoking area. Children welcome.
Directions: Leave the A165 taking the A1039 and follow to the
centre of Filey. Drive through the centre and down Cargate Hill
and turn right along the sea front. (Map 12, D8)

Individual charm and warmth

Great Ouseburn

The Crown

Great Ouseburn, York, North Yorkshire YO26 9RF
Telephone: +44(0)870 4016211
+44(0)1423 330430

If you want to visit a typical Yorkshire pub, then the Crown is an ideal place to start. It stands in a picturesque village, conveniently close to the A1, and is full of character and interesting memorabilia, notably that of the Tiller Girls dancing troupe who began their careers at this bustling and cheerfully friendly free house. Despite its traditional appearance, food is well above average for a pub, with various menus offering imaginative modern British dishes. From the extensive dining room carte you could begin with roast tiger prawns with garlic, chilli and coriander and ginger seaweed, before moving on to a memorable carpet bagger fillet steak that comes stuffed with homemade pâté, English back bacon and a whisky and scallion sauce, or rack of lamb with redcurrant and rosemary sauce. In the bar, opt for freshly battered haddock with chips and mushy peas, the Crown's legendary steak, ale and mushroom pie, or homemade fishcakes with dressed leaves. Leave room for the amazing dark chocolate and Amaretto torte or savour a fine selection of Yorkshire farmhouse cheeses, perhaps handmade Swaledale goats cheese or Richmond Smoked. The wide-ranging wine list has been thoughtfully put together and offers good tasting notes and 10 wines by the glass.

Prices: Brasserie 2-course set menu £12. Main course from £11.
Bar main course from £6.50. House wine from £9.80.
Last orders: Food: 21.30 (Sunday 21.00).
No food Monday-Friday lunch.
Closed: Rarely.
Food: Modern British.
Other points: No-smoking area. Children welcome. Garden.
Car park.
Directions: Junction 48/A1. Great Ouseburn is off the B6265,
midway between Boroughbridge and Green Hammerton.
(Map 12, E6)

Harrogate

Ascot House

53 Kings Road, Harrogate, North Yorkshire HG1 5HJ
Telephone: +44(0)870 4016350
+44(0)1423 531005
admin@ascothouse.com
www.ascothouse.com

The laid-back elegance of Ascot House makes for a very pleasant stay. Its town-centre location means it's just a 10-minute stroll from the shops, attractions and the conference and exhibition centre, but lovely gardens give it a peaceful, secluded quality. It's easy to feel at home as soon as you step into the small, informal reception. The relaxed atmosphere is reflected throughout, from the lounge filled with comfortable and inviting sofas and armchairs overlooking the garden to the attractive lounge bar, which has views on to a pretty patio balcony. The 19 very well-kept en suite bedrooms are each individually styled in soft colours, and have every extra. Further reasons to stay can be put down to some sound cooking, which caters for a wide range of tastes and offers value for money. The set-dinner menu includes grilled lamb chops with a warm red onion marmalade, and chicken breast wrapped in smoked bacon and served with Madeira sauce. A typical meal from the carte could include chargrilled vegetable terrine with a balsamic dressing, and roasted pork fillet with apple and onion chutney, and marsala wine sauce. The wine list is strong in the French department. Private car parking is another plus.

Rooms: 19. Double room from £87, single from £59.
Prices: Set dinner £17.50. House wine £10.95.
Last orders: Food: dinner 20.30.
Closed: 22 January-6 February.
Food: Traditional and Modern English.
Other points: No smoking in the restaurant and bedrooms.
Children welcome. Small garden. Car park.
Licence for Civil Weddings.
Directions: Follow signs for town centre/conference and
exhibition centre of Harrogate. This will bring you to Kings Road,
drive past the exhibition centre and the hotel is on the left,
immediately after the open park area as you drive up the hill.
(Map 12, E6)

Regional produce

Harrogate

Boars Head Hotel

Ripley, Harrogate, North Yorkshire HG3 3AY
Telephone: +44(0)870 4016351
+44(0)1423 771888
reservations@boarsheadripley.co.uk
www.boarsheadripley.co.uk

This smart coaching inn is at the heart of this historic estate village owned by Sir Thomas Ingilby, who resides at Ripley's famous castle. In 1900, all the old village pubs were closed on Sundays by the zealous Sir William Ingilby, an action that eventually left the place dry for 71 years. Yet, such was the rejoicing at the reopening of The Boar's Head in 1990, that the vicar arrived to bless the beer pumps. Today's thoroughly stylish hotel boasts every modern comfort in 25 sumptuous standard and luxury bedrooms filled with antique furniture and paintings from the attics of Ripley Castle, plush soft furnishings and homely touches such as toy boats in the baths. The best of modern British menu brings together interesting combinations such as potted Morecambe Bay shrimps with lemon grass butter and rocket salad to start and mains of cannon of pork with a mini apple and sage crumble and venison steak topped with saffron scallops and crispy shallots. Bistro alternatives include award-winning venison sausages on cranberry mash with red wine jus and salmon with guacamole and watercress dressing. Round off perhaps with dark chocolate crème brûlée topped with vanilla ice cream sauce or a noteworthy assortment of British farmhouse cheeses. Wines by the glass come from vineyards as diverse as the Murray/Darling rivers of Australia and Chile's Central Valley, home of Sir Thomas's own Reserve Chardonnay; while guests never tire equally of the choicest Yorkshire ales.

Rooms: 25. Double/twin room from £125.
Prices: Set lunch from £15 and dinner from £25. Restaurant main course from £18.50. Bar main from £10.75. House wine £12.50.
Last orders: Bar: lunch 14.00; dinner 23.00. Food: lunch 14.00; dinner 21.30.
Closed: Never.
Food: Modern British.
Other points: No-smoking area. Children welcome.
Dogs welcome. Garden. Car park. Licenced for Civil Weddings.
Directions: Three miles north of Harrogate on A61. (Map 12, E6)

Harrogate

Courtyard Restaurant

1 Montpellier Mews, Harrogate,
North Yorkshire HG1 2TQ
Telephone: +44(0)870 4016349
+44(0)1423 530708
www.courtyardrestaurant.net

It might be tiny, but this restaurant is big on quality food and style. Its setting in a former stable mews overlooking the Montpellier Quarter's cobbled streets lined with bow-fronted shops, old-fashioned gas street lamps and antique shops is very picturesque. Once inside, it's easy to be won over by the welcoming and easy-on-the-eye décor of creams and white tablecloths covering small, close-set tables. The food majors on the modern, and daily specials are posted on a mirrored wall. Pan-seared queen scallops, celeriac and fennel purée with a coriander and basil cream and classic fillet of beef with pommes Anna, buttered spinach, tomatoes, shallots and red wine jus are exquisite. A set menu offered at lunch and in the early evening is just as tempting with ham hock terrine and first-class homemade ketchup and frissée and herb salad. Follow with slow-cooked roast belly pork with a rich, unctuous sauce, served with crunchy oriental vegetables and hoisin sauce. Iced white peach parfait, pear and orange syrup makes a wonderful finish. This is good value food using fresh ingredients and based on sound cooking skills. Service is very efficient and the wine list is wide-ranging and not greedy on prices.

Prices: Set lunch and dinner £14.95. Main course from £9.95. House wine £11.50.
Last orders: Food: lunch 14.30; dinner 21.30.
Closed: Sunday.
Food: Modern English.
Other points: Totally no smoking. Garden and courtyard.
Directions: In Harrogate town centre, located in the Montpellier Quarter, near Valley Gardens. (Map 12, E6)

Helmsley

Pheasant Hotel

Harome, Helmsley, North Yorkshire YO62 5JG
Telephone: +44(0)870 4016359
+44(0)1439 771241

Quiet and quaint, the location and look of this country hotel is quintessentially English. Overlooking the duck pond, the two former cottages and the village blacksmith's shop have been merged to give guests the best of both worlds – country pub meets country hotel. In the flagstoned and beamed bar it's very cottagey, then as you move into the restaurant and lounge it becomes chintzy and exceedingly comfortable. The real surprise, in such a picturesque and rural setting, is the small heated swimming pool in one of the courtyard buildings, which is great for a few leisurely lengths before breakfast or dinner. The neatly decorated bedrooms are cottagey in style, quite roomy and well equipped, and all overlook the duck pond. With its open lounge fire and peaceful village position, you will find this an easy place to relax and slow the pace. The restaurant, partly set in a conservatory, serves a daily-changing menu of traditional British food, such as cream of asparagus soup, roast breast of Gressingham duckling with apple sauce and onion stuffing, or poached fillet of fresh Scarborough sole with parsley sauce, and blackberry and apple pie to finish. There is also plenty of seating area outside in summer.

Rooms: 12. Double room from £140, single from £70 dinner,
bed and breakfast.
Prices: Set dinner £22.50. House wine £9.50.
Last orders: Food: lunch 14.00; dinner 20.30.
Closed: December, January and February.
Food: Traditional English.
Other points: No-smoking area. Dogs welcome overnight. Garden.
Car park. Indoor heated swimming pool.
Directions: Take the A170 from Helmsley towards Scarborough.
After 0.25 miles turn right for Harome. The hotel is opposite the
church. (Map 12, D7)

Hunmanby

Wrangham House Hotel

10 Stonegate, Hunmanby, Filey,
North Yorkshire YO14 0NS
Telephone: +44(0)870 4016417
+44(0)1723 891333
info@wranghamhouse.co.uk
www.wranghamhouse.co.uk

Fomerly a vicarage, this 18th century Georgian house has seamlessly made the transition to comfortable, elegant country house hotel. Its two acres of secluded woodland provide leisurely walks, while the more energetic can head for the coastal paths or the 13 top golf courses nearby. Most of the house renovations and extensions were planned by Francis Wrangham, a correspondent of William Wordsworth. He added the current dining room and the rooms above primarily to accommodate his library. The dining room is now quite a feature with striking décor. You can dine on traditional and updated dishes such as Caesar salad or smoked trout with avocado and shrimp mousse, and move on to roasted rack of lamb with redcurrant coulis or breast of Barbary duck in a red wine, button onion and mushroom sauce. The wine list has something for most tastes, and prices are reasonable, rarely topping £15. The day rooms are tastefully furnished with comfortable armchairs and they have log fires and lovely views on to the grounds. Four of the smart, traditionally styled bedrooms are located in an adjacent converted coach house, and one on the ground floor is equipped for guests with disabilities.

Rooms: 12. Double room from £75, single from £45.
Prices: Set dinner £19.50 and £16 (2 course).
Bar/snack from £5.95. House wine £11.75.
Last orders: Food: dinner 21.30. No food on Sunday.
Closed: Never.
Food: Contemporary British.
Other points: No-smoking area. Children welcome over
12 years old. Garden. Car park. Licence for Civil Weddings.
Directions: Nine miles south of Scarborough via the A165, then
the A1039. (Map 12, D8)

Down-to-earth, friendly service

Lastingham

Lastingham Grange

Lastingham, Kirkbymoorside, York,
North Yorkshire YO62 6TH
Telephone: +44(0)870 4016426
+44(0)1751 417345
reservations@lastinghamgrange.com
www.lastinghamgrange.com

The pretty village of Lastingham is in a small valley on the edge of the North Yorkshire Moors, and Lastingham Grange is a fitting hotel to grace this peaceful, rural setting. Built of stone and set around a central courtyard in 10 acres of gardens, it exudes an air of timeless elegance. The former farmhouse, dating from the 17th century, is well maintained, from its formal gardens down to the flower baskets, and there is woodland beyond. The Wood family, who have lived here for nearly 60 years, make visitors feel immediately at home without being intrusive. The public areas and bedrooms are spacious and furnished in soft colours with antiques, ornaments, and paintings. Bedrooms and en suite bathrooms are in pristine condition and comfortable, with a timeless air about them. The dining room has a romantic feel. The menus are built around local produce and lunch may include smoked salmon with egg mayonnaise or homemade soup, with baked fillet of salmon with leek and cider sauce or honey and lemon-glazed roast chicken for main course. Dinners offer starters of smoked trout with lime vinaigrette or three-onion Parmesan tart, and mains of braised pheasant with cider and cream sauce or venison casserole.

Rooms: 12. Double room from £180, single from £95, dinner, bed & breakfast.
Prices: Set lunch £18.75 (4 course) and dinner £36.50 (5 course). Main course from £12.50. House wine £7.75.
Last orders: Food: lunch 13.45; dinner 20.30 (Sunday 20.00).
Closed: December to the beginning of March.
Food: Traditional English.
Other points: No-smoking area. Children welcome.
Dogs welcome overnight. Garden. Car park.
Directions: From Pickering take the A170 towards Kirkbymoorside for five miles. Turn off right towards Appleton-le-Moors and Lastingham; follow the road for two miles turning right by the church. After 75 yards turn left up the no through road for 400 yards. (Map 12, D7)

Marton

The Appletree Country Inn

Marton, Pickering, North Yorkshire YO62 6RD
Telephone: +44(0)870 4016217
+44(0)1751 431457
appletreeinn@supanet.com
www.appletreeinn.co.uk

Formerly a run-down pub, chef TJ Drew and partner Melanie Thornton have transformed it into a cutting edge gastropub. It not only looks stylish, from its deep red front door to its lounge and patio garden, but the food served here is something to behold. Innovative monthly menus and daily specials make the most of quality local produce, including lamb, beef and pork from surrounding farms and home-grown fruits and vegetables. This is modern in every sense as they combine the best flavours and ideas from across the continents. Arrive for dinner and start with miniature crab cakes with gazpacho dressing and Avruga caviar. Move onto locally reared beef fillet with a walnut and date crust and horseradish cream. For pudding, opt for the stunningly presented marbled chocolate pyramid with Baileys chocolate mousse, yet save room for TJ's delicious petits fours with excellent coffee. First-rate lunches range from Yorkshire blue cheese, apple and pear salad to tomato risotto and minted lamb pie. All are served throughout the informal and very comfortable bar/restaurant, with its deep red walls, heavy beams and open fires, neatly adorned with polished tables and lots of candles. In addition, expect quality wines, impeccable service, Yorkshire ales (try a pint of Double Chance from nearby Malton), and a shop counter laden with homemade goodies.

Prices: Main course dinner from £10.50.
House wine £9.95.
Last orders: Bar: lunch 14.30 (Sunday 14.30); dinner 23.00.
Food: lunch 14.00 (Sunday 15.00); dinner 21.30.
Closed: Tuesday and two weeks in January.
Food: Modern British.
Other points: No-smoking area. Children welcome. Garden. Car park.
Directions: From Kirkbymoorside on the A170 towards Scarborough, village signposted right. (Map 12, D7)

Northallerton

Lovesome Hill Farm

Lovesome Hill, Northallerton, North Yorkshire DL6 2PB
Telephone: +44(0)870 4016402
+44(0)1609 772311
pearson1hf@care4free.net

Mary and John Pearson's working farm is deep in the Yorkshire Dales of James Heriott's *All Creatures Great and Small* and *Heartbeat*'s North Yorkshire Moors. It's set in 156 acres of farmland and is just 200 yards from Wainright's Coast to Coast walk, so all in all a quite remarkable location. It's a welcoming place, with sheep, cows, pigs and hens adding to its rural charm. Expect to be well fed, from the moment Mary ushers you into the lounge with a tray of tea and homemade biscuits on arrival. Breakfast is a hearty affair with eggs from the farm, local honey, sausages and bacon, homemade marmalade and lemon curd. Dinner is cooked around local supplies too. Homemade soups, chicken in tarragon or pork with apricots, served with locally grown vegetables, and raspberry Pavlova to finish are some of the dishes you can expect to tuck into. There is one bedroom in the main house; the rest are in a barn conversion; however, this is attached to the main house, so there is no need to go outside. A neat cottage style with floral prints, some canopied beds, and neat touches distinguish the rooms, which are all en suite. Gate Cottage sleeps two and offers the flexibility of bed and breakfast or self catering.

Rooms: **6. Double room from £50, single from £28, family room £78.**
Prices: **Set dinner £18.**
Closed: **Rarely.**
Food: **Traditional English.**
Other points: **No-smoking area. Children welcome. Garden. Car park.**
Directions: **Four miles north of Northallerton on the A167 towards Darlington, on the right hand side. (Map 12, D6)**

Pickhill

Nags Head Inn

Pickhill, Thirsk, North Yorkshire YO7 4JG
Telephone: +44(0)870 4016221
+44(0)1845 567391
enquiries@nagsheadpickhill.freeserve.co.uk
www.nagsheadpickhill.freeserve.co.uk

This former 17th century coaching inn has become synonymous with Yorkshire hospitality. Good, traditional rooms, excellent food and well-kept Yorkshire ales mean it has achieved an excellent reputation. Publican brothers Raymond and Edward Boynton are just as enthusiastic about their extended inn as they were when they started out just over 30 years ago. It's popular with the racing fraternity and visitors can retreat to the beamed and comfortably furnished lounge or the tie-adorned main bar at any time of day for refreshments. Alongside the top ales, Edward offers monthly wine selections, vintage armagnacs and an array of 40-odd malt whiskies. Two blackboard menus display Raymond's varied repertoire, which incorporates the best available produce – local game in season, Doreen's black puddings and quality meats. For a bar meal, try the beef, rabbit and venison pie, the large fish and chips or a choice of sandwiches, which are available all day. Interesting and often adventurous meals extend to poached scallops on spinach with cheese-glazed potato and duck with lime and gin sauce, plus traditional puddings such as Yorkshire curd tart. Seventeen en suite bedrooms are split between the main building, the next-door house and cottage. Most rooms have recently been refurbished to a high standard and now include a stylish suite. As well as a beer garden, there is also a 9-hole putting green and quoits pitch.

Rooms: **15 plus 1 suite. Double/twin from £70, single from £45.**
Prices: **Main course from £9.95. House wine £12.**
Last orders: **Bar: 23.00. Food: lunch 14.00; dinner 21.30.**
Closed: **Rarely.**
Food: **Modern British.**
Other points: **No smoking in the restaurant. Well-behaved children welcome. Garden. Car park.**
Directions: **In the centre of Pickhill just off the A1 between Boroughbridge and Catterick. Turn off on the B6272 towards Thirsk signposted Ainderby Overnhow. (Map 12, D6)**

Good food and wine

Hambleton Stallion

at the Appletree Country Inn

Traditional handmade ale using malted barley and English hops, Hambleton Ales is a small, family-run business that has flourished since its inception in 1991. Starting in a small barn under the watchful eye of the famous Hambleton White Horse it now produces 20,000 pints a week and appears in local shops and as guest beers at pubs around the country.

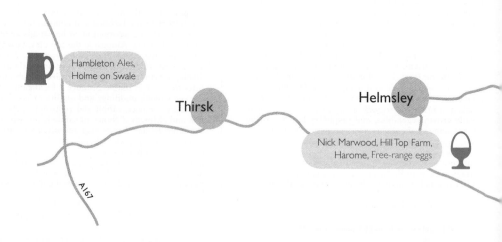

Hambleton Ales,
Holme on Swale

Thirsk

Helmsley

Nick Marwood, Hill Top Farm,
Harome, Free-range eggs

A167

One of these pubs is the Appletree Country Inn, a recent Les Routiers Dining Pub of the Year. This stylish pub in the Yorkshire moors has bundles of atmosphere, fantastic food and, of course, quality ales from Hambleton. Brewing still employs traditional methods and they claim that the local water is particularly suited to producing top quality beer with the unique and all important Hambleton flavour. It is not just available in shops and pubs, they will also deliver to your front door, be it bottles, which can be individually named, or casks, while visits to the brewery for an afternoon of tasting is also an appetising option. With accolades such as the Champion Winter Beer of Britain at the British Beer Festival it is no surprise that pubs such as the Appletree regularly feature beers like the award winning Hambleton Nightmare and Hambleton Stallion.

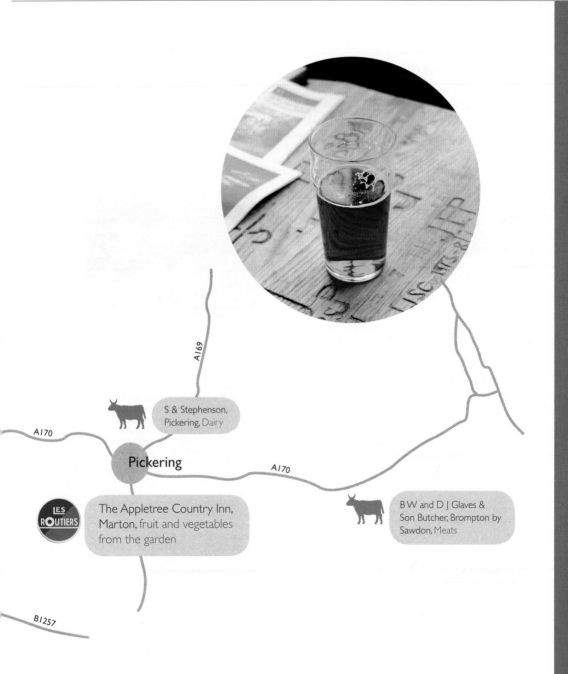

A169

A170

S & Stephenson,
Pickering, Dairy

Pickering

A170

LES
ROUTIERS

The Appletree Country Inn,
Marton, fruit and vegetables
from the garden

B W and D J Glaves &
Son Butcher, Brompton by
Sawdon, Meats

B1257

Sawley

The Sawley Arms and Cottages

Sawley, Fountains Abbey, Ripon,
North Yorkshire HG64 3EQ
Telephone: +44(0)870 4016224
+44(0)1765 620642

In a quiet village five miles south west of Ripon stands this fine old-fashioned pub whose immaculate upkeep and enduring popularity are a tribute to the work of June Hawes, who has been in charge here for over 35 years. She has built up an excellent reputation for good food, friendly hospitality and more recently for quality overnight accommodation in a newly built stone cottage. In a succession of alcoves and tiny rooms, each with winged armchairs, cushioned settles and attractive plates and prints, regulars find their preferred tables and order from June's varied menu and her tempting daily specials that are built around prime local materials, including smoked Nidderdale trout. Expect a good range of freshly cut sandwiches, delicious soups and snacks or starters like salmon, celeriac and herb pancake, and crab salad. In the evening one end of the pub takes on a more restaurant feel, and choice extends to steak pie with buttercrust pastry, braised lamb shank in Madeira gravy, and fresh Whitby cod. Available on a self-catering basis, the two very comfortable cottage suites feature spacious lounges, fully equipped kitchens and spotless en suite bathrooms with power showers and bathrobes, and plenty of cosseting extras.

Rooms: 2 cottage apartments sleeping two persons each. Prices from £250. There are seasonal price variations, please call ahead.
Prices: Main course restaurant from £10.50. Main course bar from £7.70. House wine £10.50.
Last orders: Food: lunch 14.30; dinner 21.00.
Closed: Sunday and Monday evening.
Food: Traditional and Modern British.
Other points: Totally no smoking. Garden. Car park.
Directions: Take the B62665 from Ripon and turn at Risplith into Sawley village. (Map 12, E6)

Scarborough

Golden Grid Fish Restaurant

4 Sandside, Scarborough, North Yorkshire YO11 1PE
Telephone: +44(0)870 4016415
+44(0)1723 360922
www.goldengrid.co.uk

This ever-popular restaurant is one of the best places to enjoy the freshest fish bought direct from Scarborough and Whitby fish markets. It's open all day, but it's in the evening that a top floor window seat overlooking the pretty harbour offers the best views, but you'll need to book to secure these popular tables. The restaurant has been in John Senior's family for 110 years and its consistently good quality food and friendly service attracts locals and tourists. Fish couldn't be fresher. Tuck into Atlantic cod, haddock and plaice served with mushy peas and chips, and lemon or Dover sole and halibut offered either grilled, herbed or with a meunière sauce. Shellfish includes fresh lobster, simple crab split in two and served with brown bread and lemon, and a fantastic fruits de mer platter with lobster, crab, oysters to name but a few of the shellfish delights. That old-fashioned northern tradition of high tea lives on in the Golden Grid's speciality farmhouse ham and egg tea. They also serve the Greenlay 1873, a secret sausage recipe, which features in the all-day big breakfast. Game from Wykeham Estates shoots makes a seasonal appearance, and even the butcher gets a mention on the menu, so proud are they of the quality of their meat.

Prices: Main course from £6.50. House wine £10.
Last orders: 22.30.
Closed: Winter hours are flexible due to weather.
Food: Seafood.
Other points: No-smoking area. Children welcome.
Directions: Located on the harbourside adjacent to the fish pier. (Map 12, D8)

Whitby

Magpie Café

14 Pier Road, Whitby, North Yorkshire YO21 3PU
Telephone: +44(0)870 4016463
+44(0)1947 602058
ian@magpiecafe.co.uk
www.magpiecafe.co.uk

You'd expect a fishing town to have a good fish restaurant, but the Magpie Café more than fulfills the brief. Café doesn't do justice to what is in fact a large, impressive black and white building that stands proudly overlooking the harbour. The building has long been associated with fishing, and the Café moved to this site in 1937. Its quality fish is legendary, so much so that queues have to make way for the daily deliveries of halibut, salmon or boxes of lobster that are delivered daily fresh off the boats in the quayside. Its traditional fish and chips, either haddock or cod, are renowned and come in small, regular or large sizes. But, there is much else to tempt. Owner Ian Robson has an extensive repertoire taking in fish pies and speciality recipes, such as haddock and prawns in a creamy leek sauce, salmon with lime crème fraîche, and whole oven-baked sea bass, served plain or with a garlic or a lemon butter. The meat dishes, such as local pork, sausage, egg and chips, or own-boiled ham with homemade coleslaw, and steak pie, are equally good and are made using locally sourced ingredients. In contrast, the wine list is small but offers good value and an international choice. There's a good selection of beers too. If you have room after the generous Yorkshire portions, the nursery puds such as jam roly-poly won't disappoint.

Prices: Main course from £5.95. House wine £9.95.
Last orders: Food: 21.00.
Closed: Mid January-early February.
Food: Seafood.
Other points: Totally no smoking. Children welcome.
Directions: Directly opposite the fishmarket on Whitby's historic harbourside. (Map 12, D7)

Whitby

Northbeach Café

The Sea Wall, Whitby, North Yorkshire YO21 3EN
Telephone: +44(0)870 4016465
+44(0)1947 602066
manager@northbeachcafe.co.uk
www.northbeachcafe.co.uk

The former art-deco style pavilion built in 1933 was saved from demolition and has been reborn. It is now an ideal spot for breakfast, dinner or lunch. Darren Archibald restored its original style to create a contemporary café serving light meals and refreshments throughout the day and good bistro-style dishes in the evening. In fine weather and at weekends mostly, the flat roof has a barbecue, which has proved very popular with summer visitors. Inside, the informal, light and bright ambience, combined with excellent service led by Rebecca Archibald, draws the crowds. The added attraction is being able to enjoy great views at sunset. The menu emphasis, especially in the evening, is on fresh seafood and meats plus the other ingredients that are also sourced locally. Throughout the day, you can enjoy salads, jackets and sandwiches. In the evening, the cooking steps up a gear to include local cod, homemade Thai fishcakes and grilled marlin steaks. There is a good choice of mostly modern wines and bottled beers, and prices for both food and drink are very reasonable. You will have to walk down the cliff path to reach the promenade, but transport can be arranged if needed.

Prices: Lunch from £3.95. Dinner from £5.95. House wine £10.95.
Last orders: Food: Snacks and lunch 09.00-17.00; dinner 21.00.
Closed: November-February. Open the first week of January.
Food: Modern British.
Other points: Totally no smoking. Garden. Children welcome.
Directions: Exit45/A1M. Travel on the A64 to York and then Malton and on the A169 through to Whitby. Northbeach Café and Restaurant is situated at the base of west cliff on the sea wall. (Map 12, D7)

Affordable good value

A E Wright & Son,
School Farm, Northallerton,
Meats

R J Noble, Whitby,
Shellfish and smoked produce

Herbs Unlimited,
Sand Hutton,
Salad leaves and herbs

Alliance Fish Marketing,
West Pier, Scarborough,
Fish

A168

A170

A61

Thirsk

A1

City of York

A64

Hazlewood Castle
Hotel, Tadcaster

LES
ROUTIERS

Tadcaster

Leeds

Herbs Unlimited
at Hazlewood Castle Hotel

Using local suppliers is important to Hazlewood Castle Hotel, and they have found a like-minded supplier in Herbs Unlimited. This business, based in Thirsk, sells mainly in the north, as its owner Alison Dodd points out that freshness of herbs and salad is important. And with cut herbs having a shelf-life of five days, you don't want them travelling the length of the country in containers. Herbs Unlimited grows around 23 different herbs from the popular parsley and basil through to the more unusual lemon and orange thymes, lemon and Thai basil, green and bronze fennel, sorrel and lovage. In fact, it's the chefs at top-end restaurants such as Hazlewood that want suggestions for new flavourings to try, says Alison. And in turn she looks to her seed supplier in Italy for new varieties to grow. As well as herbs, she grows a range of baby salad leaves, and chard and chicory. She has a four-acre site of poly tunnels and greenhouses and nine acres of field farm for outdoor crops. And the secret of growing herbs, says Alison, is to keep sowing so you continually have a fresh crop and good-quality leaves.

T Soanes & Son, Church Hill Farm,
Middleton-on -the-Wolds,
Poultry

A1079

Market Weighton

A614

Whitby

Quayside

7 Pier Road, Whitby, North Yorkshire YO21 3PU
Telephone: +44(0)870 4016464
+44(0)1947 602059

The fish market is only a stone's throw away, so you can look forward to the freshest local fish at Quayside. And it's all cooked in the traditional Yorkshire way with a special batter and served with its special crinkle-cut chips. Whitby cod, wholetail scampi, seafood platter and homemade fishcakes are just a few of the specialities offered by the Fuscos family. They have refurbished this three-storey quayside building, which used to house bathing and changing facilities for returning fishermen. It is in the first-floor library that it is claimed Bram Stoker wrote some of his Dracula stories. The open-plan interiors are fresh and airy, helped not only by air conditioning but a good eye for décor. The tiled floors are offset with dark green timbered walls, attractive lighting and cast-iron tables. As well as fish, the menu offers meat dishes such as homemade steak pie and vegetarian options such as cream cheese and broccoli bake. Before dining, have a drink in the contemporary upstairs bar that has fantastic harbour views. It also serves light snacks as well as heartier meals.

Prices: Restaurant main course from £6.50. House wine £8.
Last orders: Food: 20.00.
Closed: December and January, excluding 25th and 26th December.
Food: Traditional British.
Other points: Totally no smoking. Children welcome.
Directions: (Map 12, D7)

York

Four High Petergate Hotel and Bistro

2-4 High Petergate, York, North Yorkshire YO1 7EH
Telephone: +44(0)870 4016459
+44(0)1904 658516
enquiries@fourhighpetergate.co.uk
www.fourhighpetergate.co.uk

You can't help but feel you're somewhere special at this historic city-centre town house. Not only is it luxuriously appointed, it's also built into the city walls and Porta Principalis ancient gateway, once the western gateway to the old city. It also has wonderful views of the amazing York Minster. The house has been renovated beautifully by a Yorkshire racing family, and they have carefully chosen staff who can offer a high level of individual service. The elegance of the furnishings is evident from the reception with its old fireplace, polished floorboards and elegant furniture to the individually and stylishly designed bedrooms. The centrepieces are the comfortable solid beds with superb crisp linen and goose-down duvets. Other treats include power showers in the smart bathrooms, DVD players, and a beverage tray with fresh milk. Mornings get off to a great start with Yorkshire breakfasts in the bistro, and it is well worth returning for lunch or evening meal. For dinner, start with Whitby mussels, then marinated haunch of venison or Hovingham Estate pheasant wrapped in Parma ham and slow-roasted with garlic and white wine on a bed of deep-fried wild mushroom risotto. A good wine list is supported by a beer menu with tasting notes and suggested food matches. On warm evenings, head for the peaceful rear walled garden with its views of the Minster.

Rooms: 14. Double from £85, single from £50, family room from £110.
Prices: Restaurant main course from £10. House wine £10.
Last orders: Bar: lunch 14.30; dinner 23.00. Food: lunch 14.30; dinner 22.00.
Closed: Rarely.
Food: Modern British, Chilean, Classical French.
Other points: No-smoking area. Garden.
Children welcome over five years. Car park. Film library.
Directions: A19 Shipton road, follow through Bootham to town centre, immediately through ancient gateway of Bootham Bar. (Map 12, E7)

Leeds

Hazlewood Castle Hotel

Paradise Lane, Hazlewood, Tadcaster,
West Yorkshire LS24 9NJ
Telephone: +44(0)870 4016462
+44 (0)1937 535353
info@hazlewood-castle.co.uk
www.hazlewood-castle.co.uk

Off Paradise Lane, this centuries-old castle is grand and is grandly surrounded by attractive and mature parkland and gardens. Bedrooms in the main castle or the courtyard wing live up to the exteriors and are sumptuously appointed. Celebrity chef John Benson-Smith has a wonderful setting in which to showcase his fine cooking at restaurant 1086. It's named after the date the castle was first mentioned in the Domesday Book. The room is beautifully designed and spacious with tall French windows opening on to a terrace overlooking the lawns. The colour scheme is a stylish black and white and the elegant table settings get you in the mood for the sophisticated dishes that are to follow. Start with baby leaf and local Lilac Farm asparagus, truffles, Parmesan and poached quails eggs, and follow with turbot fillet with wild mushrooms, pomme Maxine and rosemary butter. Wines by the glass are suggested for each course. The strong kitchen skills are evident in the flavour and presentation. In addition to the extensive wine list, there is a long modern bar offering a selection of drinks. For more casual dining, there's the Castle's Prickly Pear bistro, which serves mainly Italian pizza and pasta and some classic hearty British dishes.

Rooms: 21. Doubles from £140, suites from £255.
Prices: Restaurant 1086 set lunch £29.50 and dinner £19.95.
Restaurant 1086 main course from £15. Prickly Pear Pizzeria main course from £4. Prickly Pear house wine £10.95.
Last orders: Food: 21.30.
Closed: Never.
Food: Modern French.
Other points: No-smoking area. Garden.
Children welcome over 12 years old. Car park.
Directions: A64 junction A1M, take A64 towards York then the first left, A659, towards Tadcaster and follow the information signs to Hazlewood Castle Hotel. (Map 12, E6)

Leeds

Mill Race Organic Restaurant

2 Commercial Road, Kirkstall, Leeds,
West Yorkshire LS5 3AQ
Telephone: +44(0)870 4016278
+44(0)113 275 7555
enquiries@themillrace-organic.com
www.themillrace-organic.com

This relaxed, laid-back organic restaurant is made up of early 19th century cottages close to Kirkstall Abbey grounds. All ingredients, including beer and wines, are certified by the Soil Association, UK Farmers and Growers, or similar international certifying bodies. Upstairs is a casual, relaxed sitting room, filled with deep sofas and it is the only place where you can smoke. Downstairs, the dining room has big windows with frosted glass at the bottom to shield customers from the traffic outside. The upbeat, contemporary menu opens with seared savoury cheesecake with four cheeses and honey beetroot salad. Main courses range from breast of chicken stuffed with almond and saffron on bubble and squeak polenta with raisin and black olive sauce to Thai noodles with peanut sauce and deep-fried tofu, served with a spicy carrot and lemon salad. Blackboard evening specials bring the likes of Yorkshire-reared pork chop with apple and sage mash with a creamy cider sauce. After this chocoholics should head straight for the triple chocolate cheesecake with dark chocolate sauce and chocolate ice cream. The well-annotated organic wine list ranges far and wide and is reasonably priced.

Prices: Set lunch/dinner £15 (Sunday-Wednesday).
Main course from £10. House wine £10.95.
Last orders: Food: Sunday lunch 15.00; dinner 22.00.
Closed: Monday, Sunday evening and Tuesday-Saturday lunch.
Food: Modern British.
Other points: No smoking in the restaurant. Children welcome.
Directions: Two miles from the centre of Leeds on the A65 Skipton road; close to Kirkstall abbey and opposite Kirkstall Leisure/sports centre. (Map 12, E6)

An alternative Britain

Moorsfresh produce

*at Four High Petergate
Hotel and Bistro*

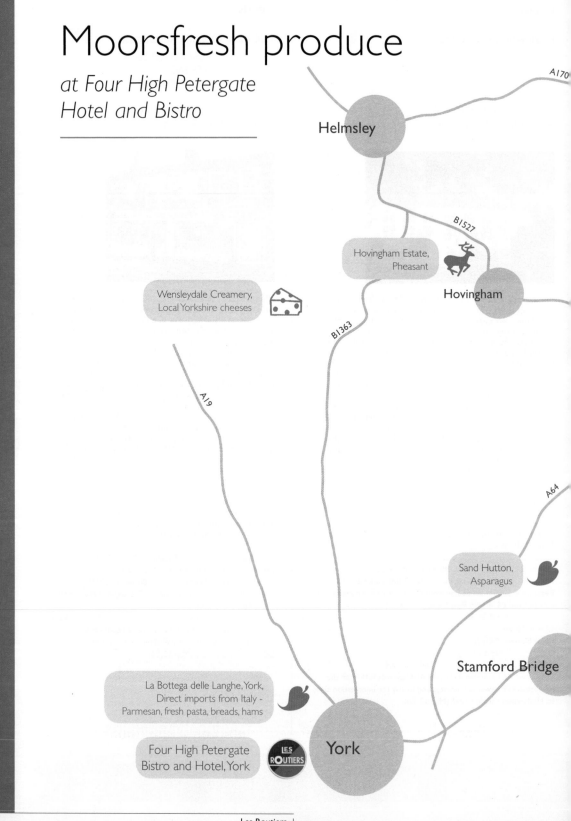

A170

Helmsley

B1527

Hovingham Estate,
Pheasant

Hovingham

Wensleydale Creamery,
Local Yorkshire cheeses

B1363

A19

A64

Sand Hutton,
Asparagus

Stamford Bridge

La Bottega delle Langhe, York,
Direct imports from Italy -
Parmesan, fresh pasta, breads, hams

Four High Petergate
Bistro and Hotel, York

LES
ROUTIERS

York

Moorsfresh, Pickering,
Sourcing local and regional artisan produce

Pickering

A169

Malton

Restaurants don't have time always to deal direct with suppliers, but still want to get the best ingredients from producers who are passionate and responsible about growing and rearing methods. Moorsfresh collects the best products in Yorkshire from suppliers and delivers them to hotel and restaurants, including Four High Petergate Hotel and Bistro in York. It has more than 40 producers on its books and offers shellfish and lobster, crabs from Whitby, rare breed meats such as Saddleback pork, Swaledale lamb, and Shorthorn beef. On the dairy side it can offer organic clotted cream, Wensleydale cheese and the much in demand Grosmont goats' cheese from the North Yorkshire moors. At Four High Petergate, they have regular orders of oriental salad leaves, rocket and dairy products such as milk, cream and cheese, plus speciality breakfast sausages come from Moorsfresh. One ingredient becoming more popular is Moorsfresh's smoked garlic bulbs, which are smoked by its smoked salmon supplier. It only takes a few hours before the garlic has a lovely smoky and milder flavour, and chefs in York just can't get enough of it.

Moorsfresh: Thornton Road Industrial Estate, Pickering, Yorkshire; 01751 477888

A166

Scotland

Whether you fancy haggis or haddock and lime risotto, you'll find the old favourites and new trendy dishes on the thriving Scottish food scene, says Anita Chaudhuri.

To the uninitiated, the Scottish restaurant scene might suggest some unappetising cliches – haggis and boiled turnips washed down with a bottle of Chateau irn-bru. In fact nothing could be further from the truth. When it comes to using nature's larder, Scotland is blessed with a vast array of quality local produce, from the ubiquitous Speyside salmon and prime Aberdeen Angus beef to West Coast scallops, lobster and langoustines.

However locally sourced ingredients are just part of the story. Scottish chefs are notoriously inventive and seek inspiration from across the globe. Even in the most obscure Highland inn, it is possible to stumble upon a menu boasting lime and haddock risotto, coriander cheese rarebit or shortbread with Drambuie sabayon. There will always be a demand for classic regional dishes though, both from locals and the significant tourist population. Cullen Skink (a creamy smoked haddock soup) is a firm favourite as is venison casserole and clapshot (a dish of mashed turnips spiked with caramelised onions).

In the major cities, particularly Glasgow and Edinburgh, there's a strong focus on atmosphere and keeping up with new trends. However tastes are fickle and the scene is fast-moving. Glasgow's first sushi restaurant was short-lived, organic mania has died down and curiously the gastropub has yet to become a feature of Scottish urban life. Even Gordon Ramsay's Michelin-starred Amarylis couldn't stay the course. Ramsay blamed the closure on Glasgow having just too many restaurants. However insiders say that the real reason was the high prices – not on the food, but on that most crucial Scottish factor – licensed victuals.

On the global front, Indian food has always enjoyed great popularity in Scotland thanks to a large immigrant community, however here too there are touches of humour and imagination. Edinburgh's Suruchi Too offers curries of haggis, venison and salmon while at Glasgow's Mr Singh's, the waiters are all decked out in kilts.

As Scots embrace the foodie mentality, many outlying restaurants are becoming day-trip destinations such as the Inn at Lathones, which serves some of the finest fish and shellfish. And not a deep-fried Mars Bar in sight...

Ballater

The Station Restaurant

Station Square, Ballater, Aberdeenshire AB35 5RB
Telephone: +44(0)870 4016333
+44(0)13397 55050

The small cream and red wooden railway station in the town of Ballater has welcomed royals and their guests from the 1860s until its closure in 1966. Balmoral is just eight miles away. Luckily, the disused station fell into good hands after it was restored. Nigel Franks, hotelier and train enthusiast, looks after the station's refreshment rooms and has transformed them into a fun, informal restaurant. Many of the original features, including wood panelling and a smoked glass ceiling, are still in place and are tastefully offset with wicker chairs and marble tables. If only all station food was this good. It's well worth arriving for breakfast as the porridge and cream is exemplary, or there's fabulous French toast or a full Scottish monty. Later in the day, the menu moves on to cakes and cappuccino and lighter dishes of sweetcorn fritters with bacon, roasted tomatoes and rocket, or a more substantial crispy beer-battered haddock with French fries and a green salad. In fact, the Station has a something-for-every-one appeal. Daily specials chalked up on blackboards extend the choice further. Ingredients are sourced locally, and there is a homely appeal to the cooking – we would return just for the straight-out-of-the-oven scones, some of the best we have ever tasted.

Prices: Restaurant main course from £6. House wine £12.
Last orders: Food: lunch 17.00; dinner 21.00. Seasonal variations.
Closed: Rarely.
Food: Scottish.
Other points: Totally no smoking. Children welcome. Car park.
Directions: In central Ballater, the old royal station. (Map 16, F7)

Arduaine

Loch Melfort Hotel

Arduaine, Oban, Argyll and Bute PA34 4XG
Telephone: +44(0)870 4016448
+44(0)1852 200233
reception@lochmelfort.co.uk
www.lochmelfort.co.uk

The hotel's claim to have the 'finest location on the west coast' lives up to expectations. On a clear day the outlook is quite magnificent as you can see right across the Sound of Jura. The core of the house is Edwardian and despite having been much extended, owners Nigel and Kyle Schofield have maintained a seamless look and atmosphere that you feel has gone unchanged for decades. A keen eye for décor includes modern and bold colours and fabrics. In the popular Skerry bistro, there's a wonderful bright and breezy Mediterranean look. Bedrooms in the main house are spacious and some have spectacular loch views. There are also cheerful and simpler rooms in the Cedar Wing. The restaurant serves good-quality locally caught fish and seafood, much of it collected straight from the boat in front of the hotel. Meat and game are also locally sourced. Dinner could include local shellfish bisque or twice-baked Dunshyre Blue soufflé, followed by grilled fillet of sea bass with sautéed asparagus and sugarsnap peas, tomato and chive butter sauce, or roast gigot of Barbeck lamb on a ring of clapshot with redcurrant jus. The wine list spans a range of styles and prices.

Rooms: 26. Double/twin room from £90, single from £55.
Prices: Set dinner £25-34. House wine £12.50.
Last orders: Food: lunch 14.30; dinner 21.00.
Closed: 4-22 January. Restaurant closed for lunch.
Food: Modern Scottish.
Other points: No-smoking area. Dogs welcome.
Children welcome. Garden. Car park.
Directions: 19 miles south of Oban on the A816. (Map 13, C3)

Arrochar

Greenbank Guest House

Arrochar, Argyll and Bute G83 7AL
Telephone: +44(0)870 4016312
+44(0)1301 702305
shirleyandsam@cluer101.freeserve.co.uk

This small 19th century house has been turned into an attractive guest house and is the ideal choice for those on a limited budget. It's set in the centre of Arrochar, which is bustling in summer and peaceful in winter. Everything is well maintained, and there's a cosy feel to the lounge and bar areas. The four en suite bedrooms are also warm and homely. The views from some of the bedrooms and the dining room are wonderful, taking in the famous Cobbler Mountain as well as Loch Long. Food is available all day, with a series of menus ranging from snacks and light lunches to a full carte. Scotch broth, mussels from the Isle of Mull, and fried Loch Fyne herring in oatmeal, and haggis and neeps are among the typical choices.

Rooms: 4. Double room from £37, single from £22 including breakfast.
Prices: Set lunch and dinner £10.95. Main course from £7. House wine £9.95.
Last orders: Food: 20.00 November-March (22.00 March-November).
Closed: Rarely.
Food: Traditional Scottish/seafood.
Other points: No-smoking area. Children welcome. Garden. Car park. Licence for Civil Weddings.
Directions: On the A83, opposite Cobbler Mountain. (Map 14, C5)

Cardross

Ardardan Estate Farm Shop & Nursery

Cardross, Argyll and Bute G82 5HD
Telephone: +44(0)870 4016343
+44(0)1389 849188
www.ardardanestate.co.uk

When a compulsory order for road widening was put on the Montgomery's Brown Egg Farm Shop on the other side of the Clyde, they put the cash boost from the council and their 20 years of experience into a farm estate some 30 minutes away. Now, after five years of hard work, their super farm shop, along with its small plant nursery, walled garden, woodland walks and working farm is drawing folk from Glasgow and further afield, as it is en route for the Highlands via Loch Lomond. The farm has sheep, free-range chickens and bantams, and a few Highland cows, and they grow their own summer fruit. In the farm shop they stock a huge variety of Scottish produce: clover and heather honey, free-range eggs, fruit and vegetables in season (not all locally grown), locally made cakes and biscuits, homemade jams and chutneys, smoked and cured meats and fish, and a wide range of organic ice creams including Orkney ice cream. There's also the option of picking your own strawberries and raspberries in season. The coffee shop next to the plant nursery serves light lunches from a menu built around traditional Scottish food such as homemade soups, and bakery goods are available.

Last orders: Shop 16.00.
Closed: Rarely.
Food: Light lunches.
Other points: No-smoking area. Children welcome. Garden. Car park.
Directions: M8 motorway, go over the Erskine Bridge. Two miles from Cardross on the A814 towards Helensburgh. (Map 14, C5)

Individual charm and warmth

Dunoon

Dhailling Lodge

155 Alexandra Parade, Dunoon,
Argyll and Bute PA23 8AW
Telephone: +44(0)870 4016337
+44(0)1369 701253
mac@dhaillinglodge.com
www.dhaillinglodge.com

It's easy to get away from it all at this attractive Victorian villa that sits along the coast road through Dunoon with restful views over the Firth of Clyde estuary and the hills of West Renfrewshire. And owners Donald Cameron and Fraser McKenzie do their utmost to make your stay comfortable. The lodge with seven individually styled rooms is immaculately looked after. All rooms come with TVs, hairdryers, beverage trays and bathrobes. One room is designed for use by those with limited mobility and who require wheelchair access. The dining room overlooks the front garden and here you can enjoy hearty buffet-style Scottish breakfasts and set menu dinners that change daily and incorporate many local ingredients. Before sitting down to dinner, you can enjoy aperitifs and canapés in the lounge. At dinner, start with Cambletown Cheddar and spring onion soufflé, followed by noisettes of new season Isle of Bute lamb on a red wine and cranberry jus, and round off with lemon and bilberry meringue roulade, and Columbian coffee or Ceylon tea. While there is no bar as such, there is a good selection of wine served in the dining room, featuring European favourites and popular new world varieties.

Rooms: 7. Double room from £60, single from £32.
Prices: Set dinner £19.50 (5 course). House wine £8.50.
Closed: November.
Food: Traditional Scottish with international influences.
Other points: Totally no smoking. Dogs welcome. Garden. Car park.
Directions: On Alexander Parade, the East Bay Promenade about two miles west of Hunters Quay and one mile east of Dunoon town centre and pier. (Map 13, C4)

Isle of Bute

Russian Tavern at The Port Royal Hotel

37 Marine Road, Kames Bay, Port Bannatynne,
Argyll and Bute PA20 0LW
Telephone: +44(0)870 4016258
+44(0)1700 505073
stay@butehotel.com
www.russiantavern.co.uk

It's one of the least likely places for a reincarnation of a Russian Tsarist tavern, but Norwegian-born landlord Dag Crawford and his wife Olga, a Russian palaeo-botanist, have achieved just that in the pretty village of Port Bannatyne. The waterfront location of this stone-built Georgian building is stunning, overlooking Kames Bay with views to the Cowal Hills. The Russian Tavern is an amiable place, the friendliness is genuine, and service relaxed. Dag cooks a brasserie-style menu that has a strong Russian accent, having researched recipes from the Tsarist kitchen archives in St Petersburg. His beef stroganoff is considered outstanding, but gets strong competition from blini with marinated herring, and spicy Russian sausage with apple, latkas, red cabbage and sauerkraut. Local produce plays a big part, notably Highland beef, game and fish and langoustines from the bay. A typical dinner of langoustine soup, halibut steak, followed by fresh fruit, cream and ice cream filled Russian Pavlova, is remarkable value. To drink, try one of the excellent real ales from Scottish micro-breweries, or a glass of Imperial Russian stout. The house wine is a bargain. Upstairs are five unpretentious, good-value bedrooms, two are en suite. There's plenty to explore and one of the top attractions is the Victorian Gothic Mount Stuart House, where fashion designer Stella McCartney was married.

Rooms: 5, 3 not en suite. Room from £22 per person, £26 for an en suite.
Prices: Set lunch and dinner £20. Main course £14. Bar main course from £5.50. House wine £5 per pint.
Last orders: Bar: 01.00 (Saturday 02.00).
Closed: 1-21 November.
Food: Traditional Russian.
Other points: Totally no smoking. Children welcome. Car park. 5 free yacht moorings. Beach. Golf course at the rear.
Directions: Three miles north along the coast road from the Rothesay (ferry) on the Isle of Bute and six miles south on the coast road from the ferry at Colintraive, Argyll. (Map 13, C4)

www.routiers.co.uk

Luss

Coach House Coffee Shop

Loch Lomond Trading Co Ltd, Luss, Loch Lomond,
Loch Lomond Trossachs National Park,
Argyll and Bute G83 8NN
Telephone: +44(0)870 4016357
+44(0)1436 860341
enquiries@lochlomondtrading.com
www.lochlomondtrading.com

Set in the centre of one of the most visited villages on
the banks of Loch Lomond, this super old-style coach
house is the perfect stop-off for light refreshments and
more substantial meals. There are plenty of specialities
to try. The shop has bags of atmosphere and is homely,
warm and welcoming. But despite having exposed
beams, a huge rustic stone fireplace, and solid wooden
tables and chairs, this is in fact a new building. Open
all day, it caters for everyone in its spacious but cosy
rooms. The kilted Gary Grove and his wife Rowena
offer an ever-revolving repertoire. Scones, cakes such
as caramel apple granny or Skeachan fruit cake, light
lunches of homebaked quiche with coleslaw, salad and
fresh bread, or stokies (traditional soft bread rolls)
filled with egg mayonnaise from their own free-range
Black Rock hens, form the bedrock of the menu.
Haggis, neeps and tatties, and bacon and courgette
pasta make filling lunch dishes, and they don't stint on
the portions. There's a separate menu offering a wide
range of espressos, cappuccinos and lattes, speciality
teas and smoothies. The coffee shop is unlicensed. And
if you don't get a chance to try their fruity whisky
cakes, you can buy some from the shop to take home.

Prices: Meals from £4.90.
Last orders: Food: 17.00.
Closed: Never.
Food: Modern Scottish.
Other points: Totally no smoking. Children welcome. Garden.
Directions: From the A82 follow the signs for Luss. The café is
next to the church in the centre of the village. (Map 14, C5)

Luss

Lodge on Loch Lomond

By Alexandria, Luss, Argyll and Bute G83 8PA
Telephone: +44(0)870 4016356
+44(0)1436 860201
res@loch-lomond.co.uk
www.loch-lomond.co.uk

Hugging the shores of Loch Lomond, it comes as no
surprise that this smart pine-clad hotel has accommodated American presidents. It's a class act, and every
window along the side of this long linear building has
remarkable views across the loch. The hotel's atmosphere is Scottish, but without a hint of tweeness. There
are 45 bedrooms in all, which range from standard
and executive rooms with sitting areas to the President
Carter Suite, which has its own separate sitting room.
In addition, all bedrooms have their own sauna, as
well as smart modern bathrooms. Magnificent views
are standard. A lack of pretension, coupled with
meticulous attention to detail, characterises the running of both hotel and Colquhoun's restaurant, which
draws on the best of local ingredients. Starters include
steamed Shetland mussels, rillettes of Bradan roast
smoked salmon or something more exotic like bonito
soup. Mains deliver the likes of sirloin Glen Fyne beef
or brochette of scallops, monkfish and prawns with
couscous salad, and a mussel and saffron nage. The
wine list is a well-annotated global tour with plenty of
good drinking.

Rooms: 45. Double/twin from £85, single from £50,
family room from £110.
Prices: Set lunch £10.95. Set dinner £23.95. Restaurant main
course from £12. Bar main course from £6. House wine £11.95.
Last orders: Food: lunch 17.00 (Sunday 16.00); dinner 21.45.
Closed: Rarely.
Food: Modern British.
Other points: No-smoking area. Dogs welcome.
Children welcome. Garden. Car park. Licence for Civil Weddings.
Directions: On the A82 on the western shores of Loch Lomond.
(Map 14, C5)

Regional produce

Rothesay

Brechin's Brasserie

2 Bridgend Street, Rothesay, Isle of Bute,
Argyll and Bute PA20 0HU
Telephone: +44(0)870 4016411
+44(0)1700 502922
info@brechins-bute.com
www.brechins-bute.com

The brightly coloured yellow and blue brasserie brings
a touch of the continent to Rothesay. Owners Tim Saul
and Ann Council have spotted a gap in the market for
an upmarket brasserie and are making their mark in
this bustling town. There is a breakfast, snacks and
hot meals menu served throughout the day, and a restaurant menu on Friday and Saturday evenings. Ann
is in charge of the kitchen, while Tim sees to front
of house. Lattes, cappuccinos and Americanos are a
good match for the selection of French pastries and
puddings. Sandwiches are filled ciabatta plus there are
salads and hot dishes such as steak and Guinness pie,
vegetable lasagne and Brechin's curry bowl. The set
dinner menus include many local ingredients, including
smoked Isle of Bute trout, smoked Bute cheese, and
smoked salmon, lamb and beef. Start with hot smoked
salmon or king prawns, followed by fillet of Scottish
steak tournedos Rossini, and finish with crème brulée.
The short wine list covers classics at reasonable prices.
This fledgling brasserie is already proving popular, and
we imagine it will soon be expanding the menu and
opening times in the coming months.

Prices: Restaurant evening main course from £7.95.
Lunchtime snack from £4.95. House wine £9.95.
Last orders: Food: lunch 15.00; dinner 21.00
(Friday and Saturday only).
Closed: Sunday, Monday all day. Tuesday to Thursday evening
Food: Traditional Scottish, English and Continental dishes.
Other points: Totally no smoking. Children welcome until 20.00.
Directions: By road to Wemyss Bay and by Calmac Ferry to
Rothesay. Situated in the town centre 400 metres from the ferry
terminal and marina. (Map 13, C4)

Tobermory

Fishermen's Pier Fish and Chip Van

Raraig House, Tobermory, Argyll and Bute PA75 6PU
Telephone: +44(0)870 4016410
+44(0)1688 302390
jeanette@scotshop.biz
http://www.silverswift.co.uk/van.htm

Jeanette Gallagher and Jane MacLean's takeaway fish
and chip van on Tobermory's Fisherman's Pier is quite
an institution. The two friends are in their second decade of serving consistently good fish and chips to regular customers that come from miles around. Their van
occupies an amazing position overlooking Tobermory
Bay, which is famous for the sinking of a galleon from
the Spanish Armada in 1588. The location is perfect
for some well-priced, al fresco dining. Park up at the
Clock Tower or on the lobster/prawn creels on the Pier
before ordering. Fish comes straight off the boats and
into the van where it is cooked to order. It is supplied
by Taste of Argyll, Oban, while the freshest local scallops are supplied by Grampian Seafood off its fishing
vessel Western Belle, which is skippered by Jeanette's
son Geoffrey. Come rain or shine, the queues are long,
but always good humoured, and the fish meals superb.

Prices: Average price of meal £3.80.
Last orders: Food: 21.00.
Closed: Sunday and January, February, March.
Food: Seafood.
Directions: On the Fisherman's Pier in Tobermory. (Map 13, B3)

Ballantrae

Balkissock Lodge

Ballantrae, Girvan, South Ayrshire KA26 0LP
Telephone: +44(0)870 4016368
+44(0)1465 831537
franaden@aol.com
www.balkissocklodge.co.uk

Once a shooting lodge, then a farm, Balkissock is now an attractive and efficiently run guesthouse. Set deep in the countryside, you will get a real taste of rural life and hospitality from Denis and Fran Sweeney. After taking on the lodge in 2001, they have just completed the refurbishment. The lounge is beautifully decorated in cream with comfy sofas, cushions and throws. A real fire adds to the cosy atmosphere. Fran has also individually designed the three bedrooms, one with an additional adjoining room that's perfect for families. Two are in the adjoining barn. Each room has en suite facilities and is furnished to high standards, and comes with extras such as TV, radio, hairdryer, beverage tray and mini fridge. Breakfast is taken in the separate dining room and offers some of the best Scottish fare, including porridge and smoked salmon and scrambled eggs. At dinner, the Sweeney's share the cooking. Fran makes the starters and puddings, which include smoked mackerel pâté, a platter of Arbroath smokies with a cucumber pickle, lime and ginger cheesecake or iced raspberry cranochan trifle. Denis devises the mains, which are a selection of excellent game, meat, fish and vegetarian dishes, using local and home-grown ingredients. Standards are excellent and on a par with some of the best hotels.

Rooms: 4. Double room from £27.50, single from £39 and family from £85. Prices are per person.
Prices: Set dinner £20.
Last orders: Dinner served at 19.00.
Closed: Rarely.
Food: Modern British.
Other points: Totally no smoking. Garden. Car park.
Directions: Three miles off the A77 near Ballantrae. On south side of Ballantrae take the turn signposted to the camp site, at T-junction turn right, bear left at fork and continue for one mile. Lodge is on the right. (Map 13, E4)

Down-to-earth, friendly service

Scottish cheeses

at Balkissock Lodge

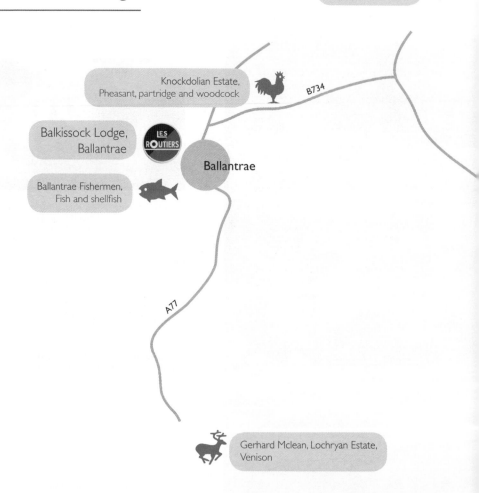

P Pieroni & Sons, Ayr, Fresh fish

Knockdolian Estate, Pheasant, partridge and woodcock

B734

Balkissock Lodge, Ballantrae

LES ROUTIERS

Ballantrae

Ballantrae Fishermen, Fish and shellfish

A77

Gerhard Mclean, Lochryan Estate, Venison

After serving a selection of Scottish-only cheeses, Fran Sweeney has never looked south of the border again. At Balkissock Lodge, Fran serves the region's specialities with a few of her own: homemade oatcakes, pear and rosemary, and rhubarb and chilli chutneys. There is a thriving market for cheese in Scotland, with more producers making farmhouse cheese. Fran gets her selection from The Tryst Farm Shop. Star attractions are the Howgate Camembert and Bishop Kennedy, a whisky-washed brie-style cheese, both of which are produced at Kinfauns Home Farm, near Perth that suppliers wholesalers and farm shops. Both cheeses are made from cows' milk and take six weeks to make. The Camembert is soft, creamy and wonderfully ripe, while the liquor-soaked brie has a distinctive earthy flavour, which only needs oatcakes as an accompaniment. These ripe cheeses certainly don't need to be served with butter. At The Tryst, you can also sample lots of other styles of Scottish cheeses such as blue and hard Cheddar-style cheeses and do a one-stop shop of other Scottish specialities such as whisky and honey.

Kinfauns Home Farm, Perth and Kinross,
Bishop Kennedy, Howgate
Camembert, Ayrshire Blue Cheeses

A714

B7027

Newton Stewart

Galloway Smokehouse,
Smoked Scottish Salmon

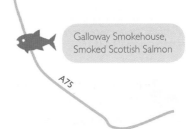

A75

Castle Douglas

Balcary Bay Hotel

Shore Road, Auchencairn, Castle Douglas,
Dumfries and Galloway DG7 1QZ
Telephone: +44(0)870 4016390
+44(0)1556 640217
reservations@balcary-bay-hotel.co.uk
www.balcary-bay-hotel.co.uk

It stands overlooking the beautiful Balcary Bay and offers space, comfort and, of course, some fine views. For nearly two decades Graeme Lamb has slowly enhanced his hotel. The entrance hall-reception leads to a large, comfortably appointed oak-panelled lounge with open fire and fine bay views. Off this is a residents' lounge, furnished in full country house rig, with a separate cocktail bar and terrace overlooking the sea – popular spots for pre-dinner drinks and good value light meals at lunchtime. Three new superior bedrooms are on the ground floor, while original bedrooms are on the first and second floors. All bedrooms are spacious and furnished and equipped to a high standard, but those overlooking the bay are the best. Fantastic views can also be enjoyed from the pastel-coloured dining room as the windows look over the sea as well as the gardens. Here, the emphasis is firmly on flavour and quality. Local produce such as Galloway beef, lamb, salmon and lobster features strongly on menus that include starters of ravioli of fresh lobster and pickled dill served with braised Puy lentils, and mains of rosette of local beef fillet and sautéed mushrooms. Similarly, the wines are well chosen and represent the classic and new wine producing areas of the world.

Rooms: 20. Double twin from £114.
Prices: Set Sunday lunch £14.75. Set dinner (5 course) £29.50.
Restaurant main course from £13.50.
Bar main course from £6.50. House wine £13.50.
Last orders: Food: lunch 14.00; dinner 20.30.
Closed: Third Saturday in December to the first Friday in February.
Food: Modern British.
Other points: No-smoking area. Dogs welcome overnight. Garden. Children welcome. Car park.
Directions: Auchencairn is on the A711 between Dalbeattie and Kirkcudbright. On reaching Auchencairn turn along the Shore Road for two miles. (Map 14, F6)

Castle Douglas

Craigadam

Castle Douglas, Dumfries and Galloway DG7 3HU
Telephone: +44(0)870 4016391
+44(0)1556 650233
enquiry@craigadam.com
www.craigadam.com

This substantial 300-year-old whitewashed farmhouse is set in its own country estate of 25,000 acres of farmland, woodland and moorland. It offers fabulous views southwards over rolling hills and distant views northwestwards to the higher Galloway hills, as well as plenty of fishing, stalking and shooting opportunities. Cecilia Pickup runs Craigadam as a charming guest house, but with the space, style and service of a country house hotel, while Richard, her husband, runs the farm that operates along organic lines. This conveys the dedication they bring to their businesses: guests benefit from the attention to detail in bedrooms and public rooms and from the quality of produce used. An excellent set dinner is served that may include locally smoked salmon, home-reared lamb, or estate game, with home-grown vegetables, homebaked bread and regional cheeses. All seven bedrooms and en suite bathrooms are generously proportioned and beautifully furnished, many have French doors opening onto a gravelled courtyard, and they are decorated with different themes, for example oriental or Rennie Macintosh style. Public rooms are also spacious, with the bay-windowed lounge being particularly comfortable. The dining room is grand with a massive communal oak table, and off this is a room with a full-size snooker table and honesty bar.

Rooms: 7. Double/twin from £76. Single from £45.
Prices are per person.
Prices: Set dinner £19 served at 19.00. House wine £9.95.
Closed: 24 December-2 January.
Other points: No-smoking area. Dogs welcome. Garden. Children welcome. Car park.
Directions: M74. Leave the motorway on the A75 to Dumfries. Follow the signs to Castle Douglas, after nine miles go through the village of Crocketford turn right on the A712. Craigadam is two miles along on the right hand side. (Map 14, F6)

Gretna

Garden House Hotel

Sarkfoot Road, Gretna, Dumfries and Galloway DG16 5EP
Telephone: +44(0)870 4016367
+44(0)1461 337621
enquiries@gardenhouse.co.uk
www.gretna-weddings.net

The Garden House is the place for modern Gretna weddings. It's an elegant setting with lovely grounds complete with a Japanese water garden and with several stylish honeymoon suites to choose from. However, spacious, well-equipped bedrooms that offer real value for money and The Sark Leisure Club with a state-of-the-art 15-metre long swimming pool with sauna and steam room, act as a lure for weary travellers too. Families, in particular, will find the hotel a useful stopping off point on a journey north or south. As well as large honeymoon suites with super-king size beds, there are 38 spacious en suite bedrooms, which come with satellite TV, hairdryers and coffee and tea-making facilities. The lounge and dining room are bright and open plan. In the latter, a traditionally robust country house menu delivers something for everyone, be it salads such as Waldorf and Caesar, meats from the char-grill, say fillet steak with crushed black peppercorn sauce, or rack of lamb with redcurrant sauce, and fish in the guise of lemon sole with basil and herb butter, or Solway salmon steak with a lemon and herb crust. Around 80 or so wines make a good effort to keep prices within reason.

Rooms: 38. Rooms from £42.50 per person.
Prices: Main course from £11. House wine £8.25.
Last orders: Food: lunch 14.00; dinner 21.00.
Closed: Rarely.
Food: Modern British.
Other points: Children welcome. Garden. Car park. Licence for Civil Weddings.
Directions: On the A74, just across the Scottish border. (Map 14, F7)

Kircudbright

Harbour Lights

32 St Cuthbert Street, Harbour Square, Kirkcudbright, Dumfries and Galloway DG6 4HZ
Telephone: +44(0)870 4016392
+44(0)1557 332322
the_harbour_lights@hotmail.com
www.harbourlights.com

You'd expect Harbour Lights to have a good view of the harbour, and it doesn't disappoint. In keeping with this town popular with artists, the restaurant has a distinctively painted mulberry front and attractive windows. Inside the single dining room is small and cosy, with homely tongue and groove panels and walls painted in soft colours. Bag a window table to watch the comings and goings in this busy tourist spot. Chef/proprietor Jill Lawrie caters for all, from those travellers stopping off before taking the ferry or locals who come for dinner at weekends. The daytime menu offers delicious homebaked cakes such as scones or crumbly shortbread with tea and coffee, and afternoon toasted teacakes. More substantial options for lunch include sandwiches, paninis, and meat and salad platters. On Fridays and Saturdays, Jill opens for dinner and offers a wide-ranging menu focusing on local ingredients. Dishes such as Galloway beef, mushroom pie and Solway salmon are excellent traditional options and for the more adventurous there's Kashmiri lamb or Thai green chicken. Leave room for fabulous homemade puddings such as tiramisu, strawberry cheesecake and Tia Maria brulée. Jill's easy-going manner and her welcome, coupled with her good cooking, has ensured Harbour Lights is streets ahead of the competition.

Prices: Restaurant main course from £5.50. House wine £9.50.
Last orders: Food: lunch 15.30;
dinner 20.15 (Friday and Saturday only).
Closed: Rarely.
Food: Modern Scottish.
Other points: Totally no smoking. Children welcome. Car park.
Directions: In the centre of Kirkcudbright on St Cuthbert Street. (Map 14, F6)

Good food and wine

Corsewall Lighthouse Hotel, Stranraer

Stranraer

Corsewall Lighthouse Hotel

Kirkcolm, Stranraer, Dumfries and Galloway DG9 0QG
Telephone: +44(0)870 4016434
+44(0)1776 853220
lighthousehotel@btinternet.com
www.lighthousehotel.co.uk

It's in a romantic setting and its interiors couldn't be more charming. Corsewall Lighthouse has been beautifully converted and what it lacks in space, it makes up for in exceptionally elegant furnishings and nice touches such as wonderfully fragrant flowers that scent the air. Extensive restoration has created six rooms and three suites, all but one en suite. Decorations offer contemporary and classically designed rooms. Each comes with extras such as TV/video, telephone, tea tray and trouser press. Great thought has been put into the food too, and ingredients are bought locally from Buccleuch, with smoked products from Marrbury Smokehouse and fish landed at Kirkcudbright. Chef Andrew Downie transforms these quality ingredients into his modern Scottish menus. Leading the set menus are baked haggis and black pudding or Marrbury smoked chicken supreme. These are followed by mains of Buccleuch Scotch beef sirloin or grilled salmon delice. Chocolate nemesis and rum and banana bread and butter pudding round off an excellent meal. After dinner, relax in the bar, to sample the good range of malts, or retire to the lounge to admire the rocky shore coastline or to watch videos.

Rooms: 9. 1 with private bathroom. Double from £130.
Price includes dinner. Seasonal price variations.
Prices: Set dinner (5 course) £32.50. House wine £13.95.
Last orders: Food: lunch 13.45; dinner 20.45.
Closed: Rarely.
Food: Modern Scottish.
Other points: No-smoking area. Dogs welcome. Garden.
Children welcome. Car park.
Directions: (Map 13, F4)

Edinburgh

40a Heriot Row

40a Heriot Row, Edinburgh EH3 6ES
Telephone: +44(0)870 4016320
+44 (0)131 226 2068
diane@heriotrow.com
www.heriotrow.com

Its rooms wouldn't look out of place in a smart upmarket hotel, so it may come as a surprise to find that this B&B is infact housed in the garden flat of a Georgian town house. It's in a fabulous location, just minutes from Princes Street. The attention to detail and style are second to none. The spacious, beautifully decorated B&B is on two light and airy levels. The long, light hallway leads to a large beautifully furnished drawing room with wall-to-wall bookcases and antiques. It's the ideal place to relax in the evening over a complimentary glass of whisky. One bedroom, a twin, is on this floor, which is a lovely cosy room with an en suite shower room and the second en suite bedroom is on the lower ground floor. Both rooms have tea trays, mineral water and a little decanter of whisky. The dining room is also on the lower level, making use of the old cellar. It is decorated with painted stone walls, bookcases covering one wall, light cream paintwork, an antique dining table and sideboard. Here, Diane Rae serves breakfast, using as much homemade produce as possible, and the local butcher and fishmonger supply sausages, bacon, and kippers. There's a tiny patio filled with exotic and unusual plants and across the road is the 3-4 acre private Queen Street Garden, to which guests have access. This B&B is a real gem, and cat lovers will be enchanted by the resident felines.

Rooms: 2. Double room from £50 per person, single from £60.
Closed: Rarely.
Food: Local Scottish.
Other points: No-smoking area. Garden. Children welcome.
Directions: From Princes Street take a left at Frederick Street and then left after the gardens. 40a is at the end of the block on the right. (Map 14, C7)

Affordable good value

Edinburgh

A Room in the Town

18 Howe Street, New Town, Edinburgh EH3 6TG
Telephone: +44(0)870 4016318
+44(0)131 225 8204
john.tindal@btconnect.com
www.aroomin.co.uk/thetown

It's what every city needs, a bustling neighbour-hood bistro serving up a good vibe and good modern Scottish cooking. Along an attractive cobbled street, it is a popular spot, drawing in customers with its bright, colourful daytime look, and by lowering the lights and serving by candlelight in the evenings. With a few exceptions all produce is obtained from small, independent local suppliers and producers, such as MacSweens for haggis and Tombuie smoked cheese from the Perthshire hills. The menu offers bistro fare with a contemporary twist: roast chicken, chorizo and couscous salad with an avocado and corn salsa, or pink peppercorn and mustard crusted tuna garnished with a chunky niçoise vinaigrette. A Highland element is evident in the cooking too, with the likes of smoked haddie and black pudding dauphinoise topped with peppered goats cheese, or crispy cod fillet on creamed tatties with haggis and smoked bacon, and cassis-soaked brambles with lemon meringue ice cream. Scottish cheeses are teamed with hot gooseberry chutney and oatcakes. Value for money is a major factor, combined with generous portions and use of fresh produce. A mixed selection of mostly new world wines includes several by the glass.

Prices: Set lunch £10.95 and dinner £21.95.
Main course from £10.25. House wine £9.95.
Last orders: Food: lunch 14.30; dinner 22.00
(Friday and Saturday 22.30, Sunday 21.30).
Closed: Second Sunday of January.
Food: Modern Scottish.
Other points: Smoking allowed after 14.00 and 22.00. Bring your own wine policy, £1 corkage. Children welcome.
Directions: Turn off Princes Street up Frederick street. Howe Street is a continuation of Frederick Street, a Room in the Town is on the left hand side down the hill. (Map 14, C7)

Edinburgh

The Blue Parrot Cantina

49 St Stephen Street, Edinburgh EH3 5AH
Telephone: +44(0)870 4016316
+44(0)131 225 2941
blueparrot@blueyonder.co.uk

This tiny little basement restaurant continues to be a popular haunt in the bustling Stockbridge area of the city. With only nine tables, the dining room can either be very intimate, quiet and cosy – usually midweek – or absolutely buzzing at weekends. The bright and simple décor gives a real Mexican feel to get you in the mood for the food. It's attractively furnished with walls painted dark blue or dark red, wooden floors, chunky wooden tables and chairs and Mexican-style iron wall candle sconces providing a stylish finishing touch. The menu might not change often but that's because Fiona Macrae finds the unusual dishes served are so popular with customers that there would be a mini outcry. You won't find the bog standards such as chilli con carne or tacos here. This is modern Mexican cooking, taking in starters of homemade bean and vegetable soup, or seafood ceviche marinated with lime and orange juice with cold avocado, chilli and coriander. Mains include strips of sirloin marinated with orange, lime juice, oregano and smoked chipotle chillies and pan-fried with capsicum and onion. Fruit chimi (kahlua liqueur with apple, banana or pineapple wrapped in flour tortillas, deep fried and served with cream), or pecan pie make good puddings. There's a good range of cocktails, tequilas, and predominantly new world wines, with the house French also being offered by the glass.

Prices: Main course from £8.05. House wine £10.15.
Last orders: Food: 22.30 (Friday and Saturday 23.00).
Closed: Monday-Friday lunch and Sunday lunch.
Food: Modern Mexican.
Directions: In the centre of Edinburgh. (Map 14, C7)

Edinburgh

Britannia Spice

150 Commercial Street, Britannia Way, Leith,
Edinburgh EH6 6LB
Telephone: +44(0)870 4016325
+44(0)131 555 2255
info@britanniaspice.co.uk
www.britanniaspice.co.uk

With contemporary interiors, a trendy Leith Docks address and an ever-evolving menu, this restaurant continues to attract new customers. It's in an attractive converted whisky bond, and en route you will see the Royal Yacht Britannia that is docked nearby. The restaurant is open plan, yet offers intimate Indian dining. In the nautically themed dining room, blonde wood tables, dark blue chairs, and sunken ceiling spots, create a sense of light and space. The restaurant has many supporters, and this could be down to its varied menu, which explores Northern Indian, Bangladeshi, Nepalese and Thai cuisines. It is constantly changing, with new dishes added every few weeks to provide the regular clientele with new choices. From Nepal there could be spicy trout roasted with fried mushrooms, tomatoes, green chilli, mustard seeds and fresh herbs, with its counterpart from Bangladesh of freshwater fish marinated in spices and herbs. Thailand supplies a popular green curry of chicken or, from North India comes chicken kebab with hot spices and a ginger-based sauce with fresh coriander. There's also tikka masala, billed as the Queen's favourite dish, in chicken, lamb and prawn versions, as well as biryanis, and a decent selection of vegetarian dishes. The wine list offers a balanced variety from European vineyards and the new world plus there's a selection of bottled beers.

Prices: Main course from £6.95.
Last orders: Food: lunch 14.15; dinner 23.45.
No food Sunday lunch.
Closed: Rarely.
Food: Indian and Thai.
Other points: No-smoking area. Children welcome. Car park.
Directions: In Leith, follow road signs for the ocean terminal or the Royal Yacht Britannia. (Map 14, C7)

Edinburgh

Daniel's Bistro

88 Commercial Street, Leith, Edinburgh EH6 6LX
Telephone: +44(0)870 4016323
+44 (0)131 553 5933
www.daniels-bistro.co.uk

Occupying a converted warehouse overlooking the revamped Leith Docks, Daniel's offers a contemporary setting for its bistro classics and the trendy Leith crowd. It's bright and modern with beech tables, chrome chairs, spotlights, and has a semi open-plan kitchen. The main part of the restaurant is almost conservatory style, as one whole wall is made up of floor-to-ceiling windows; even the roof is glass with canvas awnings to protect against the glare of the sun. A variety of all-day eating options runs from late breakfasts of croissants, Danish pastries and coffee, through a value-for-money lunch to a carte that offers French bistro classics such as moules farcies, and entrecôte steak au poivre. This is simple, direct cooking, overseen by Daniel Vencker, who comes from Alsace. He pays homage to his home by offering specialities, but he also incorporates local ingredients in dishes such as double lamb chop cutlets provençal and Scottish salmon fillet with zesty warm coarsegrain mustard seeds and balsamic vinaigrette. One of the perennial favourites is the raclette. Desserts are mainly French stalwarts: crème brulée and gateau opera, but cranachan flies the flag for Scotland. The wine list is predominantly French, but other wine-producing regions of the world get a look in. There are several available by the glass, as well as a good selection of beers available.

Prices: Set lunch £7.95. Main course from £8.45.
House wine £12.95.
Last orders: Food: lunch 14.30; dinner 22.00. (Saturday 22.30).
Closed: Rarely.
Food: Traditional French.
Other points: No-smoking area. Children welcome. Garden. Car park available evenings.
Directions: City district of Leith near the Docks and Ocean Terminal. Halfway along Commercial Street towards Royal Yacht Britannia on the right hand side. (Map 14, C7)

An alternative Britain

Edinburgh

Duck's at le Marche Noir

2/4 Eyre Place, Edinburgh EH3 5EP
Telephone: +44(0)870 4016327
+44(0)131 558 1608
enquiries@ducks.co.uk
www.ducks.co.uk

Duck's has spread its wings and has recently taken over the Kilspindie House Hotel and restaurant in Aberlady. The new restaurant is run along the same lines as the popular city original, which offers fresh, flavoursome food that is popular with the Edinburgh crowd. Ducks really are a prominent feature in Malcolm Duck's eponymous restaurant, and feature as table ornaments and as pictures on the Emma Bridgewater plates. The dining room is attractive, with bold mustard-gold walls offset by green wood panelling. It's a fairly intimate space with large picture windows allowing lots of natural light in by day, and in the evening this is changed to soft candlelight. Duck's is something of an Edinburgh institution, and has built up a loyal clientele that appreciates its modern bistro-style cooking. At lunch, there's the excellent value 'Fly By Lunch'. In the evening, the carte serves up stunning dishes. Starters may include smoked venison loin salad with Parmesan, ciabatta croûtons and blueberry vinaigrette or pan-fried haggis on celeriac mash with shallot marmalade and red wine jus. Among the inventive main courses are seared scallops with crispy prosciutto, asparagus and pecorino salad and red pepper salsa or Aberdeen Angus beef fillet with horseradish mash, red onion confit and cep jus. The carte changes monthly, and bargain set lunches change every five weeks or so. Though its strength lies in France, the wine list also contains some well-chosen new world bottles and a notable selection of halves.

Prices: Main course £11.50-£22. House wine £14.50.
Last orders: Food: lunch 14.30; dinner 22.00 (Sunday 21.30).
Closed: Saturday, Sunday, Monday lunch.
Food: Modern Scottish/European.
Other points: Children welcome.
Directions: 15 minutes walk from the city centre. (Map 14, C7)

Edinburgh

Maison Bleue

36-38 Victoria Street, Edinburgh EH1 2JW
Telephone: +44(0)870 4016319
+44(0)131 226 1900
www.maison-bleue.co.uk

Halfway between the Royal Mile and Grassmarket is this funky French bistro that has proved to be a big hit with city slickers. Its contemporary and stylish setting and relaxed, bustling atmosphere coupled with imaginative food is a winning combination. And it has proved inspirational for some diners: it's claimed that JK Rowling wrote some of *Harry Potter and the Philospher's Stone* here. The bargain set menu, available at lunch and in the early evening, is rooted firmly in France, with a style that's typified by provençal-style seafood croquettes with rocket salad, and slow-cooked lamb casserole with butter beans, spinach and white wine. But it's the banquet menus offered from 5-7pm, from which you choose two dishes plus a side dish and dessert, that has captured the imagination. From a repertoire that roams the world, you can sample boureks au crevettes, which is a calamari, roast aubergine tower, or North African chicken brochette and smoked salmon ciabatta, to name but a few specials. Le banquet grand bleu includes an extra dish of say seared tuna loin or lamb tagine and makes for a fabulous feast. The wine list offers a good selection of predominately French wines, but a few new world choices help to match the extensive range of dishes on offer.

Prices: Set lunch £9.50 (2 course). Main course from £8. House wine £9.90.
Last orders: Food: lunch 15.00; dinner 23.00. Longer opening hours during the Edinburgh festival.
Closed: Rarely.
Food: Modern French.
Other points: No-smoking area. Children welcome.
Directions: Just off Grassmarket between the Royal Mile and Grassmarket. (Map 14, C7)

www.routiers.co.uk

Edinburgh

Merchants

17 Merchant Street, Edinburgh EH1 2QD
Telephone: +44(0)870 4016317
+44(0)131 225 4009
www.merchantsrestaurant.co.uk

Once you find this restaurant on a tiny dead-end street near the Royal Mile, you'll be glad you ventured off the main drag. It's a cheery and cosy place to dine, and an attractive setting. Stone walls are painted bright red, a low-beamed ceiling, varnished floors, clever lighting and well-placed mirrors that diffuse the little light create an intimate atmosphere. The white linen, cream napkins, white crockery and fine glassware are a sophisticated contrast, but are an indication that they take dining seriously here. The set lunch and dinner menus change every week or so and local and seasonal produce feature prominently. For dinner, you could start with an imaginative guinea fowl and black grape filo pastry parcel with a sesame and honey dressing or a more traditional haggis, neeps and tatties gateau served with a whisky jus. Mains also offer some of the best Scottish produce with Angus sirloin steak topped with foie gras with a red wine and port sauce, while oriental stir fry caters for more exotic tastes. The short wine list opens with well-priced house French wines, and prices remain under £20 throughout most of its varied international selection.

Prices: Set lunch £12.95 and dinner £24.95. House wine £10.50.
Last orders: Food: lunch 14.00; dinner 22.00.
Closed: Saturday lunch and all day Sunday and 2-3 January.
Food: Modern Scottish.
Directions: In Edinburgh old town; just off the Grassmarket. (Map 14, C7)

Edinburgh

Peter's Cellars

11a-13a William Street, Edinburgh EH3 7NG
Telephone: +44(0)870 4016322
+44(0)131 226 3161

This small basement restaurant in a smart West End shopping street has built up a good following in the 20-odd years it has been open. Current proprietor Suzanne Brown is the goddaughter of the original owner and also worked as manager for the previous owner, so she knows what does and doesn't work and has got her menu down to a fine art, accordingly. Adventurous it may not be, but it serves consistent good-quality favourites. The bar is a popular local hangout, used as just that, despite only accommodating 10 people. The restaurant proper, however, is quite intimate in that most of the tables are in their own little mahogany-style booths with wrought-iron rails around the top and little checked curtains, and they are popular with couples. The short, weekly changing set menu is built around basic ingredients from local suppliers. The kitchen offers popular combinations such as chargrilled sirloin steak with sauce au poivre, and breaded pork and brie schnitzel with a lemon and thyme reduction. On the starter line-up are terrines, soups, and beer-battered cauliflower and broccoli florets with chilli jam, with individual summer puddings, or iced vanilla parfait with a blackcurrant coulis featuring among the desserts.

Prices: Set lunch £10.95. Early-bird set dinner £13.95 and regular set dinner £23. House wine from £9.
Last orders: Bar: 01.00. Food: lunch 14.30; dinner 21.30 (Sunday 21.00).
Closed: Rarely.
Food: Scottish.
Other points: Totally no smoking in the restaurant (smoking in the bar). Children welcome.
Directions: In the West End of Edinburgh. (Map 14, C7)

Individual charm and warmth

Edinburgh

Le Petit Paris

38-40 Grassmarket, Edinburgh EH1 4DU
Telephone: +44(0)870 4016321
+44(0)131 226 2442
petitparisrestaurant@hotmail.com
petitparis-restaurant.co.uk

This super little blue and white painted restaurant is idyllically situated against a backdrop of the towering rocky cliff face of Edinburgh Castle. Its blackboards help to draw attention to incredibly good-value lunch or pre-theatre menus on offer. Inside its simple rustic looks, from the old French photographs and French signs to the pretty check tablecloths, whitewashed walls and wooden floors, will win you over. You can eat upstairs or in the cosy basement room. The plats du jour menu, a bargain £5 including coffee, is available at lunch and early evening. Dishes on this menu may include grilled steak, pan-fried salmon with a Noilly Pratt sauce or sautéed lamb with rosemary jus. Equally, the main menu never strays beyond the boundaries of the French classics. This is the place to rediscover forgotten favourites such as a straightforward version of fish soup with rouille and croûtons, boudin noir with a special Limousin mustard, snails in garlic and Pernod sauce and coq au vin that is done traditionally and marinated in wine for 48 hours. Desserts follow a traditional theme too, perhaps crème brûlée, or chocolate fondue, or there is a French cheese selection. The all-French wine list is to the point and keenly priced.

Prices: Restaurant main course from £9.80. One course and coffee £5, between 12.00-15.00 and 17.00-19.00.
Last orders: Food: 22.30 (23.00 Friday and Saturday).
Winter: lunch 15.00; dinner 22.30 (Friday to Sunday 23.00).
Closed: Monday during the winter.
Food: Traditional French.
Other points: Children welcome.
Directions: In the centre of Grassmarket. (Map 14, C7)

Edinburgh

Regents House Hotel

3/5 Forth Street, Edinburgh EH1 3JX
Telephone: +44(0)870 4016326
+44 (0)131 556 1616
info@regenthousehotel.co.uk
www.regenthousehotel.co.uk

This Georgian building first became a hotel in 1942, and its new owners are gradually restoring it to its former glory. It is made up of two elegant Georgian houses that have been knocked into one and the strong period feel of the properties has been retained to give 19 bedrooms. These are a mix of family rooms, doubles and singles. In some bedrooms patchwork bedspreads add appeal to the homeliness of the establishment. Although some rooms are small and reserved for single occupancy, nearly all have en suite showers. In addition, there are family rooms catering, in one instance, for up to five. Given that the hotel is only a 10-minute walk from Princes Street and the centre of Edinburgh, this is good value for money in a city where prices can be extremely high. The main dining room where breakfast is served opens as a teashop during the day, offering traditional Scottish teas and high teas, backed up by homemade soups, sandwiches and a selection of cakes, pastries and scones. There is also a licensed bar.

Rooms: 17, 2 not en suite. Double room from £65, single from £35, family room from £70.
Closed: Five days over Christmas.
Food: Traditional Scottish.
Other points: Totally non-smoking.
Children welcome. Garden.
Directions: In the centre of Edinburgh. (Map 14, C7)

Edinburgh

Suruchi Too

121 Constitution Street, Leith, Edinburgh EH6 7AE
Telephone: +44(0)870 4016324
+44(0)131 554 3268
suruchires@aol.com
www.suruchirestaurant.co.uk

At the foot of Leith Walk is this Indian restaurant that occupies a former whisky warehouse. It's a warm and welcoming place with spicy aromas from the kitchen meeting you at the door. The decoration is a vibrant mix of Indian fabrics, mirrors, dramatically enlarged photographs of Indian scenes, and a huge leather camel adorned with Rajasthan decorations. Herman Rodrigues hails from Jaipur in Rajasthan, and his chefs have trained in India. He is intensely proud of the fact that he uses as many Scottish ingredients as possible in his menu, especially venison, salmon, and even haggis. Indeed, an Indian interpretation of Scottish produce is a unique feature here. You can choose from starters such as pakora, samosas, fritters and kebabs, and a wide range of main courses from tandoori favourites to an excellent array of vegetarian dishes such as chana masala, masala bhindi, aubergine masala, or shabnam, and chicken, meat and fish specialities, and a fabulous selection of flavoured rice. On Wednesday and Friday nights and Sunday lunchtimes, there is live jazz. And every month, the restaurant runs a food festival, which focuses on one Indian region, with cookery demonstrations and dishes to try. Alternatively, its other branch Suruchi, at 14a Nicholson Street opposite the festival theatre, offers a comprehensive carte.

Prices: Set lunch £6.95 and dinner £14.95.
Restaurant main course from £8. House wine £9.95.
Last orders: Bar: 14.00; dinner 23.30.
Closed: Rarely.
Food: Traditional Indian.
Other points: No-smoking area. Children welcome.
Directions: At the bottom of Leith Walk, walk straight over the lights into Constitution Street and Suruchi Too is 200 yards along on the right hand side. (Map 14, C7)

Edinburgh

Teviotdale House

53 Grange Loan, Edinburgh EH9 2ER
Telephone: +44(0)870 4016329
+44(0)131 667 4376
eliza@teviotdalehouse.com
www.teviotdalehouse.com

If you want to explore the capital, then head for Elizabeth and Willy Thiebaud's (she is Scottish, he is French) charming and friendly hotel. It's in a terraced house on a residential road just 10 minutes from the city centre, and it provides a quiet and restful base. All the bedrooms are individually decorated and show great attention to detail. All follow a smart, well-thought through chintzy theme, with matching headboards or pelmets. Five rooms have small compact en suite shower rooms, while the two remaining rooms have adjacent bathrooms and come equipped with bathrobes. All have hot drinks trays, TVs, and hairdryers, and large, fluffy towels. The dining room looks out through a picture window onto the back garden. It's light and pleasant and filled with light pine furniture, golfing pictures and memorabilia (golfing lessons, and green fee bookings can be arranged at 20 different courses). Breakfast is excellent, with a choice of teas or herbal infusions, porridge, compote of dried fruits, prunes in nectar, free-range eggs, Ayrshire-cured bacon, homemade sausages from the local butcher, oatcakes, and homemade scones.

Rooms: 7, 2 not en suite but private facilities. Double/twin room from £28 per person, single from £32, family from £25 per person.
Closed: Rarely.
Other points: Residents only. Totally no smoking.
Children welcome.
Directions: A720. Leave the city bypass at Straiton junction and head towards the city centre for 2.1 miles. Fork left, Mayfield Road, for one mile. Go through the traffic lights at Mayfield church and then take the first left. (Map 14, C7)

Regional produce

Musselburgh

Inveresk House

3 Inveresk Village, Musselburgh, Edinburgh EH21 7UA
Telephone: +44(0)870 4016328
+44(0)131 665 5855
chute.inveresk@btinternet.com

This large house dates back to the 15th century and it has a very special vibe thanks to its rich history. Oliver Cromwell stayed here before the Battle of Dunbar in 1653, and there are Roman remains in the gardens and resident ghosts. The atmosphere is homely and lived in, but smart and tasteful in a traditional style. Furnishings include antiques, heavy drapes and large colourful oil paintings by owner Alice Chute. Dining is a treat, not least because the room itself is enormous and you sit at a long dining table with bamboo-style chairs. Rugs cover bare floorboards and there are dark sideboards. Alice serves wholesome, hearty breakfasts. The drawing room immediately upstairs is equally large, and this has a grand piano and large comfortable sofas, antique tables, more pictures, and a fire on chilly days. Bedrooms range from a roomy family room, with antique furniture and a Victorian-style bathroom with a huge, deep bath with overhead shower, to a double room with more modern en suite facilities, plus a separate smaller double room, which also may be used by a family. A final bedroom has a double and two single beds, and its own modern shower room. All rooms have TV, hot drinks tray, large cream fluffy towels and toiletries.

Rooms: 3. Double room from £70, single from £45.
Closed: 23-27 December.
Other points: Residents only. Totally no smoking. Garden. Children welcome. Car park.
Directions: Before entering the village of Musselburgh at the top of the hill, turn sharp right towards St Michaels Church. Take the second entrance on the right; go past two cottages and follow the road round to the right, signposted Inveresk House. (Map 14, C7)

Anstruther

The Anstruther Fish Bar

42-44 Shore Street, Anstruther, Fife KY10 3AQ
Telephone: +44(0)870 4016331
+44(0)1333 310518
alison@falcotwo.demon.co.uk
www.anstrutherfishbar.co.uk

It seems fitting that two fishermen's cottages have been turned into one of the finest fish bars in Scotland. Anstruther's occupies the ground floor overlooking the picturesque harbour. Its popularity with locals and tourists is down to its consistently good fish and chips. People travel from miles around for its fare and in summer months queues outside stretch right along the street. The interiors are designed for maximum efficiency. A brass Victorian-style rail maintains an orderly queue for takeaways or you can sit in at two restaurant areas. Service keeps up with demand, and despite the hussle and bustle, you don't feel rushed. The star of the show is haddock, battered or breadcrumbed, but there are plenty of alternative fish. The catch of the day board can include monkfish, halibut, trout, salmon, lemon sole, prawns or dressed crab, all specially selected and supplied daily from Smiths' fish processing in St Monans. A popular non-fish choice is white pudding, a delicious mixture of oatmeal, onion and seasoning, pressed into a sausage shape and deep-fried. A license means you can also enjoy wine or beer with eat-in meals.

Prices: Set lunch £6.30. Restaurant main course from £4.50. House wine £7.50.
Last orders: Food: 22.00.
Closed: Rarely.
Food: Traditional fish and chips.
Other points: No-smoking area. Children welcome. Public car park opposite.
Directions: M90. Nine miles south of St Andrews, B9131. (Map 14, C7)

www.routiers.co.uk

Anstruther

The Spindrift

Pittenweem Road, Anstruther, Fife KY10 3DT
Telephone: +44(0)870 4016332
+44(0)1333 310573
info@thespindrift.co.uk
www.thespindrift.co.uk

Commissioned by a sea captain in the early 19th century, this imposing yellow sandstone house makes for a comfortably elegant guesthouse. Ken and Christine Lawson have furnished it beautifully, from the comfortable lounge with honesty bar to the dining room. At the top of the house is its most remarkable bedroom. It overlooks Anstruther harbour and is decorated as a captain's cabin, a style created by the original owner one Captain Smith, although sadly he never lived to see the house finished. Eight other en suite bedrooms make up this immaculately run guesthouse. Each has a TV, telephone and internet connections and tea tray. Breakfast is served buffet style from a central station, and Ken is an award-winning porridge maker, after winning a competition by Scott's, the well-known oats manufacturer. Set dinners revolve around locally sourced meat, fish and vegetables and speciality smoked products. Starters include homemade soup of say carrot and parsnip or Orkney herring in dill marinade, and are followed by classics such as lamb in red wine with rosemary and grilled Pittenweem haddock. Desserts also revolve around local specialities; there's Orkney ice cream, fruits of the forest crème brulée and the famous Pittenweem oatcakes with cheese. There is also the opportunity to sample beers from small local brewers, whiskies and Scottish liqueurs.

Rooms: 8. Double/twin room from £26.50 per person, single from £35.
Prices: Set dinner £15. House wine £7.60.
Last orders: Food: served from 19.00.
Closed: Christmas.
Food: Traditional Scottish.
Other points: Totally no smoking. Garden. Children welcome over 10 years old. Dogs welcome overnight. Car park.
Directions: Exit2A/M90. Approaching Anstruther from St Andrews turn right at the roundabout onto Pittenweem Road, Spindrift is the last house on the right leaving the village. (Map 14, C7)

Kincardine

Seasons Coffee Shop

7 Kirk Street, Kincardine-on-Forth, Fife FK10 4PT
Telephone: +44(0)870 4016298
+44(0)1259 730720

Leslie Mitch's tiny bistro-cum-coffee shop has a wonderfully homely, cottagey feel, and home-cooked, hearty food to eat in or takeaway is firmly on the menu. The shop is prettily decorated; an old fireplace is covered with cards and gifts, many of them local crafts, and there's a small corner shelf display, with further displays of gifts laid out on the small windowsills and hanging on the walls. It is all attractively done with the added bonus of the coffee shop being totally non smoking. The little shop front with its food counter and seating for 25 does good business serving good home-cooked food to eat at anytime during the day, and delicious and healthy takeaways too. The menu is short and straightforward, delivering soup, perhaps an excellent carrot and ginger, followed by a generous prawn sandwich made with chunky brown bread, or there are hot paninis with mixed salad, say roast beef and mustard, or bacon rolls, and filled baguettes. Cakes and homemade scones extend the range. Five wines are offered by the glass.

Last orders: Food: 16.00.
Closed: Sunday, 1-4 January.
Food: Coffee shop, sandwiches and homemade cakes.
Other points: Totally no smoking.
Directions: In the centre of Kincardine. (Map 14, C6)

Down-to-earth, friendly service

Kincardine

Unicorn Inn

15 Excise Street, Kincardine-on-Forth, Fife FK10 4LN
Telephone: +44(0)870 4016250
+44(0)1259 739129
info@theunicorn.co.uk
www.theunicorn.co.uk

Tony and Liz Budde have put this 17th century coaching inn on the map. They serve quality food in smart, contemporary surroundings. Its bar, grill and restaurant configuration means you can find meals for all occasions. The Grill Room, the more casual of the two dining areas, is on ground level. Here, you can sink into leather sofas around an open fire and enjoy coffee and sandwiches or afternoon tea with warm homemade scones. Star of the menu though is the beef from the Duke of Buccleuch estate, reared by Liz's brother Robert. It scores highly on quality and flavour. Additional selections take in roast honey-glazed pork loin with coarsegrain mustard mash or the Unicorn burger. Upstairs, and for more special occasions, is the Red Room decorated in deep red with gold-tasselled curtains and tables clothed in white linen. Nightly menus depend on the best available fresh seafood, meat and game. Start perhaps with Loch Linnhe langoustines, before moving on to sea bass baked in olive oil and crushed garlic or local venison medallions with sweetened haggis and red wine sauce. Classic puddings or Scottish and Irish cheeses round things off nicely. The wine list majors on European varieties, but also offers a few new world favourites.

Prices: Set dinner in the Red Room £26.50.
Grill restaurant main course from £7.95. House wine £11.95.
Last orders: Bar: 23.00. Food: lunch 14.00; dinner 21.00
Closed: Monday.
Food: Scottish and Irish.
Other points: No-smoking area. Garden. Children welcome.
Car park.
Directions: From the south, cross Kincardine Bridge, then take the first then the second left. (Map 14, C6)

St Andrews

Inn at Lathones

By Largoward, St Andrews, Fife KY9 IJE
Telephone: +44(0)870 4016154
+44(0)1334 840494
lathones@theinn.co.uk
www.theinn.co.uk

Beautifully restored and extended by Nick and Jocelyn White, the charming Inn has built up a sound reputation for its fine accommodation, great food and first-class wines. The stylish bedrooms were fully refurbished in 2004. Comfort and style are paramount. There are smart oak floors, goose-down duvets, entertainment systems, internet access, and gleaming new en suite bathrooms with fluffy robes and quality toiletries. In fact throughout this 400-year-old former coaching inn, the ancient and modern blend perfectly. Golf lovers will be happy to learn that St Andrews is nearby plus 40 another golf courses. The hotel is happy to arrange bookings. Traditional settings create much of the hotel's character. Part of the reception has an old-fashioned, shop-fronted bow-window room which houses Nick's extensive wine cellar, and the large lounge has stone walls, a mix of leather and upholstered chairs and bow windows. The dining room blends elegance with informality and it has a relaxed atmosphere. Here, chef Marc Guibert offers an exquisite carte built around Fife's finest produce – first-class meats, fresh seafood and organic fruits and vegetables. Dinner could open with smoked haddock and salmon fishcake with lemon and chive sauce, and move on to succulent smoked lamb shank with garlic cream and light lamb jus. Marc's puddings are legendary, so finish with a soup of Scottish red fruits or vanilla crème brulée. At lunchtime, there are some good-value choices, including soup, followed by fish and chips, say, or penne pasta with mushroom sauce.

Prices: Set lunch £12 and dinner from £25. Main course from £14. House wine £11.50.
Last orders: Food: lunch 14.30; dinner 21.30.
Closed: Two weeks in January.
Food: Modern European.
Other points: No-smoking area. Children welcome. Garden. Car park. Licence for Civil Weddings.
Directions: On the A915 midway between St Andrews and Leven, five miles south of St Andrews. (Map 14, B7)

www.routiers.co.uk

Glasgow

Art Lovers' Café

House for an Art Lover, Bellahouston Park,
10 Dumbreck Road, Glasgow G41 5BW
Telephone: +44(0)870 4016347
+44(0)141 353 4779
info@houseforanartlover.co.uk
www.houseforanartlover.co.uk

Charles Rennie Mackintosh entered 'House for an Art Lover' for a competition to design a house in a modern style in 1901. It was not built until 1989 however, and was completed six years later. Set in the heart of Bellahouston Park, it is used as a venue for corporate private dining, and on the ground level is the contemporary Art Lovers' Café that is open for all-day dining. Three large arched windows create a light, bright space, enhanced by white linen tablecloths, light wood floors and monthly exhibitions of contemporary Scottish paintings. In the summer, you can dine al fresco on the terrace. Noted for being child friendly – it offers children a separate Little Art Lovers' menu – this is a relaxed place, open throughout the day for just a coffee and pastry, or light snacks of toasted bagel with Loch Fyne salmon. Elegant three-course lunches have as much to do with good value as ability and acumen. Choices may include terrine of ham hock, braised cabbage and root vegetables, cornichons and their juices with, say, roasted fillet of sea bass, broth of fennel, mussels and tomato to follow, and an open tartlet of Bramley apples, fresh egg custard and a spicy cinnamon ice cream to finish. The short wine selection is keenly priced.

Prices: Set lunch from £13.45. Restaurant main course from £8.50. Bar snacks from £4.50. House wine £13.50.
Last orders: Food: 15.00.
Closed: Rarely.
Food: Modern Scottish.
Other points: No-smoking area. Dogs welcome on terrace only. Children welcome. Garden. Car park. Licence for Civil Weddings. Changing art exhibitions.
Directions: Exit 23/M8. At top of slip road turn left, then next right into Bellahouston Park. (Map 14, C5)

Glasgow

City Merchant

97-99 Candleriggs, Glasgow G1 1NP
Telephone: +44(0)870 4016348
+44(0)141 5531577
citymerchant@btinternet.com
www.citymerchant.co.uk

Set in the part of town where wealthy merchants used to live and work from the 17th to 19th centuries, this restaurant has plenty to offer discerning tastes today, and at affordable prices. Over his 17 years of ownership, Tony Matteo has perfected his Scottish-themed menus and focused on quality local fish. Langoustines, mussels and oysters all come from local suppliers and are used in the simple through to more sophisticated dishes. On the daily fixed price set menu, available until 6.30pm, you'll find scallop and crayfish bisque, and prawn and smoked salmon timbales to start, with mains of grilled trout fillet with almond butter, breaded haddock with chips or Merchant fishcakes. Meat is supplied by Macbeths of Forres, which comes with the stamp of approval by Quality Meat Scotland, so you can expect great steaks on both the set and carte menus. The latter delivers fancier fare: fish and shellfish soup with tomato and garlic, grilled west coast langoustines and several ways with oysters, or if you can't decide splash out on a Scottish seafood platter. Scottish stalwart haggis, neeps and tatties is also a fixture, and game is served in season. It really is worth saving space for the fab Scots puds, namely cranachan ice cream with atoll brose served with homemade shortbread or a clootie dumpling with whisky and oatmeal ice cream. The short wine list offers good value.

Prices: Set lunch £13. Main course £7.50. House wine £12.50.
Last orders: Food: 22.30.
Closed: Sunday.
Food: Seafood/modern Scottish.
Other points: No-smoking area. Children welcome.
Directions: Take exit 15, east or west bound on M8 and follow signs for Glasgow Cross. Turn right into Ingram Street, then second left into Candleriggs. The restaurant is 500 yards east of George Square. (Map 14, C5)

Good food and wine

Harviestoun Schiehallion

at the Unicorn Inn

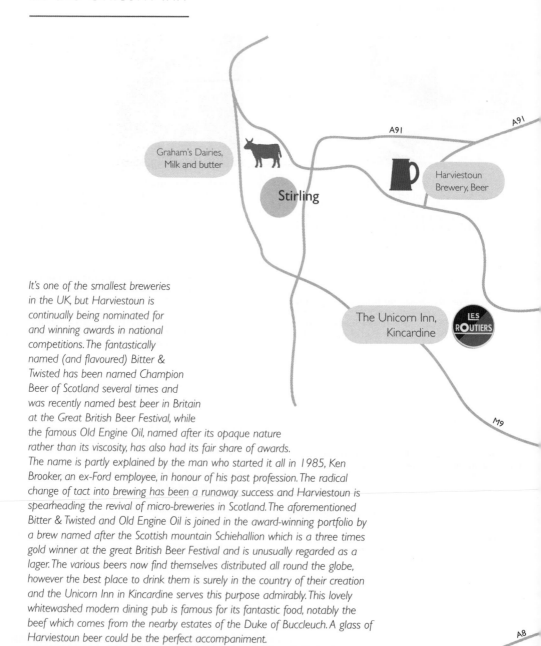

It's one of the smallest breweries in the UK, but Harviestoun is continually being nominated for and winning awards in national competitions. The fantastically named (and flavoured) Bitter & Twisted has been named Champion Beer of Scotland several times and was recently named best beer in Britain at the Great British Beer Festival, while the famous Old Engine Oil, named after its opaque nature rather than its viscosity, has also had its fair share of awards.

The name is partly explained by the man who started it all in 1985, Ken Brooker, an ex-Ford employee, in honour of his past profession. The radical change of tact into brewing has been a runaway success and Harviestoun is spearheading the revival of micro-breweries in Scotland. The aforementioned Bitter & Twisted and Old Engine Oil is joined in the award-winning portfolio by a brew named after the Scottish mountain Schiehallion which is a three times gold winner at the great British Beer Festival and is unusually regarded as a lager. The various beers now find themselves distributed all round the globe, however the best place to drink them is surely in the country of their creation and the Unicorn Inn in Kincardine serves this purpose admirably. This lovely whitewashed modern dining pub is famous for its fantastic food, notably the beef which comes from the nearby estates of the Duke of Buccleuch. A glass of Harviestoun beer could be the perfect accompaniment.

Kinross

M90

Dunfermline

A985

Crombies of Edinburgh,
Sausages

Edinburgh

Campbells Prime Meats
Buccleuch Beef

Glasgow

La Parmigiana

447 Great Western Road, Glasgow G12 8HH
Telephone: +44(0)870 4016346
+44(0)141 334 0686
s.giovanazzi@btclick.com
www.laparmigiana.co.uk

Elegant and refined, this small restaurant near Glasgow's West End, serves fine food. Everything is done in style from the purple leather bound menus to the service by well-trained and charming staff. Given the size of the kitchen, the menu is sensibly pared down and changes quarterly, drawing on what's in season. In the past, when trying to extend and change more frequently, Sandro Giovanazzi found that his regulars knew what they liked and resisted too many new recipes, demanding their favourite regular dishes back. So lobster ravioli with cream and basil, beef carpaccio with Parmesan shavings and rocket salad, or chargrilled Minch scallops with lemon and olive oil are regular starters. Good mains include escalope of veal with Parma ham, mozzarella and tomato, or risotto with porcini mushrooms, Parmesan and cream. Fish is also a reliable bet, perhaps zuppa of mixed fish and shellfish with bruschetta. Finish with crème brûlée with calvados and caramelised apples or a traditional tiramisu. Set price menus at lunch and dinner are very good value. The wine offers a good selection of Italian favourites, from a prosecco aperitifo to Tuscan vin santo for dessert, with much to tempt in between.

Prices: Set lunch £9.50 and dinner £12.50. Restaurant main course restaurant from £13.50. House wine £12.50.
Last orders: Food: lunch 14.30; dinner 23.00.
Closed: Easter Monday.
Food: Italian
Directions: Exit18/M8. Follow signs for West End along Great Western Road, travel over Kelvinbridge and La Parmigiana is on the left. (Map 14, C5)

Altnaharra

Altnaharra Hotel

By Lairg, Altnaharra, Highland IV27 4UE
Telephone: +44(0)870 4016389
+44(0)1549 411222
altnaharra@btinternet.com
www.altnaharra.com

The remoteness of this hotel makes it an ideal get-away-from-it-all choice. The surrounding area is memorable for its great vistas, spectacular mountains and numerous lochs. Altnaharra is regarded as one of the best located hotels for salmon and trout fishing in the Highlands, and it offers a truly comprehensive range of options. But there's as much of a welcome for locals and non-sporting visitors as there is for those who come mainly to fly fish and shoot game on neighbouring estates. The several public areas, lounge bar, lounge and library are welcoming with open fires, comfortable seating, flowers, plants, and fishing memorabilia. The hotel is open throughout the day and will happily provide light refreshments or meals, and the daily changing limited-choice dinner menu features locally sourced meat and game. Bedrooms are en suite and are spacious, but you have to go to the library to watch TV. Although with so much to explore on hand, we think this won't be necessary.

Rooms: 15. Rooms from £45 per person.
Prices: Set dinner £40 (5 course). House wine £14.50.
Last orders: Food: 21.30 (flexible).
Closed: Rarely.
Food: Modern Scottish.
Other points: No-smoking area. Children welcome.
Dogs welcome overnight. Garden. Car park.
Directions: From Inverness, take the A9 for Wick. At Bonar Bridge, follow the A836 towards Tongue; hotel is between Lairg and Tongue. (Map 16, C5)

Aviemore

The Old Bridge Inn

23 Dalfaber Road, Aviemore, Highland PH22 1PU
Telephone: +44(0)870 4016251
+44(0)1479 811137
www.oldbridgeinn.co.uk

The friendly Old Bridge overlooks the River Spey and the dramatic Cairngorm Mountains, and is perfectly placed for those keen on outdoor pursuits. It's been sympathetically redeveloped in keeping with its architectural ancestry, that of a Scottish Highland dwelling with steep pitched roof and bow windows. Walkers and skiers coming off the hills generally head for the cosy bar to refuel with pints of Deuchers IPA and plates of excellent, freshly prepared food. Warm red-painted walls adorned with pictures of local scenes and antique artefacts relating to winter sports, solid wood tables and cushioned settles on a tartan carpet, and a blazing log fire set the welcoming scene. Seasonal menus and the daily blackboard list modern Scottish dishes prepared from locally sourced produce. Tuck into a hearty carrot and lemon soup or salmon carpaccio, follow with venison and ginger on celeriac mash, beef and onion casserole, or an Angus rib-eye steak from the chargrill, then round off with homemade mandarin cheesecake or Scottish cheeses. Outdoor enthusiasts on a budget should book a bed in the bunk house accommodation next door. Designed to a high standard, it offers good, comfortable bunk-bedded rooms with en suite facilities, plus communal kitchens, drying rooms and a bike store – all a tired walker could want at the end of a hard day.

Rooms: 7. Double from £29, single from £12, family room from £38.
Prices: Set lunch £12, set dinner £15. Restaurant main course from £11. Bar main course from £7. House wine £11.95.
Last orders: Bar and food: lunch 14.00; dinner 21.00 (open all day at weekends).
Closed: Rarely.
Food: Modern Scottish.
Other points: No-smoking area. Garden. Children welcome. Car park.
Directions: Exit A9 for Aviemore, just off the ski road to Cairngorms. (Map 16, F6)

Banavie

Glen Loy Lodge Hotel

Banavie, Fort William, Highland PH33 7PD
Telephone: +44(0)870 4016344
+44(0)1397 712700
glenloy.lodge@virgin.net
www.smoothhound.co.uk/hotels/glenloyl.html

Built as a 1920s hunting and fishing lodge, this hotel retains the stylish look of that period. Pat and Gordon Haynes have created tasteful, individually styled rooms decorated with original artwork, ornaments and personal touches, much of them sympathetic to the period. Many of their arts and crafts pieces date from 1880. The Lodge is set by the banks of the River Loy, and its sun room is the top spot to watch the ever-changing light over Ben Nevis. The sitting room is the place to cosy up around the large log fire and relax or watch TV. Very comfortably styled bedrooms are all en suite, the majority are spacious, and they're all well equipped with a hot drinks trays with real ground coffee, mineral water and good toiletries. The set, daily changing dinner menu is given out at breakfast, so alternatives can be provided. Meals are built around seasonal local supplies, for example asparagus and smoked salmon soufflé and fillet of Aberdeen Angus steak with sherried mustard sauce, and rhubarb crème brûlée to finish. For the last two years, its cheeseboard has been recognised by the British Cheese Awards as the best in Scotland. It offers Sweet Milk and Brierly from Wester Lawrenceton Farm, mature Cairnsmore and Dunsyre Blue. The list of well-chosen wines picks off many a fine producer, especially in France.

Rooms: 7. Double room from £80, single from £40.
Prices: Set dinner £28 (4 course). House wine £10.55.
Last orders: Dinner served at 19.30.
Closed: Check Winter opening times.
Food: Modern Scottish.
Other points: Totally no smoking. Garden. Car park.
Directions: Four miles north of Banavie on the B8004. (Map 13, A4)

Affordable good value

Boat of Garten

Old Ferryman's House

Nethy Bridge Road, Boat of Garten, Highland PH24 3BY
Telephone: +44(0)870 4016370
+44(0)1479 831370

It's one of the smallest establishments in Les Routiers, but this B&B is run with some style by Elizabeth Matthews. The traditional stone-built former ferryman's cottage is just across the River Spey from Boat of Garten. In addition to four pine-furnished bedrooms, a large bathroom, a sitting room warmed by a wood-burning stove, and filled with flowers, books and magazines, there's a dining room and a lovely enclosed garden with tubs, planters and borders of cottage garden flowers. No TV is a bonus for those wanting a complete break from the norm, as are flexible breakfast times for a traditional Scottish grill-up with homemade bread and preserves, or oak-smoked kippers, Scotch pancakes, or kedgeree. Afternoon tea is also included in the B&B price, so look forward to homemade bran teabreads, shortbread and flapjacks. Residents will eat very well at dinner, starting perhaps with smoked venison and homemade mayonnaise, or cullen skink, followed by wild venison stroganoff, or organic Gloucester Old spot pork, with herbs, vegetable and salad leaves from the garden in season. Fabulous among the puddings are the rhubarb and banana crumble, or baked apples with heather honey.

Rooms: 4. 2 double/twin rooms from £46, 2 singles from £23.
Prices: Set price dinner £17.50.
Last orders: Ring to check.
Closed: Ring to check.
Food: Modern Scottish.
Other points: Totally no smoking. Children welcome.
Dogs welcome overnight. Garden. Car park.
Credit cards not accepted.
Directions: Follow main road through Boat of Garten and across the River Spey; house immediately on right. (Map 16, F6)

Drumnadrochit

Loch Ness Lodge Hotel

Drumnadrochit, Inverness, Highland IV63 6TU
Telephone: +44(0)870 4016253
+44(0)1456 450342
info@lochness-hotel.com
www.lochness-hotel.com

The solid yet romantic-looking stone Highland lodge was built in 1740, and it's set high enough to get wonderful views over the River Enrick and its valley. There is also the proximity to Urquhart Castle and Loch Ness (the hotel is part of the Original Loch Ness Monster Exhibition Centre complex). Directly opposite the hotel is a 9th century Viking battle site. The welcome is genuinely enthusiastic and down to earth, backed up by open peat fires, wood panelling, and traditional furnishings. An industrious kitchen bakes its own bread and pastries, and sources local and regional Scottish produce for a traditional repertoire that includes local Moray pork, vegetables from an organic garden in the village, game from local estates, and an excellent selection of local and regional cheeses. Expect Lochaber chicken breast stuffed with tarragon and olive emince, or tian of Moray Firth smoked salmon served with potato and horseradish salad to start. Then, perhaps, casserole of West Highland venison, pan-fried pave of West Coast salmon with mash and parsley butter sauce, or a selection of Aberdeen Angus steaks with a choice of sauces. The short, annotated wine list is global in outlook, listed by style, and reasonably priced.

Rooms: 50.
Prices: Set dinner £22.50. Main course from £8.95.
House wine £8.95.
Last orders: Food: lunch 14.30; dinner 21.30.
Closed: November-Easter.
Food: Traditional Scottish.
Other points: No-smoking area. Children welcome. Garden.
Car park. Licence for Civil Weddings.
Coffee shop and visitors centre.
Directions: Off A82 in Drumnadrochit 14 miles south west of Inverness. (Map 16, F5)

www.routiers.co.uk

Fort William

The Grog & Gruel

66 High Street, Fort William, Highland PH33 6AE
Telephone: +44(0)870 4016257
+44(0)1397 705078
greatbeer@grogandgruel.co.uk
www.grogandgruel.co.uk

Active types fed up with bagging peaks and the Clachaig Inn should head for the lights of Fort William and the Clachaig's sister pub, The Grog & Gruel, for great Scottish micro-brewery ales, hearty pub food and a lively atmosphere. Its tongue-in-cheek name reflects the relaxed and informal atmosphere of a traditional alehouse and restaurant. Wooden floors, tongue-and-groove walls, traditional bench seating and background rock music set the scene in which to enjoy pints of Atlas Latitude and Cairngorm Tomintoul Stag, 60 different malt whiskies, and all-day food from the printed 'alehouse' menu, served in the first-floor restaurant overlooking the High Street. From starters of 'Mucho Macho' nachos with hog's breath chilli beef and smoked salmon with oakcakes and dill mayonnaise, the menu extends to homemade beef burgers, Tex-Mex chicken fajitas with soured cream and guacamole, house speciality pizzas, fresh seafood tagliatelle, traditional steak and ale pie, and freshly battered cod with a generous portion of chips. If you're not partial to a decent pint, order a litre pitcher of Tequila Sunrise to accompany your beef-filled burritos. Don't miss the annual beer festivals.

Prices: Main course from £7.45.
Last orders: Bar: 23.00 (Thursday to Saturday 01.00).
Food: 22.00 Restaurant and 21.00 Bar.
Closed: Rarely.
Food: Mexican, American and Italian.
Other points: No-smokingn area. Dogs welcome. Garden.
Children welcome in restaurant only.
Directions: Half way along Fort William's pedestrianised high street. (Map 13, A4)

Glencoe

The Clachaig Inn

Glencoe, Highland PH49 4HX
Telephone: +44(0)870 4016245
+44(0)1855 811252
inn@clachaig.com
www.clachaig.com

Set in the heart of Glencoe, this 300-year-old inn is a favourite haunt of mountaineers and walkers. It has a magnificent mountain backdrop with Loch Leven not far away and the west face of Aonach Dhu rising up from the valley. The inn also stands close to the site of the Massacre of Glencoe (1692). Visitors exploring Glencoe will get a real feel of the area just through the collection of mountaineering photographs here. Huge log fires provide a roaring welcome in the cosy, wood-floored Bidean lounge bar, and in the rustic, stoneflagged Boots Bar. In the latter, booted walkers can take refuge and enjoy refreshments at a bar dispensing 120 malt whiskies and six Highland micro-brewery ales; the heather ale is a popular choice. The traditional pub food served in generous portions is perfect after a bracing walk. The wide choice ranges from filled baguettes and pasta carbonara to venison casserole and chargrilled sirloin steak with hot pepper sauce. Leave room too for homemade ecclefechan tart, a combination of dried fruit and nuts on a pastry base served hot with cream or custard. The 23 refurbished bedrooms are split between the main house and chalet-style rooms to the rear. All are contemporary in style with smart pine furnishings, and come with modern comforts, minus phones. Mountain bike hire, winter mountaineering courses and live folk music on Saturdays are all on offer.

Rooms: 23. Double room from £30, prices per person per night.
Prices: Main course restaurant from £5.85.
House wine from £8.25.
Last orders: Bar: 23.00 (Friday 24.00, Saturday 23.30). Food: 21.00.
Closed: Rarely.
Food: Scottish, American, Mexican.
Other points: No-smoking area. Dogs welcome. Garden.
Children welcome. Car park. Bike shed.
Directions: Located in the heart of Glencoe just off the A82 Glasgow to Fort William Road. (Map 13, A4)

An alternative Britain

Loch Ness

Foyers Bay House

Lower Foyers, Loch Ness, Inverness, Highland IV2 6YB
Telephone: +44(0)870 4016365
+44(0)1456 486624
carol@foyersbay.co.uk
www.foyersbay.co.uk

This large 19th century house turned guest house with stunning views of Loch Ness is as scenic a spot as any to keep an eye out for Nessie. The house is in a magical setting, located in attractive woodland grounds amid forests, nature trails, and adjoining the famous Falls of Foyer. Originally built by the British Aluminium Company for the manager of the local smelter, this solid house is now run with great enthusiasm by Otto and Carol Pancirolli. You can either stay in one of the five bright and spacious bedrooms in the main house that mix smart fabrics with good-quality furniture and gleaming en suite bathrooms or in separate lodges within the grounds. The six semi-detached lodges are geared towards relaxed self catering. Each has a large balcony, three bedrooms – a double, twin and bunk – and fully fitted kitchen complete with dishwasher, washer/dryer and food processors. The lounges are spacious and comfortable. Snacks and light meals are available in the Café Conservatory overlooking the loch. In the evenings, a set dinner menu offers specialities such as Highland sirloins and venison, West Coast smoked salmon, and an indulgent pud such as homemade toffee crunch pie to finish.

Rooms: 5. Double room from £52, single from £36.
Prices: Set dinner from £10.95. Main course from £5.95.
Wine from £7.50.
Last orders: Food: snacks 16.00; dinner 20.00.
Closed: Tuesday and Friday lunch and 6-26 January.
Food: Scottish/Continental.
Other points: Children welcome. Garden. Car park.
Directions: From Inverness take the B862 to Dores, then fork right along B852 to Foyers. (Map 16, F5)

Onich

Allt-nan-Ros

Onich, Fort William, Highland PH33 6RY
Telephone: +44(0)870 4016450
+44(0)1855 821210
lr@allt-nan-ros.co.uk
www.allt-nan-ros.co.uk

It's not only in an enviable spot overlooking Loch Linnhie, but this smart family-run hotel also has panoramic views across to the mountains beyond. The peaceful setting is perfect for a relaxing break, or if you're feeling energetic, there's riding, fishing, golfing, watersports or walking available nearby. All the spacious 20 bedrooms, bar one, offer amazing views; five on the ground floor offer disabled access and two have bathrooms fully equipped for people with disabilities. Each room varies in style, but all are decorated to a very high standard. Superior rooms have CD players as well as the standard electric blanket. The converted stables house two light, cottagey bedrooms. James and Fiona Macleod provide friendly and efficient service, helped by their long-serving staff. On colder days, a welcoming fire roars in the bar and lounge. The Macleods are meticulous about the ingredients used for their small but carefully drawn dinner menu. They source prime local foods and supplement these with their own home-grown produce. On the menu are locally smoked salmon, Letterfinlay game, the Macleods' own smoked venison and local seafood such as Mallaig cod served with wilted spinach and a homemade wholegrain mustard sauce. Their home-grown herbs provide the fresh flavourings.

Rooms: 20. Double room from £150,
single from £75, dinner, bed and breakfast.
Prices: Set lunch £15 and dinner £30. House wine £12.95.
Last orders: Food: lunch 13.30; dinner 20.30.
Closed: Rarely.
Food: French and Scottish.
Other points: No-smoking area. Children welcome.
Dogs welcome overnight (not in the bar). Garden. Car park.
Directions: Ten miles south of Fort William on the A82.
(Map 13, A4)

www.routiers.co.uk

Ullapool

Brae Guest House

Shore Street, Ullapool, Highland IV26 2UJ
Telephone: +44(0)870 4016449
+44(0)1854 612421

The longest-established guest house in Ullapool is run by Mr and Mrs Ross, who have been in residence for more than 45 years. This cosy guest house is also one of the nicest and friendliest in Scotland. The seafront Victorian property was originally two houses and two shops. Now combined, everything is of a very high standard, from the genuinely warm welcome on arrival, to the homely, comfortable bedrooms and the excellent traditional breakfast in the morning. The setting, on the front overlooking Loch Broom, is splendid and Brae House is within easy walking distance of the village centre and the Stornoway ferry. Although the Rosses no longer offer evening meals, there are several restaurants in Ullapool that they would be happy to recommend. The guest house is open from May to September only.

Rooms: 11, 2 not en suite. Double room from £26 per person, single from £24.
Closed: October to May.
Food: Traditional Scottish.
Other points: No-smoking area. Children welcome. Car park.
Directions: In the centre of Ullapool. (Map 15, D4)

Individual charm and warmth

Sleat

Hotel Eilean Iarmain

Eilean Iarmain, Isle Ornsay, Sleat, Isle of Skye IV43 8QR
Telephone: +44(0)870 4016369
+44(0)1471 833332
hotel@eilean-iarmain.co.uk
www.eileaniarmain.co.uk

It's a handsome inn built in 1888 and in a magnificent setting beside a fishing harbour. The traditional interiors tastefully combine simplicity and style. Rural chic sums up the look. The 16 bedrooms are all smartly individual, one has a canopy bed from nearby Armadale Castle, and there are four suites in the converted stables, with upstairs bedrooms with sitting rooms below. In the often bustling timber-clad An Pranban bar, you can sample more than 30 local malt whiskies, including their own blend Te Bheag, hear Gaelic spoken, and tuck into some first-rate bar food. At lunchtime, there are sandwiches and homemade soups, hearty casseroles, prime steaks and fresh local seafood such as Eilean Iarmain crab cakes served with crisp salad leaves and a lemon chive crème fraîche. The dining room with candles and flowers has a refined air and head chef Graham Smith serves fine food. Local seafood includes oysters from the hotel's own beds, shellfish from their private stone pier, and game, especially venison, is from the estate. A typical dinner may include Ord Estates rich game terrine, parsnip crisps and apple chutney, followed by cappuccino of smoked haddock and potato, then a medley of local seafood poached in Chablis and saffron with cocotte potatoes and a chervil hollandaise. Finish with a decadent dessert or selection of Scottish cheese and petits fours.

Rooms: 12. Double/twin room from £60 per person, single occupancy £90. 4 suites in restored stables at £200.
Prices: Set lunch £16.50, set dinner £31. House wine £15.85.
Last orders: Bar: 23.00. Food: lunch 14.30; dinner 21.00.
Closed: Rarely.
Food: Modern Scottish.
Other points: No-smoking area. Children welcome. Garden. Car park.
Directions: 40 miles from Portree and seven miles from Broadford on the A851. (Map 15, F3)

Glenlivet

Minmore House

Glenlivet, Moray AB37 9DB
Telephone: +44(0)870 4016442
+44(0)1807 590378
minmorehouse@ukonline.co.uk
www.minmorehousehotel.com

Set in four acres of peaceful and idyllic grounds, this fine stone house is near many local attractions. Its neighbour is the famous Glenlivet distillery, and there are many coastal and country walks for you to explore. You will be met with a warm welcome, and find it easy to unwind in the effortless elegance of the surroundings. The hallway leads through to a lovely, wood-panelled sitting room with books and a selection of more than 100 whiskies from the small bar. In the dining room, mahogany tables are beautifully arranged with fresh garden flowers, crisp white linen and soft candlelight. The set four-course dinner menus change daily and make the best of prime raw materials and vegetables from the hotel's organic vegetable and herb garden; even the water is from a natural spring – also used by the Glenlivet Distillery next door. Butternut squash soup could be followed by fresh Scottish salmon or fillet of Aberdeen Angus served with parisienne potatoes, balsamic green beans and honey and whisky-glazed baby carrots. Finish with fresh raspberry crème brulée, then coffee and heavenly Minmore chocolate fudge. Upstairs, the bedrooms are luxurious and beautifully decorated with each room named after a whisky. A capacity for making you feel at home is apparent in each room, with a collection of chocolates and a small bottle of whisky on each dressing table.

Rooms: 10. £55 per person bed and breakfast. £98 per person for afternoon tea, dinner, bed and breakfast. Suites £120 per person.
Prices: Set dinner £35 (4 course).
Light lunch main course from £7. House wine £15.95.
Last orders: Food: lunch 14.30. Dinner 20.00.
Closed: February, one week in November (phone to check).
Food: French, using Scottish produce.
Other points: No-smoking area. Children welcome. Garden. Car park. Three miles of fly fishing.
Directions: Follow A9 to Aviemore, then A95 and B9008 towards The Glenlivet Distillery; Minmore House is just before the distillery. (Map 16, F6)

Bridge of Cally

Bridge of Cally Hotel

Bridge of Cally, Blairgowrie, Perth and Kinross PH10 7JJ
Telephone: +44(0)870 4016294
+44(0)1250 886231
jeff@bridgeofcallyhotel.com
www.bridgeofcallyhotel.com

This old drover's inn is set in a lovely wooded spot and has grounds that extend over many acres along the banks of the River Ardle. It has become a popular choice because of the sports available in the area and has expanded to meet demand, accordingly. The bedroom count has increased from nine to 18, the dining room has been remodelled, a conservatory added, and new furniture introduced throughout. There's a modern fresh feeling, thanks mainly to the use of light colours, especially in the dining room. Here the colour combination of buttermilk and marigold complements chairs with oak-leaf pattern covers in pale pink. The conservatory makes the most of the riverside location, plus there's a comfortable sitting room to unwind after a hard day's hunting and fishing. The bar is warm and inviting – a fun, friendly place used by locals, and a perfect spot to enjoy a pint of Speckled Hen or one of a magnificent selection of single malts. Food is served in the bar or the dining room, with menus built around the likes of local venison sausages, wild venison, local lamb, and locally smoked trout. Start maybe with garlic mushrooms in a cream sauce and follow with confit of duck. Good-value bedrooms are nice, bright, and comfortable, with light wood furniture, modern bathrooms, and all the usual extras, except room phones.

Rooms: 18. Room from £35 per person.
Prices: Restaurant main course from £8.95.
Bar main course from £6.95. Snack from £2.50. House wine £9.95.
Last orders: Bar: 23.00 (Friday and Saturday 23.45). Food: 21.00.
Closed: Never.
Food: Traditional Scottish specialising in game.
Other points: No-smoking area. Children welcome.
Dogs welcome. Garden. Car park.
Directions: Six miles north of Blairgowrie on the A93 heading for Braemar. (Map 14, B6)

Comrie

The Royal Hotel

Melville Square, Comrie, Perth and Kinross PH6 2DN
Telephone: +44(0)870 4016259
+44(0)1764 679200
reception@royalhotel.co.uk
www.royalhotel.co.uk

Standing back from the main square in Comrie, this 18th century coaching inn exudes effortless elegance. It owes its name to the days when Queen Victoria stayed here. It was restored in the mid 90s with period antiques, paintings and stylish soft furnishings by the Milsom family. Along with their staff they provide cheerful, helpful hospitality. The cosy lounge bar, along with the wood-and-stone public bar, are the focus of the local community, offering an informal atmosphere and a warm welcome to all comers. Here, and in the conservatory-style brasserie, homemade venison and leek burgers, fishcakes with hot tomato sauce or haggis hash brown and whisky sauce may be washed down with a glass of Deuchar's IPA or one of 170 Highland malts. Dinner in the intimate Royal Restaurant can be a fixed-price, three-course affair or taken from a seasonal carte, which makes full use of the markets' seasonal produce from fresh fish, meats and game to Tobermory Cheddar, crisp tasting salad greens and luscious summer berries from the local fruit farm. The beautifully appointed bedrooms, including three four-poster suites, feature furnishings by local craftsmen, rich fabrics and luxurious toiletries that today remain fit for a queen.

Rooms: 11. Double/twin £60 per person, single £75.
Four poster suite from £80 per person.
Prices: Set dinner £27.50. Restaurant main course from £9.95.
Bar main course from £6.95. House wine £9.50.
Last orders: Bar: 23.00 (Friday and Saturday 23.45).
Food: lunch 14.00; dinner 21.00.
Closed: Rarely.
Food: Modern and Traditional English.
Other points: Garden. Children welcome.
Dogs welcome overnight. Car park.
Directions: From the A9 at Greenloaning take the A822 heading for Crieff; then the B827 to Comrie. (Map 14, B6)

Regional produce

Dunkeld

The Pend

5 Brae Street, Dunkeld, Perth and Kinross PH8 0BA
Telephone: +44(0)870 4016336
+44(0)1350 727586
molly@thepend.sol.co.uk
www.thepend.com

Set in the attractive Perthshire village of Dunkeld on
the banks of the River Tay, this hotel has much to
offer in terms of classic good looks and leisure activ-
ites. Hunting, fishing and shooting on local estates,
picturesque walks or use of smart leisure facilities at
the nearby hotel provide a full timetable of activities,
or you can just relax and enjoy the views. All rooms
are beautifully decorated, with antique furniture in
the lounge-dining room as well as in the comfortably appointed bedrooms. The traditional cooking is
based around quality ingredients from local suppliers.
The four-course dinner stars smoked salmon from
Dunkeld smokery just across the road, then there's
local Bestwick game, soft fruits from nearby farms,
home-grown vegetables and exquisite local cheeses.
Dishes may include roast haunch of Perthshire venison
in game sauce, pudding of coffee and rum gateau, and
cheese served with homemade oatcakes. There is no
bar, but a fully stocked drinks cabinet runs on an honesty basis. In the bedrooms, drinks trays come with a
selection of tea and fresh milk. There is an appealing
lack of pretentiousness about this hotel and the small
scale allows for genuine friendliness and a homely feel.
In the past, the whole house has been taken over for
small weddings or fishing and shooting parties.

Rooms: 3. £32.50 per person bed and breakfast. £55 per person
dinner bed and breakfast.
Prices: Set dinner (4 course) from £22.50.
Closed: Rarely.
Food: Traditional with French and Italian influences.
Other points: No-smoking area. Dogs welcome.
Children welcome. Car park.
Directions: 12 miles north of Perth on A9. Cross river into
Dunkeld and take second right into Brae Street. (Map 14, B6)

Perth

63 Tay Street Restaurant

63 Tay Street, Perth, Perth and Kinross PH2 6NN
Telephone: +44(0)870 4016422
+44(0)1738 441451
www.63taystreet.co.uk

It's in the cool-contemporary category, but this restaurant also oozes bags of personality. The blond
wood, white linen-clad tables are offset with splashes
of colour from the blue-upholstered chairs, colourful
murals and fresh pink lilies. What money can't buy
are the superb views across the Tay to the Kinnoull
Hills through large windows. Jeremy Wares brings all
his experience of working in leading establishments in
London and Scotland to this his first venue. His finely
tuned repertoire fizzes with lively up-to-date ideas,
and he partners traditional Scottish ingredients with
the more exotic for his imaginative line-up. Lunch
starters may be curried pea and apple soup or a salad
of sun-dried tomatoes with baby artichokes, fennel
and Parmesan, moving on to fillet of Angus beef with
choucroute, straw potatoes and a red wine sauce.
Dinner is just as interesting with starters of seared
Skye scallops with prawn tortellini and clear tomato
broth, followed by roast Perthshire pheasant with red
cabbage, celeriac purée, chestnuts and game jus. To finish, there's tantalising orange crème brulée with orange
sorbet or a heavenly hot chocolate fondant with a
chocolate sauce. Carte prices are fixed for each course,
with the same principle applied to the good-value set
lunch, so no hidden surprises.

Prices: Main course lunch from £7.50. Main course dinner
from £14.95. House wine £10.95.
Last orders: Food: lunch 14.00; dinner 21.00.
Closed: Sunday and Monday, first two weeks of January and last
two weeks of August.
Food: Modern Scottish.
Other points: Totally no smoking.
Directions: Next to the river in the centre of Perth. (Map 14, B6)

Perth

The Famous Bein Inn

Glen Farg, Perth, Perth and Kinross PH2 9PY
Telephone: +44(0)870 4016260
+44 (0)1577 830216
stay@beininn.com
www.beininn.com

This old drovers' inn is a local landmark. It stands alone in a deep, wooded glen, five minutes' drive from the M90 (J9), and it's well worth making the short detour. It has become known for its live music sessions since David Mundell took over five years ago, and it attracts some top artists. Rock music fans travel miles to experience David's Rock Bar, a museum of rock memorabilia, with signed photographs, posters, back-stage passes and signed guitar scratch plates adorning the walls. Décor is more traditional in the MacGregor Bar, with its tartan carpet, comfortable sofas and arm-chairs and old local photographs, and also in the more formal Balvaird Restaurant, replete with log-burning stove and large bay window. Food is home-cooked with the simple menus appealing to a loyal local clientele and passing travellers alike. At lunchtime, you can tuck into sandwiches and light meals such as the inn's classic beefburger, haggis, neeps and tatties, and fresh North Sea scampi or haddock. The restaurant offers starters of game and pistachio terrine and Ma Bruce's stovie cakes and mains of poached halibut steak, a choice of grilled meats and noisettes of Scottish lamb. In keeping, en suite bedrooms in the modern, two-storey extension are spotless and unpretentious, providing comfortable accommodation for passing tourists, golfers and the occasional rock fan.

Rooms: 12. Double from £70, single from £45, family from £65. Prices include breakfast.
Prices: Set lunch £14, set dinner £18. Restaurant main course from £10.95. Bar main course from £5.95. House wine £10.50.
Last orders: Bar: lunch 14.00; dinner 23.00 (open all day at week-end). Food: lunch 14.00; dinner 21.00 (Sunday food served all day).
Closed: Rarely.
Food: Scottish.
Other points: No-smoking area. Children welcome. Car park.
Directions: Exit9/M90. Exit for Glenfarg and drive through village, Famous Bein Inn is one and a half miles into the wooded glen. (Map 14, B6)

Perth

Let's Eat

77-79 Kinnoull Street, Perth, Perth and Kinross PH1 5EZ
Telephone: +44(0)870 4016423
+44(0)1738 643377
enquiries@letseatperth.co.uk
www.letseatperth.co.uk

Using the best local ingredients is a top priority for Let's Eat owners Tony Heath and Shona Drysdale, and it has paid dividends. The effort put into the seasonal changing menu has won the pair many fans, who appreciate the quality Scottish produce on the menu. Venison comes from the Rannoch Moors while nearby Eassie Farm supplies beautiful asparagus and sea kale. In fact, the menu is so full of local riches that deciding what to have is a pleasurable dilemma. Starters include seared dived Mallaig scallops with a smooth parsnip purée, white truffle oil and parsnip crisps or Isle of Skye mussels with a creamy white wine sauce, followed by pan-roasted fillet of West Coast halibut with Skye queen scallops and prawns on thyme-roasted potatoes or grilled pave of Scotch beef on the bone with a puff pastry casket. Puddings are equally impressive, especially the perfect honey, whisky and oatmeal parfait with delicious local strawberries and a tuile biscuit. The wine list is quite extensive and well priced, with a number offered by the half bottle. The restaurant is relaxed and the cheery red and grey décor creates a smart but unpretentious setting.

Prices: Lunch main course from £9.50. Dinner main course £13.95. House wine £11.
Last orders: Food: lunch 14.00; dinner 21.45.
Closed: Sunday, Monday, two weeks in January and last two weeks in July.
Food: Modern British.
Other points: Totally no smoking. Children welcome.
Directions: In the centre of Perth on the junction of Atholl Street and Kinnoull Street. (Map 14, B6)

Down-to-earth, friendly service

East Haugh Country House Hotel, Pitlochry

Pitlochry

East Haugh Country House Hotel

By Pitlochry, Perth and Kinross PH16 5JS
Telephone: +44(0)870 4016437
+44(0)1796 473121
easthaugh@aol.com
www.easthaugh.co.uk

This turreted stone Atholl Estate house set in the heart of the Scottish Highlands is picture-book perfect. Run as a family hotel by Neil and Lesley McGown for the last 17 years, it is noted for its friendly hospitality, excellent food and for shooting, stalking and fishing trips. The recent stylish refurbishment enhances its traditional qualities such as a real fire, cosy lounge and Highland memorabilia. There is a fishing theme throughout the house, especially in the relaxing upstairs bar, where guests can also tuck into hearty modern Scottish dishes. The hotel is renowned for its fabulous food, and guests can dine more formally in the modern light and airy conservatory restaurant. Neil is a trained chef and his larder is full of local game and fish plus organic, locally sourced ingredients. His modern Scottish cooking follows the seasons. Starters on the dinner menu may include twice-baked St Andrews blue cheese soufflé or Highland game terrine with orange chutney, followed by mains of roast best end of Perthshire heather-fed lamb or seared fillet of organic salmon. Puds are a sheer delight, and the Scottish cheeses also deserve a special mention. The accommodation is luxurious and all the bedrooms, named after fishing flies used to catch salmon, are individually designed and fully kitted out. Whether you come to unwind or partake in leisure pursuits, you can't fail but feel relaxed and pampered here.

Rooms: 12. Double from £79, single from £89, family room from £79. Prices include dinner, bed and breakfast.
Prices: Set dinner £35. Main course bar from £9.95. House wine £12.95.
Last orders: Bar: lunch 14.00; dinner 21.30. Food: lunch 14.00; dinner 21.30.
Closed: Christmas week, 22-27 December.
Food: Modern Scottish with traditional French influence.
Other points: No-smoking area. Dogs welcome. Garden. Children welcome. Car park. License for Civil Weddings. Bike storage. Drying room. Gun cabinets. Shooting and Fishing can be arranged.
Directions: A9 Pitlochry. (Map 14, A6)

Pitlochry

Port Na Craig Restaurant

Port Na Craig, Pitlochry, Perth and Kinross PH16 5ND
Telephone: +44(0)870 4016436
+44(0)1796 472777
www.portnacraig.com

Guests are as enthusiastic about the menu here as they are about its quite stunning setting. Nestling by the river, and beneath the Festival Theatre, the Port-Na-Craig is a rose-covered stone building that has been an inn since 1650. The elegant yet simple restaurant, accessed through a pretty cobbled courtyard, serves fine food. The building may be old, but there is nothing old and rustic about the restaurant or its owners, the Thewes family. Son Bertie is out front 'pouring', and his brother Jamie behind the scenes cooking; they make a dynamic team. The pale yellow walls of the restaurant create a lovely airy atmosphere. The dark green blinds, benched wall seating covered in subtle local tweed, and fresh flowers from the garden make a stylish impression that doesn't detract from the fantastic views of the River Tay from the restaurant's cottagey windows. Although elegant there is nothing pretentious about the place. Jamie trained at Ballymaloe and it shows in a repertoire built around seasonal local produce that takes in warm salad of fillet of beef with land cress, roasted peppers and tapenade or grilled breaded West Coast mussels with mariniére sauce. Mains are just as mouthwateringly good with Perthshire lamb, Aberdeen Angus and wild salmon all hitting the spot. Marmalade pudding with cream or yogurt and cardamon cream with strawberries make a good finish.

Prices: Restaurant main course from £9. House wine £10.50.
Last orders: Food: lunch 14.00; dinner 21.00. (Sunday 14.30).
Closed: Sunday evening, all day Monday, 24 December to late February.
Food: Modern British.
Other points: Totally no smoking.
Children welcome over eight years old. Garden. Car park.
Directions: Follow signs to Port-Na-Craig and Pitlochry Festival Theatre; restaurant just below theatre on riverbank. (Map 14, A6)

Good food and wine

Tyndrum

Green Welly Stop Restaurant

Tyndrum, Crianlarich, Perth and Kinross FK20 8RY
Telephone: +44(0)870 4016446
+44(0)1838 400271
thegreenwellystop@tyndrum12.freeserve.co.uk
www.thegreenwellystop.co.uk

If you're en route to Oban or Fort William, make a point of stopping off at this outdoor equipment shop with an all-day café-restaurant. It is a great place to savour hearty, home-cooked Scottish dishes. It's a lively, third generation family business, and they pride themselves on making everything on the premises. Local supplies dictate the menu, which offers fresh soups made daily, perhaps Scotch broth, curried apple and parsnip, cream of kail (traditional winter vegetable soup), or cullen skink. The baking is excellent, with scones ranging from plain, through fruit, treacle, and cheese, with date and walnut slice, banana loaf, Border tart and Orkney Broonie widening the tempting choice even further. Main courses include flavoursome haggis 'n' neeps, as well as crofter's stew (diced lamb with vegetables in a rich sauce) and Hebridean leek pie. Desserts include boozy bread and butter pudding or Atholl brose trifle. There's an amazing selection of whiskies, locally smoked salmon, haggis and Scottish preserves to buy in the shop, as well as snacks. With racks of waterproof gear, this is the place to stock up if the variable Scottish weather has caught you out – Barbour and green wellies are much in evidence.

Prices: Main course from £5. Snack from £2.95.
House wine £2.70 for a small bottle.
Last orders: Food: 17.30.
Closed: Rarely.
Food: Traditional Scottish.
Other points: No-smoking area. Children welcome. Patio.
Car park.
Directions: On the A82, in the centre of the village. (Map 14, B5)

Hawick

Mansfield House Hotel

Weensland Road, Hawick, Scottish Borders TD9 8LB
Telephone: +44(0)870 4016361
+44(0)1450 360400
ian@mansfield-house.com
www.mansfield-house.com

This Victorian mansion stands strong and proud overlooking Hawick. Inside, the interiors combine a softer, more traditional look with 21st century amenities. The house has been in the MacKinnon family since 1985, and they have enchanced and restored its character, successfully turning it into a comfortable, small hotel. The classic style of the sitting room brings together ornate cornicing, open fire and loungy sofas and chairs. A separate traditional bar is used for informal meals. The comforts extend to the bedrooms, the majority of which are spacious and well decorated with comfortable chairs and TVs. In the restaurant, the order of the day is up-to-date ideas using the best ingredients. Sheila MacKinnon uses seasonal local produce to ensure her menu offers only the freshest flavours. These ingredients are showcased in the regularly changing dinner menus that could take in new season asparagus with crispy Cumbrian ham, capers and black olive balsamic dressing, or plainly grilled new season lamb chops teamed with crushed new potatoes and mint. Rhubarb tart or coffee date pudding make satisfying, full-on desserts. The wine list is a good mix of France and the new world at keen prices.

Rooms: 12. Double room from £60, single from £42, family room from £75.
Prices: Set lunch £19.50 and dinner £25. House wine £9.50.
Last orders: Lounge Bar: 21.00. Food: lunch 14.00; dinner 21.00 (Sunday 20.00).
Closed: Rarely.
Food: Traditional Scottish.
Other points: No-smoking area. Children welcome.
Dogs welcome overnight. Garden. Car park.
Licence for Civil Weddings.
Directions: Take A7 to Hawick, then A698 to Denholm/Jedburgh; hotel one mile on right. (Map 14, D7)

www.routiers.co.uk

Falkirk

La Picardie

12 Union Road, Camelon, Falkirk, Stirlingshire FK1 4PG
Telephone: +44(0)870 4016330
+44(0)1324 631666

Rustic French cooking has come to Camelon and proved exceedingly popular with locals and visitors alike. This friendly and informal restaurant is run by Brian Cochrane with Ranald Davidson in charge of the cooking. They serve hearty French food at exceptionally keen prices, using local ingredients wherever possible. You can enjoy a two-course lunch for just £5, choosing from homemade pâté or creamy leek and potato soup to start, followed by garlic roast chicken or seared salmon with strawberry beurre blanc. The evening menu offers a wider choice, and even more French favourites. Simplicity is the key, and refreshingly there are no hidden extras. Bread is included in the price, water comes chilled and tea and coffee is all part of the price. Brian sources all the wine from France and the house wine is a bit of a bargain. The restaurant décor is also cosy and the space is cleverly used. As the tiny galley kitchen opens onto the dining rooms, you can see what is being prepared. The relaxed atmosphere and good food and service, all make for a very pleasant dining experience that won't break the bank.

Prices: Set dinner from £13. Restaurant main course from £7. House wine £8.99.
Last orders: Food: 21.00. Reservations required.
Closed: First two weeks of July.
Food: French.
Other points: Totally no smoking. Children welcome.
Directions: M9 and M876. One mile from Falkirk Wheel.
(Map 14, C6)

Balicanich

Stepping Stone Restaurant

Benbecula, Balicanich, Western Isles H57 5DA
Telephone: +44(0)870 4016452
+44(0)1870 603377
steppingstonehs7@tiscali.co.uk

If you arrive at this island by air, you won't miss the Stepping Stone as it's one of the first places you'll see as you leave Benbecula airport. There are regular flights to and from Stornoway, Barra and Glasgow. The restaurant gets its name from being the central island in the chain, between North and South Uist. The building is purpose built, but it's one that's been designed with style. It offers that much needed warmth and welcome in these blustery parts. Inside the wood and glass structure feels like a spacious, cheerful, light log cabin, and it's split into two eating levels. The Food Base is an informal café where you can get all-day snacks, sandwiches, takeaways and homebaked cakes, and more substantial meals such as fish and chips. Sinteag, the no-smoking restaurant on the higher level, turns out scintillating food that is based around locally caught fish. The three or five-course menus are presented in a simple style, whether it's fillet of sole with a shrimp sauce, or scallops with bacon and cheese. Other specialities beyond the fish remit include Uist venison cooked in red wine. It is owned and managed by Ewen Maclead, a chef who returned home after working in Aberdeen. His family are also in the food business and own the renowned town bakery whose oatcakes are sold all over Scotland, and, of course, here in the restaurant with delectable Scottish cheese.

Prices: Sunday lunch £11.95. Set dinner £21.75 (5 courses). House wine £8.50.
Last orders: Food: 21.00.
Closed: Rarely.
Food: Traditional Scottish and Seafood.
Other points: Totally no smoking. Children welcome. Garden. Car park.
Directions: On the island of Benbecula, on the Airport over road, 5 minutes from the ferry and the airport at Balivanich.
(Map 15, E1)

Affordable good value

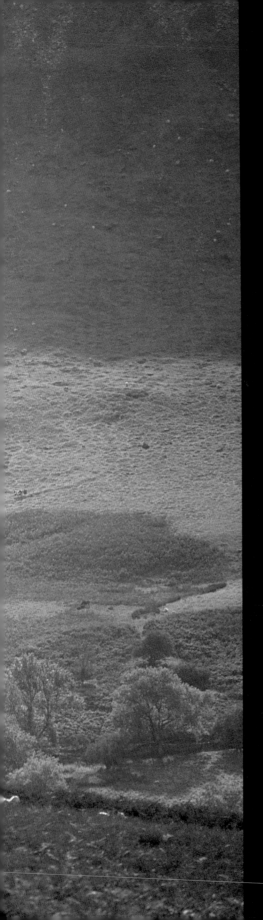

Wales

TV Chef Dudley Newbery, who hosts a cookery series on the Welsh Language Channel S4C, says Wales is home to a wide range of top-quality ingredients. He picks some of his favourite dishes to try on your travels

One of the perks of the job of being a TV chef in Wales is having the chance to travel from south to north and from east to west, visiting local producers and restaurants. Although the *Dudley* series has been running for 10 years, there are always plenty of new products and eating places springing up to provide us with plenty of scope for interesting programme content.

Most people would associate Welsh food with Welsh rarebit, Glamorgan sausage and *cawl* – a bowl of lamb and vegetable broth served with a chunk of local cheese and fresh crusty bread – very nice and traditional, but things have moved on a lot in Welsh cuisine. The shorelines of Wales have some of the finest fresh fish around from Menai oysters and mussels to Penllyn crabs and mackerel, the spider crabs of Fishguard and salmon and trout of the River Teifi. For me, the best lamb in the world is reared in Wales along with our famous Welsh black beef. We have a variety of farm-produced cheeses, too numerous to mention and a selection of organic produce. All of these ingredients are regularly used to produce fine and tasty local dishes which can be found in the best restaurants in Wales.

The most important meal of the day for me is breakfast, not your usual bowl of cereal and toast but a good, hearty Welsh breakfast, which would consist of local fresh eggs, home-cured bacon, locally made pork sausage and laverbread (*bara lawr*) rolled in oats and lightly fried with cockles from Penclawdd. This should be available at any good B&B or hotel, if they are prepared to make the effort.

If hunger pangs strike mid-afternoon, how about a teatime snack? Nobody quite beats the cakes my *mam gu* (grandmother) use to make, but *bara brith* (a fruit tea bread) and *piciau ar y mân* (Welsh cakes, cooked on a bakestone or griddle) can be found in teashops, farmers' markets and bakeries around the country.

Within this guide are many of my favourite eating places in Wales. Their chefs are all passionate about developing fresh, local food in season, and given the wide choice of products now available the scope is endless and the choices interesting.

Aberaeron

Hive on the Quay

Cadwgan Place, Aberaeron, Ceredigion SA46 0BU
Telephone: +44(0)870 4016388
+44(0)1545 570445
hiveon.thequay@btinternet.com
www.hiveonthequay.co.uk

On many a blustery March morning the winds are so strong here that's its hard to negotiate the seafront at Aberaeron's sheltered inner harbour. Yet, come Easter and the approaching summer, fishing boats float in quietly to deliver the coast's finest fruits de mer to the Holgate family's harbour-side fish shop and the freshest crabs and lobsters imaginable to their peerless seasonal quayside café. The Hive is a busy, swarming place, yet it's the production of incomparable honey ice cream the best, arguably in the Principality, that threatens to steal the show. There is, however, as much to admire in the friendly and informal all-day teashop which serves hearty lunches of daily special dishes, as there is on the splendid buffet of unusual soups and chowders, salads, free-range chicken, savoury and sweet plate pies. Don't miss the braised knuckle of Welsh lamb, or the huge black cherry meringue sundae. Smaller portions of the specials are available to any-one of any age, a delight for older customers. Evening meals are served in August from 6pm-9pm with similar menus to those detailed above. Sarah Holgate and her team make their own bread and cakes and use almost entirely organic produce, eggs and cheeses.

Prices: Main course from £7.50. Snacks from £5.
House wine £11.
Last orders: Restaurant: 15.00 from Spring Bank holiday to mid-September; Dinner 21.00 in August. Café: 17.00 (21.00 in August).
Closed: From foUrth week of September to Spring Bank Holiday.
Food: British (especially Welsh) and regional European.
Other points: Totally no smoking. Garden. Children welcome.
Licence for Civil Weddings.
Directions: At the end of the M4. Continue to Carmarthen via Llandysul to the A487 coast road to Aberaeron. Take the first left after the river bridge to the harbour and the Hive. Street parking available. (Map 7, D3)

Llandudno

Ambassador Hotel

Promenade, Llandudno, Conwy LL30 2NR
Telephone: +44(0)870 4016375
+44(0)1492 876886
reception@ambasshotel.demon.co.uk

Nigel Williams runs this hotel so efficiently that visitors return year after year. The reason it runs so smoothly may be done to the fact it's been in the Williams family for three generations. It was started by Jim and Freda Williams in 1946, and you can see why they wanted to keep it in the family. It is one of the most striking Victorian buildings in town. You can lose yourself in the spacious lounges or soak up the rays in the two plant-filled sun verandas. You'll also get a good Welsh welcome in the bar that has a convivial vibe of an evening. In the restaurant you can choose from set-price dinners that cater for most tastes, both the cautious and more adventurous. Tuck into a hearty ham or beef salad or a more swanky roast salmon with a mustard and Welsh cheese crust, mushroom sauce and horseradish mash. There's also a good value set menu at lunchtimes that is worth popping by for even if you aren't staying in the hotel. Bedrooms vary in size, but the best are spacious, so request one when you book. But you'll find all the rooms are light and decorated in soft colours and they do have that all-important sea view.

Rooms: 57. Rooms from £31 per person.
Prices: Set lunch £6.95, set dinner £15.25. House wine £9.80.
Last orders: Food: lunch 13.45; dinner 19.30.
Closed: Never.
Food: British.
Other points: No-smoking area. Children welcome. Garden.
Car park.
Directions: Leave A55 and take the A470 to Llandudno. Follow to Promenade, turn left towards the pier. (Map 7, A3)

Llandudno

Dunoon Hotel

Gloddaeth Street, Llandudno, Conwy LL30 2DW
Telephone: +44(0)870 4016374
+44(0)1492 860787
reservations@dunoonhotel.co.uk
www.dunoonhotel.co.uk

The splendid gable-ended mansion, set a block-or-two back from the seafront, is one of many fine examples of Victorian architecture that define this wonderfully traditional resort town. The charm of this old-fashioned seaside hotel has been maintained by new owners Rhys and Charlotte Williams, long-standing, second-generation friends of the previous owners. Young and enthusiastic, they have sensibly embraced a philosophy of 'if it ain't broke, don't fix it', retaining long-serving staff and an appreciation of what Llandudno did best in its Victorian hey-day. Smart oak-panelled public rooms include the Welsh Dresser Bar, which sports a magnificent cooking range. There's a relaxing reading lounge and a more intimate panelled lounge with open fire and cosy corners, in addition to a pool table and solarium. In the restaurant, chandeliers and gloriously draped windows make for elegant dining. Chef Mark Martin produces two set-price five-course dinners. This may include a salad of beef tomatoes with feta and basil or homemade chicken live pâté, mains of Welsh double chop with rosemary and redcurrant sauce or steak, kidney and mushroom pie cooked in ale, steamed ginger and rhubarb sponge, followed by Welsh and English cheeses.

Rooms: 50. Double room from £66, single from £49.
Prices: Set Sunday lunch £12.75 (5 courses+coffee) and set dinner £17.95 (5 courses+coffee). House wine £11.40.
Last orders: Food: lunch 14.00; dinner 20.00.
Closed: End of December-mid March.
Food: Traditional British.
Other points: No-smoking area. Children welcome.
Dogs welcome overnight. Garden/patio. Car park.
Directions: Turn left off Llandudno Promenade near Pier. Continue straight on at the next two roundabouts; hotel is 200 yards on the right. (Map 7, A3)

St Asaph

Drapers Café-Bar

Tweedmill Factory Outlets, Llannerch Park, St Asaph, Denbighshire LL17 0UY
Telephone: +44(0)870 4016424
+44(0)1745 731005
enquiries@tweedmill.co.uk
www.tweedmill.co.uk

Once a mill weaving tweed, the Tweedmill Factory Outlets have been graded a star attraction by the Welsh Tourist Board. As well as plenty of shopping opportunities, the outlets include the perfect spot for refuelling. The 100-seater Drapers Café-Bar is a bright and cheerful space filled with plants, pine furniture and a large, south-facing patio with beautiful views across a designated area of outstanding natural beauty. The menu changes daily and dishes are prepared using fresh local ingredients. Daily specials could take in leek and potato soup, or chicken liver pâté, grilled chicken breast filled with Welsh cheese wrapped in smoked bacon and served with a leek sauce, followed by meringue nest with fresh strawberries and cream. Snacks and light meals run to scrambled eggs with smoked salmon, cheese, chive and bacon bagel, chestnut and mixed bean savoury loaf, and filled jacket potatoes. It's a popular place for tired shoppers, but big enough to accommodate quite a crowd without the service suffering.

Prices: Main course from £4.95. House wine £6.50.
Last orders: Food: 16.30 (Thursday 19.30, Sunday 16.00).
Closed: Never.
Food: Modern British.
Other points: No-smoking area. Children welcome. Patios. Car park.
Directions: Two miles south of St. Asaph on the A525 to Denbigh. Follow the tourist signs from A55. (Map 7, A4)

An alternative Britain

Barmouth

The Bistro

Church Street, Barmouth, Gwynedd LL42 1EW
Telephone: +44(0)870 4016334
+44(0)1341 281009
bistro.barmouth@btinternet.com

It may be tiny, but this 18-seater restaurant is big on atmosphere and friendliness. It has a cheery French bistro style that takes on an intimate romantic feel in the evenings. New owners Gareth Palmer and Rosemary Heath plan to keep to the high standards set by previous owners Val Brown and her husband Gordon. The kitchen is blessed with good raw ingredients. Conwy and North Sea fish is delivered from Llandudno, the local butcher provides spring lamb and aged beef, while the organic herbs and salad come from local growers. The food ranges from good old familiar field mushrooms stuffed with garlic and parsley butter and Hereford chicken breast topped with bacon and cheese and served with a creamy cider, chunky apple and rosemary sauce to Mediterranean dishes such as Spanish chicken with chorizo and red peppers. It is also worth exploring the fish specials such as sea bass fillets with citrus butter and lemon and coriander sauce. Vegetarians are also in for a treat with dishes such as mushroom tortellini with a creamy cheese sauce, sun-dried tomatoes and pesto. Puddings are exemplary and the homemade Cointreau and Merlin ice cream is always popular as is the crème brulée. The Bistro attracts a loyal clientele, so booking is a must, especially at weekends.

Prices: **Restaurant main course from £10.50. Vegetarian main course from £9.50. Starter from £3.95. House wine £9.50.**
Special dietary requirements with advance notice.
Last orders: **Food: dinner 20.30 (Saturday 21.00).**
Closed: **Sunday to Thursday October-December. January-March. Wednesday all day.**
Food: **Traditional British with Mediterranean influences.**
Other points: **Totally no smoking. Children welcome.**
Directions: **In the town centre. Some street parking which is free at night. (Map 7, C3)**

Raglan

The Beaufort Arms Coaching Inn and Restaurant

High Street, Raglan, Monmouthshire NP15 2DY
Telephone: +44(0)870 4016269
+44(0)1291 690412
thebeauforthotel@hotmail.com
www.beaufortraglan.co.uk

Outstanding period features and excellent food set this large, handsome cream-painted 16th century coaching inn apart from your average pub. The huge fireplace taken from nearby Raglan Castle, Welsh slate floors and an impressive heavily carved oak bar in the lounge are some of the striking features. Open fires and a warm, welcoming atmosphere make you feel immediately at home at this acclaimed inn that is very much at the heart of things in this community-minded village. Renovation has introduced a complementary modern feel, best summed up in the restaurant where contemporary colours offset the heavy beams beautifully. In the kitchen, a team of talented chefs are committed to using first-class ingredients from local suppliers. Bar menus comprise simple choices such as freshly baked rustic sandwiches of Welsh ham and green salad alongside inventive modern dishes listed on the daily specials board; overall quality and presentation sets it well above average for an inn. In the restaurant, imaginative cooking produces highlights such as lemon-infused smoked salmon, torn leaf salad and dill crème fraîche, and seared, marinated lamb with fine green beans, warm basil and mint oil on a red wine deglaze. All 15 en suite bedrooms have been stylishly refurbished and all have modern comforts, and lovely rural views.

Rooms: **15. Double/twin room from £55, single from £50.**
Prices: **Restaurant main course from £10.95.**
Bar main course from £5.75. House wine £8.95.
Last orders: **Bar: 23.00. Food: lunch in the lounge bar served daily.**
Dinner: 21.00 (20.30 Sunday).
Closed: **Never.**
Food: **Modern British.**
Other points: **No-smoking area. Terrace garden.**
Children welcome. Car park.
Directions: **One minute from the junction of the A40 from Abergavenny and the A449 to Monmouth. South to Newport M4 north to the M50 M5-M6. (Map 8, E5)**

www.routiers.co.uk

Skenfrith

The Bell at Skenfrith

Skenfrith, Abergavenny, Monmouthshire NP7 8UH
Telephone: +44(0)870 4016270
+44(0)1600 750235
enquiries@skenfrith.co.uk
www.skenfrith.co.uk

Beautifully restored to its former glory, the Bell is one of the finest inns in Wales. On arrival, the handsome black and white painted 17th century coaching inn near the bridge spanning the River Monnow makes quite a picture. It's just a stone's throw from the imposing ruins of Skenfrith Castle and walks along Offa's Dyke. The Bell oozes sophisticated charm with its mix of slate floors, old settles and fireside easy chairs in the stylish open-plan bar and dining area, and eight luxuriously appointed, en suite bedrooms with lovely river or mountain views. A commitment to local produce is strong. Fish is delivered daily from Abergavenny and they cook with Welsh black beef, local lamb and regional cheeses. Bar lunches offer Gloucester Old Spot pork open sandwiches or venison steak with red onion marmalade and cranberry jus, followed by apple tart with caramel sauce. In the dining room, the set dinner menu is noted for interesting combinations of, say, pheasant and smoked bacon terrine with tomato and onion chutney, and mains of duo of salmon and sea bass, sautéed potato, wild mushroom and turmeric sauce. The impressive wine list runs from bargain Italian to Château Latour. There are also lots of half bottles to choose from plus real ales.

Rooms: 8. Double/twin from £90. Single from £75, family room from £140.
Prices: Sunday lunch £18.50. Restaurant main course from £10.20. Bar main course bar/snack from £5.50. House wine from £10.
Last orders: Bar: 23.00. Food: lunch 14.30; dinner 21.30.
Closed: Two weeks end of January and early February. Mondays from November to March.
Food: Modern British.
Other points: No-smoking in the restaurant and bedrooms. Dogs welcome. Garden. Children welcome. Car park.
Directions: From A40 at Monmouth take A49 towards Hereford. After 5 miles turn left onto the B4521 towards Abergavenny. The Bell is straight ahead of you after two mile on the banks of the River Monnow. (Map 8, E5)

St Brides Wentlooge

The Inn at the Elm Tree

St Brides Wentlooge, Newport NP10 8SQ
Telephone: +44(0)870 4016407
+44(0)1633 680225
inn@the-elm-tree.co.uk
www.the-elm-tree.co.uk

Set in the midst of the Wentlooge Flats, an area of special scientific interest offering protection to rare and varied fauna, flora and wildlife, is the stylish The Inn at the Elm Tree. Mike and Patricia Thomas's modern but thoughtful extensions have transformed this traditional old farm and 19th century barn. Confident styling mixes the old with the new – tiled flooring, muted colours and log fire in the small lounge and bistro. Here an all-day menu delivers sandwiches such as home-cooked ham and salad, or Penclawdd cockles, eggs and bacon. Afternoon tea brings crumpets and scones, and, of course, Welsh cakes, all homemade. Amid the slightly art deco look of wrought iron and glass in the dining room, a modern European carte incorporates plenty of local and many organic ingredients, such as game, organic chicken, lobster and oysters. Start with pan-seared king scallops with pea pancake, minted pea purée and tomato and lemon dressing, and follow with marinated rack of Welsh salt marsh lamb and honey-roasted parsnip purée, petite ratatouille, caper and rosemary butter. Bedrooms are top drawer and high tech with ISDN and modems. The décor ranges from a country look of solid pine to elegant iron and brass beds, waterbeds and four posters.

Rooms: 10. Double room from £80, single from £70. Family room from £120.
Prices: Restaurant main course from £12. Bar main course from £7.50. House wine from £10.50.
Last orders: Bar: 23.00. Food: lunch 14.30 (Sunday 15.00); dinner 21.30 (Friday and Saturday 22.00, Sunday 19.30).
Closed: Never.
Food: Modern British/Welsh/European.
Other points: No-smoking area. Dogs welcome overnight. Garden. Car park.
Directions: Exit 28/M4. Take A48 towards Cardiff; pass first roundabout to Asda and take next right, then at T junction turn right for two miles. (Map 8, F5)

Individual charm and warmth

Wolfscastle

The Wolfe Inn

Wolfscastle, Haverfordwest, Pembrokeshire SA62 5LS
Telephone: +44(0)870 4016272
+44(0)1437 741662
eat@the-wolfe.co.uk
www.thewolfe.info

You'll get a real flavour of quality Welsh produce at this unpretentious coaching inn. They source only the best local ingredients for the daily updated menus. The bar-brasserie is made up of interconnecting rooms of different styles. So choose between the intimate Victorian parlour, the joviality of the hunting room or the relaxed and leafy conservatory. At lunch and supper, dishes include toasted goats' cheese salad with pine nuts and pesto dressing or Hugh's award-winning sausages with creamed potato and onion gravy. The carte menu is an altogether more sophisticated affair, with home-cured gravadlax of local salmon cured in mead and dill on a crunchy green salad with a light tarragon hollandaise to start, followed by pan-roasted best end of Welsh lamb served on a bed of Mediterranean vegetables with a bramble and thyme sauce, or pheasant, port and thyme casserole, plus there's locally landed fish and seafood, perhaps St Brides Bay scallops with hollandaise. If you want to sample the best of Welsh cheeses, then you've come to the best place. Enjoy your cheeseboard with some of the good-value Italian wines that includes a 50-bin list. Draught ales and a simple snack in the front-facing bar are 'simply no problem' with low calorie, vegetarian and children's choices all readily available.

Prices: Set Sunday lunch £12.95. Restaurant main course from £12.50. Bar main course from £5.95. House wine £10.50.
Last orders: Bar: lunch 15.00; dinner 23.00 (open all day 9 April-4 September). Food: lunch 14.30; dinner 21.30 Sunday 21.00).
Closed: Rarely.
Food: Modern British.
Other points: No-smoking area. Children welcome. Garden. Car park.
Directions: Exit29/M4. Beside A40 mid-way between Haverfordwest and Fishguard. (Map 7, E2)

Wolfscastle

Wolfscastle Country Hotel

Wolfscastle, Haverfordwest, Pembrokeshire SA62 5LZ
Telephone: +44(0)870 4016358
+44(0)1437 741225
enquiries@wolfscastle.com
www.wolfscastle.com

It's been family run for over 25 years and long-serving staff provide a very Welsh welcome at this stone country house. It's highly recommended as a base for touring the fabulous Pembrokeshire coastline or a restful stop over on the way to or from the Emerald Isle. The hotel keeps pace with the times and has recently been refurbished. Bedrooms now include three executive suites that are among the most spacious and comfortable in the county. In addition to state-of-the-art television, video players, and soft furnishings that have a lived-in feel, proprietor Andrew Stirling's intriguing extras include finger-touch bedside lighting. Equally aware of current trends, daily changing menus follow an 'eat what you like, where you like' policy. Dishes incorporate the best ingredients, including fresh fish and seafood from nearby Milford Haven, local organic vegetables and herbs and Preseli lamb and beef. The choice is extensive and on the menu, you'll find traditional lamb's liver and onions sitting alongside pan-fried fillet of Welsh beef on a baked croûte. These are offered in both the clubby bar and the elegant restaurant. The day's dessert list might offer iced white chocolate and Amaretto parfait with apricot coulis and iced orange and espresso mousse with Tia Maria syrup, or tuck into a superb choice of Welsh cheeses.

Rooms: 20. Double room from £79-£107, single from £55-£75.
Prices: Main course from £8.50. House wine £10.
Last orders: Food: lunch 14.00; dinner 21.00.
Closed: Never.
Food: Welsh.
Other points: No-smoking area. Garden.
Directions: Signed off A40 midway between Haverfordwest and Fishguard in the village of Wolfscastle. (Map 7, E2)

Brecon

The Felin Fach Griffin

Felin Fach, Brecon, Powys LD3 0UB
Telephone: +44(0)870 4016273
+44(0)1874 620111
enquiries@eatdrinksleep.ltd.uk
www.eatdrinksleep.ltd.uk

A modern inn where the 'less is more' philosophy really works. This smart ochre-coloured inn ranks among that new-breed of classy Welsh pubs. Its innovative food and individually designed bedrooms are more in keeping with a chic city rather than a rural hotel. It has all those traditional features, such as flagstone floors, open fireplaces, stripped pine beams and doors and an Aga, but minus the chintz and with refreshing contemporary touches of colour and fabric. The kitchen ethos is to source fresh local ingredients grown or reared within 15 miles of the hotel, and this includes organic salads, Brecon farm-reared meats, local sea trout (sewin) supplemented by home-grown vegetables. Owner Charles Inkin, who trained as a chef at Ballymaloe, wants the food to be as fresh and flavoursome as possible and Dutch chef Ricardo Van Ede more than meets his brief. Daily updated blackboard menus may list salad of roasted asparagus, baby gem and black truffle followed by rump of Welsh lamb, lentils and chorizo and colcannon or local venison, braised red cabbage and dauphinoise potato. Rice pudding with caramelised pear, or profiteroles with whipped cream and chocolate sauce and, of course amazing Welsh cheeses make for a splendid sign-off. The bedroom quota has been increased, and the new rooms show the same flair for interiors as the others, with bright colours and an uncluttered feel.

Rooms: 7. Double room from £92.50, single from £67.50. Four poster room £115.
Prices: Main course from £10. Starters from £4.50. House wine £10.75.
Last orders: Bar: lunch 15.00; dinner 23.00. Food: lunch 14.30; dinner 21.30 (Sunday 21.00).
Closed: Monday lunch.
Food: Modern British.
Other points: No-smoking area. Children welcome. Dogs welcome overnight (£10 fee). Garden. Car park.
Directions: Four miles north of Brecon on the A470. (Map 7, D4)

Regional produce

Welsh Venison

at The Felin Fach Griffin

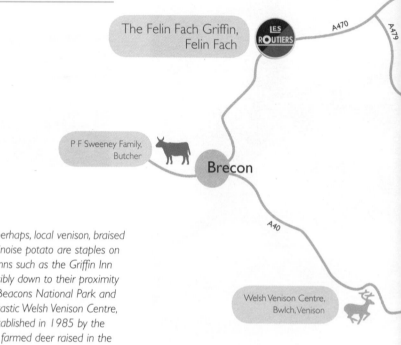

The Felin Fach Griffin, Felin Fach

A470

A479

P F Sweeney Family, Butcher

Brecon

A40

Welsh Venison Centre, Bwlch, Venison

Venison and ale pie or, perhaps, local venison, braised red cabbage and dauphinoise potato are staples on menus in classic Welsh inns such as the Griffin Inn of Felin Fach. This is possibly down to their proximity to the beautiful Brecon Beacons National Park and the existence of the fantastic Welsh Venison Centre, a family-run business established in 1985 by the Morgan family. With the farmed deer raised in the beautiful surroundings of the national park and the guarantee of superb animal husbandry, animal welfare is of the highest order, as is taste. Venison here is as tender as other red meats with a mild yet distinctive and succulent flavour, not at all like the tough gamey reputation venison often has, usually attributed to wild deer. Usually a contradiction in terms, this is also a delicious but low-fat meat. Venison is naturally lean and lower in fat and cholesterol than chicken and it has higher iron levels than other red meats, and another bonus is that it is packed with vitamins and protein.

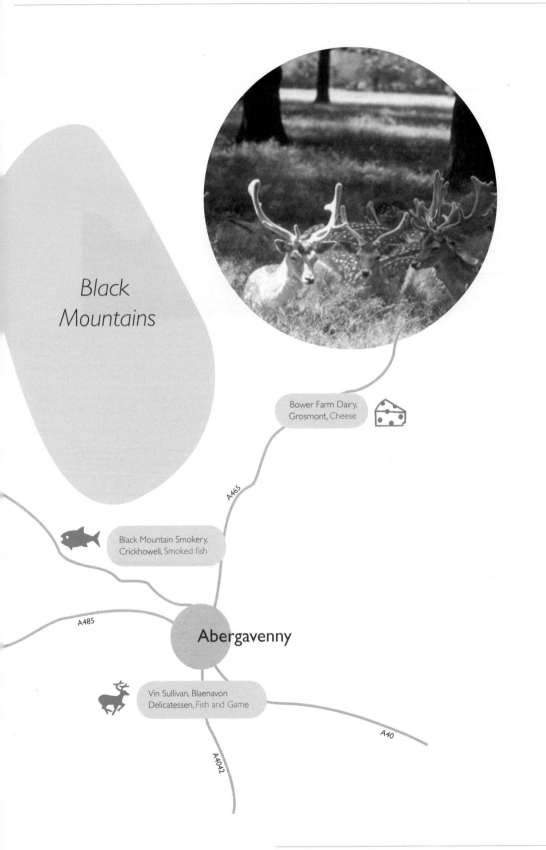

Black
Mountains

Bower Farm Dairy,
Grosmont, Cheese

A465

Black Mountain Smokery,
Crickhowell, Smoked fish

A485

Abergavenny

Vin Sullivan, Blaenavon
Delicatessen, Fish and Game

A40

A4042

Crickhowell

Bear Hotel

High Street, Crickhowell, Powys NP8 1BW
Telephone: +44(0)870 4016274
+44(0)1873 810408
bearhotel@aol.com
www.bearhotel.co.uk

The Bear remains as popular as ever and continues to offer what it has always done best – good food in convivial surroundings. It keeps an eye on the latest trends and is continually making improvements that seem to unearth even more of the traditional features of this building, which dates back to 1432. It's a nooks and crannies, beams and fireplaces sort of place; cosy, snug and friendly. Former stables have been converted into a courtyard of up-to-date bedrooms and across the sheltered rear garden self-contained honeymoon suites. Very much a hub of local community, the fiercely traditional bars always have a buzz about them. The light bar lunches feature modern dishes such as spicy Thai prawn cakes with sweet chilli dip and Welsh rarebit on toasted olive bread, or there's homely Welsh fayre such as champion sausages, Welsh black beef or rack of local lamb. Top-class cask ales and well chosen wines by the glass are ideal to complement the hearty fare. More extensive menus in the more formal dining rooms include many local ingredients: Brecon lamb and venison, fresh fish and Welsh cheeses. Dishes include fillet of smoked trout to start, followed by rack of Welsh lamb, Dijon mustard and hazelnut crust and some sumptuous desserts of which bread and butter pudding with brown bread ice cream is a star turn. Its Sunday roasts are hugely popular.

Rooms: 35. Double room from £75, single from £57.
Family room from £102.
Prices: Main course from £15. Bar meal from £7.
House wine £10.50.
Last orders: Bar: lunch 15.00; dinner 23.00. Food: lunch 14.00; dinner 21.30.
Closed: Rarely.
Food: Modern/eclectic.
Other points: No-smoking area. Children welcome.
Dogs welcome overnight. Garden. Car park.
Directions: Centre of Crickhowell on A40 between Abergavenny and Brecon. (Map 8, E5)

Crickhowell

Glangrwyney Court

Glangrwyney, Crickhowell, Powys NP8 1ES
Telephone: +44(0)870 4016454
+44(0)1873 811288
glangrwyney@aol.com
www.glancourt.com

This lovely Georgian house set in gorgeous gardens is approached by an attractive tree-lined drive. In the 10 years since she has run her B&B, it has proved to be a runaway success for Christina Jackson. Her friendly hospitality makes her the perfect host, and she is proud of her home in which visitors are treated as personal guests. The lounges, with a preponderance of chintz, are supremely comfortable. These are complemented by five opulently decorated en suite bedrooms that are romantic in style. They all have lovely views over the grounds. No meals other than breakfast are served, but the sourcing of the ingredients is impeccable. Mrs Jackson uses ingredients from the Black Mountain Smokery, and sources local honey, vegetables and fruit. At lunch and in the evening, you dine very well in nearby Crickhowell, which has plenty of pub and restaurant options. Glangrwyney Court does, however, have a residential drinks license. So, overall, this guesthouse offers excellent value for money for this level of comfort and outlook.

Rooms: 5, 1 with private bathroom. Double room from £60, single from £45. Family room £85.
Prices: Set dinner £23. Main course from £12.50. House wine £10.
Closed: Rarely.
Other points: No-smoking area. Children welcome. Garden. Car park. Boules and croquet.
Directions: Two miles east of Crickhowell off A40. (Map 8, E5)

Channel Islands

Small and perfectly formed, Jersey and Guernsey make up the delectable and unspoilt Channel Islands. And you'll find Les Routiers' members on the islands are an equally select and exquisite bunch, writes Melanie Leyshon.

Of the islands, Jersey is the most southerly, being 100 miles from the coast of Britain and just 14 from the coast of France. It is strongly linked to France and Lé Jèrriais – The Jersey Language – is still spoken in the countryside. As well as some fine French cuisine, the island has an upmarket range of European restaurants, including Italian and Portuguese, as well as Indian and fusion.

Despite being only 9 miles by 5 miles, Jersey has much to offer visitors, and with a speed limit of 15mph you will find that things move along at a leisurely pace. Unspoilt coastline, sandy beaches, lots of walking and cycling opportunities, stunning landmarks and excellent food make this a top holiday and culinary destination. Small it might be, but Jersey is pretty self-sufficient when it comes to producing quality, fresh produce, with Jersey clotted cream Jersey Royal potatoes and excellent fish and shellfish among the star attractions.

A even more leisurely break is guaranteed on the car-free island Little Sark, which is one of the tiny islands that make up Guernsey. It can only be reached by boat and day-to-day life is conducted at an easy pace. Stay at Les Routiers' member La Sablonnerie and you will arrive at your accommodation by horse-drawn cart, where some exquisite food and pampering awaits you.

Just as relaxing is Herm, which is minute at just a mile and a half long and half a mile wide. Even on a busy day you are guaranteed to find a quiet, secluded spot. On this tiny island, you will find our member The White House, which itself has enough activities and pleasant distractions to keep you entertained before you even venture into the countryside or along the picturesque coast. And once again, you'll find that the fine food is more than a match for the surroundings.

Herm Island

White House Hotel

Herm, via Guernsey GY1 3HR
Telephone: +44(0)870 4016372
+44 (0)1481 722159
hotel@herm-island.com
www.herm-island.com

Pristine beaches on its doorstep and views of the harbour and Channel Islands ensure that the White House Hotel is a breathtakingly picturesque holiday base. As the only hotel on this quiet car-free island, it sets the standard and that is pegged very high. You'll also find there's plenty to do. Wonderful walks, birdwatching, a small harbour, pastel cottages, and an 11th century chapel are within easy distance and ripe for exploration. The hotel was created from an old house in 1949 by Peter and Jenny Wood, and is now run by their daughter Penny and son-in-law Adrian. It has extensive lounges with open fires, a library, games cupboard, solar-heated swimming pool, tennis court and croquet lawn. The best bedrooms have sea views and all rooms, by popular demand, have no TV or phones. With oyster beds clearly visible from the dining room windows, local seafood is going to be as fresh as you can get, and local shellfish of, say, Guernsey lobsters, crabs or scallops, is available as a supplement to the set evening menu. Or, you could opt for set menu choices of warm pigeon and bacon salad, followed by mains of fillet of beef Rossini. The wine list, mostly pitched below £20, has France to the fore, but finds room for other wine-growing regions of the world.

Rooms: 40. Rooms from £67 per person, half board.
Prices: Set menu £22.50 (including boat fare).
Main course lunch from £6. House wine £9.50.
Last orders: Bar: 23.00; Sunday 17.00.
Food: lunch 14.00; dinner 21.00.
Closed: Second week of October to April.
Food: Modern and traditional British and French.
Other points: No-smoking area. Garden. Children welcome.
No cars on Herm Island. Tennis court. Swimming pool.
Croquet lawn.
Directions: Fly or take the boat to Guernsey. Regular 20 minute service by boat to Herm Island. (Map 4, E6)

www.routiers.co.uk

St Brelade

Chateau Valeuse

Rue de la Valeuse, St Brelade's Bay, St Brelade,
Jersey JE3 8EE
Telephone: +44(0)870 4016381
+44(0)1534 746281
chatval@itl.net
www.user.super.net.uk/~chatval

With its large windows and impressive array of balconies and windows, Chateau Valeuse is more splendid Swiss chalet in style as opposed to traditional French pile. The design allows guests to enjoy the stunning coastal views across St Brelade's Bay, one of the most attractive in Jersey. The hotel has an excellent location in other ways as it's south-facing, set back from the road and surrounded by impeccably maintained gardens. Excellent value bedrooms, many with sea view balconies, are all comfortably furnished, well-maintained and have pristine bathrooms. A sun terrace overlooking the garden is the perfect place to enjoy a light lunch or early evening aperitif, or you can relax in the Tudor Bar, while the more energetic can make the most of the outdoor swimming pool and putting green. In the restaurant, you can choose between the good four-course table d'hôte, perhaps moules marinière, or tiger prawns and mussels in garlic butter, followed by chargrilled pork fillets with tarragon and mustard cream or fresh grilled plaice. Choose your pudding from the trolley laden with delights.

Rooms: 34. Rooms from £34 per person.
Prices: Set dinner £19 (4 courses). House wine £7.
Last orders: Food: snacks 14.00; dinner 20.45.
Closed: Sunday and from November to March for non-residents.
Food: European.
Other points: No-smoking in restaurant.
Children welcome over 5 years. Garden. Car park.
Directions: From the airport take the B4 south towards St Brelade's Bay, then the B6 (La Route de la Baie). Turn left into Rue de la Valeuse; the hotel is on the left. (Map 4, F7)

Sark

La Sablonnerie

Little Sark, Sark GY9 0SD
Telephone: +44(0)870 4016373
+44 (0)1481 832061

La Sablonnerie is the ultimate get-away-from-it-all destination, and a dream break from start to finish. Set on the car-free island of Sark, which is just three and a half miles long and one and a half miles across at its widest, you will arrive by boat from Guernsey. The hotel provides a horse-drawn barouche to bring you and your luggage from the tiny harbour to Little Sark at the southernmost tip. The 16th century farmhouse and cottages are set in tranquil and extensive grounds and have been discreetly modernised for comfort. Owned and run by the Perrée family for 46 years, with daughter Elizabeth at the helm, the heart of the hotel is the low-beamed bar with its granite walls and massive fireplace that has roaring fires in winter. All the traditional charm has been maintained in the public rooms and individually decorated bedrooms. This is a magical place to dine too, as its own farm supplies fresh fruit, vegetables, dairy produce and meat for the restaurant, and locally caught lobsters, scallops and oysters are a regular feature on the menu. Dinner begins with canapés in the bar, followed, perhaps, by baby courgette flowers filled with lobster mousse with a lemon and thyme jus, then herb soup with Stilton quenelles, and a lasagne of brill and savoy cabbage filled with ginger butter on a langoustine sauce, with almond mousse and poached pears and caramel sauce to finish.

Rooms: 22, 10 not en suite. Rooms £30-£60 per person.
Prices: Set lunch £19.80 and dinner £20.80. House wine £7.50.
Last orders: Food: lunch 14.30; dinner 21.30.
Closed: Mid October-Easter.
Food: Modern French.
Other points: No-smoking area. Children welcome.
Dogs welcome overnight. Garden.
Directions: Fly to Guernsey and take the boat to Sark. (Map 4, E6)

Down-to-earth, friendly service

Food Producers

Specialist producers around the country are ensuring our farm shops are filled with quality home-produced foods. Alex Chambers talks to one such supplier, Peter Gott, who is passionate about his business of rare-breed pig farming.

Peter Gott is a proud and passionate man who lives and breaths farming and pigs. His mission is to educate and convert the ignorant and uninformed. At Sillfield Farm in Cumbria, he specialises in farming rare-breed pigs and wild boar and rears them in a natural, additive-free environment, where they are also free to roam.

He describes his pure Essex pig as 'rarer than pandas' due to all the mix breeding that has been going on and he laments the fact that we are allowing farm animals to become extinct, such as the Cumberland and Ulster pig breeds, for example. He is on a crusade along with a few other farmers around the country to concentrate on pure breeds again, and to breed selectively, humanely and as much in their natural environment as possible so that not only do they have a decent life, but also to ensure they produce the tastiest, most flavoursome meat.

This is in stark contrast to mass pig farming, which takes the piglets away from their mother too early and stuffs them full of additives and preservatives so that they are ready for slaughter at 16 weeks rather than the 32 weeks it takes at a place like Sillfield Farm. In contrast Peter has 30 pig sows, 12 wild boar sows and around 250 piglets. He is optimistic of the future however and feels that in the current climate, 'consumers are choosing to shop where traceability is apparent'.

There are 460 farmers markets thriving in the UK, which is a good sign, and these are 'awakening senses that supermarkets had closed', says Peter. You can see the fruits of these farmers' labours in Borough Market, London. Its a marvellous, treasure trove of all that is good about food. Through the bustling throng of tourists, shoppers and traders you will find exquisite meats, fish, vegetables and goodies of every variety; it really is a food lovers Mecca. We must support these food producers as much as possible and if people have the zeal and willingness to talk and share like Peter Gott then the future is in good hands.

Chester, Cheshire

The Cheese Shop

116 Northgate Street, Chester, Cheshire CH1 2HT
Telephone: +44(0)1244 346240
www.chestercheeseshop.com

Farmers' daughter Carole Faulkner opened The Cheese Shop over 20 years ago after finding it difficult to source good-quality cheese. In her quaint and packed shop, she now stocks more than 200 cheeses. You can buy the best of Cheshire cheeses here as well as quality regional British varieties. Single Estate Gloucester, Allerdale Goat, Cotherstone and Sandham's Organic Lancashire are a just a taste of what's on offer. Carole is passionate about cheese production, having once made her own Cheshire cheese, and keeps her stocks in tip-top condition in her temperature-controlled Victorian cellars. She is a big supporter of local farms such as Mr Bourne's farm at Malpas. To meet the demand of her discerning customers, she also stocks fine English wines, charcuterie, olives, breads, and much more besides. Mail order is available.

Hours: 08.30-17.30. Sunday 10.30-17.00.
Other Points: Shop. Mail order.
Directions: 50 yards from the town hall. (Map 8, B5)

Thurstaston, Cheshire

Church Farm Organics

Church Lane, Thurstaston, Wirral, Cheshire CH61 0HW
Telephone: +44(0)151 6487838
www.churchfarm.org.uk

The fact it's set in a conservation area with fabulous views of the River Dee are added bonuses, but the main reason to visit is the family-run farm shop, which stocks 2,000 lines. As its name suggests all the fruit and vegetables are organic and so too is the majority of the meats, cheese and grocery lines. You will find all the top brands stocked here, from Belvoir cordials to The Village Bakery breads and Royal Warrant holder Richard Woodall's sausages and hams. The shop sells fair trade goods where possible, and runs an organic box scheme in the Wirral area. It also offers B&B accommodation and a caravan and camping site.

Hours: 10.00-17.00 Tuesday-Friday. 09.00-17.00 Saturday. 11.00-17.00 Sunday. Closed Monday.
Other Points: Coffee shop. Parking. Plants and shrubs for sale. Easy access for disabled.
Directions: Exit 4/M53 Clatterbridge. Take the A540 Chester to Heswall. Continue until you reach Thurstaston, then follow the brown tourist signs to the farm. (Map 8, A5)

Stanhope, Co Durham

Stanhope Farmers' Market

Durham Dales Centre, Stanhope, Co Durham
Telephone: +44(0)1325 718841
katrina@bluebell30.fsbusiness.co.uk
www.teesdalefarmersmarkets.co.uk

On the fourth Saturday of the month, local producers gather at Stanthorpe's Durham Dales Centre to sell their locally grown, reared and home-made produce. It's a buzzing market that draws a crowd who come to stock up on the best foods this region has to offer. Like Barnard Castle farmers' market (below), this Teesdale & Wear Valley farmers' market is accredited by FARMA, the new organisation ensuring the genuine quality and origin of local produce sold in shops and at farmers' markets. Among the many stalls are Border County Meats, which offer rare-breed Cumberland sausages, pork products and game. For seasonings, pop along to The Herb Patch to stock up on home-grown plants, dried herbs and mixed herb dips.

Hours: The 4th Saturday of every month 10.00-15.00.
Other Points: Farmers' Market.
Directions: At Durham Dales Centre. (Map 12, C5)

Barnard Castle, Co Durham

Barnard Castle Farmers' Market

High Street, Barnard Castle, Co Durham
Telephone: +44(0)1325 718841
katrina@bluebell30.fsbusiness.co.uk
www.teesdalefarmersmarkets.co.uk

Local producers come together on the first Saturday of the month to showcase and sell their local produce. This Teesdale & Wear Valley farmers' markets is accredited by FARMA, the new organisation ensuring the genuine quality and origin of local produce sold in shops and at farmers' markets. The main stalls at Barnard Castle line the High Street. There are 25 stalls in all, offering every food item you might need, from ingredients to ready-made dishes and foods. Home-baked breads, cakes and confectionery, meat, fish and cheese, plus speciality lines are all available. Look out for Bessy Beck trout that sells fish from the River Lune and Bluebell organics, which offers locally grown organic fruit and vegetables and home-made soups.

Hours: The 1st Saturday of every month 10.00-15.00.
Other Points: Farmers' Market.
Directions: On the main High Street. (Map 12, D5)

www.routiers.co.uk

Cartmel, Cumbria

Howbarrow Organic Farm

Grange-over-Sands, Cartmel, Cumbria LA11 7SS
Telephone: +44(0)15395 36330
enquiries@howbarroworganic.demon.co.uk
www.howbarroworganic.demon.co.uk

It's a member of the Soil Association, so you can be
reassured of the organic credentials of the food stocked
at this farm shop and through its delivery service. The
farming is done without using herbicides, pesticides,
chemical fertilisers, antibiotics or growth promotors.
Choose from a fantastic array of organic vegetables,
soft fruits, an extensive array of herbs and fabulous
lamb and beef; the animals are all born and reared
on the farm. The shop stocks more than 800 lines of
organic food, and the majority is local and regional,
wherever possible. As well as running a farm trail, it
offers bed and breakfast and serves organic dinners.

Hours: Two days a week - Wednesday and Saturday 10.00-17.00.
Other Points: Farm shop. Delivery service. Bed & breakfast
and dinner.
Directions: Exit 36/M6 take the A590 and follow the signs to
Cartmel. From the village square go past the race course.
Quarter of a mile, take the left hand turning signposted cul-de-sac
after the old grammar school; the farm is at the end of the lane,
approximately one mile. (Map 11, D4)

Grasmere, Cumbria

Sarah Nelson's Grasmere Gingerbread Shop

Church Cottage, Grasmere, Cumbria LA22 9SW
Telephone: +44(0)15394 35428
sarahnelson@grasmeregingerbread.co.uk
www.grasmeregingerbread.co.uk

You can't visit Grasmere without visiting William
Worthsworth's home Dove Cottage, and the famous
Grasmere Gingerbread Shop. Tucked away in the picturesque village, this tiny shop was built in 1630 and
was originally the village school. The gingerbread business has been run by the same family for 150 years,
and the little girl pictured with her grandmother in
the photo on the shop wall is Joanne, who runs the
shop today. Many have tried to copy the world-famous
secret gingerbread recipe, but no-one has ever come
close to the intensely flavoured biscuit that is sold traditionally wrapped in a classic blue and white paper.
The gingerbread is baked daily in the little kitchen at
the back of the shop and wafts of wonderful spicy aromas greet you as you enter. You can also stock up on
locally made fudge, sticky toffee sauce and the award-
winning Cumberland rum butter. And if you can't
make it there, you can use their mail order service.

Hours: 09.15-17.30 Monday-Saturday. 12.30-17.30 Sunday.
(Shorter hours in Winter).
Other Points: Food Shop. No credit cards in shop. Mail order.
Directions: From the south take exit 36/M6, then the A590 north
on to the A591 through Windermere and Ambleside into
Grasmere. (Map 11, D4)

Regional Produce

LEEK
FLAMICHE

A rich brioche bread
dough with a filling of
local leeks, organic
free range eggs and
cream

£1·15
each

The Old Smokehouse
and
Truffles Chocolates

BRE

The
Cheese
Shop

Penrith, Cumbria

The Old Smokehouse & Truffles Chocolates

Brougham Hall, Brougham, Penrith, Cumbria CA10 2DE
Telephone: +44(0)1768 867772
enqs@the-old-smokehouse.co.uk
www.the-old-smokehouse.co.uk

Brougham Hall was once known as the Windsor of the north – a historic hall dating from the 14th century – and the current owner has spent 15 years rebuilding the outer walls. The smokery is run from two tiny rooms with a traditional smoker and best-quality oak chips. It is all done by hand and much depends on the time of the year and the temperature, as only the best ingredients are used. They smoke their own-made sausages (delicious added to soups and stews), as well as offering hot-smoked venison, pork and Mansergh lamb, and wild Scottish salmon. Wild char is listed among more unusual smokings that include Parmesan and Stilton. Handmade chocolate truffles are made next door. No machinery is used and chocolates are rolled by hand in a process that takes three days, and which creates wonderfully smooth centres and flavours. Apricot and cointreau, black Russian, and orange brandy are among the popular choices. If you can't make the trip to Brougham Hall, smokery produce and chocolates are available by mail order.

Hours: Summer 10.00-16.30. Winter 10.00-16.00. Closed for parts of January and February.
Other Points: Shop.
Directions: On the B6262, just off the A6, one mile south of Penrith. (Map 11, C4)

Cirencester, Gloucestershire

Chesterton Farm Shop

Chesterton Farm, Cirencester, Gloucestershire GL7 6JP
Telephone: +44(0)1285 653003
www.chestertonfarm.co.uk

This farm shop majors in traditional British and rare-breed meats and it is accredited by the Rare Breeds Survival Trust. It has a policy of full traceability. The butchers are happy to prepare meats and advise on recipes. Gloucester Old Spot pork, Tamworth pork, Dorset Down lamb are big draws, and its famous dry-cured bacon and ribs of beef just fly out the door. Alongside the butchers is a well-stocked fruit and vegetable farm shop offering an excellent choice of fresh produce, all locally grown. It also sells delicious home-baked cakes and frozen vegetables and fruits. Mail order is available.

Hours: 08.30-17.00. Saturday 08.00-16.00. Closed Sunday.
Other Points: Farm shop.
Directions: (4, A7)

Basingstoke, Hampshire

Manydown Farm

Worting, Scrapps Hill Farm, Basingstoke,
Hampshire RG23 8PU
Telephone: +44(0)1256 460068
www.manydown.co.uk

The Manydown Farm Shop is based on a 5,000-acre estate, which has been in the same family for the past 135 years. It stocks a range of quality meats from its livestock under a system accredited by the RSPCA Freedom Food. The Aberdeen Angus beef herd is traditionally reared and fed on home-produced silage, hay, barley and straw; the sheep graze on permanent pasture, parkland and grass leys; the Large Black pigs are reared in an outdoor system, while the chickens have free access to outside grass pens. The meat is cut and prepared by the shop's highly skilled butchery team. Manydown is a member of the prestigious Guild of Q Butchers. Also stocked are a range of sausage and meat pies made on the premises, game in season and complementary products.

Hours: Tuesday-Friday 07.30-17.00. Saturday 07.30-15.00. Closed Sunday and Monday.
Other Points: Farm shop.
Directions: One mile west of Basingstoke on the B3400 Basingstoke to Overton/Whitchurch. Four miles from junction 6/M4. (Map 5, C4)

Lymington, Hampshire

Warborne Organic Farm

Boldre, Lymington, Hampshire SO41 5QD
Telephone: +44(0)1590 688488
boxscheme@warborne.fsnet.co.uk

George Heathcote is committed to organic farming, and has a Soil Association license and awards to prove it. At his farm shop, you will be spoilt for choice, as it stocks more than 400 varieties of vegetables, everything from carrots to celeriac. It has four colours of cauliflower – orange, white, green and purple – a selection of squashes and 12 oriental salad leaves. Soft fruits available include all sorts of currants and berries. Add in superb organic lamb, beef, pork and chicken and you'll have a real Sunday lunch feast. The home-grown range is supplemented with local produce, including wines, cheese, jams, chutneys and preserves, and bread, milk and cream. Its box delivery scheme has won awards from *You Magazine* and the Soil Association.

Hours: Thursday-Saturday 09.00-18.00. Sunday 10.00-14.00.
Other Points: Farm shop.
Directions: From the A337 Brockenhurst to Lymington road follow signs for Boldre, Spinners Gardens. Pass the gardens on your right and take the first road on your left. (4, D8)

An alternative Britain

Stockbridge, Hampshire

Dairy Barn Farm Shop

North Houghton, Stockbridge, Hampshire SO20 6LF
Telephone: +44(0)1264 811405
DairyBarnShop@aol.com

It's easy to see why local customers flock here for
meats once you see the produce that's on offer. The
shop specialises in premium meat from traditional
British and minority breeds. It has built up an excellent
reputation. Top amongst its offerings are Dexter beef,
Tamworth pork, Galloway beef, Wensleydale lamb,
dry-cured bacon and gluten-free sausages. All the animals are reared on the farm, non-intensively on unfer-
tilised, herb-rich pasture or they are from small local
suppliers. Children are welcome to look around the
farmyard. As well as meats, fresh fish, organic bread,
locally grown organic fruit and vegetables, dairy products, eggs and many more items can be bought here.

Hours: Tuesday-Saturday 09.30-18.00.
Other Points: Farmers' market. Farm shop. Mail order. Delivery
service. Car park. Children's farm yard area.
Directions: Off the B3049 from Winchester. (Map 5, D3)

Corbridge, Northumberland

Brocksbushes Fruit Farm

Brocksbushes Farm, Corbridge,
Northumberland NE43 7UB
Telephone: +44(0)1434 633100
acd@brocksbushes.co.uk
www.brocksbushes.co.uk

With Brocksbushes on your doorstep you'd never have
to cook another dinner party again. Its range of homemade foods, including savoury pies to decadent puddings, are irresistible and made to order. Farm fresh
poultry and game in season is another draw, as are the
fresh berry fruits. And if you're not local, you can mail
order one of its fabulous food hampers packed with
goodies by post. Alternatively, drop by to stock up on
its fine food grocery lines, as well as fresh fruit and
vegetables, much of it organic, and wines from around
the world. This would also be the ideal place to fill
your picnic basket as there is a wonderful selection of
cheese, smoked salmon and freshly baked breads and
cakes. You can sample the farm's homemade specialities in its tearoom, which is also licensed.

Hours: 09.30-18.00 Winter. 09.30-19.00 Summer.
Other Points: Farm shop. Parking. Picnic area.
Directions: 16 miles west of Newcastle-upon-Tyne on the A69.
Entrance off the Styford roundabout. Five miles east of Hexham.
(Map 12, C5)

www.routiers.co.uk

Colston Bassett, Nottinghamshire

Colston Bassett Dairy

Harby Lane, Colston Bassett,
Nottinghamshire NG12 3FN
Telephone: +44(0)1949 81322
stilton@colstonbassettdairy.com
www.colstonbassettdairy.com

If you want to sample and buy the King of Cheeses, blue Stilton, then this is the place. The Colston Bassett Dairy has been making Stilton for more than 85 years. Its cheese is rare in that is has been awarded a trademark and is also registered as a Product of Designated Origin in the European Community. The shop stocks the finest Blue Stilton as well as White Stilton and Shropshire Blue. The Blue Stilton is incredibly creamy with distinctive blue veins, which deepen in colour as the cheese matures. The shop staff are happy to advise on storage and recipes, and are keen to point out that this cheese isn't only for Christmas, and at this quality we couldn't agree more.

Hours: 09.30-12.30. 13.30-16.00. Saturday 09.30-11.30.
Closed Sunday and Bank Holidays.
Other Points: Shop.
Directions: Three miles off the A46 to the south-east of Nottingham. (Map 9, C4)

Abingdon, Oxfordshire

Millets Farm Centre

Kingston Road, Frilford, Abingdon,
Oxfordshire OX13 5HB
Telephone: +44(0)1865 391266
www.milletsfarmcentre.com

From May to October Millets Farm has more than 50 acres of crops exclusively for pick-your-own harvesting. A choice of around 30 different fruits and vegetables can be picked throughout the warmer months, with many new varieties of certain crops extending the season. But if you'd rather someone else did the work, the extensive farm shop offers the same produce, picked fresh daily. Alongside is a bakery selling breads and cakes made from locally grown and milled wheat, a delicatessen with a good cheese counter, a butcher selling locally reared meats, and a wet fish shop. There's also a wine department. As well as two restaurants, there is a Garden Centre, Children's Zoo, Trout Lake and Maize maze. More than enough to make Millets a fun day out.

Hours: 09.00-17.00. PYO available June-September.
Other Points: Car park. Farm shop. Play area. Children's farm.
Restaurants. Garden centre. Picnic area. PYO fruit and veg.
Directions: 4 miles west of Abingdon on the A415 (follow brown tourism signs). (Map 8, E7)

Brize Norton, Oxfordshire

Foxbury Farm Shop and Butchers

Foxbury Farm, Burford Road, Brize Norton,
Oxfordshire OX18 3NX
Telephone: +44(0)1993 844141
shop@foxburyfarm.co.uk
www.foxburyfarm.co.uk

This farm shop proves you don't have to pay over the top for quality home-grown fresh produce. Foxbury's is a family-run business that sells premium meats, local fresh vegetables, free-range eggs and poultry as well as a larder full of other grocery lines, from tasty mustards to preserves. It also offers The Foxton Fast Feast Ready Made Meals, made by local chef Katherine Frelon. She uses Foxbury's meats in her recipes such as steak and kidney pie, and local vegetables in her vegetarian curry. The butchers section, run by Master Butcher John Williams and his team, is quite a draw. Meats on offer include Gloucester Old Spot pork, lamb that has grazed on Cotswold grass and beef that has been hung for three weeks. Staff are happy to advise on cuts and put together barbecue packs.

Hours: 09.00-18.00. Closed Sunday - Tuesday.
Other Points: Farm shop. Butchers shop. Mail order.
Delivery service.
Directions: Signposted off the A40 at Burford. Follow brown tourist signs. (Map 8, E7)

Hadleigh, Suffolk

Hollow Trees Farm Shop

Hollow Trees Farm, Lavenham Road, Semer,
Suffolk IP7 6HX
Telephone: +44(0)1449 741247
shop@hollowtrees.co.uk
www.hollowtrees.co.uk

From a roadside table selling homegrown vegetables, this stall grew into a fully fledged business. The farm shop opened in 1996 and is run by agriculturally trained owners Sally and Robert Bendall. They employ 18 people to work on their farm, which includes 10 acres for growing vegetables, plus livestock that provides beef and pork for the shop. Their home-grown lines are supplemented by an extensive range of locally produced bread, cakes, wines, beers, jams, chutneys and juices, as well as a range of frozen foods. Children and adults can find out more about the animals on the farm trail. In addition, quality plants are for sale plus there's the Tea Shed serving refreshments. The shop is a member of the National Farmers Retail and Markets Association.

Hours: Monday-Saturday 08.30-17.45. Sunday 09.00-17.00.
Other Points: Farm Shop. Car park. Children's play area.
Garden centre. Tea shed.
Directions: On the A1141 road five miles south of Lavenham and 10 miles from Ipswich. (Map 10, E7)

Regional produce

Needham Market, Suffolk

Alder Carr Farm

Creeting St Mary, Needham Market, Ipswich,
Suffolk IP6 8LX
Telephone: 01449 720820
www.aldercarrfarm.co.uk

Housed in an attractive Suffolk barn, you could happily do a one-stop shop at this extensive farm shop and pick-your-own business. It offers an impressive array of fruit and vegetables all year round, from the everyday to the more unusual. In an addition, it has good stocks of locally produced groceries. Its Suffolk-cured bacon, creamy breakfast milk from the only surviving herd of Suffolk Redpolls in the county and 14 flavours of delicious homemade fruit ice cream are among the main attractions. Rhubarb and ginger, gooseberry and elderflower, apple and honey, and summer pudding are some of the tempting ice cream flavours. It also offers fair trade products and the farm is run along environmentally sensitive lines.

Hours: Tuesday- Saturday 09.00-16.30/17.30. Sunday 10.00-16.00.
Other Points: Farm shop.
DIrections: From the A14/A140 junction (between Ipswich and Stowmarket) take the signs for Needham Market aand follow the brown signs. (Map 10, E7)

Woodbridge, Suffolk

Tastebuds

The Street, Earl Soham, Woodbridge, Suffolk IP13 7RT
Telephone: +44(0)1728 685557
lucie@tastebudsfood.com
www.tastebudsfood.com

At Tastebuds delicatessen, you will find all that's good about Suffolk food. This wonderful deli brings together the finest collection of local as well as regional producers, items that you are not going to find in the supermarket. There is locally smoked fish and shellfish from Orford, organic fresh produce, homemade deli foods and takeaway party foods. You can also order bespoke cakes. It's also the place to pick up weekend grocery packs or picnics, a handy service if you are on a self-catering holiday. The deli is constantly on the look out for new and interesting products, so there's always something new to try. You can sample its light lunches, cream teas and other refreshments in its attractive Coffee Yard. Another bonus is that you can buy draught beers from the brewery next door to take away in bottles and flagons.

Hours: Monday-Friday 08.30-18.30. Saturday 09.00-17.00.
Closed Sunday.
Other Points: Shop.
DIrections: On the A1120 from Stowmarket to Yoxford.
(Map 10, E7)

Esher, Surrey

Garsons

Winterdown Road, Esher, Surrey KT10 8LS
Telephone: +44(0)1372 464389
info@garsons.co.uk
www.garsons.co.uk

Farm shop, garden centre, pick-your-own and restaurant, you can easily while away a leisurely afternoon at Garsons. The farm shop with its piles of colorful fresh fruit and vegetables is quite a sight to behold and they also stock groceries from small independent suppliers. The pick-your-own section is the largest in Britain and it offers more than 30 different fruits and vegetables and flowers. You'll be hard-pressed to choose between the different crops that include raspberries, white currants, blackberries and spinach, French beans, broad beans and sweetcorn. Recharge your energy levels in the restaurant run by Elizabeth Treliving. She serves hearty, homemade specials from cakes to hot dishes.

Hours: 09.00-17.00. Sunday 11.00-17.00.
Other Points: Farm shop. Garden centre. PYO.
DIrections: Turn onto West End Lane from the A307 Esher to Cobham road or from the A244 Esher to Hersham road. Winterdon Road is a turning off West End Lane by the Prince of Wales Pub. (Map 6, C5)

Godalming, Surrey

Secretts

Hurst Farm, Chapel Lane, Milford, Godalming
Surrey GU8 5HU
Telephone: +44 (0)1483 520500
kathy@secretts.co.uk
www.secretts.co.uk

At this top-quality PYO operation you will find the old favourites, the unusual and the most flavoursome fruits not stocked by the supermarkets. The farm shop sells a vast array of locally produced speciality foods. Vegetables and salads are picked fresh every day: the farm range takes in strawberries, asparagus, bunched beetroot, baby courgettes (with flowers), spring onions, coriander, spinach, baby bunched carrots, broad and runner beans and sweetcorn. Other sections include a country bakery, chocolates, ice creams, groceries, delicatessen, and a cheese counter with more than 200 British and continental cheeses. Specialities extend to Halloween toffee in the autumn and whole hams, free-range turkeys and puddings at Christmas. A 1930s-style tea shop adjoins the shop offering an inventive menu of sandwiches, country lunches, pâtés and tea-time cakes. There are regular cookery demonstrations using the best of the season's produce, and the South West Surrey Farmer's Market is held at the farm on the third Sunday of every month.

Hours: 09.00-17.30 Monday-Saturday. 11.00-17.00 on Sunday.
Other Points: Farm shop. Flower shop and garden centre.
Ample parking. Play area. Picnic area.
DIrections: Just off the A3. (Map 5, C4)

An alternative Britain

Warminster, Wiltshire

Purely Organic

Deverill Trout Farm, Longbridge Deverill, Warminster,
Wiltshire BA12 7DZ
Telephone: 01985 841093
trout@purelyorganic.co.uk
www.purelyorganic.co.uk

Its fresh orangic trout has received much praise from
food journalists and celebrity chefs, most notably the
king of fish himself Rick Stein, and Hugh Fearnley-
Whittingstall. In addition, this farm shop run by
Tony and Eleanor Free, stocks many other organic
lines, many of them locally produced. Smoked trout,
pâté, fishcakes, watercress soup, cakes, jams and
marmalades are just a few of the 1,500 organic lines
available. All the fresh vegetables sold are organic.
In addition, Chef Dale Ingram makes the organic
Baked Delights in the farm kitchen. The farm is Soil
Association registered. You will find its products at
farmers markets and can buy them mail order.

Hours: 09.00-18.00.
Other Points: Farm shop. Farmers' market. Mail order.
DIrections: On the A350 Warminster to Blandford road, 2 miles
from Warminster. (Map 4, C7)

Harome, North Yorkshire

Star Inn Delicatessen

High Street, Harome, North Yorkshire YO62 5JE
Telephone: +44(0)1439 770397
www.thestaratharome.co.uk

Apart from its food and accommodation, The Star Inn
has another attraction in the shape of its Corner Shop,
opposite. Here you can buy all sorts of fine foods, and
delicious homemade ready meals, which are created
by the chefs at The Star, using the freshest, top quality
ingredients. You can buy takeaway soups of say carrot
and coriander or north sea fish soup, salads, terrines,
pâtés, and mains of Rydedale roe deer casserole or wild
mushroom and spinach risotto. The tarts and cakes are
equally as enticing and feature blueberry bakewell tart
and caramel slices. For home cooks, there is a fabulous
meat counter and fresh fish to choose from, as well as
other fresh produce and groceries.

Hours: Monday 08.30-12.30. Tuesday-Saturday 08.30-18.00.
Sunday 10.00-16.00.
Other Points: Delicatessen.
DIrections: The Star is two and a half miles south-east off the
A170 between Helmsley and Kirkbymoorside. (Map 12, D7)

Richmond, North Yorkshire

The Swaledale Cheese Co.

Mercury Road, Gallowfields, Richmond,
North Yorkshire DL10 4TQ
Telephone: +44(0)1748 824932
sales@swaledalecheese.co.uk
www.swaledalecheese.co.uk

Nobody is sure of the origin of this famous cheese, but
it's thought to have first been made at local abbeys by
Cisterian monks, who had travelled from Normandy.
Swaledale cheese is now handmade at Mandy and
David Reed's dairy and they produce a mouthwatering selection. The several varieties include cow's
milk, ewes' milk, goats' milk, smoked goats', organic,
Italiana and Old Peculiar varieties. They are all made
using vegetarian rennet. You will find these moist, mild
yet distinctive cheeses sold at local farmers markets in
the area; check out the website at www.swaledalech-
eese.co.uk to find out where and when. You can also
buy them by mail order.

Hours: 09.00-16.00.
Other Points: Farmers' market. Mail order.
DIrections: From Scotch Corner follow the road to Richmond,
at the traffic lights turn right up Barrack Hill. Turn left in to Gallowfields road and continue through the estate taking the second
left. The company is on the right. (Map 12, D6)

Caergwrle, Flintshire

Mike Williams

12-14 High Street, Caergwrle, Wrexham,
Flintshire LL12 9ET
Telephone: +44(0)1978 761078

There's always a lot of friendly banter going on
between the butchers and their customers at this classic butcher's shop, which has been in the same family
for 28 years. They even close for an hour at lunchtime.
What distinguishes this shop is that every piece of
properly hung meat is certified, so its origin is guaranteed. Mike Williams adheres to the Black Labelling
scheme, which proves the origin of the meat and veri-
fies that this is what is being sold. Butchers like Mike
Williams are a dying breed, but the quality of their
meat is unrivalled. Specialities include Welsh Black
and Rose beef, own-cured bacon and homemade burgers and sausages. Business comes from as far afield as
Chester and occasionally from the south. Alongside the
meat business, they also serve as a greengrocers.

Hours: 09.00-17.50. Closed on Sunday. Closed between
13.00 and 14.00.
Other Points: Speciality butchers.
DIrections: FIve miles along the A542 on the Wrexham to
Mold Road. (Map 8, B5)

www.routiers.co.uk

Drive and Dine

Enjoy a planned day out with Les Routiers. Our trips take in spectacular scenery and sights, with good food and accommodation with our members highlighted en route.

Devon and Cornwall

Exeter is the starting point for this wonderfully varied trip that takes in a cathedral city, rolling hills and windswept moorland before reaching the rugged coastline of Cornwall.

Distance: 110 miles	Map reference: Map 3-4

What better place to start than Exeter, the capital of Devon, with its majestic Norman cathedral completed in 1206 and Guildhall dating back to 1160. The city was a former Roman settlement and fragments of wall can still be seen. Dine> The Twisted Oak p93. From here take the A38 to Ugbrooke House and Park, which was home to the Lord Clifford of Chudleigh. It was built by Robert Adam toward the end of the 18th century, and now houses a magnificent array of furniture, portraits and silverware.

Continue south on the A38 to Buckfastleigh, an attractive market town. It is at one end of the Dart Valley Railway, which closed in 1962 but reopened some years later. From the church, which is reached by a climb of 196 stairs, you can enjoy panoramic views over the area. Dine/Stay> Orestone Manor p97. Follow the A38 south to Ivybridge, which is an assortment of brightly coloured houses, cottages and inns. The River Erme flows through the centre of town, which lies on the southern boundary of Dartmoor, and it is the ideal base for exploring the National Park.

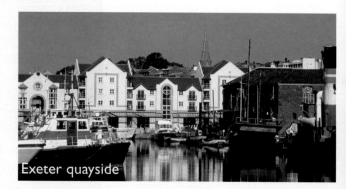

Exeter quayside

Drive further along the A38 to Plymouth. This historic naval city was extensively rebuilt after the Second World War, and it is steeped in maritime history. Old warehouses along the quay are now shops and restaurants. See how they make the famous Plymouth Gin at the Black Friars distillery in the historic Barbican area, and take a stroll on Plymouth Hoe, where Francis Drake played bowls before defeating the Spanish Armada in 1588.

Continue further south to Liskeard on the A38, then from here take the A390 and follow signposts to our next stop, which is the beautifully unspoilt little port of Charlestown. Dating from the 18th century, it is often used as a film location, most notably for the TV series *Poldark*. The market town of St Austell, is just a little north west on the A390. It has a distinctive Georgian Meeting House and Italianate town hall. The town is also closely associated with the china clay industry, and the first pits opened in 1755. They now house the Eden Project, the indoor garden project which has revitalised the area. Dine> Auberge Asterisk p75, Stay> Anchorage House p75.

St Michael's Mount

Take the A390 to Truro, which has an interesting display of Cornish history in the local museum. Its cathedral has three splendid towers that dominate the town of narrow streets. Dine> Smugglers Cottage of Tolverne p78. Before you reach Helston, take a detour on the B3297 to Poldark Mine, worked since Roman times and now a museum. Descend 200 feet to see the subterranean chambers and mining artefacts. Rejoin the A390 for our next port of call St Michael's Mount.

After the A390, follow the A394 on the Penzance road. This small granite island rises from Mount Bay, and is one of Britain's most notable landmarks. The castle on top dates from the 12th century. Just a little further on the A394, we reach Penzance, a popular holiday resort overlooking St Michael's Mount. Head to Morrab Gardens to admire some of this area's subtropical plants. Finally, take the B3311 north to St Ives. Dine/Stay> The Garrack Hotel and Restaurant p78.

North Norfolk

Beaches and salt marshes stretch for miles along the coast giving a real sense of space. Our drive also takes in the splendour of Sandringham as well as sleepy villages and towns.

Distance: 82 miles   Map reference: Map 10

Start at Holkham Beach, just off the A149. It has miles of beautiful sandy beaches and dunes, which have been used as film locations, most notably *Shakespeare in Love*, starring Gwyneth Paltrow and the wartime classic *A Matter of Life and Death* with David Niven. The beaches are reached by an avenue opposite Holkham Hall, and are backed by pine trees. Take note, the beach is a popular destination with naturists. Holkham Hall is on the south side of the A149.

Follow the A149 to Blakeney, an attractive upmarket village on an unspoilt stretch of coastline. It was an important port in medieval times and has pretty cobbled streets leading down to the quay. There are boat trips to see seals in their natural environment. Also worth visiting are the 15th century church and 14th century Guildhall.

Holkham Hall

Further along the coast, still on the A149, is Cley next the Sea. Cley, pronounced 'Cly', was a bustling port town 400 years ago. It is now a quiet, unspoilt village that lies a mile from the sea after land reclamation in the 17th century. It is charming with a legacy of fine buildings from its wealthier sea age. There's a fine 18th century Custom House, windmill, 14th century church and excellent smokery. The area is also famous for its marshland and birdlife, especially rare birds and wintering wildfowl. Dine> terroir p129.

As you continue on the A149, you will come to Sheringham Park, which was designed by Humphrey Repton in 1812 and one of his finest pieces of work. There's an elegant landscape park with mature woodlands and a large garden of exceptional displays of rhododendrons and azaleas from mid May to June.

Cromer

It's a short run to Cromer on the A149, and from there take the A148 to Holt. The town is lined with fine Georgian houses built after the fire of 1708. There is a busy market on Thursdays and flea markets throughout the summer. The main street is also home to many specialist shops. Visit> Richard and Julie Davies Fishmonger p129. Hougthon Hall is signposted after East Rudham on the A148. This splendid Palladian mansion was built for Sir Robert Walpole, Britain's first Prime Minister in the 1720s, and it retains much of its grandeur. Back on the A148, drive until you come to a right turn for the B1140 to Sandringham, where the Royal Family spends Christmas and New Year. This smart red-brick house was bought by Queen Victoria for the Prince of Wales, later Edward VII in 1862. Dine/Stay> Strattons p135. Continue north on the B1440 and rejoin the A149 at Snettisham. Our penultimate stop-off is Brancaster, near the coast. Dine> The White Horse p128, or The Lord Nelson p128. The final destination of Burnham Market is just along the A149, and you turn off right on to the B1355. It's a handsome market town with a small green and a variety of fine Georgian houses and pretty cottages.

Classic Cotswolds

This stunning drive through middle England, crosses three counties and takes in some of the prettiest towns. The most striking houses built from golden Cotswold stone were for the area's wealthy wool merchants.

Distance: 92 miles   Map reference: Map 8

Blenheim Palace

As well as being Cotswold cute, Stow-on-the-Wold has more than its share of antique shops and art galleries. It's also the highest town in the Cotswolds, and has been an important crossroads for a thousand years. After exploring, head east on the A436, then left on the A44 for Chipping Norton. 'Chippy' as it's known to locals is the highest town in Oxfordshire. It's easy to park and has a striking high street and spacious square, dotted with shops. St Mary's Church and many of the town's handsome buildings were built by wealthy wool merchants.

Head south out of town on the A44 to the next stop, Woodstock. The highlight of this attractive town is a visit to Blenheim Palace, which is within walking distance or you can drive in and park inside the grounds. It's England's largest stately home owned by the 11th Duke of Marlborough. The extensive grounds and gardens are magnificent, and that's before you even get to the wonderful state rooms, plus the Long Library, considered to be the finest room in the house. Sir Winston Churchill was born at Blenheim in 1874. It was built to celebrate defeating the French at Blenheim in 1704.

Further south from Woodstock on the A44, take the A4095 for Bladon. At Bladon Church, you can see the graves of many of the Churchill family. Most notable are the stone and marble memorial tablets for Sir Winston Churchhill (1874-1965). Continue on the A4095 to Witney, which has long been famous for its links with the wool trade, and the manufacture of blankets, which goes back over 700 years. Dine> Greens Restaurant, p143, or The Fleece, p143.

From Witney, take the B4047 to Minster Lovell, for the famous Minster Lovell Hall. Frances Lovell was implicated in the schemes of Richard III and fled after the defeat at Bosworth in 1485. After the Battle of Stoke it's claimed he hid in a secret room at the hall, which is no more than a ruin today. Rejoin the A40 and head west to Burford, known as the gateway to the Cotswolds. The broad high street with its mellow stone houses and lines of lime trees that descend down to the River Windrush create a pretty picture. There are also lots of side streets and many shops to explore. Charles II stayed here, possibly with Nell Gwynn, whose child was named the Earl of Burford. The church is another testimony to the prosperity of the wool merchants.

Burford Church

From Burford follow the B4425 along to Bilbury, described by William Morris as 'the most beautiful village in England'. Its most famous and most photographed feature is a group of 17th century weavers' houses. At Arlington Mill, you can find out all about the cloth history, as it is now a rural and craft museum. Follow country lanes west, that cross the Fosse Way (A429) to Chedworth. It has one of the best preserved Romano-British villas, built between the 2nd and early 4th centuries, and rediscovered by a gamekeeper in the mid-1900s. The site includes 4th century mosaics, two bathhouses and a water shrine. A museum houses the smaller finds.

The Lake District

Our journey includes some of the most breathtaking scenery in The Lakes, and takes in its most famous landmarks and poetic connections.

Distance: 73 miles	Map reference: Map 11

As you drive along on the eastern shore of Derwentwater on the B5289, you will have fabulous views of this 'Queen of the Lakes', as it is known. Shelley described it 'as smooth and dark as polished jet', and it is an arresting sight. The lake has been designated a site of special scientific interest and is an important site for wildlife. Stay> Seatoller House p81. At the top of the lake, turn right on to the A591 to Keswick. This attractive market town offers a variety of activities, from fell walking on Skiddaw and Saddleback to boat trips on Derwentwater, plus many other cultural diversions. Visit the Pencil factory, as the town is famous for its manufacture of lead, and the Keswick Museum and Art Gallery to find out more about the town's history.

Take the A591 south to Grasmere, one of the smaller but most picturesque lakes. It inspired William Wordsworth, who wrote most of his best poetry when he lived at Dove Cottage, just south of Grasmere. He is buried beneath one of the yew trees in the village churchyard. The rocky peaks of The Lion and the Lamb and other fells overlooking the village are prettily reflected in the still lake waters, and the scene has been painted many times. Dine> The Jumble Room p86. Visit> Sarah Nelson's Grasmere Gingerbread Shop p245.

Derwentwater

Windermere

Stay on the A591 and head south to Rydal Mount. It has amazing views across Lake Windermere and Rydal Water, and it's easy to see why Wordsworth decided to live here later in life, from 1813 to his death in 1850. The landscape gardening around the house is very much as Wordsworth designed it. Here, you can view many of the poet's personal possessions and first editions of his work. Continue on the A591 down to Ambleside, which is at the head of Lake Windermere. This Victorian town is an attractive tourist hub with good shops for outdoor pursuits enthusiasts in need of gear and retail therapy. It also has a cinema and museums.

Now head south on the A593 to Coniston. Donald Campbell was killed attempting to break the world water-speed record in Bluebird on Coniston Water in 1967. The Ruskin Museum tells the full story. For superb views of the Coniston Water take the Steam Yacht Gondola. Fit walkers should aim for the 803-metre high Old Man of Coniston above the village. Take the B5285 towards Hawkshead. William Wordsworth was educated at the grammar school in this pretty village made up of whitewashed houses and pretty squares. At Hawkshead gallery you can see many illustrations from Beatrix Potter books, as the author lived in Near Sawrey just a little further along on the B5285. Here you can explore Hill Top, the 17th century house, where she wrote many of her classic children's stories. It remains much as it was in her time. Dine> Queen's Head Hotel p86.

Rejoin the B5285, then turn right on to the A592 to Windermere, one of the most popular and well-known Lakeland spots. It's an ideal spot for sailing and for lake cruising. This is the home of Lakeland Limited, the amazing kitchenware store, which is next to the Windermere railway station. The A592 now takes you all the way to Ullswater, the second largest lake. Take a steamer along the lake or partake in canoeing, windsurfing and sailing. Walkers have the option of easy or more challenging climbs on Helvellyn. Pooley Bridge, at the northern end of the lake, is a popular spot and a good base for those wanting to fish, cycle or trek. Dine> Alan's Cafe Restaurant p87, or the Watermill p88. Visit> the Old Smokehouse and Truffles p247.

The Roman Trail

Travel back in time to an ancient Britain of Hadrian's Wall, Roman forts and Norman castles as we cut a swaithe through Yorkshire and finish in the historic city of York.

Distance: 142 miles	Map reference: Map 12

Before heading into Hexham, drive west on the B6318, which runs along Hadrian's Wall. The Romans built this wall as a fortification and as a base for raids against the northern barbarians. It stretches for 73 miles, from the Tyne to Solway and originally stood 20-feet high, with patrol points every 1,620 yards, and smaller turrets every 540 yards. Find out more about the Wall at Chesters Roman Fort that houses a museum. Now head south on the A6079 into Hexham. Its abbey was built in the 12th and 13th centuries over a crypt of an abbey built by Saint Wilfrid in AD674. Other notable buildings in town include the 15th century Moot Hall and old jail, which is now the Border History Museum.

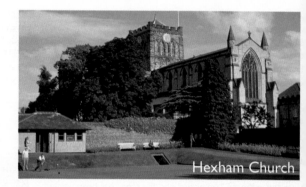
Hexham Church

Head south to Durham, first taking the A69 east, then the A68 south. Turn off to Consett on the A692, then turn at Iveston on to the A691 to Durham. A visit to the magnificent Norman cathedral is a must. It contains shrines of Venerable Bede and Saint Cuthbert. The Charter House on the east side of the cloister became a Hogwarts classroom in the film *Harry Potter and the Philosopher's Stone*, and the cloister was also featured.

The Bowes Museum

Head out of Durham on the A167 south, then turn on to the A688 to Bishop Auckland, then down to Barnard Castle. Dine/Stay> the Manor House Hotel and Country Club p72. This fine market town also has an imposing Norman castle to defend a vital river crossing. It stands on a rocky crag overlooking the town. For a cultural fix, head to The Bowes Museum, which was built in the style of a French chateau by John Bowes, son of the 10th Earl of Strathmore, in the 1860s. It has a fine and extensive collection of art, including works by Goya, El Greco and Canaletto. It also contains comprehensive collections of furniture, ceramics, clocks and tapestries.

Our next stop Ripon is reached by taking the A67 to Bowes, then the A66 south, before joining the A1, followed by the A61 into what is the smallest cathedral city in Yorkshire. The cathedral dates from the 12th century and has a Saxon crypt. And to find how the criminal mind works, visit Liberty Prison, built in 1815, which is now a Prison and Police museum, with artefacts dating back to the 17th century. Dine> Sawley Arms and Cottages p180.

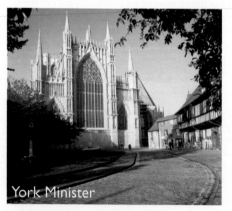
York Minister

Take the A61 south of Ripon, then the A59 to our next stop of Knaresborough, one of Yorkshire's most picturesque market towns. It too has a Norman castle, albeit it in ruins, as it was demolished by the Roundheads. The town is made up of narrow streets and Georgian houses and steep steps and alleys lead down to the River Nidd. It is also noted for Mother Shipton's Cave and its classic viaduct that strides the river. Factor in good shops and a scenic gorge, and you can while more than an hour or two here. Now take the A59 east to York. This ancient Roman city's history stretches back 2,000 years. It's filled with many fine churches and elegant buildings, none more so than York Minister. It was built between 1220 and 1470, and is the largest medieval church in northern Europe. After this head for the historic Shambles, the Viking Centre or the National Railway Museum, just a few attractions the city has to offer, as well as excellent shopping. Stay/Dine> Four High Petergate Hotel and Bistro p184.

The Yorkshire Dales

Travelling through the heart of the picturesque Yorkshire Dales, you'll come across some remarkable natural features such as cascading waterfalls, as well as historical houses and abbeys.

Distance: 62 miles

Map reference: Map 12

Hardraw Force

Sedbergh on the A684 is acknowledged as the western gateway to the Dales. The town sits beneath the peaks of Howgill Fells. Climb the steep paths to Winder and you will have magnificent views of the Pennines, Lune Valley and the Forest of Bowland. Once a Yorkshire town, it switched to Cumbria as part of county boundary changes in 1974.

Continue along the A684 eastwards to Hardraw, a left turning off the main road. This well-known Dales village is famous for its spectacular 100-feet high waterfall in the grounds of the Green Dragon pub. Hardraw Force is reputed to be England's highest unbroken waterfall, and it plunges over a ledge into a natural amphitheatre, where brass band contests are held annually.

Further along the A684, you will come to a turn off for Askrigg. It's a quiet Dales town with a long curving street of tightly backed houses running down to the very attractive market square and the parish church of St Oswald. The town's greatest claim to fame though, is Skeldale House, opposite the church. It was used as James Herriot's veterinary surgery in the TV series *All Creatures Great and Small*. In reality, Herriot practised at Thirsk, but Askrigg became the fictional Darrowby for the filming. Back on the A684 to another natural stunning water feature, Aysgarth Falls, which is one of the most popular beauty spots in the Yorkshire Dales. The falls cascade over rocky ledges on the River Ure for a mile, and create quite a spectacle in an already picturesque setting.

Rejoin the A684 for the next stop Castle Bolton, the 14th century castle where Mary Queen of Scots was imprisoned for six months in 1568. It creates quite a dramatic setting at night when it is floodlit. Further along the A684, turn right on to the A6108 at Leyburn for Jervaulx Abbey. Despite being ruins, you can still figure out the plan of the ground floor of this former Cistercian Monastery.

Ripon Cathedral

Further along the A6108, you come to another remarkable building, Marmion Tower. This splendid medieval gateway-tower with its oriel window is all that remains of the old family seat of the Marmions. It is now in the hands of English Heritage and open to the public. The best views over the village and River Ure are from the top of the tower reached by a spiral staircase. On the road into Ripon, you will see signs for Norton Conyers, a fine medieval house, with alterations carried out in the 18th century. It is reputed to be the inspiration for Thornfield Hall in Charlotte Brontë's *Jane Eyre* and well worth a stop-off. Last on our itinerary is Ripon. The rectangular market square dominates this fine old cathedral city. The cathedral dates from the 12th century and has a Saxon crypt. You can find out all about the town's history at the 13th century Wakeman's House Museum, which is claimed to be haunted. Dine> Sawley Arms and Cottages p180.

Lochs and Glens

The west coast of Scotland has a stunning array of beautiful lochs and glens. The area is also home to Britain's highest mountain, Ben Nevis.

Distance: 47 miles	Map reference: Map 14

Oban

The sheltered coastal town of Oban is the tourist centre for the Great Glen and Western Highlands region. To appreciate its true splendour climb Pulpit Hill for fine views, or choose from a range of coastal walks along this stretch of coastline. One striking landmark well worth visiting in the town is McCaig's Tower, sometimes called McCaig's Folly. But you don't have to walk there, as it can be clearly seen above Oban. It was financed by a local banker who wanted it built as a family memorial, with the aim of also helping to reduce unemployment in the area. From Oban, you can take the ferry across to the islands of Mull or Iona.

Take the A85 north out of Oban, and just off on the left, is Dunstaffnage Castle, which has magnificent views over the region. It is now in ruins, but this 13th century stronghold has a gatehouse, two round towers and walls, which are 10 feet thick. Flora MacDonald was once imprisoned here. Keep on the A85 to Tyndrum, Dine> The Green Welly Stop Restaurant p226, or turn off the A85 on the A828 for Barcaldine, which is a forested area of towering Douglas firs that line the path to Gleann Dubh. There are scenic waterfalls and caves to explore nearby. Barcaldine is made up of various houses and crofters' fields, and there is a 16th century tower house associated with the Glencoe Massacre.

Glencoe

Stay on the A828 as far as Tynribbie, then take a left turn and detour for Port Appin, a picturesque hamlet of whitewashed cottages. It also has a wildlife museum. Nearby, on an offshore island, is Castle Stalker, which dates back to the 14th century. Rejoin the A828 and continue north until you reach the junction with the A82 east for Glencoe, the most famous glen in Scotland, and well worth a short detour. It is renowned for its stunning scenery and has some of the best walking and climbing in the Highlands. The excellent visitor centre covers the history of the Glencoe Massacre of 1692 and includes information on local walks. Dine> Allt-nan-Ros p218 or the Clachaig Inn p217.

After your tour, head back west on the A82 passing Ballachulish through beautiful scenery to our final destination, Fort William. It was founded as a fort in 1690, and is named after William, Prince of Orange. Much of the town was demolished in the Victorian era to make way for the new railway. It is a real hub in the Western Highlands, surrounded by marvellous peaks and lochs. Just north of the town is Ben Nevis, Britain's highest mountain that rises to 4,407 feet. Some of the best views are from the Mallaig Road and the B8004 on the west bank of the Caledonian Canal.
Dine/stay> Glen Loy Lodge p215.

Ben Nevis

Gretna to Stranraer

A stunning collection of castles and churches line the route from the infamous matrimonial destination of Gretna to our beautiful journey's end, the northern market town of Stranraer.

Distance: 147 miles	Map reference: Map 14

We start in the town that's famous for runaway weddings. Dine/stay> Garden House Hotel, p199. Driving west on the B721, you will have spectacular views of Annan, the third largest town in Dumfries and Galloway. At the end of the High Street is Bridge House, built in 1780 and considered one of finest Georgian town houses in Scotland. Off the High Street is Bruce Street, which leads to the public park where the mounds of Robert the Bruce's 12th century motte and bailey still tower.

On to the B724, and you come to the church where the 7th century Ruthwell Cross is housed. Further along the B725 is Caerlaverock Castle, a magnificent 13th century pile with stunning views over the Solway Firth. Drive up to Dumfries, the 'Queen of the South' has long been the southwest's most important town and is most famous for its association with Robert Burns. Burns' enthusiasts should visit the Burns Mausoleum, Burns House and Burns Statue.

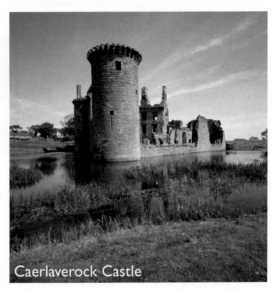
Caerlaverock Castle

Leaving Dumfries on the A710 down the Solway Coast, you will enjoy views of unspoilt countryside. Just after the village of New Abbey lies Sweetheart Abbey, the last Cistercian foundation in Scotland. It was founded in 1273 by Dervorgilla, wife of John Balliol, whose embalmed heart lies with her in the presbytery – hence the name. At Dalbeattie, take the A745 to the market town of Castle Douglas. Dine/stay> Craigadam, p198, From here visit the impressive 14th century tower of Threave Castle, sitting on an island in the River Dee. Threave Gardens, with its 64 acres of fabulous plants and flowers, is also well worth a look.

Alternatively, from Dalbeattie head south on the A711 to Auchencairn. Dine/stay >Balcary Bay, p198. From here, visit Dundrennan Abbey and move onto Kirkcudbright. From Castle Douglas, take the A75 the A711 to Kirkcudbright. Dine> Harbour Lights, p199. You are near Broughton House, the home of the artist Edward Atkinson Hornel, and also Maclellan's Castle. Out of Kirkcudbright onto the A755 then take the A75 for the pretty coastal drive to Creetown, driving through the picturesque gatehouse of Fleet and passing Cardoness Castle. When you reach Newton Stewart, a pretty market town with glorious hill walking nearby, a visit to the Bladnoch Whisky Distillery for a tasting is a most interesting diversion.

Threave Gardens

Take the A714 through the book lovers' Mecca that is Wigtown and drive down to the Isle of Whithorn. Around here are St Ninian's Cave of cult film, *The Wicker Man* fame, the ruins of Cruggleton Church and Castle and the Priory and museum in Whithorn. The A746 turns into the A747, and the beautiful coastal drive up Luce Bay. Take a left at the A75 and almost immediately to the north, lies the 12th century Glenluce Abbey. The agricultural market town of Stranraer is at the end of the A75. The countryside is breathtaking, not least at Castle Kennedy, set on a beautiful site between two lochs. After Stranraer, continue northwards on the A718 to our journey's end. Dine/stay> Corsewall Lighthouse Hotel, p201.

The Welsh Marches

The beautifully tranquil countryside of Shropshire that borders England and Wales offers fabulous walks, and has more than its fair share of castles and curiousities.

Distance: 68 miles   Map reference: Map 8

Our trip starts at Clun on the A488. In the centre of this sleepy village is Clun Castle, a Norman motte and bailey castle, built around 1090. It is set above the valleys of Clun and the Unk, and if you're looking for a spot for peaceful contemplation, then you've come to the right place as this small town was one of the 'four quietest places under the sun', in AE Housman's *A Shropshire Lad*. Dine> Bird on the Rock Tearoom p145. Continue on the A488 south to Knighton, home to the Offa's Dyke Centre. The rural market town is the starting point for Offa's Dyke Path, the 8th century defensive rampart, in Shropshire. The 30 miles of path that run through this county are considered to be the most attractive along the 177 mile-long trail. The climbs may be steep, but you will be rewarded with fantastic views. The town's neo-Gothic railway station is also worth a visit.

Clun Castle

Out of Knighton, follow the A4113, then take the A4110 south to Wigmore. Here, you can explore the remains of Wigmore Castle, which date back to 1067. It was dismantled during the Civil War and what remains forms a motte and bailey. The attractive ruins stand between the manor house and church, and Wigmore makes for a pleasant place to stop-off for a leisurely stroll. Further south along the A4110, you will see signposts to Croft Castle. The castle is in a wonderful spot overlooking the River Lugg on the hillside below Croft Ambrey hill fort. The castle was first mentioned in the Domesday book, and it is late medieval in style with elegant 18th century interiors. The surrounding parkland is well worth exploring as it includes a magnificent avenue of 350-year-old Spanish chestnuts and an attractive walled garden.

Church Stretton

Rejoin the A4110, and turn on to the A44 to Leominster, one of England's great wool towns, which has a network of quaint narrow streets lined with timber-framed houses and cottages, while the more spacious Broad Street has the stamp of the Georgian era. From Leominster, take the A49 north, and at Ashton take the turning for Berrington Hall. This late 18th century National Trust property was designed by Henry Holland and has wonderful landscaped grounds designed by 'Capability' Brown. As well as being a fine piece of architecture, the house has an interesting collection of furniture and paintings, plus you can step back in time by touring its Victorian laundry. Outside, there's a pretty walled garden.

Rejoin the A49 for Ludlow. As well as being considered one of the prettiest towns in Britain, there are several other good reasons for stopping off here. Visit the 11th century Ludlow Castle, built to keep the Welsh out, before browsing the pretty back streets lined with antique, book and craft shops and admiring the 500 listed buildings. There's a museum of geology and fossils for the curious. Dine> De Greys p146, the Clive Restaurant with Rooms p146 or the Feathers Hotel p147.

From here continue on the A49 north to Stokesay Castle, a wonderfully preserved 13th century fortified manor house that's near the pretty town of Craven Arms. Enter the castle through a black and white gatehouse with a gabled stone roof, and then admire the great hall, which is outstanding, not least for the size of its windows. From here head north, again on the A49, to the pretty town of Church Stretton, which is a good starting point for walking the beautiful heather-covered moorland of The Long Mynd. Along the 500-acre long route, you will have superb views across the Shropshire and Cheshire plains, and get glimpses of the Black Mountains in the distance. It's suitable for all levels of walkers.

Wonderful Welsh Hills

Brooding mountains, lush river valleys and dense forest make up the area around the Brecon Beacons. It is spectacularly beautiful and offers excellent walking opportunities.

Distance: 82 miles	Map reference: Map 7

North of the Beacons at the crossroads of the B4350 and the B4348 is Britain's most famous capital of books, Hay-on-Wye. Bookworms will be in paradise, as the town's streets are full of antiquarian and new bookshops. A literary festival is held annually, but there is much to see and do besides leafing between covers. The 17th century mansion, known as The Castle, and the many old buildings in its network of narrow streets are worth exploring. From Hay-on-Wye, take the B4350 north to join the A438 all the way into Hereford. Along this route you will be able to admire Golden Valley that's to the south. The River Dore runs through this picturesque countryside.

However, the most scenic drive is along the B4348, from Dorstone to Pontrilas, which is just further south. Following this route, you can either miss out Hereford or head north on the A465 to visit this bustling city. It has a small but distinctive Norman cathedral, and an interesting Cider museum at Pomona Place and a museum and art gallery on Broad Street. Out of town, take the A465 south to Abergavenny. Off this road, you can take a detour along the B4347 to Skenfrith Castle, built to defend one of the main routes between England and Wales. Dine> The Bell at Skenfrith p233. When you reach the busy market town of Abergavenny, take the opportunity to stock up on local specialities at the market and to browse the many shops. The town's Tudor buildings and 11th century castle are also worth a closer inspection, or visit the museum, which traces back the local history of the area.

Hay-on-Wye

Brecon Beacons

From Abergavenny, take the A40 north to the pretty village of Crickhowell, which is in the stunning Usk Valley. There are many good walks around here, plus a pretty 14th century church and castle ruins to explore. Dine > The Bear Hotel, p238, Stay> Glangrwyney Court p238. Stay on the A40 for the drive to Brecon. To the west, you will see the spectacular Brecon Beacons that soar to 2,096 feet above sea level. Visit the town's Information Centre for booklets about the many walks in the Brecons. And, if you've two to three hours to spare, and fairly fit, think of tackling Pen-y-Lan. Dine> Felin Fach Griffin Inn, p235.

Just off the Motorway

Take a short detour off the motorway and you will discover a world of good food and accommodation with Les Routiers' members. We've mapped out lots of tasty options on some of the leading routes around Britain.

From London to Leeds on the A1

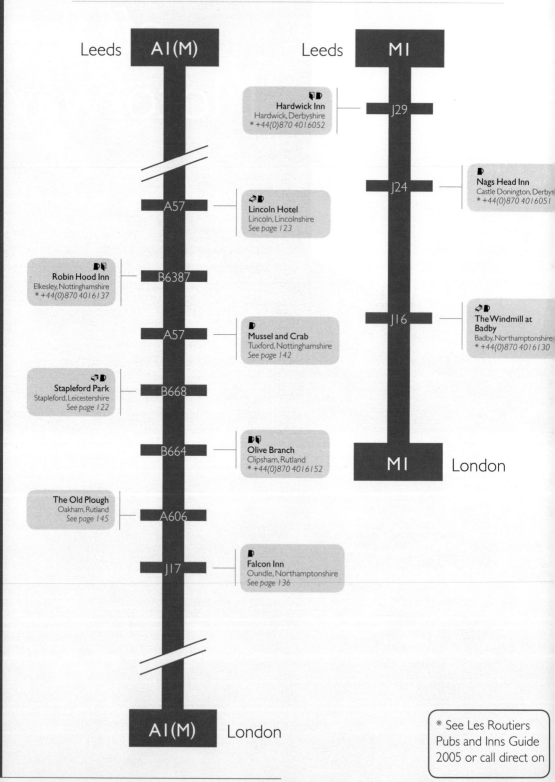

Leeds **A1(M)**   Leeds **M1**

Hardwick Inn
Hardwick, Derbyshire
*+44(0)870 4016052
— J29

— J24 — **Nags Head Inn**
Castle Donington, Derbys
*+44(0)870 4016051

A57 — **Lincoln Hotel**
Lincoln, Lincolnshire
See page 123

Robin Hood Inn
Elkesley, Nottinghamshire
*+44(0)870 4016137
— B6387

J16 — **The Windmill at Badby**
Badby, Northamptonshire
*+44(0)870 4016130

A57 — **Mussel and Crab**
Tuxford, Nottinghamshire
See page 142

Stapleford Park
Stapleford, Leicestershire
See page 122
— B668

B664 — **Olive Branch**
Clipsham, Rutland
*+44(0)870 4016152

The Old Plough
Oakham, Rutland
See page 145
— A606

J17 — **Falcon Inn**
Oundle, Northamptonshire
See page 136

M1 London

A1(M) London

* See Les Routiers
Pubs and Inns Guide
2005 or call direct on

From Leeds to Edinburgh

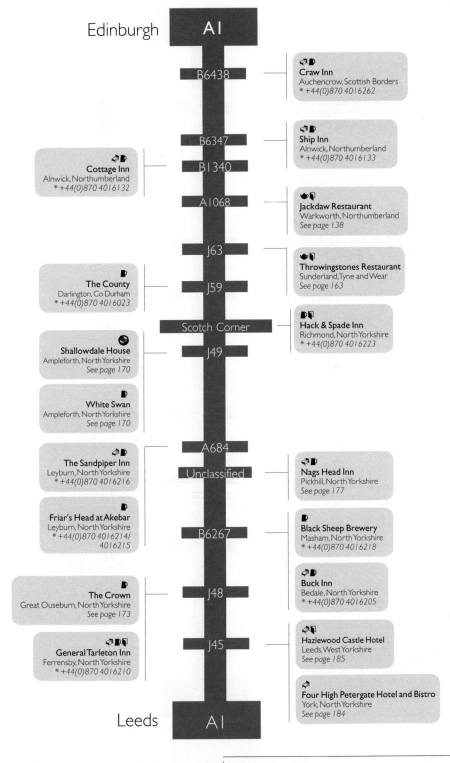

Edinburgh

A1

B6438

Craw Inn
Auchencrow, Scottish Borders
* +44(0)870 4016262

B6347

Ship Inn
Alnwick, Northumberland
* +44(0)870 4016133

B1340

Cottage Inn
Alnwick, Northumberland
* +44(0)870 4016132

A1068

Jackdaw Restaurant
Warkworth, Northumberland
See page 138

J63

Throwingstones Restaurant
Sunderland, Tyne and Wear
See page 163

The County
Darlington, Co Durham
* +44(0)870 4016023

J59

Scotch Corner

Hack & Spade Inn
Richmond, North Yorkshire
* +44(0)870 4016223

Shallowdale House
Ampleforth, North Yorkshire
See page 170

J49

White Swan
Ampleforth, North Yorkshire
See page 170

A684

The Sandpiper Inn
Leyburn, North Yorkshire
* +44(0)870 4016216

Unclassified

Nags Head Inn
Pickhill, North Yorkshire
See page 177

Friar's Head at Akebar
Leyburn, North Yorkshire
* +44(0)870 4016214/
4016215

B6267

Black Sheep Brewery
Masham, North Yorkshire
* +44(0)870 4016218

Buck Inn
Bedale, North Yorkshire
* +44(0)870 4016205

The Crown
Great Ouseburn, North Yorkshire
See page 173

J48

J45

Hazlewood Castle Hotel
Leeds, West Yorkshire
See page 185

General Tarleton Inn
Ferrensby, North Yorkshire
* +44(0)870 4016210

Four High Petergate Hotel and Bistro
York, North Yorkshire
See page 184

Leeds

A1

From London to Southampton

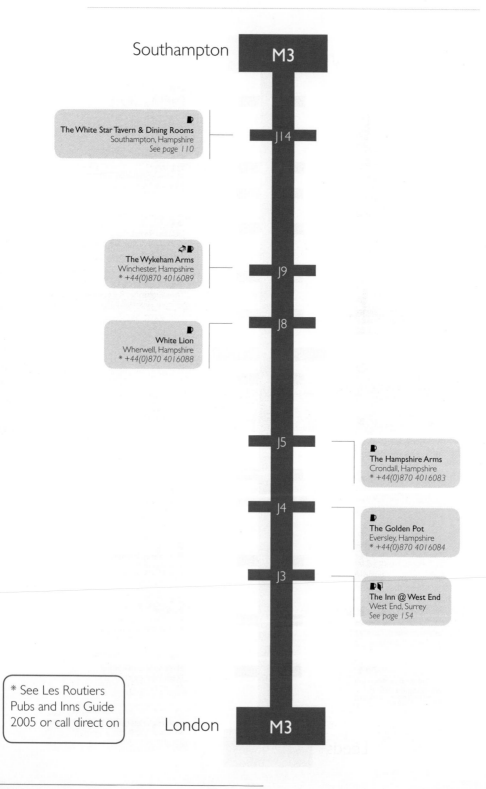

Southampton

M3

The White Star Tavern & Dining Rooms
Southampton, Hampshire
See page 110

J14

The Wykeham Arms
Winchester, Hampshire
* +44(0)870 4016089

J9

J8

White Lion
Wherwell, Hampshire
* +44(0)870 4016088

J5

The Hampshire Arms
Crondall, Hampshire
* +44(0)870 4016083

J4

The Golden Pot
Eversley, Hampshire
* +44(0)870 4016084

J3

The Inn @ West End
West End, Surrey
See page 154

* See Les Routiers
Pubs and Inns Guide
2005 or call direct on

London

M3

From Salisbury to Penzance

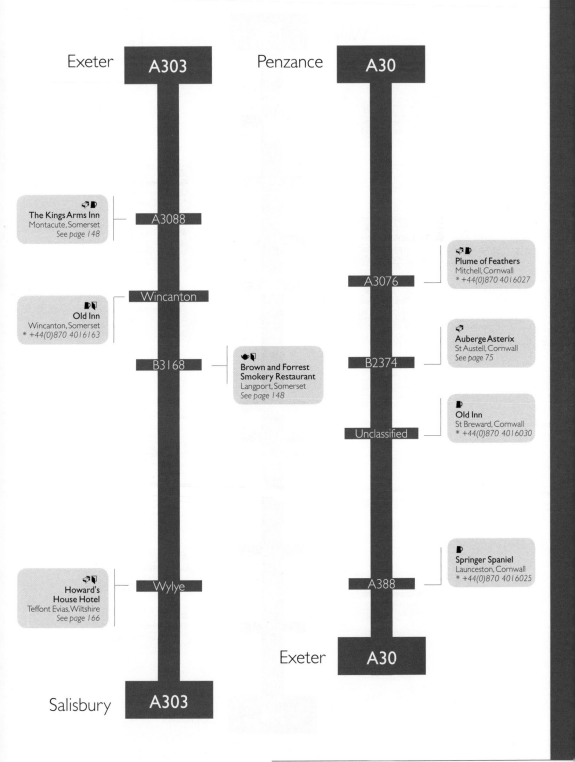

Exeter **A303**

Penzance **A30**

The Kings Arms Inn
Montacute, Somerset
See page 148
A3088

Old Inn
Wincanton, Somerset
* +44(0)870 4016163
Wincanton

Brown and Forrest Smokery Restaurant
Langport, Somerset
See page 148
B3168

Howard's House Hotel
Teffont Evias, Wiltshire
See page 166
Wylye

Salisbury **A303**

Plume of Feathers
Mitchell, Cornwall
* +44(0)870 4016027
A3076

Auberge Asterix
St Austell, Cornwall
See page 75
B2374

Old Inn
St Breward, Cornwall
* +44(0)870 4016030
Unclassified

Springer Spaniel
Launceston, Cornwall
* +44(0)870 4016025
A388

Exeter **A30**

From London to West Wales

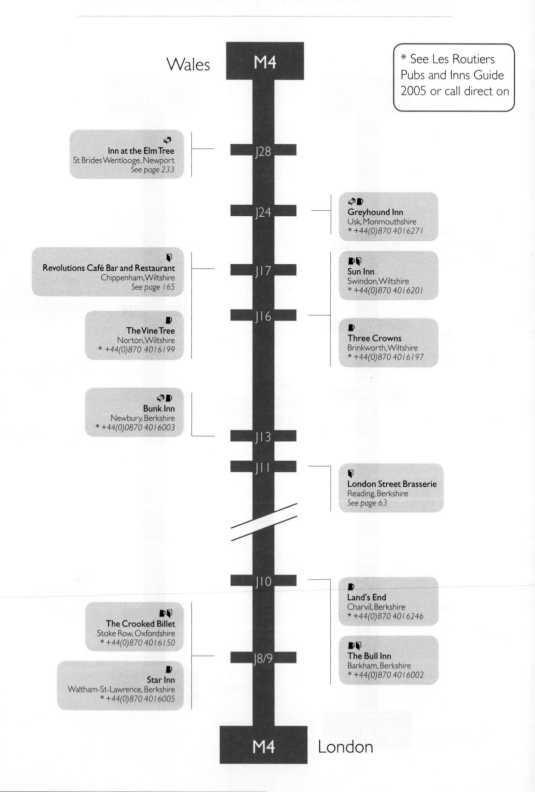

Wales

M4

* See Les Routiers Pubs and Inns Guide 2005 or call direct on

Inn at the Elm Tree
St Brides Wentlooge, Newport
See page 233

J28

J24

Greyhound Inn
Usk, Monmouthshire
* +44(0)870 4016271

Revolutions Café Bar and Restaurant
Chippenham, Wiltshire
See page 165

J17

Sun Inn
Swindon, Wiltshire
* +44(0)870 4016201

J16

The Vine Tree
Norton, Wiltshire
* +44(0)870 4016199

Three Crowns
Brinkworth, Wiltshire
* +44(0)870 4016197

Bunk Inn
Newbury, Berkshire
* +44(0)0870 4016003

J13

J11

London Street Brasserie
Reading, Berkshire
See page 63

J10

Land's End
Charvil, Berkshire
* +44(0)870 4016246

The Crooked Billet
Stoke Row, Oxfordshire
* +44(0)870 4016150

The Bull Inn
Barkham, Berkshire
* +44(0)870 4016002

J8/9

Star Inn
Waltham-St-Lawrence, Berkshire
* +44(0)870 4016005

M4 London

From Exeter to Bristol

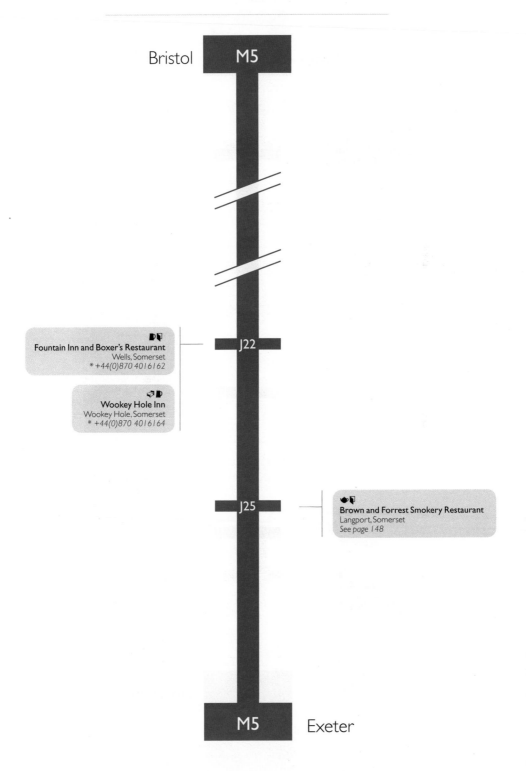

Bristol — M5

J22

Fountain Inn and Boxer's Restaurant
Wells, Somerset
✆ +44(0)870 4016162

Wookey Hole Inn
Wookey Hole, Somerset
✆ +44(0)870 4016164

J25

Brown and Forrest Smokery Restaurant
Langport, Somerset
See page 148

M5 — Exeter

From Birmingham to Bristol

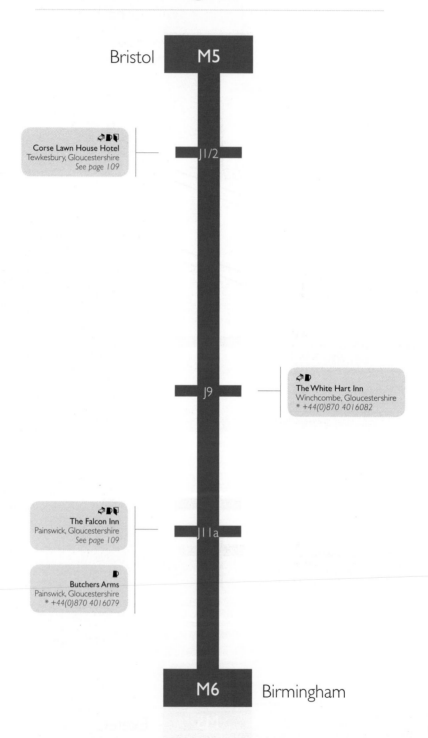

Bristol | **M5**

Corse Lawn House Hotel
Tewkesbury, Gloucestershire
See page 109 — J1/2

J9 — **The White Hart Inn**
Winchcombe, Gloucestershire
* +44(0)870 4016082

The Falcon Inn
Painswick, Gloucestershire
See page 109 — J11a

Butchers Arms
Painswick, Gloucestershire
* +44(0)870 4016079

M6 | Birmingham

From London to Birmingham

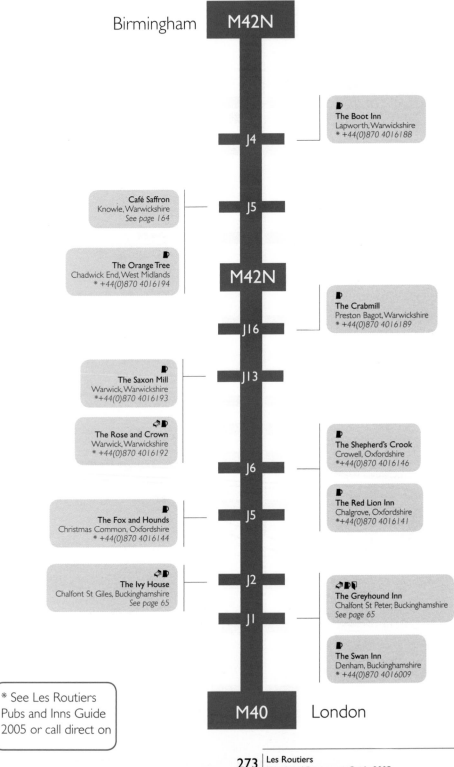

M42N

Birmingham

J4

The Boot Inn
Lapworth, Warwickshire
* +44(0)870 4016188

Café Saffron
Knowle, Warwickshire
See page 164

J5

The Orange Tree
Chadwick End, West Midlands
* +44(0)870 4016194

M42N

The Crabmill
Preston Bagot, Warwickshire
* +44(0)870 4016189

J16

The Saxon Mill
Warwick, Warwickshire
*+44(0)870 4016193

J13

The Rose and Crown
Warwick, Warwickshire
* +44(0)870 4016192

The Shepherd's Crook
Crowell, Oxfordshire
*+44(0)870 4016146

J6

The Red Lion Inn
Chalgrove, Oxfordshire
*+44(0)870 4016141

The Fox and Hounds
Christmas Common, Oxfordshire
* +44(0)870 4016144

J5

The Ivy House
Chalfont St Giles, Buckinghamshire
See page 65

J2

The Greyhound Inn
Chalfont St Peter, Buckinghamshire
See page 65

J1

The Swan Inn
Denham, Buckinghamshire
* +44(0)870 4016009

M40 London

* See Les Routiers
Pubs and Inns Guide
2005 or call direct on

From Birmingham to Carlisle

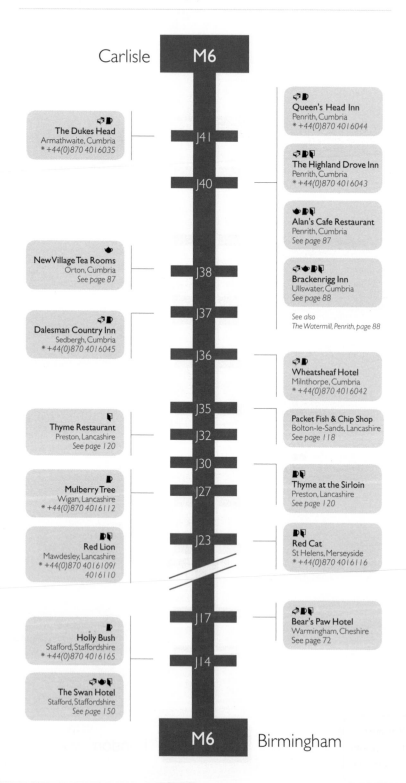

Carlisle · **M6**

J41

J40

J38

J37

J36

J35

J32

J30

J27

J23

J17

J14

M6 · Birmingham

The Dukes Head
Armathwaite, Cumbria
☎ +44(0)870 4016035

New Village Tea Rooms
Orton, Cumbria
See page 87

Dalesman Country Inn
Sedbergh, Cumbria
☎ +44(0)870 4016045

Thyme Restaurant
Preston, Lancashire
See page 120

Mulberry Tree
Wigan, Lancashire
☎ +44(0)870 4016112

Red Lion
Mawdesley, Lancashire
☎ +44(0)870 4016109/
4016110

Holly Bush
Stafford, Staffordshire
☎ +44(0)870 4016165

The Swan Hotel
Stafford, Staffordshire
See page 150

Queen's Head Inn
Penrith, Cumbria
☎ +44(0)870 4016044

The Highland Drove Inn
Penrith, Cumbria
☎ +44(0)870 4016043

Alan's Cafe Restaurant
Penrith, Cumbria
See page 87

Brackenrigg Inn
Ullswater, Cumbria
See page 88

*See also
The Watermill, Penrith, page 88*

Wheatsheaf Hotel
Milnthorpe, Cumbria
☎ +44(0)870 4016042

Packet Fish & Chip Shop
Bolton-le-Sands, Lancashire
See page 118

Thyme at the Sirloin
Preston, Lancashire
See page 120

Red Cat
St Helens, Merseyside
☎ +44(0)870 4016116

Bear's Paw Hotel
Warmingham, Cheshire
See page 72

From Edinburgh to Inverness

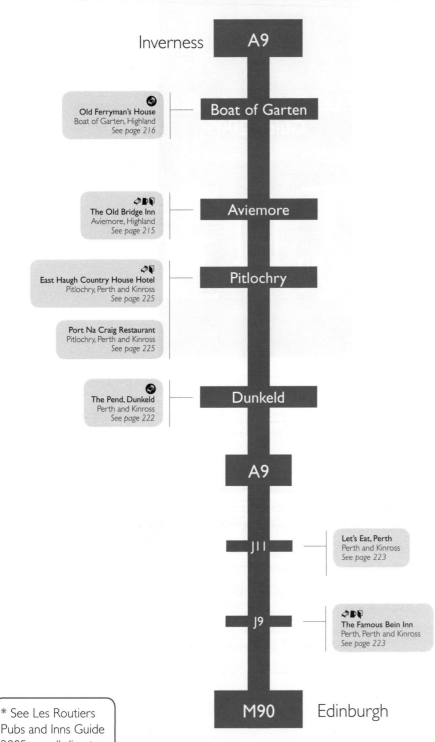

Inverness — **A9**

Old Ferryman's House
Boat of Garten, Highland
See page 216
— **Boat of Garten**

The Old Bridge Inn
Aviemore, Highland
See page 215
— **Aviemore**

East Haugh Country House Hotel
Pitlochry, Perth and Kinross
See page 225
— **Pitlochry**

Port Na Craig Restaurant
Pitlochry, Perth and Kinross
See page 225

The Pend, Dunkeld
Perth and Kinross
See page 222
— **Dunkeld**

A9

J11 — Let's Eat, Perth
Perth and Kinross
See page 223

J9 — The Famous Bein Inn
Perth, Perth and Kinross
See page 223

M90 Edinburgh

* See Les Routiers
Pubs and Inns Guide
2005 or call direct on

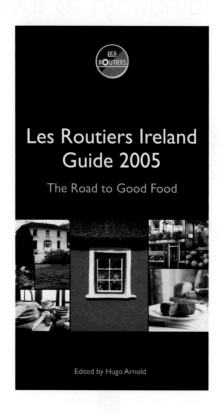

Les Routiers Ireland
Guide 2005

The Road to Good Food

Edited by Hugo Arnold

Exclusive Discount

The first ever Les Routiers Guide to Ireland - over
150 hotels, country houses, restaurants, pubs and cafes
throughout the island of Ireland. "The Les Routiers Ireland
Guide 2005 is about telling those who come to the island
how great our island is and where to find the best food
and real hospitality", says Hugo Arnold, Guide Editor.
"Don't leave home without it", says the Irish Times.
Receive this feature-packed guide at a discount of €5 by
telephoning Les Routiers Ireland:
00353 53 58693

www.routiersireland.com

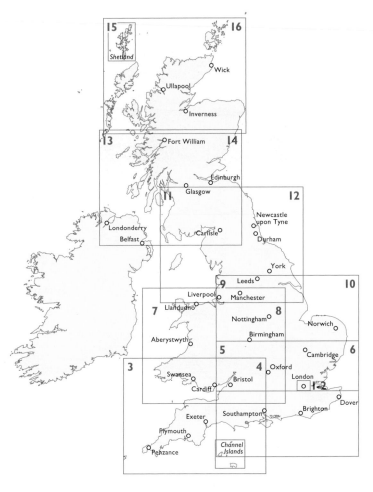

MI (Motorway symbol)	Motorway
AI (Primary A roads symbol)	Primary A roads
A4 (Other A roads symbol)	Other A roads
(Other roads symbol)	Other roads
☎ 08701 296002	Ferry routes (with contact number)
(National park symbol)	National park
(Forest symbol)	Forest
(Beach symbol)	Beach

●	Accommodation/Food
●	Food
🦐	Food Shop

Scale 1 : 1 100 000

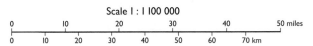

LONDON ZOO

REGENT'S PARK
NW1

KING'S CROSS

SOMERS TOWN

PENTONVILLE

BUSINESS DESIGN CENTRE

Angel

CRAFTS COUNCIL GALLERY

King's Cross St Pancras
King's Cross Thameslink

ST PANCRAS

EUSTON

BRITISH LIBRARY

ST PANCRAS

CONGESTION CHARGE ZONE

FINSBURY
EC1

FAMILY RECORDS CENTRE

THE HOUSE OF DETENTION

MARX MEMORIAL LIBRARY

CLERKENWELL

WELLCOME CENTRE

UNIVERSITY COLLEGE HOSPITAL

THOMAS CORAM FOUNDATION

SCHOOL OF PHARMACY

CORAM'S FIELDS

ORDER OF ST JOHN'S MUSEUM & LIBRARY

FARRINGDON

WARREN STREET

UNIVERSITY COLLEGE

RUSSELL SQUARE

DICKENS HOUSE MUSEUM

WC1 BLOOMSBURY

UNIVERSITY OF LONDON

CENTRAL MARKETS SMITHFIELD

ST BARTHOLOMEW'S HOSPITAL

BRITISH MUSEUM

GRAY'S INN

HOLBORN VIADUCT

NEWGATE

BROADCASTING HOUSE

WALLACE COLLECTION

OXFORD CIRCUS

SOHO

HOLBORN

INNS OF COURT & CITY YEOMANRY MUSEUM

LINCOLN'S INN FIELD

CITY THAMESLINK

EC4 CITY

ST PAUL'S CATHEDRAL

SELFRIDGES

Bond Street

WC2

ROYAL COURTS OF JUSTICE

FLEET STREET

LUDGATE HILL

QUEEN VICTORIA ST

BLACKFRIARS

OXFORD

ROOSEVELT MEMORIAL

SOTHEBY'S

COVENT GARDEN

THE TEMPLE

WHITE LION

THE FARADAY MUSEUM

ROYAL ACADEMY OF ARTS

PICCADILLY CIRCUS

NATIONAL GALLERY

NELSON'S COLUMN

CHARING CROSS

STRAND

SOMERSET HOUSE

VICTORIA EMBANKMENT

BANKSIDE GALLERY

MILLENNIUM BRIDGE

OXO TOWER

Green Park

ARCHITECTURE FOUNDATION

INSTITUTE OF CONTEMPORARY ART

ADMIRALTY ARCH

THE MALL

EMBANKMENT

SOUTH BANK CENTRE

HAYWARD GALLERY

BFI LONDON IMAX CINEMA

SOUTHWARK

Southwark

SPENCER HOUSE

ST JAMES'S PALACE

CLARENCE HOUSE

GREEN PARK

HORSE GUARDS

MOD

BANQUETING HOUSE

MINISTRY OF DEFENCE

JUBILEE GARDENS

BRITISH AIRWAYS LONDON EYE

SHELL CENTRE

ROYAL NATIONAL THEATRE

WATERLOO

WATERLOO EAST

THE BOROUGH

WELLINGTON MUSEUM APSLEY HOUSE

Hyde Park Corner

WELLINGTON ARCH

CONSTITUTION HILL

BUCKINGHAM PALACE

THE QUEEN'S GALLERY

QUEEN VICTORIA MEMORIAL

ST JAMES'S PARK

FOREIGN & COMMONWEALTH OFFICE

CABINET WAR ROOMS

WESTMINSTER BRIDGE

COUNTY HALL

WATERLOO INTERNATIONAL (EUROSTAR)

BRITISH RED CROSS SOCIETY

KNIGHTSBRIDGE

ROYAL MEWS

GUIDE HERITAGE CENTRE

WESTMINSTER

SW1

MIDDLESEX GUILDHALL

QUEEN ELIZABETH II CONFERENCE CENTRE

WESTMINSTER CENTRAL HALL

WESTMINSTER ABBEY

HOUSES OF PARLIAMENT

FLORENCE NIGHTINGALE MUSEUM

ST THOMAS'S HOSPITAL

LAMBETH NORTH

ST GEORGE'S CATHEDRAL (RC)

BOROUGH

VICTORIA

WESTMINSTER CATHEDRAL (RC)

RHS LAWRENCE HALL

RHS LINDLEY HALL

QUEEN MOTHER SPORTS CENTRE

ST JOHN'S SMITH SQUARE

HORSEFERRY RD

LAMBETH BRIDGE

LAMBETH PALACE

LAMBETH

LAMBETH PALACE

MUSEUM OF GARDEN HISTORY

MUSEUM OF THE ROYAL PHARMACEUTICAL SOCIETY

IMPERIAL WAR MUSEUM

ST GEORGE'S ROAD

CHRIST CHURCH & UPTON CHAPEL

Elephant and Castle (Bakerloo)

VICTORIA COACH STATION

SLOANE SQUARE

VAUXHALL BRIDGE RD

TATE BRITAIN

MILLBANK

PIMLICO

SE11

CONGESTION CHARGE ZONE

SE1

PIMLICO

GROSVENOR ROAD

VAUXHALL BRIDGE

VAUXHALL

VAUXHALL CITY FARM

KENNINGTON LANE

KENNINGTON

RIVER THAMES

SW8

VAUXHALL

FLOWER MARKET

NINE ELMS LANE

KENNINGTON PARK

OVAL CRICKET GROUND

Oval

SE11

KENNINGTON

CALVARY CHURCH OF GOD IN CHRIST

BATTERSEA PARK

NEW COVENT GARDEN

BRIXTON ROAD

CAMBERWELL NEW ROAD

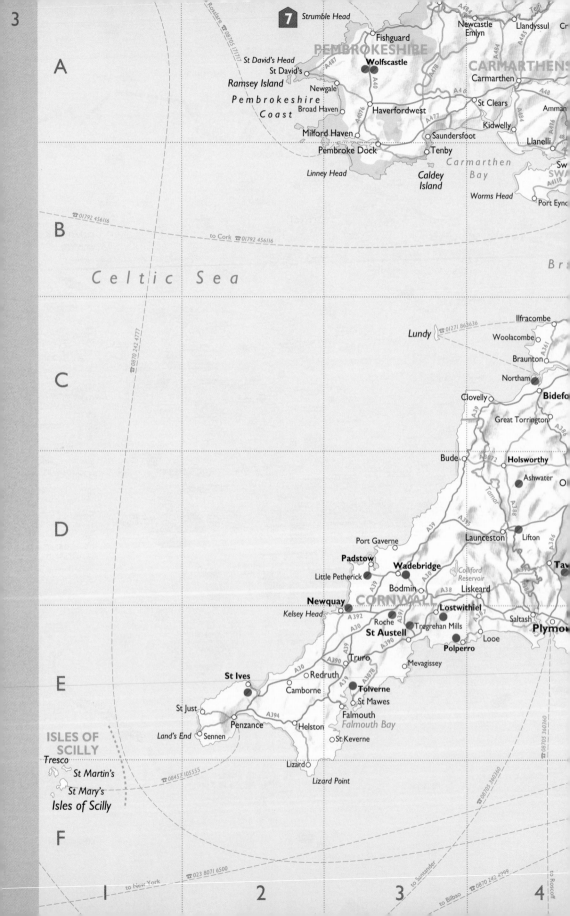

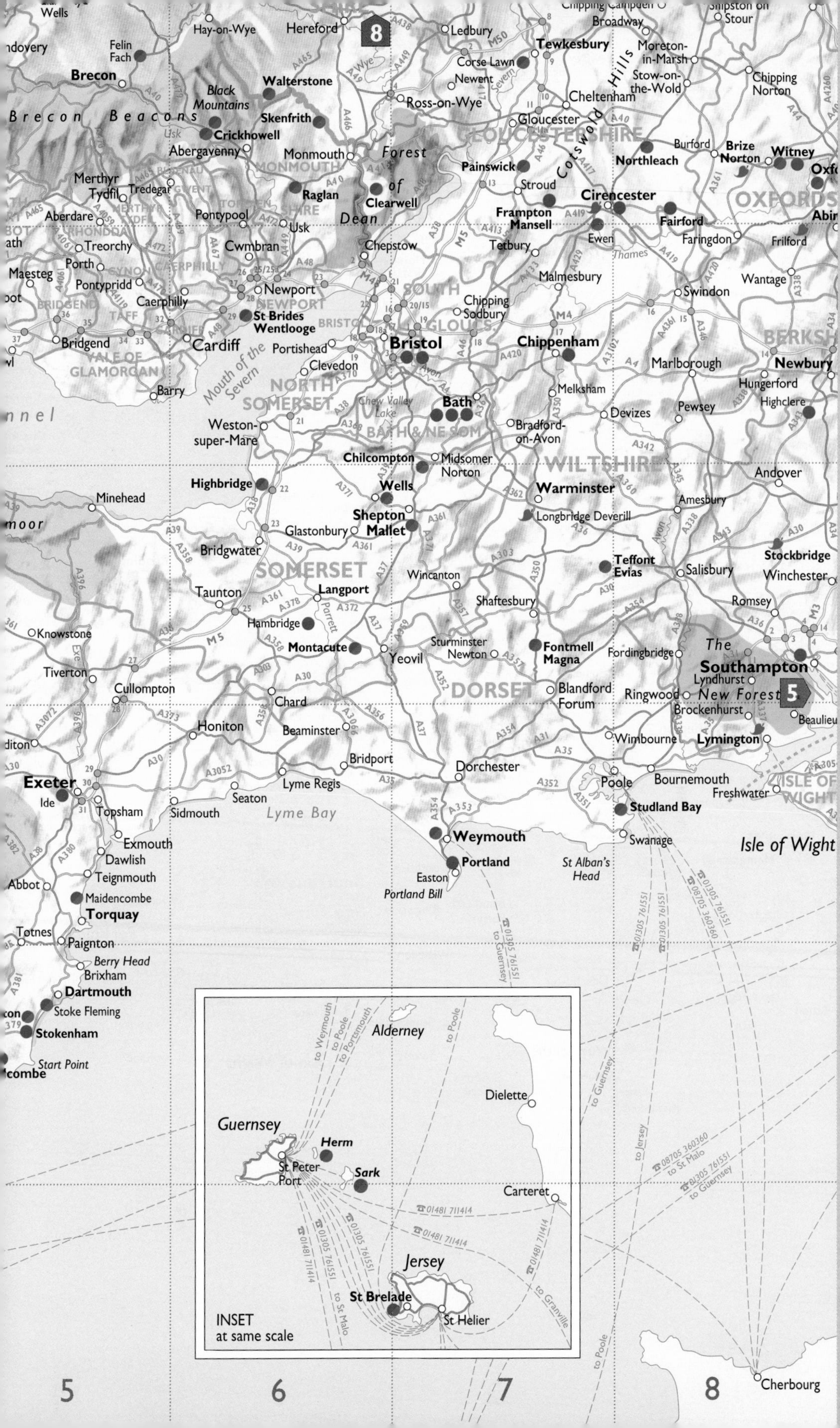

Wells
Felin Fach
Hay-on-Wye
Hereford
8
Ledbury
Chipping Campden
Broadway
Shipston on Stour
ndovery
Brecon
Walterstone
Tewkesbury
Moreton-in-Marsh
Stow-on-the-Wold
Chipping Norton
Black Mountains
Skenfrith
Corse Lawn
Newent
Ross-on-Wye
Cheltenham
Brecon Beacons
Crickhowell
Abergavenny
Usk
Monmouth
Gloucester
Burford
Brize Norton
Witney
Oxf
Raglan
Forest
Painswick
Stroud
Northleach
OXFORDS
Clearwell
of
Cirencester
Pontypool
Dean
Frampton Mansell
Fairford
Abir
Merthyr Tydfil
Tredegar
Cwmbran
Chepstow
Tetbury
Ewen
Faringdon
Frilford
Aberdare
RHONDDA
Pontypridd
Newport
Malmesbury
Thames
Wantage
BOT
ath
Treorchy
Porth
Caerphilly
SOUTH
GLOUS
Chipping Sodbury
Swindon
BERKSH
Maesteg
Bridgend
St Brides Wentlooge
BRISTOL
Bristol
M4
Marlborough
bot
BRIDGEND
TAFF
Portishead
Chippenham
Newbury
Cardiff
VALE OF GLAMORGAN
Clevedon
Melksham
Hungerford
Highclere
l
Barry
Mouth of the Severn
NORTH SOMERSET
Weston-super-Mare
Chew Valley Lake
Bath
Bradford-on-Avon
Devizes
Pewsey
Andover
BATH & NE SOM
WILTSHIRE
Minehead
Highbridge
Chilcompton
Midsomer Norton
Wells
Warminster
Amesbury
moor
Glastonbury
Shepton Mallet
Longbridge Deverill
Bridgwater
SOMERSET
Wincanton
Teffont Evias
Salisbury
Stockbridge
Winchester
Taunton
Langport
Romsey
Knowstone
Hambridge
Sturminster Newton
Shaftesbury
Fordingbridge
The
Tiverton
Montacute
Yeovil
DORSET
Fontmell Magna
Southampton
Cullompton
Chard
Blandford Forum
Ringwood
Lyndhurst
New Forest
5
Honiton
Beaminster
Wimbourne
Brockenhurst
Beaulieu
Exeter
Ide
Topsham
Bridport
Dorchester
Poole
Bournemouth
Lymington
ISLE OF WIGHT
Exmouth
Dawlish
Teignmouth
Lyme Regis
Seaton
Sidmouth
Lyme Bay
Studland Bay
Freshwater
Abbot
Maidencombe
Weymouth
Swanage
Isle of Wight
Torquay
Portland
St Alban's Head
Totnes
Paignton
Berry Head
Brixham
Easton
Portland Bill
Dartmouth
Stoke Fleming
con
Stokenham
Start Point
combe

INSET
at same scale

to Weymouth
to Poole
to Portsmouth
to Poole
Alderney
to Guernsey
Dielette
Guernsey
Herm
to Jersey
St Peter Port
Sark
08705 260360
to St Malo
Carteret
☎ 01481 711414
to Guernsey
☎ 01481 711414
☎ 01481 711414
☎ 01805 761551
Jersey
☎ 01805 761551
St Brelade
to St Malo
St Helier
to Granville
to Poole
Cherbourg

5   6   7   8

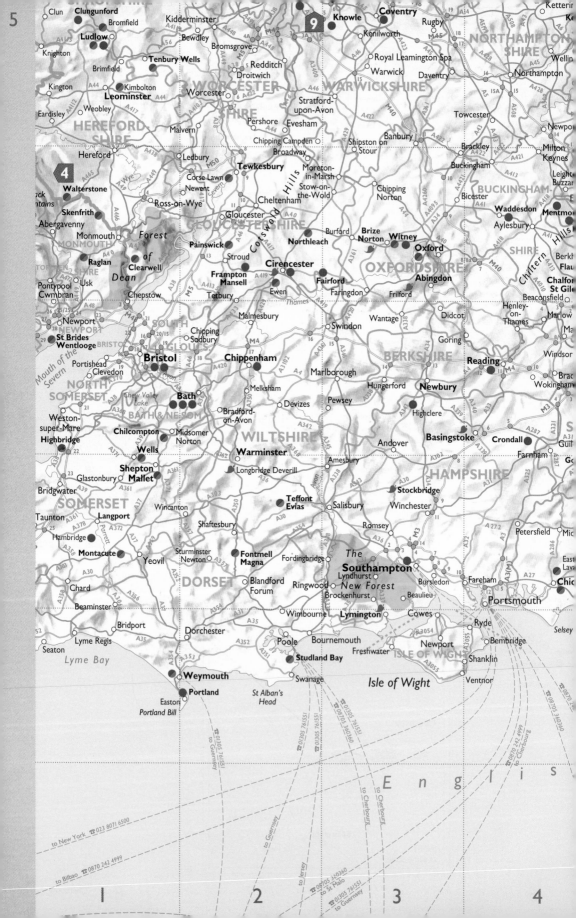

6

CAMBRIDGESHIRE

HERTFORD-
SHIRE

GREATER

LONDON

SUFFOLK

ESSEX

KENT

EAST SUSSEX

South Downs

SUSSEX

Ely
Mildenhall
Thornham Magna **10** Eye Fressingfield Southwold
Halesworth
Huntingdon
St Neots
Bury St Edmunds
Newmarket
Madingley
Cambridge
Earl Soham
Stowmarket
Needham Market
Aldeburgh
Hundon
Lavenham
Orford
Haverhill Cavendish
Sudbury
Hadleigh Ipswich
Woodbridge
Orford Ness
Royston Saffron Walden
Halstead
Woodbridge
to Esbjerg
☎ 08705 333222
Felixstowe
☎ 08705 333222
to Cuxhaven
Stevenage
Bishops Stortford
Braintree
Colchester
Manningtree
Harwich
☎ 08705 707070 to Hook of Holland
Hertford Harlow
Little Canfield
Coggeshall
Fingringhoe
The Naze
Epping
Witham
Mersea Island
Clacton-on-Sea
St Albans
Chelmsford
Maldon
Woodford Green
Brentwood
Burnham-on-Crouch
West Hampstead
Basildon
Barking Romford
Southend-on-Sea
London
Woolwich
Canvey Island
Mouth of the Thames
Chiswick
Barnes
Tilbury
Sheerness
Margate
Wandsworth
Gravesend
Isle of Sheppey
Herne Bay
North Foreland
Sutton
Rochester
Whitstable
Ramsgate
Croydon
Swanley
Gillingham Sittingbourne
Faversham
Epsom
Maidstone
Canterbury
Deal
Leatherhead
Sevenoaks
Ashford
South Foreland
St Margaret's at Cliffe
Reigate
Royal Tunbridge Wells
Biddenden
Dover
☎ 01304 210949 to Dunkerque
Dorking
East Grinstead
Bewl Water
Tenterden
Folkestone
☎ 08706 000600
☎ 08705 711711
☎ 08705 240241
Rusper Crawley
Turners Hill
Crowborough
Channel Tunnel
Calais
Haywards Heath
Heathfield
Rye
Uckfield
Battle
Dungeness
Lewes
Hailsham
Hastings
Strait of Dover
Worthing Hove Brighton
Newhaven
Bexhill
Eastbourne
Beachy Head

Channel

Dieppe

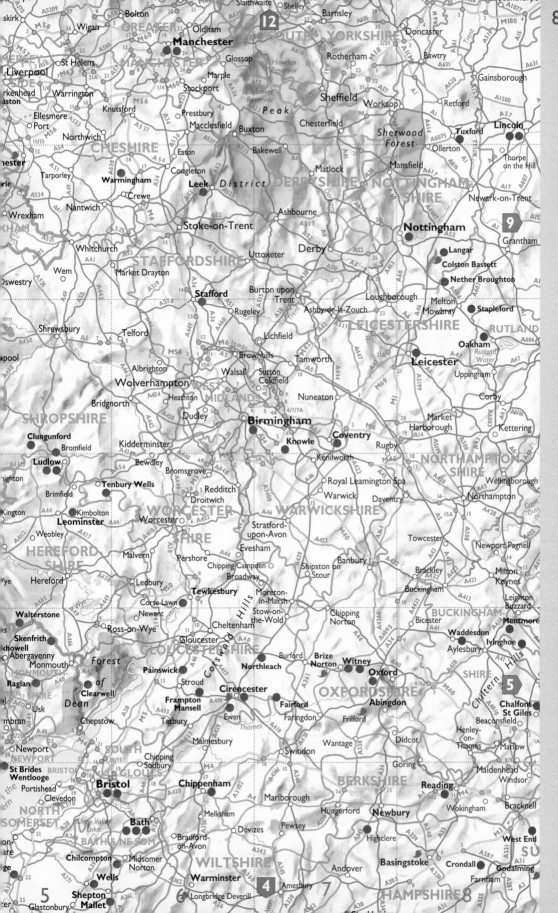

Grid numbers: 1 2 3 4

12 Leeds

Poulton-le-Fylde, Longridge, Clitheroe, Keighley, Tadcaster, Bever…, Preston, Blackburn, Hoghton, Burnley, Bradford, Selby, Howden, Goole, Barton-up Hum, Lytham St Anne's, Leyland, Ramsbottom, Halifax, Sowerby Bridge, Dewsbury, Wakefield, Castleford, Pontefract, NORTH LINCOLNS…, Southport, Rochdale, Huddersfield, Slaithwaite, Shelley, Barnsley, Scunth…, Ormskirk, Bolton, Wigan, Oldham, Manchester, Glossop, Rotherham, Doncaster, St Helens, Stockport, Marple, Howden Reservoir, SOUTH YORKSHIRE, Bawtry, Gainsborough, Liverpool, Warrington, Ledbower Reservoir, Sheffield, Worksop, Retford, Birkenhead, Knutsford, Prestbury, Peak, Chesterfield, Sherwood Forest, Tuxford, Ellesmere Port, Northwich, Macclesfield, Buxton, Ollerton, Thorpe on the, Chester, CHESHIRE, Eaton, Bakewell, Mansfield, Caergwrle, Tarporley, Congleton, Matlock, Newark-on-Tren…, Warmingham, Crewe, Leek, District, DERBYSHIRE, NOTTINGHAM…, Wrexham, Nantwich, Ashbourne, Nottingham, Oswestry, Whitchurch, Stoke-on-Trent, Derby, Langar, Colston Bassett, Wem, Market Drayton, STAFFORDSHIRE, Uttoxeter, Nether Broughton, Shrewsbury, Telford, Stafford, Burton upon Trent, Loughborough, Melton Mowbray, Stapleford, Rugeley, Ashby-de-la-Zouch, LEICESTERSHIRE, Oakham, RUTLA…, Lichfield, Oakham, Rutland Water, Albrighton, Brownhills, Tamworth, Leicester, Wolverhampton, Walsall, Sutton Coldfield, Uppingham, Foth…, Bridgnorth, Heathton, Nuneaton, Corby, Dudley, Birmingham, Ketter…, Clun, Clungunford, Bromfield, Kidderminster, Knowle, Coventry, Rugby, Ke…, Ludlow, Bewdley, Kenilworth, NORTHAMPTON SHIRE, Knighton, Brimfield, Tenbury Wells, Bromsgrove, Royal Leamington Spa, Welli…, Kington, Kimbolton, Redditch, Droitwich, Warwick, Daventry, Northampton, Leominster, Worcester, WORCESTERSHIRE, WARWICKSHIRE, Weobley, Stratford-upon-Avon, Towcester, HEREFORDSHIRE, Malvern, Pershore, Evesham, Banbury, Brackley, Newpo…, Eardisley, Ledbury, Chipping Campden, Shipston on Stour, Buckingham, Milton Keynes, Hereford, Broadway, Moreton-in-Marsh, BUCKINGHAM…, Walterstone, Tewkesbury, Chipping Norton, Bicester, Leight… Buzza…, Skenfrith, Corse Lawn, Newent, Stow-on-the-Wold, Waddesdon, Mentmo…, Abergavenny, Cheltenham, Burford, Brize Norton, Witney, Aylesbury, Monmouth, Gloucester, GLOUCESTERSHIRE, Northleach, Oxford, SHIRE, Chalfon St Gil…, Forest of Dean, Painswick, Stroud, Cotswold Hills, Fairford, Abingdon, Berk… Flat…, Raglan, Clearwell, Cirencester, OXFORDSHIRE, Beaconsfield, Usk, Frampton Mansell, Ewen, Faringdon, Frilford, Marlow, Pontypool Cwmbran, Chepstow, Tetbury, Thames, Didcot, Henley-on-Thames, Newport, Malmesbury, Swindon, Wantage, Goring, Windsor, St Brides Wentlooge, Chipping Sodbury, BERKSHIRE, Portishead, Clevedon, Bristol, Chippenham, **5**, Reading, Bracknell, Wokingha…

7

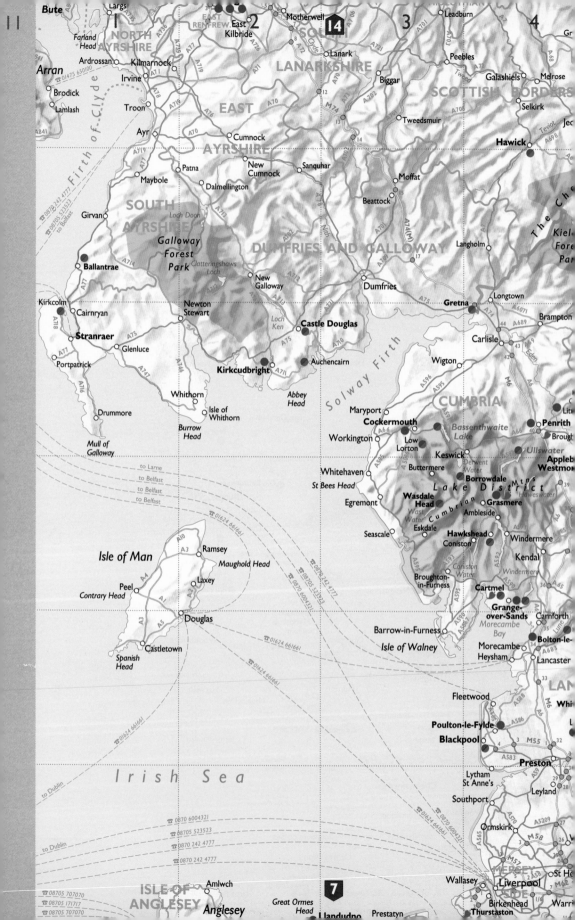

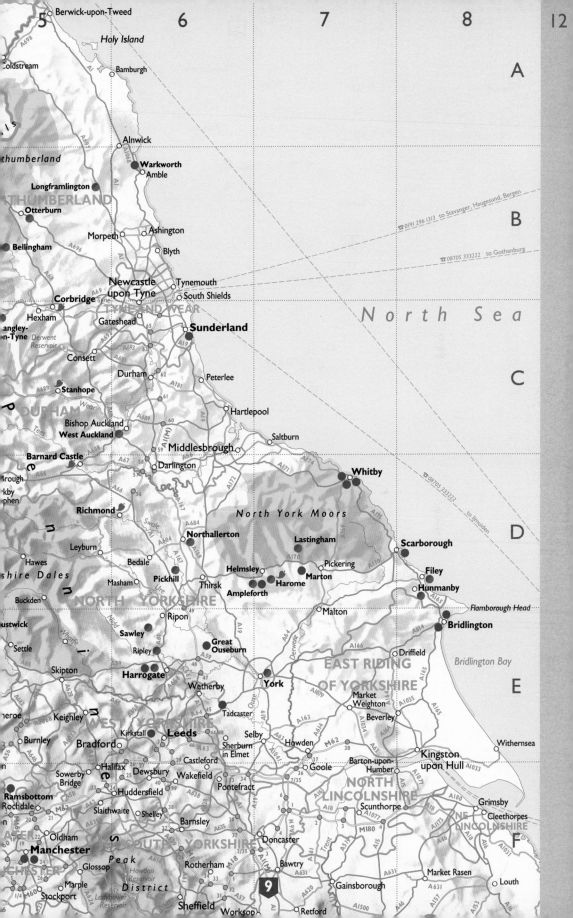

A

B

N o r t h   S e a

C

D

E

F

Berwick-upon-Tweed
Holy Island
Coldstream
Bamburgh
thumberland
Alnwick
Warkworth
Amble
Longframlington
Otterburn
Morpeth
Ashington
Bellingham
Blyth
Newcastle upon Tyne
Tynemouth
South Shields
Corbridge
Hexham
angley-
n-Tyne
Derwent
Reservoir
TYNE AND WEAR
Gateshead
Sunderland
Consett
Durham
Peterlee
Stanhope
DURHAM
Hartlepool
Wear
Bishop Auckland
West Auckland
Saltburn
Barnard Castle
Middlesbrough
Darlington
rough
Tees
A66
Whitby
kby
phen
Richmond
Swale
North York Moors
Leyburn
Northallerton
Lastingham
Scarborough
Hawes
Bedale
Helmsley
Pickering
Filey
shire Dales
Masham
Pickhill
Harome
Marton
Hunmanby
Buckden
Thirsk
Ampleforth
NORTH YORKSHIRE
Ure
Flamborough Head
ustwick
Ripon
Malton
Bridlington
Settle
Sawley
Great
Ouseburn
Driffield
Bridlington Bay
Skipton
Ripley
EAST RIDING
Harrogate
Wharfe
OF YORKSHIRE
heroe
Keighley
Wetherby
York
Market
Weighton
Withernsea
Burnley
WEST YORKSHIRE
Tadcaster
Beverley
Bradford
Kirkstall
Leeds
Selby
Howden
Kingston
upon Hull
Halifax
Castleford
Sherburn
in Elmet
Sowerby
Bridge
Dewsbury
Wakefield
Goole
Barton-upon-
Humber
Grimsby
Ramsbottom
Huddersfield
Pontefract
NORTH
LINCOLNSHIRE
Cleethorpes
Rochdale
Slaithwaite
Shelley
Scunthorpe
LINCOLNSHIRE
Manchester
Barnsley
SOUTH YORKSHIRE
Doncaster
Oldham
Peak
Market Rasen
Glossop
Rotherham
Bawtry
Louth
Marple
Howden
Reservoir
Gainsborough
Stockport
District
Ladybower
Reservoir
Sheffield
Worksop
Retford

Spey
Braemar
16
Ballater
Banchory
A957
Stonehaven

Grampian Mountains
Loch Laggan
Dalwhinnie
Moy
Loch Ericht
water
rvoir
Loch Rannoch
Blair Atholl
Loch Tummel
Loch Laidon
Tay Forest Park
Pitlochry
Bridge of Cally
Aberfeldy
Kenmore
Loch Tay
Dunkeld
Blairgowrie
Glen Lyon
Loch an Daimh
Killin
Lochearnhead
Loch Earn
Comrie
Crieff
KINROSS
Perth
ndrum
rich
och Lomond the Trossachs
Loch Katrine
Queen Elizabeth Forest Park
Loch Lomond
Arrochar
Callander
Glen Farg
Auchterarder
FIFE
Dunblane
Inverbervie
Brechin
Montrose
ANGUS
South Esk
Kirriemuir
PERTH
Forfar
Friockheim
Red Head
Arbroath
Carnoustie
Buddon Ness
Dundee
St Andrews
Cupar
Largoward
Crail
Anstruther
Isle of May
Glenrothes
Earlsferry
West Wemyss
Kirkcaldy
Leven
Dunfermline
Glen Farg

STIRLING
Stirling
CLACK
Kincardine
Falkirk
Grangemouth
Cumbernauld
WEST LOTHIAN
Alexandria
Dumbarton
Kirkintilloch
Glasgow
East Kilbride
Paisley
nstone
RENFREW
Motherwell
SOUTH LANARKSHIRE
Lanark
Biggar
Burntisland
Firth of Forth
☎ 020 7431 4560 to Zeebrugge
North Berwick
East Linton
Dunbar
Haddington
EAST LOTHIAN
Eyemouth
Edinburgh
Musselburgh
Livingston
Roslin
Bonnyrigg
Leadburn
Peebles
Greenlaw
Duns
Berwick-upon-Tweed
Coldstream
Galashiels
Melrose
Kelso
SCOTTISH BORDERS
Selkirk
Jedburgh
Tweed
Tweedsmuir
Hawick
Teviot
The Cheviot Hills
Northumberland

EAST AYRSHIRE
Cumnock
Patna
New Cumnock
Sanquhar
Moffat
Beattock
Langholm
Kielder Water
Kielder Forest Park
Otterburn
12
Bellingham
North Tyne
NORTHUMB
Dalmellington
bole
rnock
DUMFRIES AND GALLOWAY
Nith
Langholm
Longtown
Gretna
Brampton
Corbridge
Hexham
Langley-on-Tyne
Derwent Reservoir
South Tyne
Galloway Forest Park
Clatteringshaws Loch
New Galloway
Loch Ken
Dumfries
Carlisle
Wigton
Eden
Alston
Newton Stewart
Castle Douglas
Auchencairn
Kirkcudbright
Whithorn
Isle of Whithorn
Abbey Head
Maryport
Workington
CUMBRIA
Cockermouth
11
Low Lorton
Bassenthwaite Lake
Keswick
Penrith
Brougham
Melmerby
Little Salkeld
Cow Green Reservoir
Tees
Solway Firth
Burrow Head
5
6
7
8

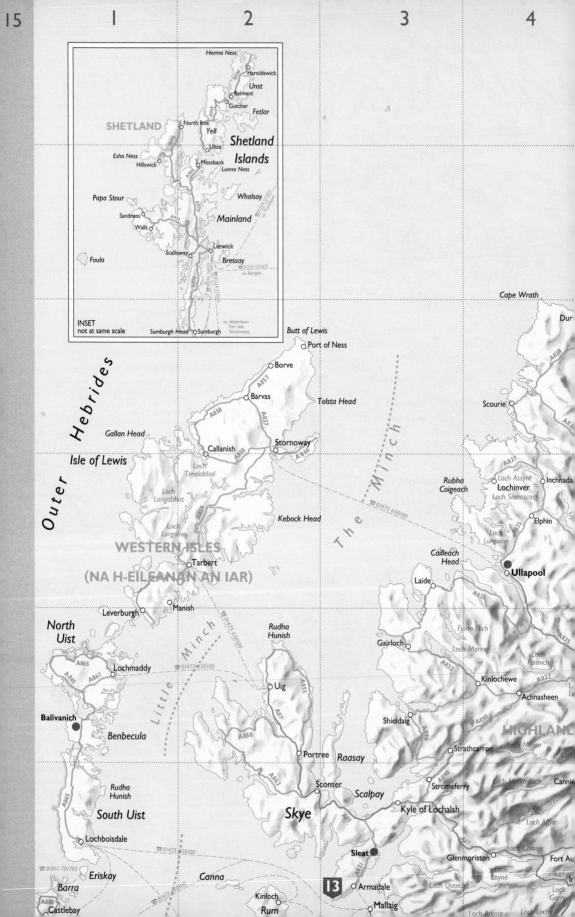

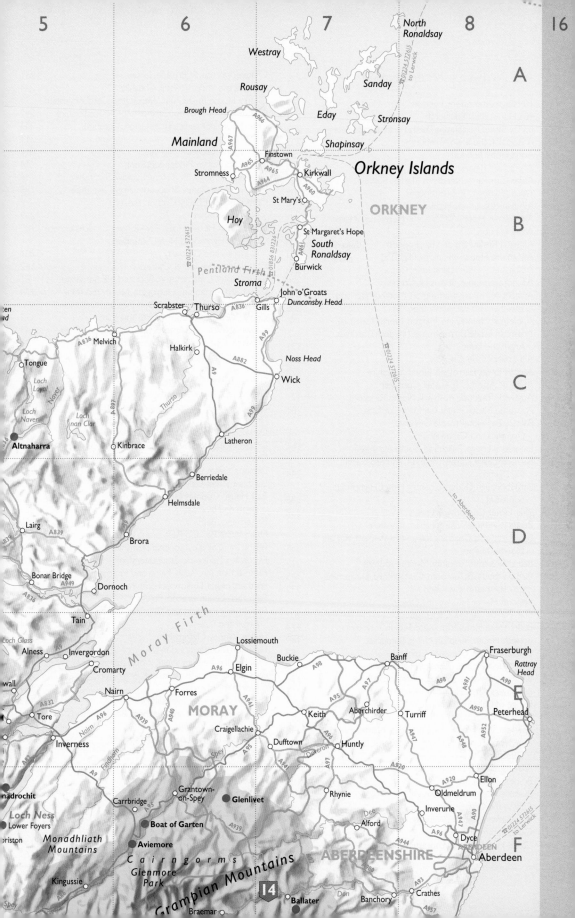

A-Z by Establishment Name

A-Z by Town

Index

To the Editor, Les Routiers Guide 2006
Report Form

☐ From my personal experience the following establishment should be a member of Les Routiers.

☐ From my personal experience the following establishment should not be a member of Les Routiers.

Establishment   PLEASE PRINT IN BLOCK CAPITALS

....

Address ....

....

....

I had   ☐ lunch   ☐ dinner   ☐ stayed there on (date) ....

Details ....

....

....

....

....

....

....

....

....

....

....

Reports received up to the end of May 2005 will be used in the research of the 2006 edition.

☐ I am not connected in any way with management or proprietors.

   Name

Address ....

....

....

As a result of your sending Les Routiers this report form, we may send you information on Les Routiers in the future.
If you would prefer not to receive such information, please tick this box ☐

To send your report...
Fax: Complete this form and fax it to 020 7370 4528
Post: Complete this form and mail it to
The Editor, FREEPOST, Les Routiers, 190 Earl's Court Road, London, SW5 9QG
E-mail: info@routiers.co.uk

To the Editor, Les Routiers Guide 2006
Report Form

☐ From my personal experience the following establishment should be a member of Les Routiers.

☐ From my personal experience the following establishment should not be a member of Les Routiers.

Establishment   PLEASE PRINT IN BLOCK CAPITALS
....

Address
....

....

....

I had   ☐ lunch   ☐ dinner   ☐ stayed there on (date)
....

Details
....

....

....

....

....

....

....

....

....

....

Reports received up to the end of May 2005 will be used in the research of the 2006 edition.

☐ I am not connected in any way with management or proprietors.

Name
....

Address
....

....

....

As a result of your sending Les Routiers this report form, we may send you information on Les Routiers in the future.
If you would prefer not to receive such information, please tick this box ☐

To send your report...
Fax: Complete this form and fax it to 020 7370 4528
Post: Complete this form and mail it to
The Editor, FREEPOST, Les Routiers, 190 Earl's Court Road, London, SW5 9QG
E-mail: info@routiers.co.uk

Les Routiers establishments invite you to join them for a complimentary glass of wine

Les Routiers would like to offer all its readers the opportunity to have a complimentary glass of wine on us. Thanks to the generosity of a number of our establishments across the country, we are inviting you to go in and enjoy a free glass of wine at one of the participating Les Routiers establishments.

To take up this offer, simply look for the wine symbol ♆ alongside the individual establishments name. Only those with wine symbols will be participating in this 'free glass of wine' offer. Then, cut out one of the vouchers from below, and take it into the establishment, ordering your free glass of wine at the same time as presenting your voucher.

Terms and Conditions
1. The offer will be valid during the individual bar opening hours of each establishment.
2. Offer valid until 1 September 2005.
3. The free glass of wine, made available for this offer, will be chosen at the discretion of the establishment.
4. Voucher holders are entitled to upgrade on the glass of wine offered and pay the difference.
5. One voucher entitles the bearer to one glass of wine only.
6. Only one voucher is valid per person.
7. The vouchers may only be used once, and must be given up upon redemption.
8. A maximum of two vouchers are valid per group/visit.
9. This offer cannot be used in conjunction with any other offer.
10. Les Routiers accepts no responsibility financial or otherwise for the misuse of this voucher.
11. All participating establishments reserve the right to refuse admission.
12. The vouchers have no monetary value and are non-transferable.
13. Photocopies of the vouchers will not be accepted.

 Les Routiers **Free glass of wine**
This voucher is valid until Sept 1st 2005
Subject to availability 1 voucher per person

 Les Routiers **Free glass of wine**
This voucher is valid until Sept 1st 2005
Subject to availability 1 voucher per person

 Les Routiers **Free glass of wine**
This voucher is valid until Sept 1st 2005
Subject to availability 1 voucher per person

 Les Routiers **Free glass of wine**
This voucher is valid until Sept 1st 2005
Subject to availability 1 voucher per person

 Les Routiers **Free glass of wine**
This voucher is valid until Sept 1st 2005
Subject to availability 1 voucher per person

 Les Routiers **Free glass of wine**
This voucher is valid until Sept 1st 2005
Subject to availability 1 voucher per person

 Les Routiers **Free glass of wine**
This voucher is valid until Sept 1st 2005
Subject to availability 1 voucher per person

 Les Routiers **Free glass of wine**
This voucher is valid until Sept 1st 2005
Subject to availability 1 voucher per person

 Les Routiers **Free glass of wine**
This voucher is valid until Sept 1st 2005
Subject to availability 1 voucher per person